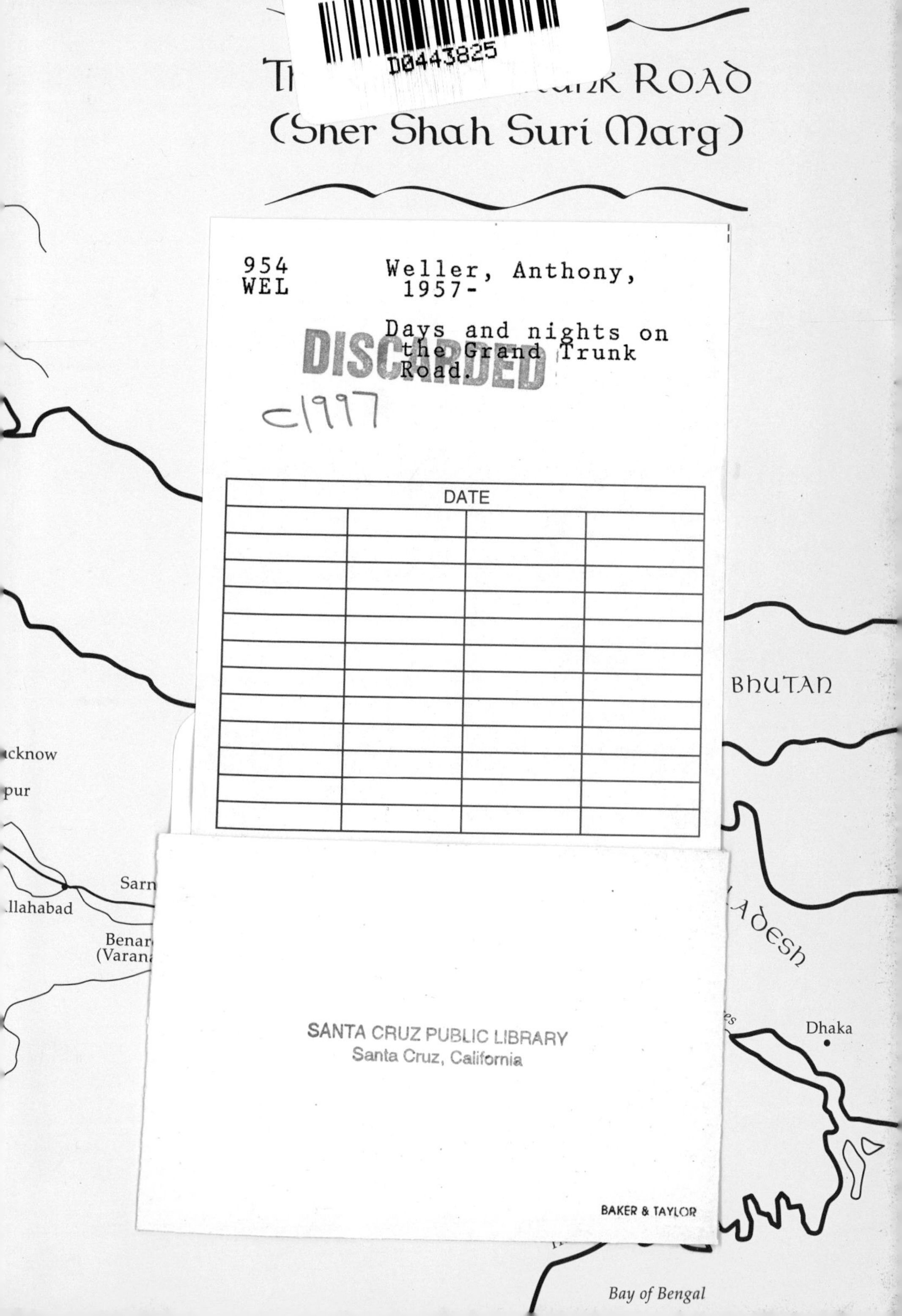

Th... ...unk Road
(Sher Shah Suri Marg)

Days and Nights on the Grand Trunk Road

Also by Anthony Weller

The Garden of the Peacocks

Days and Nights on the Grand Trunk Road

Anthony Weller

Marlowe & Company
New York

Published by
Marlowe & Company
632 Broadway, Seventh Floor
New York, NY 10012

Library of Congress Cataloging in Publication Data

Weller, Anthony, 1957-
Days and nights on the Grand Trunk Road / by Anthony Weller.
p. cm.
ISBN 1-56924-751-X (cloth)
1. India—Description and travel. 2. Pakistan—Description and travel.
3. Grand Trunk Road (India and Pakistan) I. Title.
DS414.2 97-25270
954-dc21 CIP

Manufactured in the United States of America
First Edition

for

Emmett Thomas

Geo Beach

Paul & Jane Weller

many miles, many years

Contents

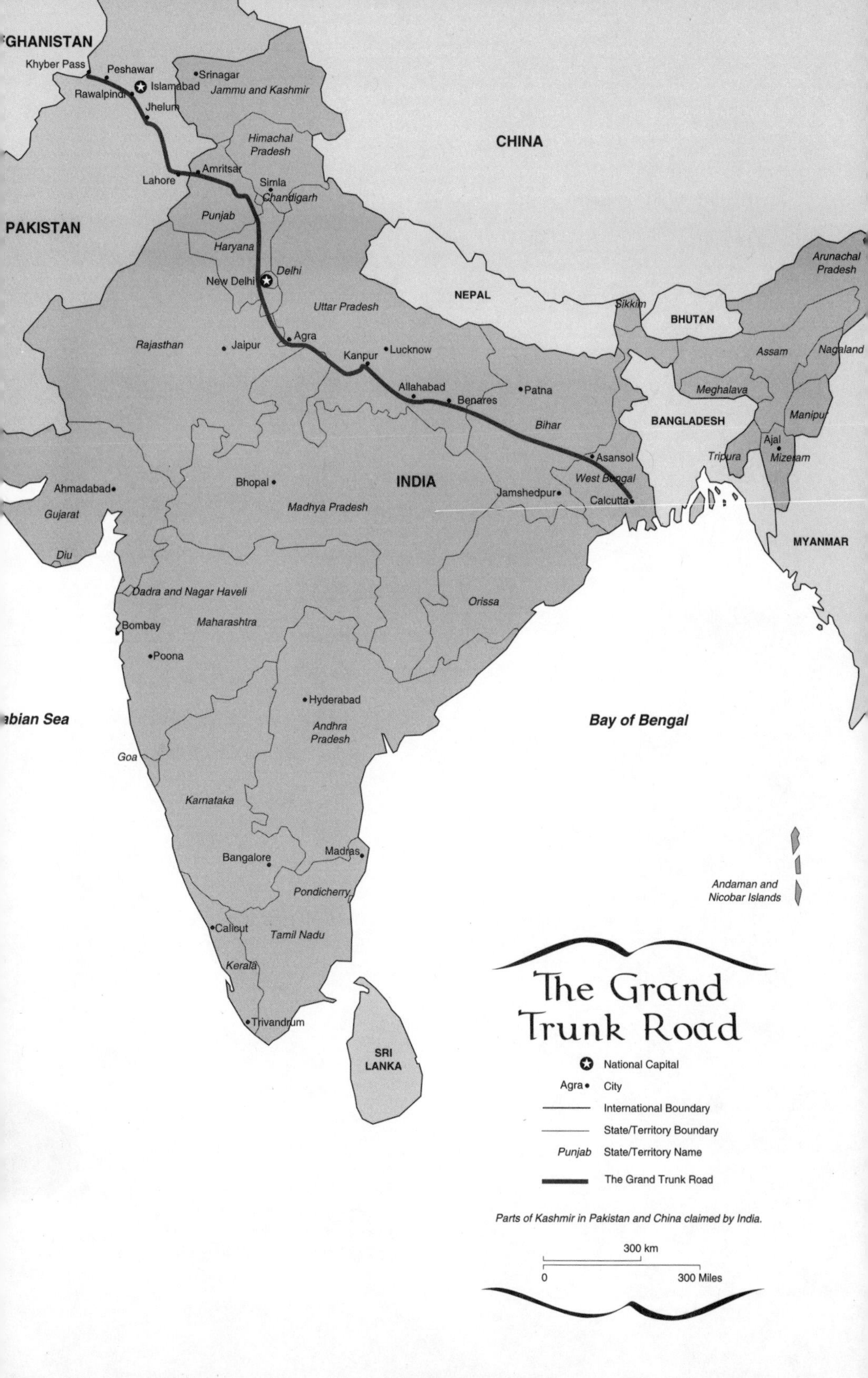

FGHANISTAN
Khyber Pass
Peshawar
Rawalpindi
Islamabad
Jhelum
Srinagar
Jammu and Kashmir
CHINA
Himachal Pradesh
Amritsar
Lahore
Simla
Chandigarh
PAKISTAN
Punjab
Haryana
Delhi
New Delhi
NEPAL
Uttar Pradesh
Sikkim
BHUTAN
Arunachal Pradesh
Rajasthan
Jaipur
Agra
Kanpur
Lucknow
Assam
Nagaland
Allahabad
Benares
Patna
Meghalaya
Bihar
BANGLADESH
Manipur
Ajal
Asansol
Tripura
Mizoram
Ahmadabad
Bhopal
INDIA
West Bengal
Jamshedpur
Calcutta
Gujarat
Madhya Pradesh
Diu
MYANMAR
Dadra and Nagar Haveli
Orissa
Bombay
Maharashtra
Poona
Hyderabad
abian Sea
Andhra Pradesh
Bay of Bengal
Goa
Karnataka
Madras
Bangalore
Pondicherry
Andaman and Nicobar Islands
Calicut
Tamil Nadu
Kerala
Trivandrum
SRI LANKA
The Grand Trunk Road
National Capital
Agra • City
International Boundary
State/Territory Boundary
Punjab State/Territory Name
The Grand Trunk Road
Parts of Kashmir in Pakistan and China claimed by India.
300 km
0
300 Miles

Days and Nights on the Grand Trunk Road

The wheeling months go round

And back I come again

To the baked and blistered ground

And the dust-encumbered plain

And the bare hot-weather trees

And the Trunk Road's aching white;

Oh, land of little ease!

Oh, land of strange delight!

—British Army Engineer, engaged in the
Grand Trunk Route Survey,
Calcutta to Delhi, 1830

> I had always supposed this place a melancholy, or at least a staid and soberly-coloured spot, a gray record of bygone days. Instead, I find it one of the most... startlingly radiant of places full of bustle and movement. Constantinople or Naples are simply dull and quiet by comparison.
>
> — Edward Lear (1873)

1.

Calcutta

At the beginning of a long journey it is easy to find omens everywhere—especially under a low sky packed with heavy clouds. The air here feels unexpectedly alert, suffused with that tropical awakening which follows a deluge. I have, of course, timed things very badly with the August rains.

Omens: while I was checking in late this afternoon at a modest businessman's hotel just off Chowringhee Road, a fellow guest—an Indian in a suit and tie, his eyes bulging with emergency—leaned over and warned me from the corner of his mouth, "Trust me, sir, you must avoid the food here at all costs."

It wasn't his advice that was alarming, but the fact that at first I thought he'd muttered, *Avoid the road*.

Not having been in India for several years, my last impression—a country of people ever waiting, some patient, some listless, many trapped in anger or bathed in hopeful belief, but all always waiting—

was echoed on arrival again. This time everyone seemed busy waiting for the monsoon to make up its many minds.

Calcutta at evening eerily resembled the London of black-and-white films from just after the war. Through a fog of pollution the weak headlamps glimmered, and extravagantly hued film posters looked down on people waiting for transport. Ghosts of once-grand buildings loomed in calm decay above the food stalls and the overlit fabric shops and the Calcuttans barely moving in purposeful confusion on the glistening streets.

So many more, the hopeful and the desperate, arrived here daily to try to make their way. They came to Calcutta from its own state of West Bengal, from neighboring Bihar, from Uttar Pradesh. They saw it as a city of prospects, a city with a future. They reminded me that I'd come here only in order to leave, once I located the beginnings of an ancient road.

In daytime to equate Calcutta with "horror" seems unfair. Much of it appears no more crowded than any other city, though a morning walk is like exercising wrapped in hot towels. Against an overcast, swollen sky the monumental buildings of the British Raj do look dingier and more weatherbeaten than they would under admiring sunlight. They dwarf the restless, energetic life of the sidewalk: bare-chested porters with interminable loads, twisted beggars lying on their blankets like blotched human pretzels, and people jabbering, hurrying, embracing, gesticulating, bargaining in the heat.

Calcutta was the capital for the British in India from 1774 until 1911. At first it looks as if some inarticulate catastrophe has engulfed London's Pall Mall, so the British have abandoned it and gone away. Perhaps Maugham was right: "India was lost in the public schools of England." In a kind of frenzied Victoria-meets-Akbar style, all the emblematic institutions are here: a High Court, a National Library, a Race Course, a Zoological Gardens, a Stock Exchange, a Bengal Club and a Tollygunge Club and a Royal Calcutta Turf Club, even a St. Paul's Cathedral with dozens of whirling electric fans, at whose services white men are rare. The columned buildings stand shoulder-to-shoulder like massive gravestones in an overgrown imperial cemetery.

At first the *maidan*, the three-mile square green, seems as benevolent in spirit as Hyde Park, and it is easy to imagine gentlemen strolling it in top hats and heavy frock coats. But the British kept it open only to have a clear stretch for cannon fire in the event of a native uprising, and now its fringes have been turned into a dumping ground.

I stopped at a corner stand to buy sunglasses. Just in from the boulevard, down a muddy side street, a crowd seemed to be assembling for a riot outside a moldy cinema; they were shoving desperately to get into the day's first performance of some film with a Bengali title. That was one morning excursion I instantly abandoned. Besides, I hoped I was going to need those sunglasses.

"First time in India, yes?"

"No."

"First time in Calcutta, no?"

"That's right."

"Aha! Beautiful city. Poor people. You like sunglasses, sir?"

"Very much."

"Let me look, sir. You are too handsome in those."

"I don't think so. What about that pair—"

"You are going to Delhi? Beautiful city, Delhi. Better. Not so many poor people. Try these instead. Let me put them on, I am professional, sir. And going to Agra, yes? To see Taj Mahal? You will need ultra-radiation sunglasses to look at Taj Mahal! Otherwise you are going blind! Aha, not your size perhaps. Just one moment. Only last week, sir, English woman—you are English, no? American? Only last week American woman approaches me, familiar, familiar, she says, 'Remember me? Remember you warn me not to look at Taj Mahal without sunglasses? And do I listen? Now look at me, for I can no longer look at you! I cannot find my way, I am lost, where are children, where is husband—' You see, those are much better. Ultra-radiation type."

"They look a little expensive."

"They are not one bit expensive! Only five hundred rupees."

That was about fourteen dollars. "Much too expensive."

"Four hundred, sir. How much you are paying?"

"The fellow a street over sells the same ones for half."

"I know that chap. He is a charlatan, sir."

"Money is money."

"His are not ultra-radiation, sir. Trust me, I am professional. Three hundred rupees, sir. You are rich. I cannot abandon my wife and children."

"One hundred."

"Two-eighty, sir. Please."

"One hundred twenty. I'm not rich."

"Two-seventy. That is my Maginot Line, sir."

"I can walk back a street and buy them for one-fifty."

"You are inventing, sir. For that price you would have purchased them from him."

He was right, of course: a tactical error. Clinging to the wreckage, I said, "But I like you. I didn't like him. Two hundred."

"Sir, I must make a profit. I am not making a profit at two-seventy. It is morning price, first sale of the day, very lucky if it is to foreigner."

The grass blade bends to the hurricane; I gave in and bought the sunglasses at about twice a fair price. A week later both lenses fell out.

"You are going on to Delhi, sir? I am from Delhi."

"Farther than that. I'm going all the way to Amritsar. By car."

I didn't mention Pakistan.

He became very solemn. "Watch out on the GT Road at night, sir. Most of those truck drivers—not all of them, mind you—they are out of their heads. On opium, sir. They put a ten-kilo rock on the accelerator, they fold their legs and close their eyes and they don't care what happens. You must take every precaution." He sighed, shook his head, then brightened. "Perhaps you are wanting second pair of sunglasses? Wraparound? For dust, sir?"

I'd first come to India via the past—captivated, as a boy who liked to read, by the history. Whether the modern region went up in flames meant nothing to me compared with invasions of five centuries ago, seen through a veil of romance: Tamerlane on horseback, bringing bloodshed and enlightenment. As a child you take sides in such struggles, switching allegiances shamelessly. As an adult you wonder, centuries later, what traces remain.

And there was the ancient process, discontinued now, of brave new ideas quietly making their way out of the subcontinent even while things were falling apart within. It is three countries today—Bangladesh, India, and Pakistan—but those are modern names and recent divisions of a jumble that goes back many centuries.

I didn't actually visit the region until my twenties, while trying to earn a living in New York as a writer and a musician. I finally got sent to India on a magazine assignment. A month's visit, to Delhi, Simla, and Kashmir: I went home dissatisfied and uneasy, with a sense I'd failed, even more than the journalist's usual failure, to get under people's skins. This felt doubly frustrating in a country where a stranger is instantly made welcome and spoken to candidly.

I knew I'd been stirred by India's beauty and its difficulties, but I also knew that I was unable to grasp it. I did not realize then that this sense of an enormous revelation about to occur—but not quite yet—is simply fundamental to the Indian experience.

I found myself wondering if there might be a way I could approach the subcontinent as a whole. The more I read, the more fragmentary it seemed; to even think of it as one place was absurd. Still, wasn't there anything, apart from ways of living brought on by climate and geography, that linked not just India, but Pakistan as well—its sundered, smaller half brother? A journey that made sense, unifying this vast region's present and its past, so an outsider could emerge with perhaps a sense of the future?

Over the years I came to know other parts of Asia. The idea of crossing the subcontinent, larger than Europe and in most ways more diverse, stayed with me. Today it contains nearly a fourth of the world's people, galvanized by Hinduism and Islam, with the potential every day for war. The greatest paradox of this schism is that while Pakistan is the second largest Muslim country on earth, India, Hindu India, trails it as a very close third.

Often the places that stay with us the most, that possess our imaginations, are the ones we have failed to understand. I knew I was looking for a way out of the purposeless confusion of my first visit. I realized there was an ancient route, staring out at me from maps in old books: the Grand Trunk Road. It flows as a shared idea across India and Pakistan, the only man-made artery that now joins the divided subcontinent—apart from the railroad line which follows the road like a shadow. But the trains are a foreigner's contribution and relatively young in local terms, while the road has witnessed several millennia.

Travel can be as much an experience of time as of distance. In both India and Pakistan there are still subsistence farmers living like their ancestors did three thousand years ago, while an hour's drive up the Grand Trunk Road the well-off in cities are leaving their computers to visit health clubs, and medieval darkness rubs shoulders with the crashing looms of the early industrial era. Along the Grand Trunk Road I often had the impression that all the distinct ages of man were crowding the wayside and flourishing in its dust, sheltered by its shade trees.

The Grand Trunk begins in Calcutta, and heads resolutely northwest for about 1,925 kilometers (1,195 miles) across India's chest—through Benares, Agra, Delhi, and the Punjab. It then crosses into Pakistan for another 530 kilometers (330 miles), to

Lahore, Peshawar, and the Khyber Pass. There it takes on another persona as it leaves the subcontinent and enters Afghanistan.

It struck me that the violent act of Partition was now a half century gone, India and Pakistan having been surgically divided and given their independence from Britain in 1947. The way to see them both was clearly the most traditional way, along the Grand Trunk. I guessed it might take nine, ten weeks—and I had time on my hands. I'd recently finished a novel and had nothing new in mind; and musical work around Boston (I am a guitarist) was scarcer than usual for this time of year. It seemed an ideal moment for a long journey. It was one that no local, no Indian or Pakistani, could legally make—but their travel restrictions wouldn't apply to me.

As natural as a river by now, the Grand Trunk Road has been the principal route across the subcontinent for at least thirty-five centuries. Countless invaders have used it like a whip laid across the fertile treasure of the vast Indo-Gangetic plain. Like a whip the road has punished and controlled the subcontinent; like a whip it has stimulated. Four great religions—Hinduism, Buddhism, Jainism, and Sikhism—were born and grew up along the route. The Islamic idea of a single God spread down it. Empire after empire has fought for the road and its treasure, held them for a time, and been swallowed either by the next conqueror or by the subcontinent's insatiable hunger for outsiders. Two centuries seems each empire's maximum efficient duration, in a strange echo of the old Indian proverb which says of foreigners dying swiftly from the climate: Two monsoons is the life of a man.

Those invaders had always come out of the west heading east. I thought it might be more intriguing to do the journey in the opposite direction, from Calcutta to the Khyber Pass, finishing up where so many outsiders had started.

At times the road must've been little more than a track through woods and fields and jungle, tolerant of carts in places, difficult on foot in others. The Grand Trunk, under many names, has felt the steps of Krishna, of Buddha, of Alexander, of the Mogul sword of Islam, of European traders and travelers, of Kipling, of the British Raj, of Gandhi. Its dust contains the bones of maharajahs and emperors, of forgotten holy men and wasted soldiers—a dust beaten down by the monsoon each year as it whittles at the road.

Today it is ruled by neither soldiers nor holy men, but by truckers careening in an uncontrolled life-and-death struggle through thousands of forgotten villages.

The British had built Calcutta from scratch, as wishful thinking given architectural form. The City of Palaces, they'd called it, congratulating themselves on its echoes of Greece and Rome; their viceroy's palace boasted busts of the Caesars and six thousand servants. It was a gleaming dream of Londoners in stinking, tropical Asia.

Attracted by Dutch and Portuguese successes with the spice trade in the East Indies, the first British traders had arrived on the subcontinent at the end of the sixteenth century. When Queen Elizabeth chartered the East India Company in 1600, she allowed this group of ambitious merchants "exclusive" exploitation rights to an unknown land twenty times the size of Britain, with nearly six hundred princely states, fifteen languages and a thousand dialects, and a few rival European powers to compete with, not to mention the Mogul Empire. But John Company, as it would be known, at that time had practically no interest in India, no ideas of military expansion. Nor did the Crown. These were simply merchants going after the Java trade, which the Dutch had already wrapped up. India was only a consolation prize for the Spice Islands contest.

The British started in the south, acquiring control one way or another of settlements that became Surat, Bombay, Madras, and later Calcutta. They built trading posts, hired Indian mercenaries, formed alliances with some local rulers, subdued others. The Moguls left them alone in return for a promise to protect their shipping interests. After all, a few British traders hardly posed a threat to that vast Islamic empire in the northern subcontinent. At the time the Mogul emperor's annual income was over 50 million pounds sterling, more than a hundred times the revenue of the Crown.

The trade itself was largely in cotton and other cloths, sugar, indigo dye, silks, and saltpeter. In return Indians wanted mostly silver bullion, and in such quantity that the Company nearly failed. But by the turn of the eighteenth century there were only two powers for the Company to contend with: the French, who were commercially far less competent, and the Marathas, a Hindu kingdom that controlled central India. Mogul rule in northern India, after two centuries, was in disarray. By the mid-1700s the Company had seized the prize of Bengal from the local Nawab, thanks to the skill of the manic-depressive (and later suicidal) Robert Clive, a merchant mercenary who led a tiny, outnumbered army of a few hundred British and several thousand Indians.

Clive resembled many other Company bigwigs who, unlike their ill-paid clerks, got so rich on the subcontinent, usually keeping their own personal trade in diamonds and opium going on the side, that on their return home they were considered a separate class, the Nabobs. The Nabobs' new money in turn disrupted the English landholding system as they bought up country estates, baronetcies, and Parliament seats. They also persuaded a lot of people to go out to India.

Private corruption within the East India Company made it look uncomfortably like the decaying Mogul throne. Yet the Company's charter with the British government to control the India trade kept being renewed, even as they verged on insolvency and flirted with empire-building. This lack of control inspired the India Act of 1784, which effectively put John Company under the political thumb of the Crown.

No matter who was really running India, it was an unhealthy place for a foreigner. Annual deaths in Calcutta at one point reached 74 percent per year among Company employees, due as much to the Anglo-Saxon diet (mutton pie, lamb, soup, cheese, Madeira) in hot weather as to Indian diseases.

Still the city grew, and became the center of power for the British Indian Empire. "So it spread," wrote Kipling in *The City of Dreadful Night*. "Chance-directed, chance-erected..." The architecture, which must once have seemed the natural order of things, looks preposterously artificial and stagey now, and the political slogans scrawled everywhere on the brick and stone are the signatures of people who can write whatever they want on the old bosses' walls. The dream ran out of control: since Indian independence in 1947, Calcutta has become a humid hallucination of London. It is a low city, built on swampland, but crammed to skyscraper density, for its mostly one-, two-, or three-story buildings sustain about five thousand people per acre.

In 1900, Calcutta's population was well under a million, and even just before the Second World War, it still hovered at around a million and a half. Today the population has easily passed thirteen million, should overtake sixteen by the turn of the century, and is projected to reach thirty million by 2025. By then those figures will seem as acceptable as the present ones. As a result Calcuttans have become some of the most adept city dwellers on earth, with rarefied techniques of survival in an inferno of heat, mud, traffic, disease, other people, and human and animal muck. Only half of Calcutta is sewered, and none of it adequately.

So many millions exist like this on the Indian subcontinent—vulnerable to weather in tent houses of plastic sheets and flayed tires pulled skintight over a bamboo skeleton—that their poverty sometimes seems a whole other idea of life, one which involves permanently camping out. Especially in Calcutta, the first impulse is to see India only as a crowd, and think: there is always someone poorer.

Unexpectedly, the city's modern subway works well, and as the centerpiece of communal pride, it stays spotless, perhaps because it doesn't invoke any questions of inheritance or identity. "It is ours and only ours," a shopkeeper told me. The underground stations have plants and murals and ancient sculptures and color TVs showing cricket matches and Laurel & Hardy films; it is like descending into an alternate universe. Foreigners may worry about the destiny of Calcutta, but locals fret about the appearance of their metro.

More intellectually vital than anywhere else in India, this city built by and for merchants has also become a city of coffee houses and theaters and film societies, of dynasties of poets, painters, and musicians, of literary journals and clever talk; one estimate counts over two thousand locally published magazines. In this sense it does echo London, though Bengalis prefer to call themselves "the French of the East." Calcutta wears a touch of the injured dignity of a down-on-his-luck aristocrat. The people still carry themselves with the manner of those who inhabit a national, even an imperial capital—albeit a fallen one.

Through the hotel I have hired a car and driver for the first stretch of the Indian road. It seems wisest to do the journey in stages, changing cars like tired horses and taking fresh ones from time to time; drivers in India are notorious for not venturing out of their own territory. The road will be dangerous enough without the added anxieties of a driver uncomfortably far from home.

My original plan was to convince a trucker to let me accompany him, since the Grand Trunk is almost exclusively the domain of trucks. But of course they're doing the route as quickly as possible. My intention is to travel slowly, stopping for whatever catches my eye. To try that with jam-packed public buses would be absurd. An Aussie would probably walk the entire road barefoot (*Ten Toes Up the Khyber!*), but I'm not that durable.

So a rented car it will be. This means a rented driver also—

foreigners in India essentially aren't "allowed" to drive hired cars. This is advice that's virtually rule of law, and I've never been able to determine whether it's from safety, or to assure more work for Indian drivers. Or because of a tradition that foreigners, naturally wealthy, aren't drivers, but the ones driven.

Or the ones taken for a ride.

With the recent currency devaluations, over thirty-five rupees to the dollar now, it is more inexpensive than ever for a Westerner to equip himself here. Who knows which items may have their day on the GT? In the Upper Basement of the Air-Conditioned Market on Shakespeare Sarani—lucky name—I bought airtight plastic food jars, bed linen, electrolyte salts in case of diarrhea, a black umbrella, tinned cheese, and a case of bottled water, having first confirmed that the tops hadn't been cunningly re-sealed.

This afternoon Abdul drove me to search for the beginnings of the Grand Trunk Road over in the slum-suburb of Howrah, on the other side of the Hooghly River, a tributary of the Ganges. A light rain was falling, merciful compared to the coming monsoon, which will leave many of the city's roads knee-deep in water for days at a time. These are the worst months of the year for people living unsheltered on the streets.

We rode in a patched old cream Ambassador, an Indian version of a bygone British Morris Oxford from the early fifties. A cozy grandmother of a car, round-nosed, wide-eyed, and comfortably upholstered, capable of making a tremendous gooselike honking to get its own way. The ideal vehicle for the Grand Trunk Road: solidly constructed, it doesn't give up or flip over easily, and spare parts are available everywhere.

Abdul—a small, resourceful, and imperturbable Muslim, with swift, streetwise motions in his soiled smock—has evolved a quick-thumb klaxon technique that makes honking as natural as braking, and indeed he would rather slam on the horn than stop. He looks molded into the compact sofa of his driver's seat, but his enthusiasm at leaping out as soon as we pull over, then his courtly gesture of opening the door for his passenger, make me worry he'll do this in villages on the road. I suppose to imagine one can be white-skinned and stop unnoticed in an Indian village is naive. Still, I hope to convince him that I can open a car door myself.

Abdul's other quirk is that he has removed the sole windshield wiper out of fear of thieves, no doubt a legitimate concern, and he keeps the wiper safely in the glove compartment. It takes a great deal of rain to make him bother to get it out again and attach it; he prefers peering blindly through a windscreen of running water to screwing the valuable wiper in place.

He makes up for this with a calm in the face of oncoming, honking, certain death, and an unlimited deviousness as he negotiates the traffic like a pinball gliding impossibly between bumpers, never touching.

Geographically and socially, Howrah is to Calcutta rather what Queens is to Manhattan. Many Calcuttans like to pretend Howrah doesn't exist. Given the choice, they don't go over the river any farther than the Howrah Railway Station, which is Calcutta's only rail link with the rest of the subcontinent.

Abdul took me across the great Howrah Bridge high above the river, through buses painted in Day-Glo detail and yellow-and-black taxis moving like water bugs among them. The bridge is all gray steel girders in strict geometries, a cage for the savage traffic. Sluggish buses are outweighed by trams, outfoxed by taxis. There are few private cars, even in the heart of this giant city. Slogans everywhere encourage moral behavior in the proletariat toward the bridge:

THE VERY SIGHT OF IT DETERMINES CALCUTTA'S IDENTITY
KEEPING IT CLEAN IS YOUR RESPONSIBILITY.

There is some question exactly where this part of the Grand Trunk Road starts. Prior to the British the road didn't run down to this corner of Bengal, since Calcutta didn't exist. (In ancient times it followed the Ganges all the way east to Sonargaon, the Village of Gold, near what is now Dhaka.) Calcutta was founded by the British in 1690, but they waited a hundred and forty years before deciding they needed to link their eastern port to the prior timeless road.

The road's origins probably lie with the subcontinent's Aryan settlers, who came in waves from the west, beginning around 1500 B.C. The present GT can be seen as a collaboration of conquerors, centuries apart: Sher Shah, the last Afghan ruler of north India, who interrupted the Mogul Empire from 1539 to 1545; and the British governors-general of the mid-nineteenth century.

Sher Shah revived the existing ancient road, planting trees, erecting caravanserais and distance markers called *kos minars* (many of these obelisks still stand), and establishing a postal system of runners inherited by the Moguls, who kept up the road for a time.

The GT received little attention from the British until they'd been in India for nearly two centuries. The East India Company did practically nothing to maintain the subcontinent's extensive roads, which had fallen into severe disrepair and were impassable by carts during the monsoon. They were also beset by highwaymen like the murderous Thugs, a sect, who honored the goddess Kali by happily strangling twenty to thirty thousand wayfarers a year.

But beginning in the 1830s, the British cleared, repaired, extended, and paved the GT. The benevolent Lord Bentinck, Governor-General from 1828 to 1835, was obsessed with the idea of restoring the road and thus linking Calcutta to Peshawar, near the Khyber Pass and the Afghan border—several months' arduous march for a regiment then. (Bentinck was also a proponent of a postal service, steamboat transport, tea and coffee plantations;

and he outlawed *sati*, the ritual immolation of Hindu widows on their husbands' funeral pyres that still persists.) He pushed hard for funds to cut the old road out of the jungle, level or raise it, prop up the embankments, and plant shade trees along it.

Subsequent governors-general followed Bentinck's example, using convict labor much of the time. In those days the journey from Calcutta to Peshawar, by horse, horse carriage, and palanquin, could take two months. A saying later arose that if the British ever quit India, the only monuments they'd leave behind would be the GT and a pyramid of empty beer bottles.

Paving the GT between Calcutta (then the capital) and Delhi commenced in 1839. Links between other major cities soon followed. The railroads, begun in 1853 under Lord Dalhousie, actually encouraged the swift completion of a paved road as far as the Khyber, to support and feed and give constant access to the trains. Within twenty years the road was known as the Grand Trunk, meaning the big road that linked all the branch roads. But throughout the subcontinent, as often as not, it was and is still called the Sher Shah Suri Marg—Sher Shah's Road. It was three tree-lined lanes wide then, with a faster, broader carriageway in the middle. Wheeled bullock carts largely replaced pack animals and porters, but (at a top speed of two miles an hour) they couldn't possibly compete with trains for large-scale transport. It took modern trucks to bring back the GT's old commercial clout as a long-distance cargo route.

For the British the restored road's importance was proven during the 1857 Mutiny—known to Indians as the First War of Independence—when it made large troop movements possible in a hurry. For Indians the Grand Trunk opened and eased local trade and communications, as it had centuries earlier. For both British and Indian minds it came to exist as a rediscovered unifying idea, sewing the subcontinent together along a single wobbly thread.

• • •

Within South Howrah, where it starts, the GT has the status only of a neighborhood main street. It winds through what once must've been a separate village but has now turned into an area of cheap, ready-made clothing shops fronting *bustees*—literally "habitations," in fact slums; there are over five thousand bustee compounds in Calcutta. The road is narrow, fit for two lanes of traffic, with usually another flexible lane of dispute between.

Rain was threatening and food was frying; people stood about waiting in the oppressive humidity, children cradled in their arms. Cows wandered the road and dogs lay asleep with gently folded limbs in their private ditches. Here and there brimming lakes of watery filth glistened, as thick as asparagus purée.

I'd hoped it would be a matter of simply following the address numbers right down to #1 to find the road's nineteenth-century beginning. But street numbers in India often make no sense, or in this case, run backward. (The local joke is that the city maps are deliberately all wrong, in order to confuse the Pakistanis when they invade.) The G.T. ROAD (SOUTH) HOWRAH, as it first appears on addresses posted over shops, begins with #4 and actually counts higher as you follow it to its start, traditionally held to be the old Botanical Gardens.

The G.T. Road numbers continued to mount into the 300s. This was a district of food stalls, furniture dealers, "watch handlers," granaries, tailors, tiny snack shops, with palm trees and more tightly pressed bustees behind. After a level railway crossing the road continued, but under names that kept rapidly changing—College B. Road, then Botanical Gardens Road.

The gardens themselves came about two ragged miles farther down this mysterious tributary of the GT, in Sitpur. From massive stone walls they seemed to overflow like a bountiful green island. A sign before the high front iron gate said: INDIA BOTANIC GARDEN, EST. 1787. The road flowed right into the gardens, though no car traffic was allowed through the gates.

Abdul insisted the Grand Trunk Road's true beginning was at

the back gate of the Botanical Gardens—where, in theory, this now-pedestrian road through the gardens surely led. We went winding along tortuous side lanes and at last came to the back gate. Just inside sat three guards in khaki uniforms and matching berets.

Behind them rose a universe of dripping tendrils, a complex forest that was one single two-thousand-legged banyan tree, the largest certainly in India, and probably in the world. AT LEAST 235 YEARS OLD (said a conveniently undated sign) and 425 METERS IN CIRCUMFERENCE AT ITS BROADEST REACH (then).

I pointed out to Abdul that the gardens had been established by the British, around the tree, at least a good half century before they had extended the Grand Trunk Road to Calcutta. So how could the little road that led circuitously *through* the enclosed gardens be considered the original beginnings of the GT?

Well, said Abdul astutely, it depended on when the gardens were actually walled in.

He had a point. Maybe the gardens hadn't been so big then.

I asked the guards here at the back gate where they thought the Grand Trunk Road began.

One said it began, as the changing street names indicated, back at the railway crossing.

One said it began at the front gate of the gardens.

One said the road had originally run all the way through to this very spot.

Originally?

The second guard said that in this case, it would mean it was no longer the Grand Trunk Road, except as far as the front gate. The problem was the signs and the names; signs and names in India were always a problem.

The first said that proved his theory. Where the name changed, the road changed. Otherwise all roads would have one name, since they led into each other, no?

The third guard said it wasn't all that simple.

A man on a bicycle came over and said he knew it began somewhere else, but he wasn't sure where. The four men started arguing in Bengali.

Abdul took me aside and insisted the GT began here at the back gate, in which case its glorious commencement is now marked by a dilapidated soft drinks stand.

To me it seemed most likely that its start was back a few miles, where the road crossed railroad tracks that led to nearby docks on the Hooghly River. Trains and river and road would have served each other, for the city's importance had grown from the status of its port, over on the east side of the river. Though ninety miles up the Hooghly from the Bay of Bengal and not nearly as accessible as rival ports like Madras, Rangoon, Karachi, or Bombay, Calcutta had accounted for nearly half the imports and exports in British India.

Still, as soon as the railroads spread all over the land in the 1850s, Calcutta became hindered by its disconnection from the rest of the subcontinent. (Until Howrah Bridge's completion in 1943, there'd been only a sole bridge of boats across the river.) India's two main exports, tea and jute, are still processed and shipped from here, but Calcutta's port today is sadly out-of-date, the Hooghly all silted up, and access more limited than ever; only its location in Bengal keeps it alive.

Abdul drove me back the way we'd come. In one garden a young woman sat in a straight-backed chair while her mother combed her dark hair with long, slow strokes. At the gate of an ochre stone house by the railway crossing I asked the blinking man who lived there if he knew where the GT began. He shrugged and shook his head.

"How far does it go?"

"From Howrah," he said. (We were in Howrah.) "I don't know. It comes from there and the road goes on over there a bit more."

For him the Grand Trunk was only a local street.

An august elderly man on a bicycle, sensing a discussion, pedalled over and said, "There used to be a sign, you know, just on the other side of the level railway crossing. The sign read, THE GRAND TRUNK BEGINS HERE. AND FROM HERE ON WE ARE CALLING IT B COLLEGE ROAD. The sign must have come down, or someone took it away. Not so long ago, either. I have been living here for only twenty years."

Since rain had begun to spatter the road and people who no doubt had different opinions on the question were running for shelter, I was prepared to take the stance that (since the mid-nineteenth century, at least) the GT has begun here at the railway crossing. But I wasn't prepared to argue with anyone who wanted to begin the road symbolically under an enormous banyan tree.

The Grand Trunk may lead everywhere, but it begins nowhere.

That evening the city underwent a bombardment of rain. En route to dinner from my hotel, in no time I found Little Russell Street transformed into a channel a foot deep in the center, and every water-gliding Ambassador became Chitty-Chitty-Bang-Bang.

It's been pointed out that India is above all a land of ruins; now I see that Calcutta is simply one of the more recent. Perhaps the city needn't have gone this way, but nearly everything in India takes on a daunting inevitability. Bengalis themselves speak of how susceptible and gullible Bengalis are, artists and writers and talkers by nature, not natural organizers or pragmatists. They tend to look down upon mere businessmen, and this makes them natural victims of someone like my sunglassses vendor. Or of themselves—no wonder the Bengali filmmaker Satyajit Ray (1921-92) created one of his masterpieces, *The Music Room*, around a nobleman who squanders his entire fortune for the sake of music and dance.

Because Bengalis are easily taken advantage of, Calcutta has acquired little of the forward propulsion of Bombay. The city may have little future in the sense of "progress," but it survives—which is miracle and future enough.

Other cities around the world, gradually but relentlessly, are developing their own neighborhood Calcuttas, and anyone who wants to see what the next century will look like has only to come here. In this sense it really is the world's future. The daily hardships of Calcutta street life have already arrived in parts of Mexico City, Bangkok, Nairobi, Rio, and Moscow, but they have also appeared in New York and Rome. Around the turn of the millennium there will be nearly thirty cities the size of Calcutta today. This is its destiny—to be reincarnated overseas like an unwelcome urban deity.

The difficulty with looking at severe mass poverty on an Indian scale is that it seems to force ready-made conclusions on you, especially when it appears accepted, and even organized. For a Westerner, it is difficult to pass beyond instinctive responses of outrage and pity. One reason may be that urban Indian poverty, and Calcutta in particular, sometimes seems to mock him through its architecture: those grand decayed buildings are like a parody of the eighteenth- and nineteenth-century European culture from which he springs.

But you can't begin to understand a place until you understand what its people take for granted. In India this is nearly impossible. So an outsider sees the director-writer-composer Satyajit Ray as a freak Calcutta genius rather than as the tip of the iceberg, and goes away content to think of the city as a crowded canvas of human misery in which he can glimpse any conclusion he wants.

Meanwhile, the Calcuttans swap poems, argue, wade through rivers of shit, and go to the movies.

Dinner at the nearly empty Grand Hotel, out of a last-minute worry over food along the road. Without question the most lavish establishment in Calcutta, formerly a Victorian boardinghouse, recently acquired by an international chain and given a top-to-bottom surgical renovation. Unbelievably white, protected from the surrounding squalor by judicious colonnades and cunningly closed old entrances. The usual embarrassing doormen done up as grandiose servants from some hodgepodge of British Raj, Moguls, maharajahs.

The hotel has several pretentious restaurants, including Indian, where I ate for the price of a couple of drinks back home. A few musicians—singer, veena, sitar, drums—played beautifully, but at an absolutely deafening volume. I told the manager that, as a musician, I appreciated their expertise, but couldn't they play more quietly? Surely he noticed people leaning across tables to shout conversation at each other?

The manager wobbled his head. "I cannot simply turn them down, you know. I cannot simply do that." He added firmly, "It is *not* as simple as you think."

> I have seen no country in the world where provisions are cheaper than in this; but it is muggy, and those who come from Khorasan call it, "a hell full of good things."
>
> —Ibn Batuta (1345)

2.

Foreign Survivors

In early morning heat Abdul and I drove across Howrah Bridge, the airiest place in Calcutta. Pedestrian traffic on both sides and even a man on horseback. Another lump of a slogan, written in both Bengali and English:

> THIS IS A UNIQUE ART FORM OF TECHNOLOGY—
> SHOULDN'T WE SEE IT ALWAYS REMAIN BEAUTIFUL?

We joined the Grand Trunk Road again, heading away from Calcutta past engineering works, auto-parts warehouses, barber "saloons," and weigh bridges for trucks. Walls were aglow with the living-color splendor of Indian film posters: couples lasciviously embracing, villains brandishing curved daggers. The road took us past smaller remains of the British era. Lost among carpenters' stalls and butcher shops were ornate mansions in ruins, with rusted iron balconies and crumbling stone columns. A few men still lay asleep on raised wooden platforms by the roadside, sharing the shelter of a yellow awning. Cows patrolled and dogs napped before small temples decorated like fancy pastries.

India is a land of inspired mottos. On the back of a red truck just ahead, existence was split between the two gates:

LIFE IS DRAMA	MAN IS ACTOR
WORLD IS STAGE	GOD IS DIRECTOR

The most popular motto by far, way ahead of pragmatic wisdom like HORN PLEASE or USE DIPPER AT NIGHT (meaning dimmers) was the happy farewell inscribed on the back of practically every truck, just above the plate numerals, to be read as it roared away and left you in the dust:

OK! TA-TA!

The Grand Trunk Road was severely potholed as it ran alongside the Hooghly, separated by shop stalls from the river. I soon became an admirer of these little stilt-stalls on stunted plank legs, shutters flung open, sheltering in the lee of a tree, barely large enough for a man to fold himself into on one of his shelves. Their roofs usually extend far out to keep the rain from dripping or being blown in, and they look the safest and most private dwellings in a land of hardly any safety or privacy.

The mud-brown river was perhaps a mile wide here, lined with tall palms, smoking factories, and the pocked remains of great houses. Already buses and lorries ruled the road, horns blaring, lights glaring, scattering puffing rickshaw cyclists, innocent wayfarers, and pedestrian rickshaws moving loads of wood or hay. These hand-pulled rickshaws, with whipcord men hauling passengers or goods on foot, are now unique to Calcutta. Even China, which introduced them here a century ago along with immigrants to handle them, no longer permits any.

Calcutta, on the other hand, has perhaps sixty thousand barefoot rickshaw-wallahs. Many are untouchables from Bihar who sleep on the streets, sending their earnings (about a dollar a day) back home. The high wheels put enormous strain on the men's bodies; they are forced to fight to keep any heavy load from lifting them in the air. Only a few thousand human-powered rickshaws are licensed, so the opportunities for the police to collect bribe money from the unlicensed ones are irresistible. A recent attempt to abolish them met with enormous protest from the rickshaw-wallahs themselves—several hundred thousand people would lose their means of support, it was argued—and under investigation, it turned out that 80 percent of the rickshaws were owned and leased out by the police. Far more Calcuttans use them than the expensive immaculate subway, where fares start at about ten cents.

Children were bound for school: girls in red and white uniforms and boys in blue and white, their dark hair neatly slicked back. Half-starved cows wandered along at their own leisurely pace, walking anatomy lessons. As it began to rain faintly on a makeshift market one woman whipped a sacred cow with a straw handbroom to shoo it away from her tomatoes.

Auto centers proliferated, elephants' graveyards of eyeless, wheelless, faceless dead or dismembered Ambassadors. Water pooled everywhere, ready to slop over the little stone canals lining both sides of the narrow road. Soon the GT left Calcutta behind, but not before one last warning:

DON'T CREATE CHAOS

Until the late sixteenth century this part of the subcontinent was mostly thick mangrove and malarial swamps, steaming, tiger-infested, and barely penetrable. The Hooghly was the only feasible long-distance route then, Bengal's "swift, untaxed highway of trade and commerce." For thirty miles north of the city the river is lined on both sides with remnants of foreigners—the Portuguese, Dutch, French, Danish, and British predecessors of Calcutta.

European possessions along the Hooghly would start with a fort, mills, and a church, then add fine houses, schools, and cultural institutions. Along today's river, Indian temples and *ghats* (wide staircases into the water) significantly outnumber the colonial-era jute mills, mansions, and church spires. These European towns still emanate a gentrified peace quite removed from the common hurly-burly of the road, and a Peter Pan aspect too—like the "lost boys" who didn't have to grow up as Calcutta had, downriver.

Serampore, once the principal Danish settlement (1755-1845), was a bustling town, known today for a weaving college. The most striking Danish survivor was gigantic St. Olaf's Church, tall out of all proportion to the Indian buildings. 1805 was carved in stone above three huge sets of doors framed by muscular columns. The church was shut tight and young men were playing cards in the shelter of the roof overhang, staying out of the rain. On the elongated steeple a clock had stopped at 8:23, though not that day.

The Indian Public Works Department had thoughtfully propped up a dozen blackened Danish cannons in a triangular park just before the church, around a weird waterless fountain of leaping dolphins more suited to a miniature golf course.

Two centuries ago Serampore, called Fredericsnagore by the Danes, had been more successful than Calcutta. Denmark, a neutral European state in the Napoleonic Wars, briefly dominated the India trade, as its ships, cash, and merchandise (mainly cotton and silk) were safe from attack by other European powers. The British finally bought the town from the Danes, and Serampore still manufactures jute sacks used for grain all over the world.

In a drink shop across the way I asked who'd built the church. The shopkeeper thought for a strenuous moment. "American," he said finally. "The Americans."

After Serampore we emerged into countryside, the road well worn away and its original stones exposed. On both sides green fields soothed the eye. Roadside stalls and hovels were thatched, with walls of plaited bamboo. The downpour grew steady, the tentative forefinger of the monsoon; soon rain would be sovereign over all India. On the Grand Trunk Road it was benevolent, softening the exhaust fumes and the pollutants and keeping the dust in its place rather than in your throat.

The day's rain turned creeks into rivers. People washed clothes near the embankments, and on a sodden field with goalposts, soaked boys were kicking a ball around. The road kept traversing railway tracks. We averaged perhaps fifteen miles an hour, but in villages we crawled along. Five-minute traffic jams were common, even blessed events compared to the alternative, which inspire a particularly Indian litany of boasting.

"Don't think you can impress me with your traffic jams. Two hours we were stranded. A line of trucks ten kilometers long. Are you listening? Like the coils of a snake. You think perhaps I am exaggerating? I am not exaggerating even one little bit."

"That is nothing. Once for seven hours I did not even turn on my engine. And the line of trucks was thirty kilometers long. *Thirty.* Water on all sides. You could not walk anywhere. Like an island. The chap in the lorry in front got out to relieve himself and *ffft!* We never saw him again."

In these villages and even on bare crumbling patches of wall in the countryside, the ubiquitous emblem was a version of the hammer and sickle plus star which signifies the C.P.M., the Communist Party of India (Marxist). As the ruling Bengali party since 1957, and the first democratically elected communist government in the world, its leaders and policies are increasingly paradoxical. They are naturally antithetical to the caste system, and apparently against nationalized companies; in favor of foreign capitalist investment as well as small individual landowners (as opposed to cooperative farms); and staunchly behind the idea of entrusting village councils with unprecedented local power. This is a very Indian Marxism.

They also like unusual statues along the GT.

The first was in Baidyapati: a wise, talkative Mao Tse-tung, larger than life. The black statue stood on a pedestal just off the road, wearing a double garland of red flowers around the collar of the trademark suit; a red armband had been painted on. Right hand upraised, Mao indefatigably addresses every passing worker on the Grand Trunk Road. Was it Nabokov who said that political art is always kitsch?

"Chairman Mao," the keeper of the little store beside the statue told me helpfully.

I said I recognized the Chairman. Had the C.P.M. paid for the statue?

"No, sir. All Baidyapati pay. The whole village itself puts up the whole statue."

If so, an act of genuine sacrifice in such a poor place.

In Champdani, beneath a lamppost in the center of town, stood a funny toy statue of Mahatma Gandhi—the first of many genial Gandhis on the road. Carved in cartoon lines out of white stone, he stood on an enormous Bauhaus pedestal that dwarfed him many times over: smiling old grandpa in robes, with a walking cane, as if he'd had a good day fishing.

"Gandhi happy mood," said Abdul.

Any white foreigner standing in a Bengal village square is surrounded immediately by a throng of curious men pushing forward and asking, "Country?"

Here in Champdani, a small sinewy young man—barefoot, dark-skinned, in ragged clothes—spoke English pretty well. What did he do? I asked. "Nothing," he said. "No work to do here."

Was it like that for everyone?

"People is weak here. No work."

"This Grand Trunk Road—how far does it go?"

"Peshawar," he said, flicking his hand as if the Khyber Pass were just around the next bend. "Peshawar."

The first to give me that answer, in fact.

A couple of miles on, we passed a columned, faded school whose courtyard was colored by a lifesize statue of Subhas Chandra Bose. An aggressive leader, elected president of the Indian National Congress and later ousted by Gandhi, Bose was a self-styled general who then fought against the British for the Japanese with his own cobbled-together army and died on Formosa during World War II. Taken as a symbol of nationalism by the Bengalis, with separatist overtones, and recently rehabilitated in Delhi by the Parliament as a great independence leader, he is gaudily omnipresent. In a Calcutta street market I'd seen him on rainbow posters in the guise of Shiva on a horse, in full military regalia, medals and all. Here, natty in his suit, he had his arm up for the passing trucks. A day later he would turn up again in white stone in an unflattering fey pose, one arm flung up high, wrist turned out as if he were modeling designer watches.

Chandernagore was the next of the ex-European towns, and the relic most resplendent with the past. The French had left more surviving memorials than the Danish in Serampore or the Portuguese in their settlement Bandel across the river. The GT entered the town through a stone gate, still known as the Porte Royale and evidently sometimes used as a *pissoir*, with the insignia of France and LIBERTÉ, EGALITÉ, FRATERNITÉ divided between the two portals. The gate looked centuries old, but it'd been dedicated on Bastille Day, 1937, according to an inscription in ungrammatical French—surely one of the final monuments erected by a colonial power.

It was significant that it'd been allowed to remain, since so many of the colonial powers' paeans to themselves have been carted away. One reason was that Chandernagore had got here first—it was established by the French in the 1670s, a good decade before Calcutta, and was never British. By the mid-1700s it was the most prosperous of the European mill towns; French ships negotiated the Hooghly to take on cargos of indigo, sandalwood, spices, and cotton goods. In 1756, when the local Nawab briefly seized Calcutta from the East India Company, Robert Clive, one day to be governor of Bengal, took matters into his own hands and rather irrelevantly bombarded Chandernagore from the river as part of his declaration of British control. Even so, it remained a French possession right through the 1947 independence of the rest of the country. Two years later it was allowed by Paris to vote to become part of India.

What survived of France here, near the river, still looked quite French, benevolent, and well kept. An ochre church stood in blooming gardens, with a white Jeanne d'Arc statue out front. A sign proclaimed the hours for mass. Chandernagore's small Christian community maintained a nearby school, and there were two active French-built colleges. Facing the river, a solemn governor's *palais* had been converted to a French-funded cultural institute, museum, and library. There was even an Hôtel de France with a peaceful garden and French-speaking waiters.

The Indian town still had the country elegance of a small provincial capital in France, a gentle reminder of how assiduously the colonial powers had managed to reproduce their home scenery in this unlikely setting. Chandernagore must've been even stranger at the height of French commerce, as outlandish as Hindu temples and a Gandhi statue would be in the heart of Bordeaux.

Just down a tree-shaded road I reached the esplanade which ran along the waterfront. It was dominated by a proud gazebo like an icing-covered gâteau, engraved in memory of a M. Roquitte, Légionnaire d'Honneur, etc., died in Benares in 1898. The confidence of the inscription was astonishing—how stubbornly the French had kept up an unblinking presence in this tiny place, even after the British had taken possession of the subcontinent! It reminded me of a remark by R. P. Gupta, the patriarch of history-minded intellectuals in Calcutta. "If only the French had conquered India, instead of the British," Gupta had said. "At least we'd have had better food."

Abdul doesn't want to risk his faithful old Ambassador any farther on the GT, so I've had to find another car and driver for the stretch to Benares. At the hotel's suggestion I'm trying Israfel, another Muslim, and his lowslung and more recent Contessa Classic, of predominantly Japanese origin. His English is pretty basic, unfortunately, but the hotel concierge claims he's every bit Abdul's equal.

Israfel is a Bihari, not a Bengali, so theoretically he should know the road. About fifty, with the face of a worried clerk. He has not washed his hair for years. He has the utmost confidence in the prowess of his car, but as a driver he lacks Abdul's brass enthusiasm, and he is obviously terrified of trucks. With good reason, but his hesitation is dangerous, and his anxiety contagious. At the most momentary halt he leaps out, checks under the hood, and starts energetically polishing his car, which already looks as world-weary as he.

The Contessa's furnishings are excessive. Two small bottles of lavender and yellow cologne ride the dashboard like a do-it-yourself salad dressing, and a small TV hangs from the plush roof. I am reluctant to ask Israfel if it works for fear it might. The Contessa also has air-conditioning, though to use it raises the hire-price by several rupees per kilometer. Cheaper to roll the windows down and enjoy a breeze—like leaving the oven door open.

Hooghly-Chinsurah was once two villages which, being so close, became hyphenated. A lavish movie theater in a Bengali art deco style was showing *Lost Empire*. The title fit, for Chinsurah was Dutch from 1628 until 1824, when (along with Malacca and other Dutch holdings in India) it was exchanged to the British for

Sumatra. Thus Fort Gustavus got turned into one of the longest courthouses in the British Empire, and the colonial powers lost their little upriver Amsterdam where Danes, French, English, Portuguese, and Dutch could forget their differences, knock back beer, wine, and cheese in Free Mason lodges, and try to ignore the Bengal heat.

A few British houses remained, and an Armenian Church as testimony to Dutch free-thinking, but little else that wasn't Indian. Chinsurah had a stately architecture throughout, however, for Bengalis of means copied the foreign styles. This made it more a village of high ruined townhouses than of low new hovels.

There was one surviving Dutch eminence near the river. Behind high walls it stood hidden in trees, a deep reddish mansion in the grand style. Nowadays the home of the Indian District Commissioner, before that it had been the residence of his British equivalent, and presumably a mansion of similar standing in Dutch times. It was covered in British concrete, but one recognizably Dutch part was the entrance hall. I slipped in while the guard went to consult with another guard about denying me permission to look around. The floors were elegant black-and-white marble, and above a domineering double staircase was the date: 1687.

Outside again (the guard was gently insistent) I wandered through the disarray of what must once have been a glorious garden, now grown weedy and wild. A little money would keep the gardens healthy, but probably much of the house inside wasn't looked after either. Sometimes it is difficult to grasp how little in India of a nonreligious nature is maintained. Only the means of transport, of the body or the soul, are kept up.

When the Calcutta bypass spliced into the GT, Israfel and I were overpowered by a stampede of trucks. Many hoods wore fringes, tassels, bells, feathers, and whistles, giving them a just-married look. Usually GOODS CARRIAGE and occasionally PUBLIC CARRIER was gaily painted on their fringed and heavily made-up foreheads, and often a slogan, like TRUST IN GOD, or a nickname, like KING OF THE ROAD or ASSAM MAIL. Almost invariably NATIONAL PERMIT was painted above the windshield along with a list of states that particular truck was permitted to carry goods through. On the GT this means West Bengal, Bihar, Uttar Pradesh, Delhi, Haryana, and the Punjab. Most trucks' permits included more states, like Rajasthan, Gujarat, Orissa, Kerala, Jammu & Kashmir, and others.

In another country these trucks might be termed very large lorries. They invariably have six wheels, two in front and four along a single axle in back, and they are almost always overloaded. More than a million such trucks hurtle down Indian roads, and it is an open question how many drivers have licenses.

These truckers were the knights of the Grand Trunk, lancing full tilt on diesel-driven chargers, jousting at each other like honor-maddened champions and daring the enemy with honked oaths to face them down or turn aside in cowardice. It was almost surreal how people were perpetually waiting everywhere else in India but hurrying on the GT. The road was like a deadly version of a video game in which obstacles and other vehicles come at you constantly. Lives, trucks, and valuable cargos were risked to gain a few feet's advantage over one's opponent. Heavily overloaded trucks swung out to pass even if more trucks were careering out of control from the other direction. No driver would relinquish his place without a struggle and a loud, maniacal cadenza of honking protest.

Those initial miles were a baptism by fire. At first it shook me to see one truck in the correct, left-hand lane and two passing it on the right, straddling the road, jockeying for position while other trucks charged straight at them at top speed. By a mere week later it had become a rule of profound wisdom that, even though most of the time the GT was barely two unmarked lanes narrow, with judicious steering and courage it could still be dominated down the middle. Why not try? Let Shiva help the poor fool thundering toward us with the same determination! What made it preposterous was that the road was usually so bad, the jousting took place at a maximum of 30 miles per hour.

Apart from the trucks and buses, there were almost no cars on the road, only brave motorcycles, rickshaw vans, and foolhardy bicycles ("the noblest invention of mankind"—William Saroyan). There were also strange amalgamations; few vehicles remained pure for this localized village-to-village traffic. Some were missing a windscreen here and a door there, but many had been taken apart and ingeniously grafted. Wagons were towed by motorcycles, bicycles had sidecars attached, ground-level unicycle go-carts tugged plywood platforms on wheels. And, as always, oxen and horses were gamely pulling wagons in slow march time.

A few villages later we were halted by lowered barriers at a crossing and a train jolting past. After the barriers opened the country opened. On the right, past occasional shop-stalls, rice fields busy with black buffalo stretched to the river, and the road became a corridor through village life, a shaded colonnade of trees, magisterial and evenly spaced. Presumably some of the oldest trees were planted under the aegis of Lord Bentinck, who instigated the road's nineteenth-century renewal.

Bentinck was operating under the auspices of the East India Company, which at this time ruled a little less than half the subcontinent—"the strangest of all governments . . . for the strangest of all empires," as Macaulay put it. The Company by now had its own military and civil services; it could undertake tasks like the restoration of an ancient road or the building of a railway system. As the reigning power in Asia it controlled one-fifth the world's population and produced revenue greater than that of Britain; the Crown itself wouldn't officially take possession of India until after the 1857 Mutiny. This became the only time in two millennia when the entire subcontinent was united under one rule, and that idea—an imposed, British idea—was so unnatural it lasted only ninety years.

• • •

Few stretches of the GT stay deserted for very long. Villages are close enough that there are almost always people walking, carrying something, often barefoot, the women balancing a load on their heads, children in tow and a baby in their arms.

Frequent along the GT, now, are *dhabas*—open-air restaurants for truckers, generally set well back from the road, behind a dusty apron of open ground. They sell food and drink but invariably provide braided-rope cots free, as a come-on, and some other extra—free air for tires, perhaps. Often a shop-stall perches on stilts nearby, selling cigarettes and candy. Sometimes the dhabas have names; sometimes they even call themselves hotels. Generally they proclaim their food as vegetarian or "non-veg."

In the evening, lit by lanterns or open fires, the dhaba becomes a cozy haven, with trucks parked along the road and the drivers chatting away on the *charpoi* cots where they'll sleep at least part of the night. Dhabas have replaced the caravanserais of Mogul times, just as trucks have partly replaced long caravans of pack animals tramping this same road. Prostitutes are always available, with the inevitable result of AIDS being efficiently spread all over India. Thanks to the truckers, the disease has become the latest invader along the Grand Trunk Road.

No doubt the road has changed most radically since the advent of the gasoline engine, but the GT must always have had a similar urgency—it would be just as dangerous to get run down by several thousand oxen four centuries ago as by a Tata truck tomorrow morning. The road's wooden *ekka* carts and *tonga* carriages are probably much the same as ever, though their wheels are rarely wooden now, but usually salvaged from bicycles. During British times certain traditional professions of the road died out, like the servant whose job was to carry money for his wealthy master and die defending it—though nowadays anyone risking certain parts of the GT at night needs an armed bodyguard. Some timeless professions of the road, such as animal driver or herder, must have changed little over the centuries.

Another is the nomadic performer. Israfel stopped by a small crowd gathered between villages. The center of attention was a dark-skinned young man leading a bear; he wore a loose, open shirt and plaid sarong and carried a little drum and a yellow sack. Zakir had a practiced ease with the attention his bear drew, the result of long experience in assessing his audience, though he looked only in his mid-twenties. His black bear was, he said, about three years old.

The bear, secured to its master by a rope through its snout, went snuffling and digging by the side of the road for worms. About forty people had materialized by now. Every couple of minutes the bear would unleash an enormous shriek of frustration or rage, brought on by a cunning tug of Zakir's rope, and assault his master. The crowd always started back in delighted terror, and Zakir would give a satisfied smile, for the bear was attacking his walking stick. The only way to enjoy the spectacle was to ignore how such bears are trained—hot irons applied to the tender parts of the anatomy, or weeks spent on a metal platform with a fire beneath it to teach the bear to dance when a drum is struck or a particular tune played. Some parts of their bodies are valued as aphrodisiacs in East Asia, as well, so bears are dying out in India.

"How far will you be walking?" I asked Zakir.

"I'm staying in Bengal, you know. I won't go as far as Bihar, people are poorer there. So I'll turn back toward Calcutta soon."

He made his living walking the road, performing, perhaps doing a little dance with the bear, keeping people entertained awhile, then asking for money. He looked puzzled when I asked how he'd chosen this way of life; it was the wandering family circus he'd been born into.

"My father did this until he died," said Zakir simply.

When I offered him fifty rupees—a dollar and a half—he refused the money with a smile. He said confidently, "Wealthy people should give a hundred. Ninety at least. No, no, if fifty is all a wealthy fellow like you is going to offer, I don't want it."

The crowd watched the bargaining as if it were ping-pong. Eventually Zakir accepted the fifty, the crowd dispersed, and he hit the road again in flip-flops.

At Burdwan it began to rain and instantly the streets were full of water, the car ploughing through a shallow canal where the Grand Trunk had been. Side streets grew to torrential rivers in minutes. Once a little water was added to the overworked drainage system, it all backed up onto the street in a flood.

The men in these parts were wiry, small, and very dark-skinned, almost black; they hurried. The women were graceful and refined in their movements; they took their time.

A narrow paddy ran along the road, a field of water bordered by thin trees and mists. A chain of men and women were planting rice in the pelting August rain for a December harvest. Clumps of green rice plantings in neat bundles lay waiting on the strip of built-up mud that traversed the paddy. The men and women stood up to their thighs in the water and mud and almost flung the arrows of green down, so quick was the gesture.

When the rain stopped suddenly they stopped too, and walked up the road to the low mud-and-thatch houses of their village, alongside new pools of welcome rainwater.

A large truck carrying wheat husks from Delhi south to Burdwan had ploughed off the road, creating a four-foot ditch in the mud around its front tires. Only an isolated tree had prevented it carrying on down the slope and into the fields. Two recovery trucks were working together, blocking much of the road, trying to haul the injured truck out with steel cables attached to the front of the frame. A boy had climbed into a low crooked tree to watch. The usual Indian crowd had gathered, willing to wait a long time to see if anything would happen next; perhaps nothing would happen next. As an accident this was tame, for trucks tipped on one side are common along the GT, or lying on their backs like gigantic upended insects, their tires turned helplessly every which way.

In Panagarh I bought oranges and Israfel and I ate them as the road ran on toward the end of the afternoon.

Durgapur, where we spent the night (Israfel sleeping, as customary on the road, in his car), is the site of giant steel mills. Back in 1962 these mills were the first project completed by the government's Public Industrial Sector. For a time they were successful; for a time India led the world in steel production. But they have been defeated in the last two decades by their own inefficiency. They lose extravagant amounts of government money, and eventually they will either have to be shut down or go private. A few years ago, hundreds of coal workers up in Bihar went on strike to protest modernization—lower employment, greater production—and managed to stop traffic on the GT by aligning their bicycles across it. With few exceptions the Public Industrial Sector projects in India have been disasters.

This was the beginning of the Coal Belt, really an Industrial Belt, that extends for hundreds of miles across Bihar, the next state. The area has been called the Ruhr of India, and Durgapur, despite its steel works' failure, still looked more prosperous than any town thus far—a series of concrete house cantonments strewn across tracts of grass with horses grazing among them. Smoke rose from twin-chimnied mills in the distance. Many houses were brick and looked new, or built in the last twenty years: this meant they were probably newer. Often in India I'd think *what an old wreck,* then spot a date like 1946 above the door.

Wrecked old houses, wrecked old landscape. In one day I had traversed nearly four centuries of factories in India, from the jute mills of the early 1600s to the steel mills of the late 1900s. Back then the air must've been cleaner; now the laborers had TVs.

Durgapur even had a businessman's hotel with some pretensions to luxury. A marble staircase, telephones in the rooms, electricity that only failed once or twice, and decent food. All night from the hotel room, beyond the air-conditioner's whine, I heard trucks getting jammed-up in arguments that were settled only after a litany of hoarse blares, desperate bleats, and toodling fanfares.

Dawn on the Grand Trunk Road. No roosters crowed, but trucks honked and grumbled to welcome the day.

> It is better to go to the villages of a strange land before trying to understand its towns, above all in a complex place like India. Now, after traveling some eight thousand miles around the country, I... have a somewhat more detailed and precise idea of my ignorance than I did in the beginning.
>
> — Paul Bowles, *Notes Mailed at Nagercoil* (1952)

3.

The Usual Paperwork

In morning light vultures reigned from the trees, not actively menacing but flapping from one strategic perch to another, waiting with macabre patience for a truck to murder some dog crossing the road. One sees, actually, as many dead trucks as dead animals.

Outside Durgapur mounds of culm (waste coal) were piled a hundred meters off the road around low thatched dwellings, a pasture of black dust that in the mildest breeze made a face mask necessary. The culm is used for cooking or heating fuel and, transported elsewhere in India, can be expensive.

We passed the Raniganj coal fields—served by the Coal Field Hindu Hotel, which looked just as scarred as the landscape. After twenty miles of fields and villages, we came to the iron and steel works town of Asansol. I get that designation from the books; the real business of Asansol is business.

The largest town since Durgapur, Asansol was an unholy din of hammering, wrenching, sputtering, inflating, clanking, patching, battering, and honking. As in every town and village thus far, the GT was the main street, running right up the middle, so that the buildings clung like layers of coral accumulated along a life-giving reef. Nowhere else had embraced the road so wholeheartedly or quite so opportunistically.

A few buildings had the arches of an older grandeur, but the rest were sagging concrete bunkers, goods or tool shops. Any sober description is inadequate to the ugliness of most Indian architecture of the last four decades; to be fair, this ugliness is not uniquely Indian. The same style covers much of the Middle East, a concrete diarrhea that splatters itself everywhere and is impossible to stop.

Here, right in town, the GT was so badly kept up the paving had worn away from the road's foundation bricks. On both sides was a dirt esplanade, then the shops; mounds of steaming or petrified cow dung lay fragrantly everywhere. Piles of bananas and empty mustard oil tins lashed together were waiting to be carted off. A rank of bicycle rickshaw-wallahs rang bells to attract passengers—shrill bird cheeps against the catcalls of trucks and buses.

On foot in such a vehicular place, after a while it becomes second nature at each sudden honk to step out of the way without looking. You soon learn how to tell which banshee shriek has your name on it, and if someone thinks you are worth honking at, it is probably worth your while getting out of the way.

I took an amble about the center of Asansol. Overlooking all was the George Telegraph Training Institute, devoid of students. According to a sign, a medical clinic was dispensing oral polio vaccine every Wednesday morning. The Bengal Marble House stood next door to Bose's Gun House, quintuply padlocked and caged tight. The Asansol Paper House had no stock that I could see, only a sedentary barefoot proprietor, comfortably leafing through a newspaper beneath a rapid fan. A little farther along was the Mama Hindu Hotel, its dingy snack bar in front promising a more profound dinginess within.

It would be presumptuous to suggest, in a country as ancient and talkative as India, that the British awakened any love of language, but they certainly gave Indians a new vocabulary to which they could adapt their natural gifts. No House of Commons speaker in London can possibly match the level of eloquent rhetoric and nineteenth-century grandeur (or wind) that occurs daily in the New Delhi Parliament; and what takes place in Washington, by comparison, is only the empty rustle of dead leaves.

Even shop signs could bring happiness. Here in Asansol, just past a Furnishings Emporium and Disco Tailors, Nu-tronix sold "voltage stabilisers and booster inverters," whatever those are. Imperial Vulcanizing and their trained staff of puncture-wallahs specialized in "Tyre Tubes Fitting," just near the Hero Bicycle Store. (My favorite trinity of Indian signs was the Venus Paying House, a hotel; Abdul Hazur, Brain Surgeon; and King of Kings Karpets, "formerly King of Krokodiles.")

Meanwhile the din on the Grand Trunk was like an unrelenting Wild West shootout. To ease the strain I decided to investigate a shop full of electric fans. A wide-bladed ceiling model seemed a bargain at 900 rupees—only $26, but a month's wages for some people, though perhaps not those with the electricity to run it. Still, the proprietor assured me he sold plenty.

I said, "I bet you have to lower your prices in winter."

"No, sir. I am never lowering my prices. There is not the need. There is simply not the necessity, so I am maintaining my profit margin without stress and strain."

Asansol's walls were covered with orange and white film posters that looked restrained after the suggestive big-city ones that show several photo stills from the film. *The Sin of Adam & Eve*, rated for "adults only," was playing for four days. The poster soberly guaranteed it was "full of sex"—this probably meant a wet T-shirt. It would be followed, fortunately, by *The Armour of God*.

• • •

To escape the heat I walked into Phillips House, an electronics shop specializing in products by the Dutch company of that name. I was immediately greeted by air-conditioning and then by Mr. Ranjit Cope, store manager, who offered me tea and spoke English well.

"Is Asansol always this hectic?" I asked.

"Always."

"Even at night?"

"Not so hectic at night. At night the trucks use the bypass road. So we can all get some sleep."

"It must be good for business."

"Business is always good here. This is the GT Road, eh? It goes to Delhi. No, the Punjab. Today we are selling four hundred radios a month, my friend. In 1982 I was the top dealer in India. I sold more than six thousand Phillips radios that year."

Five hundred a month, twenty a day: it seemed impossible in such a poor place. When I voiced my disbelief, he indicated a gold-framed certificate on the wall, confirming his top sales.

"Then the television came along in '84. So now we sell less radios than before, but we are selling sixty to seventy TVs a month."

Mr. Cope very graciously took me through his stock. A large color TV ran about 23,000 rupees ($660)—this included a lower sticker price plus several thousand rupees to compensate for recent currency devaluations. An ordinary portable radio was similarly about twice the U.S. price—mainly the result of high import taxes. An outsider in India sees poverty first and foremost; what he should also see is a huge middle class, arguably the largest on earth.

"Who buys them?"

He spread his hands, palm upward, as if the explanation were self-evident. "Everyone. The colliers buy the radios. And we sell many p.a. systems and refrigerators. But, my friend, but, *but*—thirty years ago a sack of rice cost fifty paise. Now—now—it costs eight rupees or more. Something must be done about that."

A man who could boast of selling two televisions a day, priced at a year's wages, was complaining about the cost of rice.

"Are the coal workers that well paid? It seems unbelievable."

"You see, they smuggle their coal. To Bangladesh or Bihar. Or all over India." He shrugged. "They have money."

Down a side street, narrowly dodging water blindly sluiced out of a doorway, I was surprised at how muffled the GT din became only a few steps away. The world grew quiet again, humane.

A bony old man, bare-chested, was pottering around the veranda of his rather stately house. I asked its age; he answered by saying he had lived there about forty-five years, and that he was long retired from the insurance business.

"What do you do to keep busy?"

"I do nothing. What do you want me to do at eighty-five?"

"Has the town changed since you moved here?"

"Not at all," he said firmly. "Not at all."

Underway again, we kept passing trucks loaded with brand-new cars and scooters straight from the Maruti factories. As the Indian-made line of Japan's Suzuki, Maruti manufactures some thirty thousand scooters per day that get sucked up by the Asian market like plankton. Trucks were headed south carrying potatoes and wheat from the Punjab, headed north carrying coal, coke, petrol, and propane to the Punjab. Apart from trucks, the only other vehicles on the GT going any distance are the local buses. Petrol is an expensive commodity in India, around 22 rupees per liter, meaning $2.40 a gallon. This makes a middle-class family with a car think twice about using it if a bus is feasible; and if Indians want to cross the country they take the train.

Two huge Tata buses swept past us, a society on the move with arms and legs hanging disembodied off the roof, and a Toyota bus in pursuit. According to the manufacturers, the Tatas carry only about thirty-five seated passengers, the Toyotas about twenty. But seats are shared, and most buses accommodate as many people illegally on top, their rumps fitted snugly against the metal railing running round the roof, their limbs dangling over. The buses all have ladders hanging off the back to enable people to clamber up, and if the roof is full then another ten cling precariously to the ladder like mountain climbers, or to the doors and even the windows.

Thus a bus built to seat thirty-five people can seat up to ninety counting the roof, with another twenty crammed in the aisles and perhaps a dozen hanging off the back and sides, and not counting very small children and animals. It is likely that the insides of Indian buses are the most crowded places on earth, which is why when a single bus plunges off a bridge (a popular item as filler in the newspapers), the casualties are often in three figures.

To drive behind such a potential disaster alarms me, as I have no confidence in Israfel's sluggish reflexes, and he insists on following as closely as possible, as if sheltering for protection from trucks in the lee of a big bus. Someone told me a well-meaning anecdote of a little girl falling from a bus's rear ladder, getting run over by the following car, the villagers falling on the hapless driver and passenger and beating them to death.

In a private car we are at the mercy of the larger vehicles that make up almost all the traffic. The trucks, which for good luck have either an old shoe dangling on a chain from a bumper or else the evil eye insignia painted on the side, treat automobiles like irritating insects, to be swept aside or crushed.

Only a short distance to the Bihar border. We reach it after a series of banked fields where a lone woman walks, apparently on air, carrying two nude children in her arms. Her purple sari swirling.

• • •

By midday the heat had me drugged. Barakar, the last town in West Bengal on the Grand Trunk, was calmer than Asansol. It had a border-crossing feel—the sense of last-chance and first-chance shops and canny bartering with no nonsense and no wasted energy. Border towns know the value of everything.

A bit stupefied, I went into a low squarish white building, cool and blue-walled on the interior, with a wooden desk covered in papers, official-looking books piled alongside, and a makeshift sofa. In an adjoining shadowy room were several cots and a couple of men asleep. A ceiling fan stirred the forms on the desk. I sat in the welcome current of air and waited. This was the office of the Government of West Bengal's Director of Commercial Taxes, Barakar District.

A tall young man hurried in, slightly unshaven, with a beak of a nose, black-rimmed glasses, and a shock of black hair. Nirmala Bandyopadhyay was, at twenty-six, not only an amiable inspector of commercial goods coming into West Bengal but also a penny-in-the-slot dispenser of useful information.

He called for cold drinks and said, "Please, ask me anything you want and I will do my best to answer accurately if I can. I will try, let us say that."

"What do you do here?"

"I am an inspector. I inspect Notified Goods. This is defined by three Acts. In 1941, 1954, and 1956. If someone is going to import Notified Goods into West Bengal, they are going to have to declare these goods. The persons importing must go to our principal district office in Durgapur and fill out forms 30A, or forms 34A and 34B. When the consignment of Notified Goods comes to West Bengal, the driver brings the forms to us here and we inspect the goods and endorse the permit. Taxes are paid on Notified Goods, naturally. Shall I go on?"

"Give me some examples of Notified Goods."

"I can show you the official list, if you'd like." He reached for the stack of books.

"A few would be fine."

"Iron and steel," he said. "Lumber. Paper. Medicines. Hides and skins. Photographic films. Aluminium. Motor parts. Shall I go on?"

"Any foods?"

"Poppy seeds. All spices. Canned fruit. Fresh fruit, though, is *not* Notified Goods." He paused. "Drinks with air in them."

"Soft drinks?"

"Soft drinks."

We were sipping Notified Goods, 7-Up and Pepsi; new competition for India's Limca and Thums Up, which a friend once described as tasting like something you'd use to remove a tattoo. Indian soft drinks sometimes advertise themselves as containing *Absolutely no natural ingredients!*

"And some non-Notified Goods?" I asked.

"Rice. Wheat. Most fresh foods."

"What's the level of taxation?"

"You see, we have a four percent central sales tax. Then there is an eight percent general rate of tax. But it depends on the goods, you see."

All this paperwork, these taxes from state to state—all these limitations on free trade that use up hours and hours of human effort at every border: to simply follow the rules was made as complex as possible. No doubt this was an earnest attempt to combat the Indian genius for anarchy, but it struck me as one of the most dangerous inheritances from the Raj. A British obsession with "form" and the way things must be done, combined with an Indian spiritualism and ability to find ways to be sure that nothing was done, had produced a manic love, almost a worship, of official forms and rules and coagulating paperwork that utterly defeated the people they were designed to serve.

"It sounds as if you work pretty hard."

He smiled. "We do try to work hard. There are two inspectors like myself on each shift. And two shifts per month. From the first to the sixteenth, and from the sixteenth to the thirty-first. When I am not working, I go to live with my parents in Calcutta. I am from there originally, I did all my schooling there and I am still studying there."

"Will you keep working for the government after you finish school, Mr. Bandyopadhyay?"

"In some capacity, yes. My father also worked for the Reserve Bank, you see. I believe I will continue my schooling at least until age thirty."

For most graduates such a safe government job would be the top of the ladder.

"You haven't married yet, then."

He grinned a bit sheepishly. "I haven't yet been so fortunate. You know, in India these matters are settled by parents. Perhaps my parents will be choosing me a girl sometime and, thanks to God, perhaps we will be falling head over heels in love afterwards. But at the moment I am not married."

"You seem like a man of many interests."

"I would say my only hobby, really, is reading. All kinds of reading but literature especially. I like very much to read poems and I write poems myself. I have published several poems in Calcutta magazines."

That was the other ambition for a Calcuttan.

"What sort of poems?"

He blushed. "Love poems."

"And who are your favorite poets?"

"I like the Sanskrit poetry, especially. And let us say nineteenth- and early twentieth-century poets. Tagore, for one. I like his love poems."

"Do you like to go to the movies?"

He bobbed his head enthusiastically. "I do go to movies. I go mostly to Hindi and Bengali movies. I like, for example, the films of Satyajit Ray. I like what you might call 'offbeat' films. I think these films are really the ones about real life. But most films in

India are fairy tales. With a hero like Superman who can do everything. So I prefer the 'offbeat.'"

He was a typical young Bengali: scraping by through commerce, living through art, and believing almost proudly that there was no way that art and business could go hand in hand.

"It's been very generous of you to speak to me like this."

"Not at all," he said, standing up to accompany me outside. "In India we say: 'Guest is God'."

It is a curious people. With them, all life seems to be sacred except human life. Even the life of vermin is sacred, and must not be taken. The good Jain wipes off a seat before using it, lest he cause the death of some valueless insect by sitting down on it. It grieves him to have to drink water, because the provisions in his stomach may not agree with the microbes.

— Mark Twain, *Following the Equator* (1897)

4.

Followers of the Mountain

On a high bridge over a winding river three elephants trudged past, carrying betel in sacks. Women on the curved beach below were spreading their washed clothes to dry on the pale sand.

The countryside was wilder and greener than in Bengal, the people wilder and poorer; many were Bihar's tribals, or forest dwellers. It was a chaotic landscape, hellish with coal dust blowing and great highlands of coal behind the barren ground of the near distance. Patriarchal trees at regular intervals shaded the GT. Green paddies luxuriated in water with austere mountains behind; few villages were set near the road. It seemed the deep, impoverished, and secret heart of the country.

Bihar as a region has some of the richest history in India, and in natural resources it is richer than West Bengal. In actual wealth

Bihar remains one of the poorest states, feudally and corruptly run. Most of the elected officials have criminal records, and many businesses and roads are under perpetual threat from *dacoits*, armed gangs working for hire or independently. Though official India likes to boast that it is the largest democracy on earth, Bihar—like several other states—is a different story.

So much of the Indian corruption only makes sense in terms of caste. Out of about 600 million eligible voters, about 500 million are of the lower castes. They are the ones most easily swayed or bought; they are the ones most susceptible to strong-arm tactics. Bihar provides more woman and child labor than any other state, and male hard labor in places like the coal fields and construction. These are men earning, say, seventy cents a day for a ten-hour shift. Women may earn less, sixty cents perhaps, and the children working illegally as little as ten or twenty cents a day.

The figures are meaningful not as a mark of low income, which is after all only the extreme end of a commonplace, but of utter vulnerability. The choice is to work or to starve, just as in Bihar it also becomes to vote or to suffer. The state is run by *zamindars*, the feudal landlords who control jobs and land and elections. Many of their workers are bonded laborers, struggling to pay off loans taken out by their parents or grandparents. The police work in league with the *zamindars* to run things smoothly.

This means that it is possible to travel through a quiet Bihari town as if it were in the Guatemalan highlands, without having the slightest idea that this morning a dozen men died from suicide while in police custody, or that two thousand died during riots against zamindars in the last month, or that during the last elections recalcitrant voters had been kidnapped or roughed up or murdered; or else sometimes inventively tortured (bicycle spokes through the eyeballs, acid applied to the wounds afterward) or else the votes easily secured through stealing of vote slips at the polling booth or (more difficult) through the inconvenience of mass graves. As one zamindar in charge of local elections (won handily by the Congress Party) boasted on television, "First we bribed them, then we beat them, and after that we killed them." This process, used on all sides, is known as booth-capturing. The more backward the region, the more people deprived of their vote—in places as high as sixty percent.

But Bihar had other lessons in power and how to wield it.

Small towns in Bihar generally make less urban sense than in Bengal: they appear meager settlements that simply accumulated more people. Parasnath is strung out along the GT for miles and nearly every building looks only half completed, with irregular roofs of clay pot-halves and overgrowth everywhere.

Curious weapons were displayed for sale outside rude lean-tos: spears and axes on bamboo poles, curved swords in scabbards, and almost as an afterthought, bamboo walking sticks. These were connected with the Jain pilgrims. In the old days, to go up the Jains' sacred mountain, also called Parasnath, could be dangerous, due to cheetahs, tigers, wolves, jackals, and wild boars. ("Bears are numerous round this spot," warned my 1898 *Murray's Guide.*) The animals which survive today avoid the pilgrims.

We circled off the GT on a quieter road around the broad mountain. At a railway crossing an antiquated British-era shack still served, with its reassuring sign: COMPLAINT BOOK WITH GATEMAN—who also still served, no longer in uniform.

Behind the mountain we crossed another bridge high over the Barakar River at a bend. Just up the green riverbank on the other side stood the white temple marking the spot where Mahavira, the father of Jainism, had his moment of enlightenment in the sixth century B.C. The river curved serenely past the white temple into low green hills flagged with smaller and simpler shrines downriver.

Mahavira, born into a semi-aristocratic family in 599 B.C., gave up his wife, daughter, and position at age thirty to become an ascetic. For twelve years he fasted and meditated while squatting, and went naked in the heat. Enlightenment came to him here, and he became "without ties." For thirty years he traveled on foot up and down the Grand Trunk Road, through Benares and Allahabad, and eventually died of self-starvation, aged seventy-two. The story goes that for all this time he never spoke to anyone, ate only raw food, and swept insects from his path to avoid trampling them. He may have kept silent, but the Jains credit him with endless itemized lists of beliefs and duties they rigorously follow.

Though Jainism existed before Mahavira, he is considered the greatest (and last) of its twenty-four saints, the *tirthankaras*, some of whom are probably mythical. Its roots go deep in antiquity's war of good and evil, the darkness versus the light, that appears in ancient Persia's Zoroastrianism, in the Judeo-Christian Cain/Abel and Saul/Esau battles, and the conflict of the Two Brothers in Egypt. But most important, the tirthankaras represent fulfilled *men*: free, enlightened individuals, liberated spirits, with none of the human failings of the Hindu gods. They cannot save or intercede, but they are shining examples.

The shrine compound seemed rather lighthearted and modest to commemorate the spiritual awakening of the leader of this ancient, puritanical, almost obsessional religion. And the shrine wasn't nearly as old as it looked, built only in 1930. After a pale blue guardian building and a courtyard, an interior gateway was fronted by two jolly green sculpted elephants. Near the elephants, two stones bore the outsize footprints of the Lord Mahavira. Religious heroes of the Near, Middle, and Far East always had huge feet.

The shrine itself, with a little veranda, resembled a square white country cottage. Yellow and green niches were paired on outer walls. Some held statues or framed pictures of Jain mystics, others held flower offerings. A few niches were tiled in abstract zigzag patterns that looked extremely out of place.

I asked the temple keeper if there was any particular meaning in the niches' decor.

"Not at all. Just good designs, you see," he said.

Jainism is a religion without a god; or perhaps not truly a religion, but a strict monastic order. As one Jain text puts it, "Man, thou art thine own friend; why seekest thou a friend beyond thyself?" Instead of escape via God, the Jains believe in escape through enlightenment—essentially, the perfectibility of man.

In the Jains' extremely ordered, eternal universe, patterns with very particular meanings come and go in detailed forty-thousand-year cycles, relentlessly repeating. All things, from rocks to elephants and trees and mountains and insects, have equal souls. Not only are all serious Jains vegetarian, but in a monastery, ants and snakes and rats are scrupulously fed; fortunately, Jains believe the tigers in the woods around Parasnath are likewise vegetarian. In areas with many Jains, like Bombay, you can see men carried around on beds all day—paid to provide human food for bedbugs.

Non-killing is the primary Jain duty. An annihilation of self and original action controls their sometimes circular logic. One proverb runs, "He who lights a fire kills living beings; he who puts it out kills the fire." The ultimate Jain goal is a death by fasting, owning nothing, the soul finally freed into an uneventful heaven from the *karma* (actions) of imprisoning past existences.

Easy as it is to mock their precautions about killing wee bugs, the Jain ideals of non-violence and non-action spring from a source that still runs deep in the Indian soul, deep enough to have been converted into a very effective political doctrine by Gandhi. The financial success of the Jains, which is nearly as old as the religion, came about because, forbidden from entering traditional occupations like farming because of various taboos, Jains naturally became middlemen, moneylenders, and merchants. In this respect they are often called the Jews of India, and have similarly always been known as patrons of the arts. Unlike Jews, the Jains have limited their own professional options, rather than having them limited by others. And unlike Judaism, Jainism has become a creed that effectively excludes the lower classes, though

Jains claim to put no value on landed property or possessions.

Yet they are economically very strong indeed—many of the country's leading industrialists are Jains, and they have the cotton and banking businesses nearly sewn up—and they probably have a higher rate of literacy than any other group in India. They are enthusiastic builders of hospitals, libraries, schools, and orphanages; in ancient times their stone-carving and temple architecture were of the highest sophistication. They are known also for their charity, and probably unavoidably, they are always endowing animal hospitals. I found it hard to make head or tail of an austere, pedantic system which treats suicide as a sin yet in which the strains of suicide are very strong, and whose generous adherents grow rich dreaming of blissfully having nothing, being nothing, at the top end of the universe.

In the shrine's inner sanctum, flowers were laid neatly as offerings in a sculpted scale model of a temple. The walls and doorways were dominated by identical tiles which showed a Hokusai-style view of Mt. Fuji. Perhaps an argument could be made that Fujiyama is to the Japanese rather what the sacred mountain here at Parasnath represents to the Jains, but it looked more as if they simply got a good price on some tiles. Clearly the spot and hence the shrine on the spot mattered to them, and little else. I found it a bit disconcerting—my limitation—that they can be so purposeful about not injuring protozoa in their drinking water but so casual about the decor of their leader's shrine.

There is nothing casual about the Jain faith, but many of their famous strictures have been gradually abandoned over the years or else given over to individual choice. Nowadays, Jains fast only on rare occasions: gone are the days when a normal Jain death was a gradual suicide by starvation, spread purifyingly out over a decade. And though Mahavira emphasized absolute poverty, ownership of absolutely nothing, Jains—evolving as merchants over many generations—don't see a contradiction between being good in business and good in their religion. The Jains have survived so long because they never threaten anyone; instead they try to help. Rather than going after political clout, their power is based on wealth, which in such a poor country is better than fleeting political power.

I asked the genial temple keeper why Jains did so well. His answer was by-the-book, and though a Jain, characteristically he didn't include himself in the praise.

"They concentrate," he said. "And by being religious-minded, being good people, why, naturally, good things come to them."

It was late afternoon now, and because in Bihar it isn't wise to be on the roads in darkness, I left abruptly and reluctantly.

In Parasnath I'd spotted a *dak* bungalow set back from the road—a British government motel built by the Raj for its traveling sons, easily recognizable with its stone arches and capacious garden and courtyard. Kipling wrote of these hostels in *My Own True Ghost Story:* "Some of the dâk-bungalows on the Grand Trunk Road have handy little cemeteries in their compound—witnesses to . . . the days when men drove from Calcutta to the Northwest. These bungalows are objectionable places to put up in. They are generally very old, always dirty, while the *khansamah* [steward] is as ancient as the bungalow. He either chatters senilely, or falls into the long trances of age. In both moods he is useless."

The Public Works Department or sometimes the military has taken most of these over as government rest houses, but I couldn't convince the man running this one even to turn on the lights so I could see the rooms. He didn't want the nuisance of a little business, and I had a strong impression of unseen scampering rodents, so we drove a good ten miles, outside of Parasnath proper, to find an alternative as darkness seeped down.

My hotel, at a hundred rupees a night, was a series of blue concrete bungalows a couple of decades old, each with its own bathroom, set along a ridge overlooking the GT. The kitchen (which was too filthy to be worth the risk) and the loud generator were down the hillside beside the owner's busy dhabas. I boiled up some bottled water in my portable kettle and added a packet of powdered minestrone for dinner. There were no other guests. I hadn't been crazy to buy those sheets in Calcutta; the dingy mattress was bare. Soon after I turned in, the generator was shut down, the ceiling fan stopped, and the room began to bake me. I spent the night taking intermittent cold showers by flashlight to cool off.

The principal destination of Jain pilgrims is not Mahavira's temple but Parasnath, the sacred mountain. Behind it an entire pilgrims' complex has arisen. The mountain pilgrimage is usually a day trip and rarely an overnight affair, though there is a water storage tank on top, and the few Jain monks and nuns who live there keep food supplies. With a summit at 4,500 feet it is no easy walk up, and many Bihar tribals make their living as porters, carrying out-of-shape or elderly Jains on palanquins up the mountain. The trip usually consumes most of a day and is probably the single most significant experience of the religion.

The simultaneous beginnings of Buddhism are nearby, just up the GT in Bodh Gaya, and from a distance Jainism can seem like a sort of difficult, misbegotten Buddhism. As one Indian intellectual put it, in a sense Jainism stayed on the mountain while Buddhism managed to spread across the plain. Of the two, Jainism has stayed more faithful to its origins, but in India it has always been vulnerable to one-way marriages with Hindus—outtalked and outnumbered by the pantheon. Its shrines survived the centuries of Muslim invasions better than Buddhist temples, because the Jains (who have a strong pragmatic streak) very cannily incorporated Islamic designs and miniature Mohammedan tombs into their architecture.

In the country of their birth, both Buddhism and Jainism are still only small drops in the Hindu ocean and are often classified as sects of Hinduism by Hindus, scholars, and census takers. The Jains very specifically reject, however, the *vedas*—the earliest Sanskrit scriptures, sacred and fundamental to Hinduism—and the entire caste system, including the Brahmin priests. The Mahavira and Buddha stories have much in common—the son who rejects his wealthy family and, about to attain nirvana, is nearly seduced by evil. Both propose the simplicity of meditation as an answer to the elaborate Hindu rituals. Appearances to the contrary, Jainism is probably less passive, preaching "exertion" to purge the soul of its harmful desires. The name Jain means someone who has conquered himself.

Though Buddhists outnumber Jains about three to one in India today, the Jains are more significant because of their financial clout. Most are in Gujarat and Rajasthan, a result of the Muslim invasion wiping out the religion elsewhere in the subcontinent a thousand years ago. The Jains have sacred mountains in all their locales, echoes of Parasnath.

The narrow road to the pilgrims' complex dips and winds through stretches of serene rice fields and woods, until it ends in a sudden rash of buildings on the fringes of Madhuban ("honey forest"). There was no one but the Jains here behind the mountain. Madhuban was a cluster of temples, *dharmsalas* (guest houses), and shop-stalls that cater to the pilgrims' simple needs. It made little architectural sense. Some buildings were lavish, with sculpted dancing figures; others were cinder-block quickies, still with that Jain carnival aspect. A small Jains Resort Center was being constructed—the design ornate, the execution flimsy—and near it a huge, hideous hall.

An older building functioned as a chamber of commerce for pilgrims. At the entrance several ragged tribal children lay around with fevers, and in the long open patio a light rain came and went. The patio had rooms mounting on both sides as second and third stories were being built; these rooms were for monks staying several weeks or more. One monk, P. Ratnabhooshan Vijay, knew English and consented to speak to me just outside his small room.

We sat leaning back against the worn walls. An extremely old man, also in simple white robes, perched on a hassock nearby. A massive, robed and bearded middle-aged monk stood to one side and stared at me, intoning prayers.

P. Ratnabhooshan Vijay's head sprouted only a few gray hairs, but his mustache was full and dark. (Part of a Jain monk's initiation is having his hair pulled out by the roots.) He kept a small white handkerchief neatly folded in one hand to press to his mouth to prevent any stray insects flying in to their deaths. Frequently he would rub two fingertips of one hand together as if some truth lay between them and had to be gently coaxed into being.

In a small voice, he said, "I am happy to have a conversation with you."

"Please tell me about yourself."

"We are Jain monks, Jain *sadhu*, spending four months here during the monsoon."

"And what is the duty of a Jain monk?"

"The duty of sadhu is in our life. We spend our days studying. In early morning we are waking, we are doing our worship. Afterward, we are reading our religious books, studying them. This old man next to me was, before this summer, my father. Now he is our guru, you see, and we are his disciples."

"You mean he really is your father?"

"My father. His name is Muni Jaibhooshan Vijay."

"And the gentleman with the beard?"

"He is my younger brother. His name is Muni Kulbhooshan Vijay. Our father is eighty-seven. I am fifty-five, my brother is fifty-one. For thirty-four years we are joining this life. Before this life we lived in Calcutta, running a shop. A sort of—" He paused. "Department store."

"Do you ever go back to Calcutta?"

"I was April and May in Calcutta. Before, in Ahmedabad. Our guru in Ahmedabad is ninety-six years old, governing five hundred male sadhu and fifteen hundred female sadhvi. You see, we have five principles we are practicing: non-violence, non-stealing, non-having things, celibacy, truthfulness . . . . "

The Jains love numbers. Nine actions of merit, eighteen of sin, fifty-seven actions in all; five kinds of knowledge; five stages of the soul; six transcendental colors of the soul, three good, three bad; five principles of right conduct. There are even two principal kinds of Jains, for soon after Mahavira's death a schism occurred, resulting in the sky-clad (meaning naked) and the white-clothed. I never saw any sky-clad—who deny, by the way, that women can attain nirvana. It was Mahavira who gave women the possibility of enlightenment, inspiring the now far more plentiful group, the white-clothed. (The sky-clad generally stick to southern India.) It was the sky-clad that Alexander's Greeks encountered in 326 B.C., two centuries after Mahavira's death. The Greeks called them gymnosophists—naked philosophers.

"Do you fast all the time that you're here?"

"We are fasting sometimes during this time. Perhaps for one day, or two days, or one month. Only hot water, nothing else. And after sunset we take not a single drop of water."

"Are there many Jain monks like yourselves?"

"In all India, about five thousand men and ten thousand women. Here, now, staying at this moment are eight men and six ladies."

Jains number about two million, literally a drop in the large sea of a billion—he was speaking of full-time monks and nuns. Many at Parasnath were taking a week, a month, or six months off from their professional lives to make pilgrimages. Only a monk or nun can become enlightened.

I asked about a little white pouch he kept beside him on its own sandalwood stand.

"Our rule is that any religious worship we must do in the presence of our guru. When guru is not here, then we are doing it in presence of this. Just like guru." He made a small settling gesture with his hand toward the pouch, as if brushing away all worries.

"May I see what's inside?"

He nodded with contentment. He untied the pouch: five white seashells lay on a small cushion, the largest in the center, the others as four compass points.

"And your little broom, what's that?"

Its filaments were silver threads, attached to a long cotton-wrapped handle, I assumed so one could use it without much stooping.

"This broom is for the protection of all creatures. If any creature is passing, with this I protect it. It is called *rajoharan*, which means 'to clean dirtiness.'"

"And doesn't it hurt insects if you brush them with this?"

"It doesn't hurt them. It is very gentle."

"Jains have many precautions."

"We don't use metal vessels of any sort. Only wooden vessels." He smiled with deep pleasure. "This is by the orders of Lord Mahavira."

He handed me his set of wooden bowls, neatly fitting into each other in ascending sizes, lacquered in orange with black outlines. "They are carved by hand from one piece of wood each, from a desert tree. Someone else carves them. We Jains do the color ourselves."

"Does the color have any significance?"

"Not at all. It is simply the color they are having in the market and we are buying."

"And the prayer beads?"

"We have one hundred eight beads for doing our mantra. We do the mantra one hundred eight times."

One hundred eight is a magic religious number in India, shared also by Buddhism and Hinduism.

"Have you made this pilgrimage to Parasnath before?"

"Twice before. But never in the monsoon. You will see, oh, one month from now for several months it will be full, full, full here. The high season is September to March. Every day we go up the mountain as we feel suitable. We are leaving around four-thirty or five A.M. and coming back by four in the afternoon. By foot only."

"What does the mountain mean to Jains?"

"The mountain is salvation. They want to clean themselves of what they did in past life."

"And what do you do on the mountain?"

"We spend the day studying. Just a moment, please." He went into his darkened monk's room and came back with a thick wad of religious manuscripts. He set the immaculate pages reverently on his knee: hundreds, thousands of hours of human effort, written proportionally like poetry and centered according to the length of each line.

He said, "This is our *agam*. It is handwritten, on handmade paper. The durability is eight hundred years, near about. If you put it in water it can't fade. We don't do these ourselves, we pay professionals to write them."

"And what's your father got in his pot?"

"Sandalwood powder. For blessings."

All this time the old man had sat there, legs folded beneath him, rocking back and forth and reading a little pamphlet-size book of prayers and humming them quietly to himself. I couldn't tell how acute his hearing was, if our conversation was bothering him, or if he understood English. It would be unusual for a former Calcutta shopkeeper of his age not to.

"Tell me more about what you believe."

"For purifying our soul we have four ways: non-killing, fasting, meditation, and knowledge. Without pure knowledge nobody can get on the real path. Lord Mahavira preached that if anyone wants salvation, he must leave his earthly life."

"I've heard this, but I've also heard that Jains are the best businessmen in India, and that they're a very rich community. Isn't this a contradiction?"

"Lord Mahavira preached that those who are unable to leave their earthly life must support and maintain their blood relations. They can't beg—they must *support.* They earn and pass their lives earning, but they believe that this is all only for maintenance. Not to become rich."

"Are there Jains all over the world? In the U.S.?"

"Oooh! There are so many Jains in America. Business people. And a Jain temple in New Mexico. Twice a month they are gathering and preaching. And New York, New Jersey—"

"And is Parasnath a good place for anyone to come to? Even someone who isn't a Jain?"

"Of course. Jains and non-Jains are both coming here and getting results. One of our saints said, 'When you have difficulties, think of me and I will remove the difficulties.'"

I liked the pragmatic line: it seemed to sum up the kindness which, beyond all the complications, is at the heart of Jain thought. An irony of iconography is that the swastika seen on Jain temples to represent the life-force was reversed, stolen, and used by the Nazis—a cherished symbol of people who won't harm a bug appropriated by people who treated humanity as insects.

"It's been very kind of you to give me so much time."

"Not at all. Give me your address in America and I will be sure the Jains are sending you some more information directly."

"Of course."

"There are over three hundred books in English about Jainism, you know."

The hands clasped firmly as in prayer, a slight bow of the head in respect; I did this over and over in India, but never properly, and never with ease.

A dripping rain started as we left Madhuban. An hour after Parasnath the GT became impassable. A short bridgeway over a very shallow creek was being dug up; large pipes lay exposed in the creek bed. A half-dozen trucks were stopped to one side, the drivers taking a rest before turning back to take a long bypass route.

Here the villagers had dug a steep dirt ramp in the earth on both sides. A truck couldn't fit down it but a car could. It would simply mean driving across pebbles and several pipes and through a few inches of water. I got out and Israfel, in great distress, directed by a sort of tugboat crew waving their hands and encouraging, inched his car down the ramp, across the creek and up again.

While Israfel was negotiating the crossing I was arguing with the villagers, who wanted a toll, naturally. A headman said it was they who'd dug this earthen ramp on both sides, not the Public Works Department. They deserved some payment. (Israfel said later that he didn't believe this. He thought the PWD had dug the ramp in order to lay the new pipes, and the villagers were just taking the opportunity to collect a toll before everything was put right.)

They were certainly ambitious. Two-part tickets on flimsy paper had been printed up, and (a nice legitimizing touch) the headman insisted on taking down our license plate information. The fee sounded a little high. He wanted 75 rupees, but when I checked the accounting in his booklet of ticket stubs the figures for prior cars were 25 or 35 rupees. Still, it seemed worthwhile to pay a foreigners' surcharge to have more of the road to ourselves, at least until the truckers' alternate route joined the GT again. It is part of the Indian paradox that you can travel down much of the country's principal highway and be the only foreigner to come along for a month or two.

The headman duly took my money, signed the receipt stub, tore it off and handed it over.

Surely, I asked, in a situation as serious as a broken bridgeway, surely someone official would come look at the problem?

"You cannot be serious," the headman answered. "The prime minister has been in Bihar for fifteen days and he still hasn't come." He paused, spat. "No one has come."

"More people will have to die on the roads, if our nation is to develop any road sense at all!"

—Vasu, in R. K. Narayan's *The Man-Eater of Malgudi* (1962)

5.

Where the Truckers Eat

We pulled over for tea at a dhaba where eight or nine trucks were stopped. The dhaba had a little open shop next to it selling odd truck parts and supplies, stereo speakers and cassettes, tools, and cigarettes. There was also a niche shrine to Shiva and a narrow hovel of bare walls labeled *PCO*—one of India's new Public Calling Offices—where drivers could make a call or send a fax, though the antiquated telephone looked as if it had barely made it through the Raj.

Perhaps twenty drivers, most of them turbanned Sikhs, sat around companionably enfolded on braided cots, sipping, chatting. They noticed the foreigner immediately, but Sikhs have an almost blithe self-confidence; they are the Scotsmen of India, good at sports and war. They went on talking until I managed to strike up a conversation with one trucker. Then they all stopped to enjoy the alien entertainment, and eventually ambled over.

At twenty-three, Hardip Singh had been driving professionally for eight or nine years. He supported a wife, a daughter, and a son. He was hired directly by the companies for whom he transported goods, usually via family relations, with no middlemen. Shaggy-haired and easygoing, turbanless, he talked like a student who can relax because he has the system all figured out.

On this trip he was carrying steel plates from Durgapur to Benares; on the return he'd carry sugar from Benares to Calcutta. He could do the round trip in five days. He worked with another driver, a boy of eighteen who'd been driving for only six months. The boy had a plump grinning face, the baby fat still on him, and was quite nattily dressed in a clean smock. I assumed he was a relation of Hardip's, following the custom of keeping available work in the extended family.

Hardip laughed when I told him that after only a week on the GT, it seemed to me that a trucker's life was nothing but problems. Which were the worst?

"At night, it's thieves. There are more thieves in Bihar than in any other state. Well, Uttar Pradesh can be bad too. At night they try to hijack your truck. They block the GT with stones, or put nails in the road. They've got guns, knives, the works. They just kill the driver and the conductor and that's that."

By "conductor" he meant the assistant driver—in the Punjab the poor guy's called "the cleaner" because that's his other job.

"So what do you do?"

"All we can do is take care. Drive with other trucks at night."

Another driver, an older Sikh named Sandal, said, "In the daytime, the big problem's the police, asking for money. Lots of headaches. Or the bicyclists who don't know how to ride. And near the cities, cars get in the way."

"What are the headaches with the police?"

"All trucks are overloaded," said Hardip. "You're allowed ten tons. That's the truck and the cargo, together. But everyone carries extra cargo, and you're usually around fifteen tons, sometimes even seventeen. So the police stop you and make a fuss about the extra five tons and you have to give them five hundred rupees to let you go on. This happens all the time."

"In the old days," said another driver, "you could give them a hundred rupees and that was plenty. Now they're greedy, they're talking in the thousands of rupees for a normal bribe."

"The trick," said Sandal, "is you try to get the trucking company to pay for the bribe. If they pay seventy-five percent you consider yourself lucky. I try to get a bribe fund in advance, and maybe lie a little afterwards, so I keep what's left over."

Two drivers working in shifts, Hardip said, could keep rolling most of the night. Whiskey wasn't so easy to drive on, and illegal in some states. Opium was illegal too, but if you ate it and washed it down with tea, you could keep driving for twenty-four hours.

The trucks all have a built-in bunk, for one driver—usually an ornately decorated berth running crossways close to the roof—but a few hours every night invariably got spent resting at a dhaba. There's no charge for the cots, since everyone pays for a meal and tea. Some dhabas even had an astrologer available for twenty rupees.

"What are the worst months to drive in?"

"June to September. You get the fiercest heat followed by the fiercest rains. Probably all year-round the eastern part of Uttar Pradesh is the most difficult part of the GT. The road's bad, the police are bad, and there are thieves. Nearly as many as around here."

A small man named Randawa said, "Yes, yes, the worst part is around Varanasi, for two hundred kilometers on both sides." He stared around at everyone as if expecting an argument.

Sandal murmured, "I saw a trucker get his head cut off in an accident there. Cut through the neck."

The Sikh next to him said, "A friend of mine got his legs cut off up there."

I tried to change the subject to traffic jams.

Another driver said, "But for traffic jams there is no worst part. If you block this road for five minutes anywhere between Calcutta and Amritsar, you'll have fifty to a hundred trucks piled up on each side. Day or night."

"How do you get paid?" I asked Hardip.

"Some of us get paid by the load. And the miles. For me this trip, about four hundred eighty rupees per ton."

Around $14, to carry a ton of cargo a distance of around four hundred miles. Fuel came out of the truckers' pockets.

"The heavy trucks are all diesel," said Hardip. "Fuel is still expensive, though. At the moment, nine rupees per liter. Out of our pockets."

Some math: suppose seven tons of cargo at $14/ton is $98 earned over five days. Take away fuel and dhaba costs, arrive at—what? $25 earned per driver, for five concentrated days of road hell? A hundred bucks a month? Still, it was as much as an ordinary civil servant earned, and these weren't educated men. In India it was not a bad living—and these men had a sense of movement, a kind of independence.

"We make money," said Hardip, "but we also enjoy the life. You only get scared when you see an accident."

"How do truckers afford the trucks? Do you lease them?"

"A lot are privately owned—truckers own their own trucks. We buy them going through a private financier, at about sixteen percent interest. It takes most of us only a few years to buy back a truck."

Another kind of independence.

At that point an argument ensued, the gist of which—when I got Hardip to translate it for me—was that he was in fact the exception. Not one of the other drivers owned his own truck. They were all working on salary for trucking companies, at a wage of about $35 a month; but they were able to triple that by carrying the odd passenger or an extra load here and there—say, ten buckets of vegetables from a village to a market town.

"And what happens if there's an accident? Who pays?"

Hardip shrugged. "The companies have insurance. The rest of us, well, some do, and some—" He laughed. "I do."

He pointed out that accidents were probably caused less often by a collision than by swerving to avoid one. Trucks overloaded by seventy percent go out of control easily, or else one of the two axles breaks and the truck overturns.

"How about the procedure of getting a license?"

He said, "Well, the first one you're allowed isn't until age twenty. That's for light vehicles only. After a year you can get your second license, for heavy vehicles. But it's much more difficult to get your second license than it used to be. Now you have to show a blood certificate and prove you had schooling up to the tenth class. Then they want training."

"But you started driving at age fourteen."

He grinned. "I don't have a license."

Neither, in fact, did his fellow driver. I took a quick poll—as I feared, very few of the truckers had driver's licenses. Still, what better training could there be for the road than the road itself? And part of the attraction was inevitably that, even though most of the drivers were Sikhs, it was a profession that ignored caste, according to Hardip—there were plenty of Muslim drivers as well as Hindus and Sikhs. Every caste, he reiterated. I thought that was probably a bit of an exaggeration, but this attitude was undoubtedly some of the work's appeal. It gave the truckers something in common with the Buddhists.

I asked Hardip the question you're supposed to ask truckers everywhere, regardless of continent.

"Which dhabas have the best food?"

"The worst drivers are in Haryana!" said a man who hadn't spoken before.

"Yes, but the police are worst in the Punjab!" said Sandal.

"The best dhaba food is in the Punjab, though," said another Sikh. "But dhaba food is always nice, because it's fresh every day."

"No," said Hardip. "The older eating places are much better. No matter where." He smiled sadly. "This one's not old, not new."

The dhabas were nearly always run by men, so I asked the other question. The truckers were often away from home for a month or two at a time; they insisted they didn't have a problem with this.

"Ten years ago I went for the ladies," said one. "Then I got married."

Yes, there were many road signs on the GT warning truckers about AIDS; no, not one of these men had ever had a blood test. Bars and brothels were still illegal on the road, but you could have a woman at any dhaba for fifty rupees—a dollar twenty. Or less. "Even in the jungles," said one, "you can find whatever you want." Yes, they would certainly use a condom; after all, these cost only a rupee. Or else, said a man named Givan, "If we need a woman, we'll go to someone we know." But it didn't seem to occur to him that someone else might know her too.

I doubted a lot of what they said, because the fact is that the rate of infection is about ten times higher among India's five million truckers than the general Indian population, and maybe as high as three in ten. Several of the men I was speaking to would eventually die of AIDS, but didn't realize—much less fear it.

Nor did they realize the extent to which they were killers.

Infected truckers, maybe a million of them, were spreading the virus at incredible speed all over the country, with the collaboration of casual prostitutes who hung their saris on tree limbs as advertising and were available for a few rupees. The average trucker had between one and two hundred sexual partners a year; and casual homosexual relations, quite accepted, between drivers and their younger partners, made the rate of infection escalate. As the roads were the long arteries of the country, the truckers were literally putting the disease all through the bloodstream. A new Asian calamity: by the turn of the century India will probably have 10 million cases of infection. It has already surpassed the African countries in having more HIV carriers than any other nation.

I wasn't telling Hardip and his colleagues anything they hadn't heard before. Yet I felt they saw something comic in an American asking if they wore raincoats when they dallied with dhaba girls.

I said, "You do realize that some of you are dead men, right?"

Sandal smiled. "All of us are dead men. Maybe we die in bed, maybe on the road. Maybe we die at a dhaba. What's the difference?"

He spent his life driving one of the most dangerous roads in the world; he'd seen a friend decapitated in a truck last year. It finally got through to me that there wasn't much information I could add to his general perspective on the fragility of human life.

I crawled up into one truck's cab—a glass dome of calm from which to survey the hullabaloo of the road below. The interior walls and the seat fabrics were in a matching sixties checkerboard style, though the vehicle was new. Behind the two spacious driver's seats were two more passenger seats, above them the sleeping berth. Little blue curtains kept out excess sun. A statue of Shiva with a bull rode the dashboard, and there was a sticker of Kali, who slays men and protects travelers, on the windshield. Cassettes were scattered everywhere—Hindi and Punjabi music entirely. One driver turned on the tape player and music blasted through the confining space.

"Big song," he shouted.

> After renouncing his home, Gautama repaired to the quiet jungle resolved to solve the mystery of life in his own way! He arrived Bodh Gaya at the peepul tree and sat down in deep meditation facing the east. A titanic struggle between the Good and the Evil ensued within himself! The spirit of sensuous desires tempted him with the pleasures of the flesh followed by other evil temptation, all of which he conquered, and finally, as the day broke, the light of knowledge burst on his mind and he became the Fully Enlightened. Thereafter he kept meditating on the bliss he had attained, spending one week each at seven different places round the Bodhi Tree.
>
> — *Illustrated Tourists' Bodh-Gaya Guide* (Delite Press, n.d.)

6.

Under the Branches of Wisdom

Twisted trees, low misted mountains; freshened by the first rains of the monsoon, the landscape breathed more easily. Only the women displayed any talent for color in their clothing. Irregular rice fields tinged with yellow were being planted by bent people from biscuit houses growing right out of the ground.

The death-wizened masks of old women; the innocent faces of young maidens; the adult, world-weary faces of little girls.

At intervals we passed stone obelisks, distance markers about fifteen feet high. These kos minars were remnants from the Mogul era, the legacy of Sher Shah. There weren't enough left to suggest the order they must've once given the GT, set at kos intervals of about two and a quarter miles each, like reminders of my perpetual question—if there is any connection between all this history in ruins and these people who seem profoundly without any sense of that history. Or is it all invisibly stirring somewhere, beneath their skins?

One sure way to find out, a historian told me. Relieve yourself on the edge of someone's property, tell them you're a Muslim, and watch the past come alive.

Just after the river we turned off the GT for the few miles to Bodh Gaya. Without the hindrance of trucks, we raced along past flat rice paddies marked off by spectral trees. Presumably in ancient times the GT would've run through rather than simply near the important city of Gaya. Back then little Bodh Gaya was only forest, which is why the Prince Gautama went there from the city to meditate, and had his moment of enlightenment, and became the Buddha. The temple honoring that moment has made it the most important pilgrimage spot in the Buddhist world; my 1898 *Murray's Guide* states: "If it were possible to ascertain by any means what particular spot on earth is the most sacred in the opinion of mankind, there is every reason to think that the majority of votes would be given in favour of Bodh Gaya."

Bodh Gaya was deceptive. Set back from the country road in trees was an archaeological museum, but apparently no town. Then the road curved and straightened, and from the trees emerged jumbled monasteries, guest houses, and snack-stalls where shaven-headed monks in saffron robes milled around sipping soft drinks. All the structures had the architectural profiles of Tibet, of Japan, of China—pointed and curved pagoda roofs, outlandish colors. They were like religious embassies, diplomatic missions from the countries where Buddhism is strongest, to the very spot where it had first come to life and long since become relatively inconsequential.

Buddhism here is stronger now than it was fifty years ago; it remains attractive partly because twenty-five centuries later it still remains heresy, at least in India. Both Buddhism and Jainism stand counter to the enormous Hindu pantheon, establishing a single figure either as sage or god. Both show a strong compassion for nature, for all living beings. And both were revolts by their individual founders against the structures and castes of Hinduism.

A half-dozen buses for Buddhist tourists were parked near the entrance to the temple compound. Possibly because a fundamental idea in Buddhism is that everything wrong springs from desire, there was a self-imposed limit to commercialism engulfing the place, which had a peaceful, holy-campground atmosphere.

The Tibetan Temple and Rest House was an ornate wooden monastery in high style, its roof projections aswirl with color. I walked in to have a look and was shooed away, but not because I didn't look Tibetan, or Buddhist. It was lunchtime, and lunch was taken very seriously at these rest houses: no non-guests were welcome. At the Burmese Rest House next door I got the same treatment, though I'd have been invited to stay for several months, Buddhist or not, Burmese or not, after lunch. I saw only a couple of non-Asians here, both French—still, the first Westerners I'd encountered along the road since Calcutta.

I was welcomed, however, at the rather dignified Madhobadi Society Buddhist Rest House, built at the height of Empire in 1901. It resembled a very grand local library of the Raj. There I met Dorje, a strapping dark-haired man of about thirty, from Sikkim. I thought him another backpacker, and asked how he liked visiting.

"Look at this heat rash! Are you kidding? I live here," he said jovially. "But what a great place to live. And what a great place to exchange ideas with people from all over the world, eh? It's like a school too, you know, at the same time."

He turned out to be an assistant manager of the guest house, which is the "official" one here. Like any hotelier he showed me around the cafeteria and warned me about the peak season (October to March) with fifty to a hundred twenty people staying at any one time. His guest house, a complex of colonial-era and newer buildings, offered rooms with attached baths for seventy-five rupees ($2), but fifteen rupees would get you a bed in a large dormitory.

Across from the gate to the temple grounds, the shop-stalls sold prayer beads made from wood or bo-seeds and images of the Buddha, many quite delicate. Some sculptures showed an elderly emaciated Buddha, self-starved, with his bones sticking out. Known as *The Buddha In Hard Penance*, this image of Buddha's willingness to suffer is mimicked by the unwilling on every corner in India; it is sometimes difficult here to guess who is fasting by choice and who is simply going hungry. Religions like to bestow the mark of holiness on suffering, and this skeletal Buddha is certainly as brutal and garish an image as Jesus nailed to a cross. Graham Greene says somewhere that the features of Buddha cannot be sentimentalized like the features of Christ, but I always felt this suffering old Buddha to be exactly that, and a kind of taunt as well, with its implied can-you-suffer-as-I-have message.

On a pedestal by the temple entrance stood a little bust of Gandhi, eager in his blue hat and black eyeglasses, lost among the red and yellow-robed pilgrims.

Like everyone else, at the front gate of the temple compound I removed my shoes. Just inside was a receiving line of pleading beggars in rags, many of them women. I wondered if they did better with pilgrims on the way in or on the way out. Which was a more generous frame of mind: the anticipation of a sacred spot, or its realization? India confronts you with so many beggars that it helps to have a rule-of-thumb for rewarding misery. I gave exclusively to the deformed.

And because there are so many, any sense of making reply is easily lost. Of course a negligible amount of money would send the beggar away happy. But you can't help them all, so to give or not to give soon produces an automatic response—a question of loose change. Each encounter becomes more an experience of self than of the needful person before you. Whose stare, whose plea gets through the hardening armor of self-protection? How much can you turn away from and still remain humanely yourself? Occasionally you do remember: not all beggars are professionals.

Yet most are, you tell yourself. But professional suffering can still be suffering, you argue back. Many of those deformed were deliberately deformed at birth, wage-earning cripples for life, to be sold or rented to pimps of charity. Don't they even deserve the price of a postage stamp? Or what about those children who run so unerringly after foreigners, weeping, imploring—great dramatic actors, Gielguds of anguish who scamper gleefully offstage with huge grins the instant they receive a ten-rupee note. Absolute powerlessness corrupts absolutely: still, precious little of that income stays in their pockets.

In India you are constantly confronted with sights that anywhere else would shake you to your toenails but which, at the rate of one or two a minute on these beleaguered streets, fail to awaken any response other than a horrified shrug. Your mind has shifted into another gear. Slow deaths in the form of deformed limbs, diseased faces, stunted growth, intense suffering to which the sufferer has had to become accustomed, scenes of utter human desperation, all rarely grip you here, because you soon realize they have been robbed of their effectiveness along with their singularity. Soon the deformed beggar's pleas come to seem part of a professional technique; not desperation, but theater and strategy. To be a cripple, no matter how extreme, becomes simply the crippled man's way of scraping a living off the sidewalk. Were he not a cripple he would be forced to find another way. And an outsider learns not to consider that the unfortunate is "missing a normal life," because who in India has a normal life, in an outsider's terms?

It's only when you return from India that you realize you must downshift for another world, one in which to be deformed, or to be a beggar, is to be noticeable, and even extreme. To be extreme is commonplace in India: it is the most fundamental fact of the place. To the outsider, the moment of enlightenment does not occur there, but in those first few days after returning home. Perhaps a form letter arrives—begging en masse, your ability to help now made appetizing, not excruciating. Perhaps it's merely the fact that you are out walking on such undramatic streets, quietly left alone. A flash of awakening like the crack between two lives; it soon fades.

Tourist attraction: on the path to the principal temple, a monk with a costly camera was asking a blonde Frenchwoman, "May I take your photograph? You are beautiful like the goddess Venus."

The Bodh Gaya temple stands in a hollow: a tall, squared-off pyramid mainly of mud and brick, but so weather-darkened it looks entirely of stone, its surface covered with abstract niches and circles, geometric columns and protrusions—the result of dozens of additions, restorations, and well-meaning damage over twenty-two centuries. The temple is not large, but impressively steep, with detailed lotuses carved up to the enormous angular stupa on top and the lower quarter covered in ornate, multiplying friezes of the Buddha in his several postures. Some friezes are golden, but for Buddhists it is the temple's site that matters, not the masonry. Paths, staircases, and shaded walkways lead everywhere through the lovely gardens; a second white pyramid temple dominates one hill. Signs indicate where the Buddha meditated and walked.

A large pond with stairs leading down was covered with lotus blossoms and packed with fish. Pilgrims were bathing in it anyway. This was the Mucalinda Lake, the Abode of the Snake King. A cobra statue with a female image in its open jaws reared from the center of the pond. A sign said:

LORD BUDDHA SPENT THE 6TH WEEK IN MEDITATION HERE. WHILE HE WAS MEDITATING SEVERE THUNDERSTORM BROKE OUT.

TO PROTECT HIM FROM THE VIOLENT WIND AND RAIN
EVEN THE CREATURES CAME OUT FOR HIS SAFETY.

A stone walkway about twenty feet wide girdled the temple. I sat propped against a pillar beside a young South Korean monk who gave me a big smile of hello, told me he'd been there a year, then went silent. A few of these sandstone pillars near the sacred Bodhi Tree were original, but most of the ancient ones were in the museum. From another part of the gardens, beneath tents, came the hammering and scraping of men at work on replacement pillars.

On another side of the vertical temple was the Cloister Walk, with stone lotuses representing the Buddha's third week here (out of seven), which he spent "walking up and down in meditation." The lotuses indicated where "the Lord's feet rested while walking."

A stocky Tibetan in T-shirt and rolled-up trousers was pulling himself barefoot along the walkway. He would prostrate himself on his chest at full length, his hands stretched out together like a diver, then pull himself forward, stand up, flex his toes, make a gesture of obeisance or prayer, and prostrate himself again. In this caterpillar way he pulled himself unhurriedly around the temple. His T-shirt was dirty; he'd been doing this for hours, or maybe days.

The sacred fig tree, or peepul—"the tree under which you cannot tell a lie"—is also known as the Bodhi Tree, because it grows enormously where Buddhists say the original tree grew which the Buddha sat under when he had his Moment of Enlightenment around 590 B.C. Saffron robes were draped around its trunk; smaller yellow, red, and saffron cloths hung from them, to form a saffron quilt for the tree's lower body.

The original *ficus religiosa* lived for three hundred years. During that time the daughter of Ashoka (the ruler who united much of India in the third century B.C. and accomplished, by royal decree, the spread of Buddhism) took a sapling as a gift to a ruler in Sri Lanka. The original Bodhi Tree died; the present one is a descendant of a cutting of that first Sri Lankan cutting, brought back here and nurtured. The tree isn't in particularly good health, but it has spread, with some branches supported by posts. Other branches push insistently against the temple wall.

Beside the tree a geometrically carved stone bench marks where the Buddha sat and had his illumination. A pilgrim, or anyone else, can sit and share the very spot. You cannot see the devout prostrating themselves before the tree, or asking the tree's caretaker to let them in the little enclosure to be close enough to touch it, without feeling a tug of the idea of wisdom, of encouragement, that so possesses them. There is no pretense here, no trumpeted glory, no cathedral pomp: just the idea of a man sitting under a tree and thinking the world into himself.

The Bodh Gaya temple wasn't in the hands of Buddhists at all for most of the last eight hundred years, and it doesn't belong to Buddhists even now, though they oversee it. Since 1949, the temple has been controlled by an all-Indian advisory committee composed of two Hindus and two Buddhists. This is the first say Buddhists have had in the temple's fate since they were largely driven out in the thirteenth century by Muslim invaders. After that, for several centuries the temple reverted to and was saved by jungle.

Bodh Gaya is deeply sacred to Hindus as well, because they believe Buddha is the ninth incarnation of Vishnu, the Preserver—one of the all-powerful trinity of Hindu gods alongside Shiva the Destroyer and Brahma the Creator. (With the coming of Vishnu's tenth incarnation the world will end.) On the approach walk to the temple entrance, off to one side, stood a set of four small rude Hindu temples, really just little rooms, with a concessionary air. An old Hindu man standing in one doorway, with the overeager manner of a hawker, had little success beckoning pilgrims over. He talked and talked, and no one paid any attention.

• • •

A Sri Lankan monk named Wimala Thero took me in hand. He had penetrating dark eyes, a mostly shaven head, and a sweet manner, rather like an affectionate but firm older brother. He said he was an avid amateur photographer. Small, fortyish, with a wiry athleticism even in his billowy saffron robes, he spoke English well. He ushered me past workmen repairing the main doorway of the temple into a sort of high-ceilinged front hall, turned on a standing fan, and sat me down at a small table, facing him. On both sides stone stairways were roped off and marked CLOSED.

Behind him, in the flickering darkness of a few candles, a golden Buddha loomed high and shining, a few saffron-robed monks before it. An old shaven-headed Tibetan prayed on his knees.

"What about the closed stairways?" I asked.

"I can let you go up," said Wimala Thero. "But for two hours, not for ten minutes! We only allow people to go up if they intend to meditate on the next level."

I felt he was speaking allegorically. "The next level?"

"What we call the first floor. We call this the ground floor. They meditate, oh, three hours sometimes. Sometimes more. So the next level's not *really* closed."

"Is this so the meditating people aren't disturbed?"

"Not really." He hesitated. "You see, we had an accident there last year, that's all."

The rumor was that it'd been a suicide. In fact a small boy, trying to tear a few leaves off the sacred tree to sell as souvenirs—they are readily available—fell the single story to his death on the stone seat of enlightenment.

"Do you stay open all night?"

"The temple is closed at night after eight. At the front gate where you took off your shoes. Whether it is snow falling, or rain, or one hundred thirty five degrees fahrenheit in the shade, at seven thirty we have our final prayers. And at eight I close the temple and I take the key with me." For emphasis he plonked a ring of several dozen keys with a clatter on the table. "At five A.M. I open the temple. In wintertime, many people will come as early as three A.M. There are wonderful vibrations here—this is really the place where Buddha got enlightenment. We have so much faith and knowledge here, you know, there is no place like it. That I am sure of."

"And how long have you been here?"

"Myself, I have been here nineteen years. Twenty-three in India, in all."

"It must be a profound experience to live here."

"Nowhere in the world can you find a more attractive place. I have seen other countries also. By the blessings of the Buddha this past winter I got a free air ticket to Scotland and England. And I may go back there this next year if I am given another free air ticket, by the blessings of the Buddha. But this place, there is nowhere with such a wonderful good karmic vibration as Bodh Gaya. You are blessed even as a non-Buddhist being here, I promise you."

"Can you tell me about the Buddha's visit?"

"He stayed forty-nine days here. One week in one part, one week in another, seven weeks in all. All the spots are marked around the temple. I would show you myself but it would take two hours at least.

"Then he walked on to Sarnath, up the Grand Trunk Road. You see, the Buddha had been fasting for all this time. Then after his moment of enlightenment he started eating again—and five who were with him—" He paused an instant to count off names on his fingers. "They were disappointed. They did not realize he had had his enlightenment. And they left for Sarnath ahead of him. But—when *he* went there, no one has such power as he has." He smiled and his eyes looked into me like a camera shutter opening and staying open for longer than one expects. "After that, he disclosed to them that he had had his enlightenment."

As soon as he said this, he began to chant something quietly to himself for about forty-five seconds, glancing around at the pilgrims coming in. When he finished he looked back at me.

"From this moment on, he had no teachers. The Lord Buddha said, 'I can't see any teacher equal to me. I cannot see anyone equal to me.' You have to believe this.

"He then preached at Sarnath. And people began to understand. You see, he is neither deity nor savior. He is *teacher*. And anyone who says he is deity or savior is not following the teachings of the Lord Buddha. He is a teacher. And he says, 'I am the Lord Buddha, I have had my moment of enlightenment, and if you do what I say then you can become enlightened also. I was just an ordinary man, so if I can do it, you can do it.'"

He was defining, in fact, the major schism in Buddhism, between the Lesser Vehicle and the Greater Vehicle.

The Greater, which took hold soon after the Buddha's death, considers him a deity and savior; the Lesser follows the Buddha's instructions more precisely and considers him a teacher. The Greater admits a divinity and considers the Buddha the last representation of it. The Lesser, rather like the Jains with Mahavira, admits no divinity and, in an atheist structure (or monastic order) in which a teacher is the highest position, considers the Buddha the teacher without parallel.

Both vehicles launch their concentration in his direction; both consider him the pinnacle of their system of beliefs. Generally speaking, Japan, China, Korea, and Tibet follow the Greater Vehicle. Sri Lanka, Thailand, Burma, and Bangladesh follow the Lesser. India, the land of the Buddha's birth, follows both, depending generally on where people are located in relation to frontiers. Ashoka, the Mauryan emperor of India—who converted to Buddhism only after destroying most of his enemies, then sent Buddhism up the GT and all over the subcontinent—raised the first temple here in the third century B.C. and considered Buddha a deity. Ashoka was trying to create a kind of Holy Roman Empire with Buddha at its heart.

Walking around the gardens I fell into conversation with a Sri Lankan on a whirlwind bus tour of Buddhist sites in India with fellow pilgrims from his village. I kept asking how he was enjoying his journey, and he kept saying, "Do you know about Buddhism? Would you like me to explain it to you?" It took some doing, but I managed to extract his itinerary. His tour group had only fourteen days to cover enormous distances; having arrived in Madras three days earlier, they were going tomorrow up into Nepal. I told him it sounded a very tiring trip, though doubtless fulfilling.

"It is *not* tiring. That is the point. We have waited all our lives to make this trip. So it is *not* tiring. Not one bit."

Where my mind resisted was exactly where the Buddhist mind took flight. I found myself thinking: He didn't walk steadily up and back, up and back, all week; he didn't really take such even steps; he didn't really sit under a tree there, the spot got confused over the intervening 2,500 years.

I wasn't skeptical of the wisdom in his ideas—a quest for happiness through the elimination of desire, an almost psychoanalytical attempt to recognize and deal head-on with sensual urges of the human. I could see why these pilgrims followed that path of contemplation with enormous passion. I was a little skeptical of the cult of personality, the historical significance given to what seemed to me all metaphor, and which led these pilgrims to care so much that they were walking in the actual steps of the Buddha, and to derive strength, inspiration, and even wisdom from that sensation.

This was my inability, though. The capacity to pass from the actual to the metaphorical whenever it suits them, and without any sense of distance between, is a Buddhist strength. They treated the fable of Buddha's birth (which resembles that of Jesus) as pure poetry—born out of the side of a young virgin, having been conceived by a white elephant. If they followed Buddha's footprints a little dogmatically, it was because their sense of the world as an actual poem was total, and liberated them.

A night in the tourist (as opposed to pilgrim) hotel in Bodh Gaya. Overhead fans in the room, a central garden with mosquitoes on the warpath in the stifling breezeless heat. A group of Japanese tourists filed into the tired decor of the restaurant as I left. I wondered if they would notice the small rat that enjoyed taking its evening constitutional across the floor throughout dinner. At the front desk, the antique telephone switchboard looked like an upright piano, with wires everywhere and the paper-obsessed assistant manager yelling over an air-force headset, trying to hear and be heard.

Gaya, easternmost of the seven sacred cities of the Hindus, was a mishmash of narrow muddy streets and tumbledown shops. The journalist Khushwant Singh once accused it of being the dirtiest city in the world, and he may still be right. Full of urgency and little grandeur, Gaya was in great disrepair, even relative to other Indian cities. It hugged the river—a tributary of the Ganges—in a jumble of collapsing mud, brick, and concrete houses, and the rare elaborate mansion stood out sharply.

In ancient times the religious centers and the trading centers overlapped; but whereas modern Benares has retained much of its old economic power, Gaya lost its during the Mogul era, if not before. The Moguls built nothing here, and Gaya struggled on only as a religious center for Hindu pilgrims. All its old financial clout was gradually lost to speed. With the railways and a paved GT, no one needs to stop here anymore, and Gaya has become an end-of-the-line place, long fallen.

It was so sweltering you could nearly hear the heat. I was passed by a rickshaw of four bare-chested monks on their way to the Vishnupad temple, which I wasn't allowed into. The temple entrance was off a courtyard that even in early morning was taking the full impact of sun. The temple's chief tourist attraction was a silver footprint of Vishnu, 13 inches long by 6 inches broad (according to my faithful old guidebook). NO ADMITTANCE FOR NON-HINDUS, said a small sign, and the temple guides hanging around the entrance pointed it out in case I'd missed it. Imagine a sign in Paris at Notre-Dame, saying NON-CATHOLICS KEEP OUT.

Here, at least, Gaya was thriving. Along the white walls of the temple ranged dozens of souvenir stalls aimed at Hindu tourists. Down a side street past metalworkers, at the river the devout in yellow and saffron robes were descending ghats into the shallow muddy water. They immersed themselves, washing the Ganges laboriously over their shoulders and through their hair, then finally swallowed.

The lanky boys, smiles brimming, treated the Ganges as a playground, leaping across the little sand banks and plunging. The young women were of a dark somber beauty, their mothers worn and withered: in India forty often looks like sixty. Girls shampooed their long hair and men soaped themselves vigorously in the dirty sacred water. A goat bleated and nosed around, exploring the saris, the undershirts, and the bras laid out to dry on the wide stone steps. In Gaya no one was trying to sell you anything; I could watch the devout performing their ablutions without having to fend off rapacious guides and boat touts and trinket salesmen.

Along the Grand Trunk north of Gaya rice paddies were filled with rain; inland lay man-made reservoirs. They created a watery world of lakes and fields reflecting uneven hills in the distance.

A little farther on was the same landscape wholly deprived of water, burning and gasping in the heat. A Jekyll-and-Hyde quality to the subcontinent at monsoon time, depending on who has received the magic elixir of rain and who hasn't.

Remarkable that Buddhists of both Vehicles can worship together. The abyss between people who take one man to be a man and other people who take him for a god would seem unbridgeable, no?

Pilgrims of all religions here are in saffron robes: saffron is the shared color of holiness or devotion. Though both Hindu and Buddhist pilgrims wear it, the difference is that in Buddhism, *only* monks can wear it, while in Hinduism ordinary plain folk can. The Sikhs have adopted the color for turbans some of the time; it was also worn by the Rajput princes when they rode out to be gloriously slaughtered by the Muslim invaders. This suggests some unity to the way that people in the same geographical (hence the same visual) context see colors. In this case, saffron arouses specific emotions, of, let's say, an intense and higher passion.

What matters most, evidently, is to show that one is a person of devotion, rather than of *which* devotion. Whereas in the West, the depth of one's devotion is private, and the particular religion the more important public matter. A Catholic is a Catholic first, devout or lapsed second; he will still, when pushed, describe himself as Catholic. Here, it seems, publicly a passionate pilgrim is a pilgrim first, but apparently Hindu or Buddhist second.

> It is well that Indians are unable to look at their country directly, for the distress they would see would drive them mad. And it is well that they have no sense of history, for how then would they be able to continue to squat amid their ruins, and which Indian would be able to read the history of his country for the last thousand years without anger and pain?
>
> — V. S. Naipaul, *An Area of Darkness* (1964)

7.

Tomb of a Lion

Here where the Buddha walked, the road ran straight for many miles. Most villages were set way back, in trees.

Anangabad was a purposeful truck-stop town, the road so throttled with trucks that the Contessa could barely squeeze past. Schoolchildren, bickering bicycle-rickshaw drivers, and a thronging, overspilling smoky market were all subservient to fumes and horns.

The outskirts of every town grew wild; broken houses stood overgrown in a bowl of devastated hills.

Stone quarries began a few miles before Sasaram. Slabs cut out of the hillsides lay along the GT, trucks were being loaded with rock, and the air was full of hammering and clinking. Building materials were strewn higgledy-piggledy around grinding machinery. Rivers of mud slurped at the sides of the road.

Sasaram had the insulted look of a tough town: argumentative, full of swagger and spoiling for a fight. An aggressive cacophony made it a sonic hell of vehicular crossroads. The town square had a small bust of Gandhi grimacing at the noise—head only, as on a platter, and absurdly out of sight on a pedestal thirty-five feet high. Maybe it was easier, or cheaper, to make a tall pedestal than a tall statue.

Down a brief side street, though, unexpectedly glorious, was one of the supreme achievements of Mogul-era architecture. This was the mausoleum of Sher Shah Sur (c. 1505?–1545), the last Afghan ruler of northern India, remembered in the familiar name given to the GT: the Sher Shah Suri Marg. The Pathans, the predominant tribe of eastern Afghanistan and Pakistan's North-West Frontier, consider him their great hero. They still speak of what might've been, that vanished dream of a Pathan dynasty in the subcontinent; and over a thousand miles up the road, in Peshawar, I would find postcards of this building as a reminder of that vision.

His tomb rises in sober stone from its private lake about a quarter-mile square, lined generously with jacaranda trees on the banks. Half great fortress, half palace, it looms high-walled, with domed delicate kiosks at the corners of all eight sides. In the center an enormous dome rises more than a hundred feet, the tallest in India after the Taj Mahal, which it inspired. It is a noble, dignified design; the elegant kiosks set off the simplicity of the dome, which in turn relieves the severe geometry of the octagonal body. The dome holds echoes of the lotus, for the mausoleum implies a deep Hindu influence—besides having been built by Hindu craftsmen.

Sher Shah was a remarkable postscript to the long list of Afghan conquerors of the Indian subcontinent. They had come in destructive Muslim waves down the Grand Trunk Road since the late tenth century. Overthrowing each other, defeating the independent Hindustan kings, they eventually plundered and slaughtered all the way to Bengal. By the early fourteenth century they controlled most of the subcontinent, but that unity soon broke into its natural disorder. Tamerlane, a Turkic-speaking Central Asian who claimed descent from Jenghiz Khan and who had already conquered Persia, seized the moment, marched down the GT and proclaimed himself Emperor of India, outdoing his predecessors in blood.

Tamerlane's death gave India another century of chaotic, squabbling individual kingdoms. A more sophisticated descendant, Babur (1483–1530), in the early sixteenth century again conquered northern India via the GT, founding the Mogul Empire. Like Tamerlane, Babur came from near Samarkand, but (like all the Moguls) his culture was Persian.

In 1539, a decade after Babur's death, Sher Shah—a kind of Pathan version of Alexander the Great—came in and temporarily wrested northern India from Babur's bookish son Humayun. (In one account Sher Shah's attitude to the Moguls came from having his table manners derided by Babur at a banquet.) The next sequence goes like a game of checkers. After Sher Shah's death *his* successors were in turn defeated by Humayun, and India remained Mogul until that empire crumbled in the hands of the British two centuries later. There was one final irony: Humayun, whose passion was collecting illuminated manuscripts, died in Delhi after falling down the steps of a library built a few years earlier (surely you guessed) by Sher Shah.

From Sher Shah's point of view, Babur and Co. were upstart interlopers, intruders on Pathan territory; he was simply taking back what his Afghan predecessors had been invading and squabbling over for five centuries. To us Sher Shah looks like an interruption to the Mogul scheme of things. Yet all these conquerors were Muslims, and eight centuries of Hindus living under Islam, no matter how peaceably, explains a lot of resentment and violence.

Still, Sher Shah in only a few years (1539 to 1545) showed a kind of bureaucratic genius for dealing with a fundamentally anarchic situation. He was a natural administrator, devising a system of land revenues which survives today in northern India. To impose governmental order rather than organized bloodshed on the subcontinent was a new idea; he also brought his own mercenary countrymen together. He encouraged cultivation, built roads and *serais* (huge highway rest houses) all over the place, abolished village-to-village tolls, set up a police force, and cleared, linked, and defined the Grand Trunk Road once and for all. It deserves to bear his name, and had he not been killed in a freak explosion while attacking a fortress, the history of India might have been quite different.

His tomb was very much a living monument—people still knew who Sher Shah was, and that he had spent his youth here. They came in the cool relief of afternoon to stroll in his park and enjoy the view of his mausoleum, which in earlier centuries commanded the horizon and was visible for miles. Once you could only reach it by boat; now a walkway across the lake, planted with yellow lilies, connected to a tall outer staircase of the mausoleum. And perhaps because of what the town had become, people seemed to take unusual pride in the monument. After all, Sher Shah had provided them with a peaceful garden, now also used as a public latrine, that Sasaram otherwise wouldn't have.

I spoke to a white-haired man with clumps of black hair growing surreally out of his ears. Ram Nandan Prasad was dressed so simply that I assumed he must be a gardener come to cut the grass, which he was pulling up in large handfuls and collecting in a sack. In fact the grass was to take back home to feed his cows. Was he a farmer? I asked. No, no—in town, he said (as if we weren't in town) he kept a small clothing shop, with cows. He knew the legend about how Sher Shah as a young man, rather like King David, "slew a lion or a tiger with his naked sword" and was brave enough to deserve his moniker, which means Lion King. It also means the Milk King.

Think of northern India as a giant playing field where bullies from all over came to play their own sports, shoving the locals onto the sidelines, with holy men given the thankless task of refereeing.

First the Greeks came and decided that the field, though green and attractive, was much too uneven and not worth their time, so they went home.

Then the Afghans arrived, yelling bloody murder and tearing around, playing that game on horseback with the human head wrapped up as a ball.

Then a few Turkic Mongols swooped in, dealt with the Afghans very efficiently, got bored at the lack of local challenge, and wandered off in search of tougher opponents.

After a brief flurry from another short-lived Afghan squad, a new team calling themselves Moguls—and looking suspiciously like the old T.M.—showed up. They settled in as a home team, learned the local rules and decided, after several seasons, to turn the playing field into a huge, stylized chessboard.

The Europeans had been filtering into the stands, a few here, a few there. In the end the British outnumbered the rest; they stomped on the chessboard, swept the pieces away, and transformed the playing field into a cricket pitch, leaving a large number of maharajahs (with season tickets for the most select seats) cheering wildly.

When the Brits realized that the natives were starting to beat them at cricket, they handed back the playing field—though not before it was decided to establish firm boundaries and divide the local players into opposing teams for a little friendly competition.

So much for sport.

Kurma: the pleasing silhouettes of an Indian village, fragments of ruined temples against a blue pastel sky at the end of the day.

Glycerine music of unison strings and a virginal singer.

Telephone lines ran straight along the road, leading the trucks like a single-minded convoy past barren earth-mound houses and gaunt, spectral trees. By clusters of thatched dhabas, trucks were pulled over in twos and threes, the men sitting in flexible postures chatting over tea. As the last light was sipped away across the watery fields, the bulbs hung on wires came on in the little lean-tos, giving the road a festive air before night obliterated everything but headlamps and taillights.

As night settled down a rain began, thickly and slowly. No one honked; rain kept the drivers much more courteous, less competitive. Just before the Uttar Pradesh border, two trucks lay overturned with men sitting atop them. Grain sacks were all over the road. One truck's bonnet had a painted face, the tongue sticking out to scare off the evil eye.

The road improved immediately after we crossed into U. P. Over a bridge into Mogul Saray—in Mogul times there must've been a rest house here to serve the GT. A village blurred to a series of wobbling stall lamps and figures squirming away from the wet.

Trying to enter Benares on this rainy evening, we ran afoul of a nightmare of jumbled traffic. In the desperation of bad weather, a narrow muddy elbow of the road had gotten blocked. With the tempest it was as if we were all underwater in a crowded night sea; motorcycles moved around the stalled trucks like pilot fish around sleep-addled sharks. Above us a rogue electrical wire whipped in the wind, crackling and sending off eerie sparks. At the slightest gap, a truck would surge forward three feet and immediately clog all progress. Driving on the wrong side of the road became the only escape, so a second traffic jam developed parallel to the first.

This Dantean purgatory of night, rain, and vehicles that went nowhere lasted for us for nearly two hours. We were lucky enough to be stuck in its throat; for many miles behind us the coils of the serpent's body would be knotted all night.

Lit by sudden lightning, a dead cow at the side of the road was being carved up. The people crouched over it had pulled back half the sacred skin as if they were peeling a potato.

> We travelled by the Grand Military Road, riding the first part of the stage, and finishing it in the buggy. . . . At last we arrived in Benares. For ten days I could scarcely move, so much was my body bruised. . . . My recovery was brought about by having four women to shampoo me for five hours daily, and by going into a vapour-bath belonging to the Rajah of Benares. In the bath the women shampooed, and twisted, and pinched my limbs, until I could walk without assistance—that vapour-bath was a great relief.
>
> — Fanny Parks (1829)

8.

The Sacred City

A Benares hotel bed: I woke to memories of rain last night, the maelstrom of engine fumes, a cow methodically licking a man asleep on a roadside cot while trucks growled on. Did the man keep dreaming? Or was he awake and believed it a blessing to be licked by that Sacred Tongue? Like having the Ganges come to you.

A fitting question in Benares—also called Varanasi—the most sacred city in India, and probably the most consistently visited sacred city on earth. Every year for centuries, millions have realized their dream by coming here to bathe, gargle, drink from and be cremated in the Ganges. It is like a Hindu Miami, full of the elderly. They do not wait passively for the end, they busily and energetically ready themselves. To die within a fifty-mile holy radius of Benares is to be on the certain road to heaven, and seventy thousand pilgrims arrive every day just to be sure. Or at least to wash away the sins of previous lives.

For all that Christians speak of a hereafter, they do not have a select departure lounge attached to the belief. There is no holy turnstile, no Checkpoint Eternity; Lourdes is only a repair shop. This would be a devastating test of modern Christian faith: give it a Benares, a last bus stop, and see how many true believers take up the offer and spend every single penny on going there when they feel their final days nearly upon them.

In this concentrated city bulging with well over a million residents, the steady transient business shows. Places that earn their living off religion either deepen or grow cynical, and here an unflinching business sense has developed alongside the unwavering religious sense. As Mark Twain put it, "Religion, then, is the *business* of Benares, just as gold-production is the business of Johannesburg.... India flocks thither on pilgrimages, and pours its savings into the pockets of the priests in a generous stream, which never fails. A priest with a good stand on the shore of the Ganges is much better off than the sweeper of the best crossing in London."

The ageless Benares—the idea of Benares—is often compared to Athens as it was in ancient times. Both are about 2,500 years old, and it might be argued that the progress of thought stopped in each at about the same moment. Modern Benares is, like modern Athens, a tough and congested city. The difference is that the belief that built Benares has only grown more populous. Here as nowhere else, an outsider is buffeted by the full hurricane force of Hinduism.

Part of that onslaught of spirit is architectural. A century ago an Englishman started counting the temples in Benares and gave up after fifteen hundred; no one yet has surpassed his persistence. On the way to the river from my hotel, I passed the former British regimental cantonment with its clusters of barracks and officers' bungalows. The British parade ground was divided from the old city by the largest university in India, known as Hindu U. but secular in tone, and by Sanskrit U., a center of Sanskrit learning housed in a Victorian Gothic structure (once known as Queen's College) that looks designed by Edgar Allan Poe. All together they were only a token presence against the concentrated force of Hindu Benares. The ideas they represented were simply not the main show here, however vital they might be in Calcutta.

Nearby, the graceful but faded Hôtel de Paris from the last century seemed to be waiting for someone to restore it. Perhaps that would be pointless, because few foreign visitors stay more than a day in Benares, and for most of them the modern luxury hotels will do. The Hindu comes for a leisurely bathe in the Ganges, immersing himself profoundly day after day; the foreigner comes for a quick dip in Hinduism and tries to get no more than a toe wet.

As I headed for the ghats that morning, a bicycle rickshaw swept by. Two men rode nonchalantly in the back holding a shrouded corpse tightly wrapped in white robes across their laps, on the way to its cremation. This is the eternal, obvious symbol of Benares. You are continually making way for this same corpse, borne by a flowered, chanting procession here, a hired and silent rickshaw there. Cremation has always seemed far better to me than being feasted on by worms, but I never got used to seeing the death of a loved one surrounded by so much satisfaction.

Benares has for centuries been a center of textiles, silk brocade, copper and bronze work, and small wooden toys, and its narrow streets are honeycombed with minute shops and factories. Near the river the back alleys are dense with stalled or charging cows, meticulously painted temples, sleeping or dying pilgrims smeared with holy ash from burned cow turds, and deformed trees, all hemmed-in by lavender and ochre and even blinding white walls—astonishing flashes of color in a place whose filth is proudly the most timeless filth on the subcontinent. Cows are a nuisance everywhere in India, but in Benares' labyrinthine lanes they are as dangerous and sure of their power as trucks on the GT.

Descriptions of Benares' ghats along the muddy Ganges always sound the same. From a layered jumble of prickly-pear temples, umbrellas, collapsed balconies, tree-sprouting roofs, and ziggurat houses, a sequence of interknit staircases descends to the opaque, sacred, and semi-solid, semi-gaseous water. Here the blessed buzz and bathe and gossip like single-minded creatures busy at the waterhole. The stench is encyclopedic and hypnotic. Women go through their elaborate windings and unwindings of saris without showing much flesh. Men bathe nearly naked, with splutterings and vigorous depth soundings. Boys leap off the boats, flashing like porpoises. A white-haired man, in the courageous prime of old age, cleans his gums with Ganges water, darting several fingers around his mouth to make sure the river penetrates every cavity.

To submerge oneself in the shallows is enough; you rarely see anyone going for a real paddle. The place is a sacred public tub, not a holy swimming pool. Entire families are encamped on houseboats or in rope-strung tents on the ghats. Out in the swift river several twin-prowed flatboats lugging a few tourists are poled or rowed along the swirling currents.

By one ghat no one was bathing. Boats were piled high with logs to be used in cremations. Men unloaded the boats by piling wood atop their heads on little cushions of wrapped rags and then staggering up the ghat. In a courtyard near the steps, men split wood continuously while other men carted it away to pyres. Monkeys scampered across the rooftops, and beneath a gnarled spreading tree, children playfully shattered the remains of old statues.

Comparisons are odious, but Benares naturally reminds one of Venice. It makes you consider how rarely the Venetians go swan-diving off their doorsteps. There is much the same panorama of a long honor guard of palaces kneeling to the questionable water, though the Ganges is more sedate and less excitable (unless in flood) than the polluted Venice lagoon. Also the same dismay at the most profound human feelings being pandered to for ten rupees squeezed here, five hundred lire extorted there. You can easily guess which children will grow up to become pilgrims and which pilgrim-touts.

Like every other wide-eyed non-Hindu, I hired a narrow wooden boat to pole and drift me down along the waterfront—the gainful employ of two oarsmen and one majordomo. My chief boatman, Lachman Prasad, remained unmoved by all I said once a price was agreed upon. He dragged out our discussion of what I wanted to see, letting the boat drift swiftly, so no matter how I protested, he managed to start me halfway downriver. When I asked to go in closer, he made excuses about the current while his faithful oarsmen seemed bewildered. When I insisted we slow down, he claimed the current was too strong to fight and his oarsmen looked deeply offended.

Anyway, as every Hindu knows, the Ganges has a will of its own. You pass along the helter-skelter of temples at the river's speed and try to memorize the waterfront as it goes by like a reel of film. A house with roaring statues of yellow tigers. The Shanti Guest Lodge, with water in its basement. A mosque either put up to annoy the Hindu temples next door or vice versa. A Nepalese temple with gold stupa and erotic carvings—"Visitors need not see them if the attendant is discouraged from pointing them out," assured my 1898 guidebook. All the while, blackened bits of ex-bodies spin in the ash-muddied water, and on stone platforms a level above, other corpses burn off smoky exhalations of human souls.

There is, however, little surprise attached to these sights: to use this turbid water as a dumping-ground for cremated bodies seems absolutely appropriate; there are about forty thousand of them a year. There is even a new electric crematorium, though this has not stopped people from tossing in dead, uncremated animals. Just down from the temples stands a hospital, and in the most suitable location in the world. I can think of nowhere better to speed up either the healing or the ailing process, for the ultimate result of both is evident everywhere.

For Hindus cremation is the last ritual in a life of rituals, from birth to initiation, marriage, childbirth, death; and though there is no single Hindu regimen, each day generally has its ritual of prayers that involve offerings of flowers, food, incense, and other gifts for the gods. The goal is to live honestly and dutifully to reduce your bad karma (which has incarcerated you in your present caste) and raise your status in the next reincarnation. The idea of duty had resulted in the Widows' House I was now drifting past, where widows went to officially remember their late husbands. In the old days many would have burned themselves in mourning.

According to chief boatman and social critic Lachman Prasad, I was apparently getting the wrong idea about the population of Benares, which he claimed was nearly balanced—40 percent Muslim, 60 percent Hindu.

"Not fair," was his judgment, representing the majority. "Too many Muslim people."

So how did all those Muslims earn their living? I asked.

"Making saris for Hindu people."

He meant the complex brocade and embroidery for which the city is famous, but he said it the way a gentleman in Edwardian London might have accused someone of making his own trousers.

The boat let me off at the Raj Ghat; with misgivings I watched the fatigued oarsmen snap to energetic life for a swift row back against the current toward more business. Near the Raj Ghat, untouchables—who of course no longer exist as a caste, caste having been abolished in India by government decree in 1951—were building a large new temple of their own. Practically overhead arched the great railway bridge whose upper level is the GT.

Sita Ram was a bent old man in flip-flops, carrying a bamboo cane and a rolled-up seat mat. His full gray beard was tied in a neat knot, his hair bound up in a makeshift turban. He was a mendicant, without profession, attached to an ashram in Allahabad. At seventy-eight he had come by bus on the GT a day earlier, specifically to see a guru named Nirmal. He would spend three to four days in Nirmal's ashram. Sita Ram's regular guru in Allahabad didn't let him leave very often; still, he figured he came to Benares about once a year. His smock looked worn thin from such a life.

"I'm all right," he said, without much conviction. "I usually come by road, which takes about three hours. But sometimes I come by train. I lost all my money yesterday, I got pickpocketed on the bus."

He'd bathed in the Ganges that day at four A.M. It was about nine now, and he hadn't eaten anything yet. Though he didn't ask for alms, I pressed a little money on him.

He was from Benares originally; as a farmer, he'd once owned a bit of land near here. But he'd lived in Allahabad for forty-five years, ever since giving up his family life. His wife and two sons had presumably understood his reasoning. People abandon families for a half century, after all, out of less justifiable reasons than a search for enlightenment.

I asked how he felt to be back in Benares.

"My life," he said by way of answer, "is going on pilgrimages and being reverential to my guru."

His determination reminded me how in centuries past even India's regional princes, the maharajahs, made pilgrimages to Benares at least once in their lives, if not more frequently. When the maharajahs traveled it was with enormous retinues, great processions of elephants and horses, servants, wives, hangers-on. The normal traffic of the Grand Trunk Road, herds of several thousand oxen or camels perhaps, would be compelled to get out of the way, and the chaos must have been colossal. Usually the maharajahs also carried their own lavish tents and accommodations with them. If not, they would take over any serai in their path. And if it was the Mogul Emperor himself on the move, the displacement was even more titanic. The Imperial camp made up about a twenty-mile circle, and involved giant red pavilions, sentries, tents arrayed in ordered streets from nobles down to shopkeepers. This great lordly organism could progress at about ten miles a day and took four hours to set up; and when I imagined it coming down the GT to Benares, it made my notion of a traffic jam look amateurish.

A mangy limping dog arrived at the ghat, carrying something. As it shook its head triumphantly I realized with horror that in its jaws the dog held a small, pink human body: an already headless baby, recently born, still with hands and legs.

Only the corpses of small children, holy men and women, royalty, and those who died diseased may be put in the Ganges without being cremated, a sign of great holiness. Normally they're weighted down with heavy stones.

This baby—perhaps born dead, perhaps a girl smothered soon after birth—had probably been floated in the river only a few hundred yards away, twenty minutes earlier, then washed ashore to be retrieved by the dog. Someone was grieving still, but with the knowledge that the Mother Ganga had safely taken her child.

It was almost too much to look at, so I tried to write it down.

The few people standing around the ghat were as horrified as I was. They threw stones to get the dog to drop the baby, but the cur ran off successfully with the little headless body in its mouth.

Today's Benares lies to the south of the bridge; Kashi, City of Light, the original ancient city, was to the north. Centuries ago the ferryboats poling across the river must have been roughly in the vicinity of today's bridge. The Buddha, then an unknown, had bypassed Kashi because he knew his heretical ideas wouldn't be tolerated. Instead he'd preached on the outskirts of town and continued up the GT to Sarnath.

Kashi grew up at the holy junction of the Varuna and the Ganges rivers. Almost nothing is left, for it was razed by the

Afghan invader Mohammed Ghori around 1194. After its destruction people used its bricks for the new city Varanasi, and avoided the original location. Now the site is only a featureless delta with a temple or two, plenty of cows, and a Krishnamurti Institute. A few scattered brick ruins lie along the shore, but the steep and overgrown hillsides doubtless conceal ancient walls.

Every foreign tourist who visits Benares eventually makes the same lame remark about how he doesn't want to gulp down the Ganges or gargle with it like the devout, much less bathe in it. An unexceptional drop contains cyanide, arsenic, lead, decomposed holy men and cows, zinc, lead, chromium, and mercury.

Journalists go further. They make somber remarks about the diseases in the water, then quote Indian scientific sources that claim that though terribly polluted elsewhere, in Benares the Ganges has been proven absolutely, miraculously hygienic. (Western science at the service of Eastern magic.) This despite the fact that every day raw sewage is pumped into the river by the city, that at times the filth inshore is so thick pilgrims use ladders to climb across it before taking a dip in the middle. Belief must remain stronger than what observation tells us: this is the lesson of Benares.

All these joke-cracking visitors do themselves an injustice. Even in one of the better restaurants in town, in one of the better hotels, full of Italian, British, and German tourists, I still managed to swallow my share of the sacred river. Imagine my surprise, my joy, my grave excitement to learn that the ice in my drink—unlike the hotel's sterilized tap water—came from the Benares marketplace!

Because that meant it had come directly from the Ganges.

> The ordinary traveller who 'does' India, sees Bombay, Calcutta, Benares, Agra and Delhi, but the vast spaces between these noted places he sees nothing of.... They were there when we arrived in India, they were there when the Mohammedans came, and were probably on the same spot when Alexander crossed the Indus. To this it may be added that these villages will still be there when we leave India, whenever that may take place.
>
> — William Simpson (1861)

9.

Of God and Kipling

The Grand Trunk ran by the Benares Railway Station and, at the edge of the countryside, past stone carvers in rude brick or mud houses, chiseling and chipping away.

Thanks to my hotel, I had a new driver—Shambu Singh, a young, timid, very correct Hindu with a comfortable Ambassador.

Just four miles north of Benares and seven dusty miles off the GT, Sarnath is where the Buddha delivered his first sermon and laid the foundation of the faith, "turning the wheel of the law"—an act known as *Dharmachakrapravartna*. His proximity to the heart of Hinduism was no accident, but a deliberate challenge. The Buddha's sermon here, on the heels of his solitary moment of enlightenment in Bodh Gaya, was given to five ascetics who had previously spurned him in his quest. Following his speech, they became his earliest disciples.

Go forth, O Monks, and wander forth for the gain of the many; for the welfare of the many; in compassion for the world . . . preach a life of holiness, perfect and pure.

To Buddhists, Sarnath—the Deer Park—is at least as important a site as Bodh Gaya. Stone monuments were raised here by Ashoka in the third century B.C., and Sarnath survived until about the twelfth century, when Buddhism virtually disappeared from India. After that the place was ransacked and ravaged until the 1830s, when British archaeologists stepped in. The famous Lion Capital of Ashoka—four elegant, sculpted, whiskery lions gazing at the cardinal points, which once topped a pillar—is no longer in the park and exposed to the elements but inside the museum. The museum was closed because it was Friday (a logic I didn't grasp) so I missed one of the masterpieces of ancient India. This symbol of a brief Buddhist Empire is now used, with no deliberate irony, as an emblem of the Indian Union: at the center of the flag, on the five-rupee note, on the one- and two-rupee coins.

The enormous Dharmekha Stupa—about a hundred feet high, and nearly as large in diameter—supposedly marks where Buddha preached that first sermon in the forest. Having replaced an earlier one, this huge sixth-century stupa is carved with a design of flowers and zigzags of lightning which carry more power than the bland mass of stone itself.

The rest of the park at Sarnath is mostly ancient uneven brick embankments a few feet high. Much must be yet covered by grass and dirt. Hiuen Tsiang, the Chinese pilgrim who walked along the GT in the seventh century, saw thirty monasteries here, three thousand monks, and a lifesize brass Buddha busy with Dharmachakrapravartna. When the artist and nonsense poet Edward Lear visited in 1874 he described the place accurately as "isolated eminences with some lumpy ruins, all hideous and utterly unbearable, however valuable to archaeological minds. . . . " There must've been more to see in his day.

In the park three old men squatted, cutting the grass with lazy windmill sweeps of their dark scythes. A few Tibetan monks were wandering about. Down one path a man pulled himself along on his hands like a spider, his legs bowed toward me. He wasn't a monk dragging himself forward in a posture of obeisance, only a hard-working beggar with arduously twisted legs.

Following my rule of giving only to the deformed, I handed him some money and he thanked me courteously, in good English.

He said, "I am glad for all the help I can get, sir. I have been like this since I was three."

The gardens at Sarnath were well kept, and the site indeed serene, but hardly charged with the wonder of Bodh Gaya. I got no sensation of being at a "power place," and leaving by the back gate, through thickets of souvenir salesmen marketing unusually dismal Buddhist kitsch, I longed for the beautiful forest Sarnath must once have been.

At Mriz Murao we stopped for *chai* (tea). The driver's idea. Might as well keep Shambu happy.

The road here was impeccable, with big-headed trees. At Parao a truck had had a flat and, leaned over precariously, was being propped up only by a single thick bamboo limb stuck very optimistically into the ground.

Vikranpur, Mahrajahgan, Tiuri, Kuriyaman.

These unmapped and drowsy villages speckled the road like dust-brown pebbles. Between them were villagers on bicycles, carrying cheap carpets or riding sidesaddle. Always the trees stood up gratefully in water. The rains had made even the local dogs look healthy, and in India that is a miracle.

Kothara, Handia, Lalabazar. Thatched lean-tos, and stray brick walls without meaning.

Suddenly a town, corn being barbecued and fruit sold off wood carts. The loving attitudes of cows and empty rickshaws, and the every-man-for-himself attitude of pigs. Black crows pecking at a dead black dog. People asleep on rope cots by the GT.

White eucalyptus trees stood tall in a parched land hanging expectantly on the cusp of the monsoon. The British had brought these from Australia in the nineteenth century, thinking they prevented malaria. Soon we were in rain-blessed country again, and the paddies were like lakes where green lawn was starting up.

Coming into Allahabad on the long Shastri Bridge over the Ganges we passed a procession, mostly women in yellow, scarlet, purple, and saffron saris. Far below, the Ganges was unusually broad, swollen from meeting the Jamuna. This holy conjunction of the two great rivers—joined also by a third river, the heavenly, mythological Saraswati—makes the city very sacred.

Here the GT split into two carriageways for the modern bridge, with a barrier between. The horde of women was chanting, while a young man accompanied them by interrogating a weird single-string keyboard with a plectrum. There were also two men beating drums, and a boy shaking a kind of local maraca.

These people were from Jhusinghi village, on their way to the Ganges to bathe a long pole with a banner. They'd then plant it before Hanuman's temple on the other side. Hanuman, the monkey-headed God of Strength, often shown wielding a mace (as Prince Rama's powerful aide in the *Ramayana*, he helps defeat the evil demon-king), tends to be very popular with Hindu villagers. Their pole was about thirty feet high, and bent in the breeze; its banner was a rich red, brocaded with gold. Three supporting ropes, as around a maypole, helped keep it upright as the villagers slowly walked it along.

The procession, perhaps two hundred strong, let out cheers every now and then, shouting *"Bajarng Bali Ki Jai!"* (Victory for

Hanuman!) More music, amplified by a megaphone, wailed behind them. Every few cheers the procession flung up their hands, oblivious to the buses rolling past, the lorries carrying clay bricks.

As a mother runs
close behind her child
with her hand on a cobra
or a fire,

the lord of the meeting rivers
stays with me
every step of the way
and looks after me.

The procession was a tiny echo of another Allahabad event, the massive festival of Kumbha Mela, held in various incarnations every year and most massively every twelve. This can easily mean 4 million people bathing here on a single day, and up to 20 million in one month—the largest ceremonial gathering of humans on the planet. Ever since the 1954 disaster of hundreds of pilgrims trampled to death, the religious fair, which centers on an embankment where the rivers meet, has become as organized as the authorities can make it: tents, special trains, pontoon bridges, first-aid posts, "fair-price shops," cholera inoculations, floodlights, trench latrines.

Tradition dictates other rules. The festival always attracts sadhus, religious ascetics. Some sects go naked, grow their hair in dreadlocks, smear themselves with ashes; these are generally the first in the water. For the sects' leaders there are often chariots, glittering palanquins, spears, the fanfare of drums and trumpets. Mark Twain, visiting Allahabad ("Godville") in 1896, speculated that there might be only one more Kumbha Mela. ("It will be like shutting down a mint.") Yet the January festival still flourishes, much as it did when Hieun Tsiang witnessed it twelve centuries before Twain. Among the greatest beneficiaries of a Kumbha Mela are the barbers, since any Hindu who gets his head shaved above the sacred union of the two rivers receives a year in Heaven for every hair that falls into the water.

Allahabad was a college town, with dozens of bookstalls and students reading as they walked. Much of the British sector seemed intact, full of fantastical old buildings like the Palace—a cream yellow cinema with winged, scantily draped muses in stone just above the modern poster of that forbidden image, an Indian couple kissing hungrily. The atmosphere here was softer, less scarred and ruinous than Calcutta, with evocative Raj arches everywhere and a gorgeous university in an Anglo-Mogul melange of styles.

Allahabad's many schools and its university in particular were, however, long-standing centers of student unrest. Or so a local barrister informed me.

"They are hotbeds of hooliganism!" he thundered.

Political unrest? I asked.

"Mere hooliganism, sir!"

Two weeks after I left, I read in the *Times of India* that all Allahabad's educational institutions were closed for "an indefinite period" after police "fired on an unruly mob of students."

This unrest was a great Allahabad tradition, too, for many of the roots of the Indian nationalist movement are here. Jawaharlal Nehru (1889-1964), the first prime minister of independent India—as well as father and grandfather to prime ministers Indira Gandhi and her son Rajiv, both assassinated in office—had been born and brought up here. His Victorian family mansion, the first Indian home in the city to have electric lights, has been turned into a museum-shrine to politics. Nehru's elitism, shaped in England at Harrow and Cambridge, had been inspired by these lavish surroundings—his father sent his laundry all the way to Paris—but some of Nehru's dynamism and sense of historic events came from Allahabad itself. For here, in 1858, from thousands of miles away, Queen Victoria had formally declared the East India Company dissolved, and India itself now part of the British Empire—the jewel mine in the crown.

Shambu was mystified. I led him for two hours in a clueless search around the avenues of the British-era town, looking for the last offices in India where Rudyard Kipling worked. This was as a young star on the staff of the *Pioneer,* from November 1887 until March 1889, when Kipling left for England. The daily newspaper, still flourishing—India has more than four thousand dailies in a hundred languages and dialects—had long since moved to Lucknow, and no one in Allahabad seemed to know where its old premises had been. I got led around the British lines on repeated wild-goose chases because Indians are at once so helpful and yet so unwilling to admit they don't know the right answer to your question.

At last, in front of the old University Arts Faculty mansion, I found what remained of the Allahabad *Pioneer*. The skeleton was barely standing—a mottled, low, round-arched building on which every conceivable violence had seemingly been enacted, from fire to riot. Its burnt stones were the color of rust, with a few fancily tiled hearths inside still standing. One surprise of the British Raj is how grand the buildings were even for workmanlike institutions.

Kipling's only prior newspaper office had been in Lahore, up the GT in Pakistan, from 1882 to 1887. For those important years when Kipling wrote his first mature poems and stories, he was working for the *Pioneer*'s subsidiary, the *Civil and Military Gazette*. Lahore was a setting for Kipling's fiction in a way Allahabad never was, but to come here to work for the *Pioneer,* the most prestigious newspaper in India, was the prize promotion that led to exposure, acclaim, and England. If Lahore formed the writer, Allahabad made the author.

The great paradox of Kipling (1865–1936) and India is that, for all that they seem inseparable, he had only twelve years here in all. Born in Bombay, he wasn't yet six when he was sent away to England for schooling—where he was shocked by his first sight of a white woman performing manual labor. He returned as a hard-working young journalist, arriving "home" in India at age sixteen and leaving for good at twenty-three. Except for a brief visit just before his twenty-sixth birthday, he never saw India again.

I had always thought of Lahore as Kipling's city; I had no vision of Allahabad from his work. The burned-out relic of his newspaper was suggestive. In *Something of Myself* he writes of how he was put in charge of a weekly supplement to the *Pioneer* and suddenly had plenty of space for short stories not of twelve hundred but of five thousand words: "My pen took charge and I... watched it write for me far into the nights... I made my own experiments in the weights, colours, perfumes, and attributes of words.... " In one of his masterpieces, *The Man Who Would Be King,* his narrator, a newspaper editor, complains how "every dissolute ruffian that ever tramped the Grand Trunk Road makes it his business to ask for employment as a proof-reader."

During 1888, on assignment, Kipling got to Agra, Benares, and Calcutta. At year's end he sold the rights to a book of verse (*Departmental Ditties*), a book of short stories (*Plain Tales from the Hills*, likewise written in Lahore), and six other books of stories written for the *Pioneer Weekly*. These were astutely put out by the publisher who owned the bookstalls in train stations all over India. Kipling, who always suffered from fever and dysentery in the subcontinent, could now afford to leave it.

Naturally Indians resent many of his attitudes. One subtle reason for this is that Kipling's sympathies were resolutely, as he admitted, with Muslims. This had largely to do with his years in Lahore: "My life had lain among Muslims, and a man leans one way or another according to his first service." Few Hindus in his stories emerge in a positive light. Nevertheless he remains the fairest-minded creator of fiction set in India at that time, for the bulk of English fiction coming from the Raj then was dogged jingoism. Thanks to him we know what the experience of the subcontinent was for the soldiers and engineers, the doctors and traders, the cannon fodder and working middle class of the Raj—and for their wives.

His stories can be trusted in this regard because Kipling the artist was never far from sight of Kipling the journalist, and the richness of his language never outweighs the accuracy of his eye. He was too much a writer of short breaths, a sprinter, to achieve the single large work his subject matter might suggest. Even *Kim* reads like a patchwork quilt of episodes; journalism denied him the novelist's architectural sense of a compelling structure. His universe comes to us in vivid bits and pieces like chunks of an Indian bas-relief broken off a vast temple; it is up to us to put it all together. The economy of his approach, the speed and arresting seizure of a scene, were partly a result of his writing for years for an audience who knew intimately the places and the sorts of characters he was writing about. Thus he could leave a lot out, he could assume great understanding on the part of his readership, and he was forced to describe unforgettably or not at all.

Writers must be forgiven the aspects of their work, the aspects of themselves, which they cannot help. The racial bigotry that from time to time stands out like a curse in his work can still make us wince, but it also reveals the assumptions of that era of the Raj. The sad irony is that many of Kipling's objectionable stereotypes are still painted just as broadly by both Hollywood and Bollywood, in Indiana Jones as well as the Bombay cinema. At least from every page of Kipling there shines a deep love for the place and its people, if only as types, that transcends his era.

Kipling's success was to take him away from India even as writing about it insured his success. That meant for him a kind of private partition. He always seems to be wrestling with the fact that his Indian upbringing can never defeat his Englishness—for the

Anglo-Indian boy Kim, running free in the bazaar, is a dream version of himself, the Ruddy who wasn't sent all the way to cold England for his education. In the end what Kipling loves about the Raj is the fact that it functions smoothly; when it doesn't, he has little use for it. For deep down, from early on, he was a critic of British society and its internal hypocrisies in India, and not its blind exponent—the one British imaginative writer of that time of whom this can be said.

Indian critics today often take Kipling to task for an almost nostalgic sentimentalizing of the bullock cart and the bazaar, especially in *Kim*. Part of this was genuine homesickness in the author, for the novel was written more than a decade after Kipling had left India. (When analyzing his attitudes, it also should not be forgotten that most of his Indian short stories were written before he was twenty-five.) But the critique also has to do with the Indian intellectual's dismissal of all things folklorically Indian. Elite, educated India wants to be above village India, rural India. This is unlike the literary situation in the States, where the difficulties of country life are ever glorified and made into myth.

For the same reasons the novels of R. K. Narayan (b. 1906), all set in the imaginary village of Malgudi, get short shrift in India. One hopes that Narayan—to my mind, in the Chekhov league—will not be as ignored by Indian posterity as he is presently marginalized in the West, where few luminaries (with the exception of Graham Greene, who first got him published) have recognized his greatness. It is too easy to say, as V. S. Naipaul suggests, that Narayan's weakness is to portray the denizens of his fictional village without question, without presenting a critical judgment on that village life. Why should he? This is the historian's task, not the artist's. Narayan's magic lies in the transparent clarity of his portraits, the exact unfolding of thought and event and gesture. It is up to generations of readers to judge Narayan's villagers for themselves. His genius lies in letting us experience them, and in trusting to his portraits and our understanding enough to leave it at that.

What Narayan and his few colleagues and their many heirs have working against them is that, despite the culture's extraordinarily rich literary past, Hindus for centuries have been largely a two-book people—though this puts them way ahead of most Muslims. The *Ramayana* and the *Mahabharata* of antiquity—the two great Hindu epic poems, of gargantuan length—have been a Great Wall of India that kept out invaders. That India has always been a predominantly illiterate country has helped them live on; with their tremendous human wisdom and openness to interpretation, they are the largest set of myths from an ancient civilization that are still being followed in a traditional way.

Yet societies that depend on one set of myths, no matter how vast, produce people with a disregard for history and a resistance to that which does not conveniently fit the canon. The one-book mind finds that book, usually first encountered aurally, so much more interesting than a restless, relentless, and new examination of the present or the past, especially since everyone knows it.

An encounter with a book is thus a group activity, and not an adventure of the imagination in private. The *Mahabharata* and the *Ramayana* in all their richness are recounted, performed, painted, memorized, beloved, danced, and discussed all across India, from nomadic actors in the tiniest villages to serials on nationwide TV. They are the longest-lived best-sellers of all time, and the longest. This popular dependence on two huge works cannot be exorcised after several literate generations: the effects are sunk deep, like oil wells, in the society. They limit what comes up.

Imagination is partly hunger, an appetite of mind. In a people the questioning imagination can be almost a physical need, the healthy dissatisfaction of a society with what it already has. Yet the one- or two-book mind is a fully satisfied mind. Such giant texts have the effect of fulfilling all needs, because the need for difference has never been allowed to develop. The appetite is sated, crammed to bursting, before it ever learns what hunger is.

So the damage of these masterpieces is to smother, even to kill, curiosity.

The result is people who live in a never-never land somewhere between fable and fact, often flexible of mind—all those myths to reinterpret—yet strangely inflexible in their doctrines and lives, with little capacity for change. The point of ritual is to stabilize and renew a people; but if a society simply accepts, and fails to produce new myths to set alongside the old, it develops little muscle for change.

As Nehru put it: "This imagined history and mixture of fact and legend became widely known and gave to the people a strong and abiding cultural background. But the ignoring of history produced a vagueness of outlook, a divorce from life as it is, a credulity, a wooliness of the mind where fact was concerned."

He was speaking of the Hindu storytelling achievement. It struck me that what Kipling—a minor poet but one of English literature's great short-story writers—nearly added up to, taken all together, was a would-be Anglo-Indian epic. He too was writing for a woolly-minded, wholly credulous audience, living in the never-never land of an eternal Raj. And at least some of the cracks in the mural of British India that Kipling painted were deliberate ones. Nowhere meant as much to him: he wrote what he saw, and sometimes he saw even more than he realized.

Just outside Allahabad we came across a camel munching away contentedly by a truck lying on its side. The truck had been carrying hay; the camel was very wisely dealing first with the hay still on the truck. Later he would have time to deal with the wealth scattered on the road or lying in clumps against a tree.

Listen, O lord of the meeting rivers,
things standing shall fall,
but the moving ever shall stay.

When anyone of my generation speaks of Cawnpore he means those two shattered barracks with the earth wall round them. That was where Wheeler, with his ramshackle garrison, had been holding out against an army for two and a half weeks. There were nine hundred people inside it when the siege began, nearly half of them women and children; of the rest four hundred were British soldiers and civilians, and a hundred loyal natives. They had one well, and three cannon; they were living on two handfuls of mealies a day, fighting off a besieging force of more than 3000 mutineers... if you'd had both legs blown off you were rated fit only for light duties.

— George MacDonald Fraser,
Flashman in the Great Game (1975)

10.

Kanpur

North of Allahabad—just over a third of the way to the Khyber, I calculated—the road divides for four hundred miles, until Delhi. The newer British branch, also called the GT, makes an easterly sweep via Aligarh. I decided instead to take Sher Shah's older branch, which follows the ancient route via Agra.

Dust swirled about the towns where the GT charged through. The markets were hot, the air sodden, heavy with an impending rain and relief that hadn't come.

The off-white Ambassador Nova, with Shambu Singh at the wheel, raced along the smoothest stretches of road so far. In this heat, even in a car I felt extremely indebted to those who'd planted so many shade trees. Thankfully my stomach, which had been making jokes since the Benares ice fiasco, stopped threatening and left me alone. By now I'd settled into getting by on two meals a day—omelette in the morning and something innocent, like a curry or chicken tikka, in the evening. It was hard to feel hungry around people who weren't ever getting enough to eat.

A peacock took sudden fright and flight at a passing car and was immediately, loudly in the air.

Teams of black bullocks pulled preposterously overloaded carts. Monkeys crept cautiously among the trees by the road but kept away from the dhabas. The towns seemed dissolute and unkempt and the light changed from dust to gold as the afternoon wound on.

Coming into Kanpur—formerly Cawnpore—we passed miles of vast city dump, with vultures glued to every limb of every tree, watching the human figures pick through the refuse first.

Kanpur is one more place whose spelling has been altered to erase the British past—ditto Simla, now Shimla; and Bombay, now Mumbai. Cawnpore had endured one of the bloodiest events of the 1857 Mutiny, when a thousand British soldiers and civilians were pinned down by Indian fire for three weeks, then killed during a promised safe passage on the river. This particular massacre had a rare awakening effect on the British public; the Mutiny resulted in the shutting-down of the East India Company and the formal, long-delayed annexation of the subcontinent, with Queen Victoria's viceroy, answerable only to her, replacing the Company's governor-general.

The former Memorial Church—now All Souls Church—was paid for largely by public subscription in India and England after the Mutiny. In a somewhat ornate Romanesque style, with leafy columns and ceiling fans whirring, it still has the air of a monument, and is undoubtedly the building in the best condition in all Kanpur.

I couldn't climb to the belfry for the view because a service was in progress. Sunday mornings it was in English, about a dozen people attending, dispersed through the church in ones and twos.

A marble tablet on the inner wall, near the back, said:

This tablet
In memory of an excellent son,
Is erected by his afflicted parents, Admiral and Mrs. Martin, to
John Nickleson Martin
Lieut. Bengal Artillery
Who, Whilst Gallantly Fulfilling His Duties,
Was Treacherously Killed By the Mutineers
In the Boats At Cawnpore,
On the 27th of June, 1857, in his 18th year,
Respected and Beloved By All Who Knew Him.

"The Lord Gave and the Lord Hath Taken Away,
Blessed Be The Name of the Lord."

TEEKA RAM SCULPT. CAWNPORE

What resonated most was the Indian engraver's name at the bottom.

After the service I spoke with the minister, Father Carroll. A white-haired, athletic man, he took my arm gently as if we were walking, though we stood still. He was clearly Anglo-Indian, not in the mixed-blood sense but in the original meaning of the term: he looked British but his voice had the intonation of someone brought up in India. The plight of the Anglo-Indian is to be neither this nor that in a country where people are defined in stone as either this or that; where, due to the Indian mania for compartmentalizing, one is asked to define oneself quicker than in any country I know.

I asked Father Carroll about his background here.

"I have been a member of this church for twenty-three years. I was an engineer originally, then I joined the ministry."

The church was part of the Christian Church of India, which still has associations with the Anglican Church back in England.

"Where were you born, Father?"

I was trying to be delicate. I might as well have said: Tell me who your parents were.

He said, "I was born in Bombay—my family was from Yorkshire. A long story. But that's all part of history now."

He had explained much, far more delicately than I'd asked.

In India much fervent media attention is paid—either in approval or disapproval—to how the upper class often plays at being Europeanized; mostly, that is, Anglicized. Yet the role of the Anglo-Indian (in the present, mixed-blood meaning of the term) is to be somewhat ostracized. The facts of his birth condemn him because he is, genetically, what others and especially the upper class wish to become socially: half English. And more often than not he does not have the economic means to support the popular vision of that ideal.

So he remains a kind of outcaste.

The many memorial tablets in the church, en masse, told much of the British side of the story. My unanswered question was why there are so few monuments—not only here but throughout the entire country—to the Indians who died fighting for or against the British in the nineteenth century. Why not a statue in Kanpur somewhere of the Unknown Mutineer? After all, fifty years have gone by since independence: plenty of time to erect such monuments. Perhaps it's that India feeds only on the cult of a specific personality; witness the number of statues of Bose everywhere. Apart from the battle-minded Sikhs, who have a detailed sense of military sacrifice, the Indian unknown soldier remains truly unknown.

There is still a roundabout controversy regarding the term "the Mutiny." Many Indians find it disparaging, and consider the uprising the first shots fired, literally and symbolically, of the

Independence Movement. The opposing argument is that the Mutiny consisted only of scattered, unconnected outbreaks: high-caste *sepoys* (native soldiers) in the Bengal Army as at Cawnpore and Lucknow, Muslims in Allahabad and Delhi, peasants in the countryside. There was no unified "movement," it led to nothing.

But it's only a few decades from the Mutiny to Gandhi, surely. After eight centuries of nearly constant outsider rule, the Mutiny proved to Indians that they could have an effect, and on the strongest force of all.

No other foreign power had ever occupied the subcontinent totally. The great British expansion had come at the turn of the nineteenth century, under the governor-general's fist of Lord Wellesley, the Duke of Wellington's equally military older brother. The Moguls were exhausted; India was incoherent once more. Politically it was as fragmented as when the first Afghans or Moguls had come in centuries earlier—a series of henhouses waiting to be raided. Wellesley bit at the feudal territories methodically, knowing the Company's government overseers—to whom he had to answer—were too far away and too distracted by Napoleon to stop him. By the time he was called home in 1805, a third of the subcontinent was British.

It was during this time that they acquired Delhi. It had been plundered decades earlier by several Persian invaders whom the Marathas, at immense cost, had at last defeated. The British now picked the Marathas apart, treaty by treaty. Only northwest India remained outside of East India Company control, the domain of the Sikhs and of Afghan and Nepalese tribesmen. All fought unsuccessful wars against the British in the next few decades.

The last Mogul monarch, stranded like a snail on a crumbling sandcastle in Delhi's once-sumptuous Red Fort, lived off the glory of his title and a huge British pension. Millions of Indians still thought of Bahadur Shah as the Emperor of all India, with his innumerable servants and wives and bodyguards and children, while he aged and wrote verses and told himself that he could turn into a fly if danger arose, and buzz his way to safety. He was worse off than the five hundred sixty princes with their separate states which never became British property, who worked out their individual land, trade, protection, and power deals, and survived. As an old man many years later, having chosen the losing side in the Mutiny, exiled to die in Rangoon, Bahadur Shah would write

On seeing me, no eye lights up,
no heart near me finds solace;
serving no use or purpose,
I am but a handful of dust.

The numbers are laughable: fewer than forty thousand British versus a local population of about 150 million. But the subcontinent was all diversity—not a nation, but an agglomeration of peoples disunited by race, religion, language, caste, and personality. Too many Indians were ready to join John Company's military forces against other Indians. At the time of the Mutiny the British army was made up of about 34,000 European soldiers and 257,000 locals.

This era before the Mutiny was, curiously, when the British gave the most to India; when the Grand Trunk Road was restored, and the Thugs wiped out, and widow-burning banned, and the railroads begun, and more money spent on education than would be spent in England for decades. It was when Macaulay—who sneered at a local culture of "kings 30 feet high and reigns 30,000 years long"—worked for two years in Calcutta coming up with an innovative penal code that honored Hindu and Muslim customs to the letter, abolished flogging, regulated the punishments for a few thousand offenses, and was a half century ahead of Britain's laws in recognizing women's rights to own property.

What the British did not recognize in these decades before the Mutiny was how much their approach to India had changed. It had now become too much like England, with *memsahibs* who felt at home in a house full of servants, and Christian missionaries who felt they were long awaited here no matter what the Orientalists warned. The new presence of trains was felt by many Indians as a violent upheaval. A racism and disdain had crept into the relations between Englishman and Indian, a misunderstanding of the repercussions of small gestures.

Besides the meddling missionaries, what sparked the Mutiny was the use of a new rifle which required grease, made from tallow fat, on the cartridges. For Hindus, beef fat in the grease would make handling the rifles absolutely taboo; for Muslims the taboo was pork fat. A terror of all grease spread swiftly through the sepoys, especially the high castes in the Bengal Army. In May 1857, eighty-five sepoys in the Meerut garrison were given ten-year jail sentences for refusing to use the new Enfield rifles.

By the next day the British were engulfed in carnage. What was happening was unthinkable—that friendly young Bengali who took the memsahib out riding every Saturday had just murdered the memsahib in her bed, along with the children. The sepoys went wild, killing every European they found in Delhi and in Meerut, where the ghastliness of the murders far outweighed the numbers (thirty-one). The Mutiny was confined mostly to this central area of north India.

The bloodlust moved on to Cawnpore under the direction of a local billiards-playing prince, Nana Sahib. After three weeks' siege of General Hugh Wheeler and his men and the gathered white population in the horrific entrenchment, Nana Sahib relented; safe passage in boats on the river would be permitted. The siege was lifted and the survivors escorted to the Ganges. After all, only a few soldiers were left alive; it was mostly women and children. As they clambered into the boats the sepoys opened fire.

• • •

Outside, in the churchyard, was a blue and white tiled tablet in an enclosure of its own:

In Three
Graves
Within This
Enclosure
Lie The
Remains
of Major Edward Vibart, 2nd Bengal Light
Cavalry, and About Seventy Officers
And Soldiers Who, after Escaping from the
Massacre At Cawnpore On the 27th June 1857
Were Captured By The Rebels At Sheorajpoor,
And Murdered on the 1st July.
IN MEMORIAM

Wheeler's Entrenchment, where the thousand-odd British soldiers and civilians were pinned down, was the area around the church for some distance, all so flat and vulnerable it was hard to envision it as a place to be besieged in.

Behind the church was an enormous monument, an angel with spreading Gothic stone arches, that had been moved here from above the famous well, a couple of miles away. The well was where the bodies of the butchered women and children had been found—those pulled from the boats, imprisoned, then executed two weeks later.

This act, equalled in Lucknow, set off a year of widespread British carnage in reprisal. Mutinous sepoys were bayoneted or hanged or blown from cannon, having been made to lick bloody ground clean first, or to swallow beef or pork to be damned after death. There were no fair trials, only revenge: Macaulay's code of law, written years earlier, did not come into effect until 1860. By then India would be a colony, not a trade zone.

Atop the so-called Memorial Well now is a statue of Tantia Tope—an Indian leader in the Mutiny.

Inside the church, around the marble altar were seven tall marble tablets, put up

In memory of more than a
thousand Christian people, who
met their deaths hard by,
between 6th June and 15th July
1857.

A somber poetry in that phrase, "hard by"—but the dignity and restraint of such grief made it difficult to stand in this quiet spot and reconstruct that time in which British and Indian notions of each other exploded. The romance of the past is easy to enter, but not its assumptions; not the world it took for granted.

Looking over the tablets, I struck up a conversation with a man who turned out to be a major in the Indian Army, down from a hill station to spend fifteen days in Kanpur's heat. Here, as in many of the important towns, the Indian Army has largely taken over the cantonments, the self-enclosed British areas, for their own use.

I asked, "What do you think of all these British memorials to the Mutiny?"

He said softly—not imposing his point of view, but smiling—"We are Indian. So it is the First War of Independence for us."

There was another Anglo-Indian echo to the church, that I realized only later. The architect of that memorial angel was Henry Yule, whose brother had died in the Mutiny. I knew him as one of the two authors of *Hobson-Jobson,* the massive Anglo-Indian dictionary first published in 1886—a pendulous fruit of two word-obsessed cultures. In a thousand pages, four centuries of linguistic collaborations, marriages, adulteries as well as family trees are treated in a way that makes a writer weep for all that English has lost of what it once had. For me to say:

> *After my shampoo I sat on the bungalow's veranda in my khaki pajamas—a dandy sipping toddy and smoking a cheroot—counting my loot, savoring my cash, awaiting my curry and punch, knowing my muddles were behind me, that those muggers in dungarees who count me a scavenger would one day be pariahs themselves, and receive the juggernaut of this pundit's typhoon...*

would be quite impossible if the British had never come to India. These words are still alive; most of the entries in *Hobson-Jobson* are gravestones, the verbal equivalent of all those marble tablets.

The other Mutiny site in Kanpur is the Satichaura Ghat, where the few hundred survivors of Wheeler's Entrenchment were killed as they tried to clamber into their boats. Perhaps 125 women and children had lived to be taken prisoner and later slaughtered, cut up, and thrown piecemeal down the well.

The ghat descends to the Ganges, here about a mile and a half across. In the river water buffalo were bathing; the Massacre Ghat was only a few stone steps, a most unimpressive place considering the mark the event made on the British imagination. Several more recent square temples were built against curved old brick balconies rising up over the water.

The church and the surrounding gardens of the entrenchment may spiritually still belong to the British, but the river belongs to the Hindus. By the ghat people were making bread, chanting, and performing their submarine ablutions. A woman sold flower petals; offerings were made to statues of old gods set in old niches. Monkeys capered about in packs, aggressively.

On the way out of Kanpur, by a truckers' quarter, stretched a block of garbage in which rude shack-tents had been erected; the garbage was being meticulously sifted by its denizens. I saw it as a newer kind of cantonment, of hovels made of mud, shit, thatch, bits and pieces. It still had order, even if living conditions in each shack-tent were crowded—an outward sense of property and territory inherited from the Raj. Here, among some of the poorest people I have ever seen, the British concept of cantonment and containment had survived in a severe parody of itself, a collaboration of two highly class-conscious societies.

I was glad to get out on the road.

Throughout all Uttar Pradesh I frequently saw a three-wheeler gutbucket jalopy, usually all black except for a yellow forehead off the roof. Called a "tempo," it functioned as a taxi. It could hold perhaps seven people comfortably besides the driver, but frequently carried upward of twenty squished in. It resembled an experiment a few kids had put together on a dare, with a worn-out grille that dipped out over the single front wheel like a protruding, misshapen jaw. This tipped open like a hatch to reveal the engine when undergoing repairs.

From any angle the elongated body looked pulled out of shape, and the main roof was generally only a tarp stretched over an iron frame. Beneath it were two seats (or four, if the tempo was extra extended) with passengers facing each other, if there wasn't already a small crowd wedged in between. The rear of the tempo stuck up like the prow of a troop carrier, and sometimes did carry a small regiment hanging on bravely. Crawling down the road without a muffler, it made a harsh gallumphing sound that could be heard even above a Tata truck horn.

Tall cornfields, a wide-eyed camel being chucked to a trot.

Tea at a dhaba near Bhaoli. An elephant carrying leaves was being ridden by a man with a painted face.

• • •

After ten days on the road, accidents seemed almost commonplace; with one every couple of kilometers, I'd rapidly become a connoisseur. To see a truck flipped over with cargo spilled, or rusted and abandoned, or in a ditch, now left me unmoved. But about thirty miles from Agra, we came on an accident that had just happened. A truck had lost a wheel, crossed to the other side of the road, and gone off the road, down the embankment, and crunched into a tree. It'd been carrying animals to be sold in Firozobad, the next town. Most of the animals had been thrown into the field, and presumably the buffalo tied to a tree ten feet from the truck was a survivor.

One white calf lay dead in the back of the leaning truck, another lay dead on the ground; nearby the mother was dying. A man poked the injured animal's spine and it jerked and shifted in pain.

The two truckers lay in the field beside the dead animals, surrounded by a horde of villagers. Each had a leg bound up with handkerchiefs. Flies droned about, though I saw no blood. One trucker was in shock, his head flung back on a cushion like someone posed smoking a cigarette.

The other lay near him, one leg curled up and across, held by a hand under his thigh, next to the other driver. They looked like a pair of lovers after the act. They didn't talk much. Bystanders jostled and pushed to get a good look at them. Everyone but the truckers spoke, all at once, or poked at the dead and dying animals.

Apparently a third man, the actual driver of the truck, had run away after the accident, or been taken off somewhere. These two men had been in back with the animals—mostly buffaloes and donkeys to be sold.

I was shaken by the lack of involvement and initiative from the villagers; they might as well have been watching TV, or observing the aftermath of a flying saucer crash and wounded aliens from Mars, for all the active interest they took. Fascinating, but not their responsibility.

In this sort of situation the truckers are dependent on charity—there is no road "rescue service," no state troopers to radio for assistance, probably no telephone and no ambulance and often no hospital or clinic nearby. I watched a government vehicle pass with a total lack of interest.

I couldn't think what else to do, so I paid a tempo to take them to a hospital in Firozobad, a sand-colored building of some stature, where a doctor and orderlies got to work on them right away. These men were lucky: neither was seriously injured, perhaps one had a broken leg. They could've lain there a long time, though.

I did not wonder what would happen to the animal carcasses as soon as the drivers had been taken away, around a bend in the road.

> I had twentie daies journey to another goodly citie, called Agra, through such a delicate and eeven tract of ground as I never saw before, and doubt whether the like to bee found within the whole circumference of the habitable world. Another thing also in this way beeing no lesse memorable than the plainenesse of the ground; a row of trees on each side of this way where people do travell, extending it selfe from the townes end of Lahore to the townes end of Agra.... I traversed afoot, but with divers paire of shooes, having beene such a propateticke... that is, a walker forward on foote, as I doubt whether you have heard the like in your life....
>
> — Thomas Coryat (1616)

11.

An Ice-Storm of Architecture

In the countryside near Agra, a bus swerved to avoid a bicyclist, nearly hitting another bus. Both drivers jumped out and took turns methodically haranguing the bicyclist. A trucker coming from the other direction noticed the dispute and stopped just to enjoy the show. The trucker got out; he soon found himself embroiled in the argument, taking the side of the bicyclist.

By now the bicyclist had righted his upended vehicle, and during the commotion he pedaled away. The trucker in turn refused to back up so the two buses could leave. By this time more trucks were pinned behind the catty-cornered buses. No one could or would move, and another massive traffic jam was off to a mile-long start.

I first saw what Twain called "an ice-storm of architecture" tiny through the trees, from amid garages and dumping grounds on the GT a couple of miles outside the city.

Several points about the Taj Mahal that astonished me:

1. How big it is
2. How clean it is
3. How symmetrical it is
4. How many of the visitors are Indians, not Westerners
5. How mysterious it should be that those shapes, in those proportions, should be the perfect ones
6. How repetitive all descriptions of it are
7. How many people take the same photo
8. How as you get closer, you see there is curlicue writing all over it
9. How it seems one of the few buildings (along with Haghia Sophia seen from inside) whose foundations were designed not to hold it up but to keep it from floating away
10. How much it matches all its photographs

Rather like a movie star who, surprisingly captive beside you on a ten-hour airplane flight, manages to look just as beautiful as she does in the cinema right from takeoff to landing.

Appearances are misleading, for the Taj is besieged. Humidity is corroding it, rain is leaking via cracks into the domes, monsoon deluges weaken the foundations, the principal platform sags from the crowds on free-admission days, and the river beside it is crud. Thieves (hired as restorers) are stealing the inlay. It is under attack from bird dung and beehives, and graffiti, and the stains of betel-juice saliva and hair oil. Worst of all, seventeen hundred factories, foundries, and refineries in the Agra area are spewing filth into the Taj's air, creating a polluted Taj-sphere. Despite efforts to protect it either by making another three hundred factories switch from coal to gas, as the Delhi Supreme Court has just ordered, or scrubbing the surface with toothbrushes—a debatable approach—the gorgeous mausoleum still has that modern disease known as "marble cancer."

• • •

Having read great writers' often interminable accounts of their first visit to the Taj, I found that the most eloquent ones were often those registering disappointment. First, the laudatory—W. Somerset Maugham, in 1938, sees the Taj and writes:

> I was a trifle scared. I can only put what I felt into words that make no sense: I seemed to hear the noiseless footfall of the infinite.

But it does make sense, at least if you're there. Edward Lear, visiting in 1874, concludes a very long description with

> Henceforth, let the inhabitants of the world be divided into two classes—them as has seen the Taj Mahal; and them as hasn't.

I am inclined to agree, but Aldous Huxley, on his way to Burma and Japan and China in 1925, trounces them both. He is not so far from those early Englishmen who had wanted to dismantle the Taj for its marble. First Huxley points out that whenever he disagrees with everyone in the world, he asks himself if he can possibly be right. He decides he can and goes on to list the deficiencies of the Taj, starting with "a poverty of imagination." He hates the fact it cost so much ("It is a swindle!") and he hates especially the minarets. He hates the proportions, he hates the flowery reliefs ("they are frankly bad"), and he hates all the inlay of precious stones. "Marble, I perceive," he concludes, "covers a multitude of sins."

One man's opinion, you say. More convincing is that of the Scottish landscape painter William Simpson in 1860, on his three-year and 23,000 mile jaunt through India. He finds the Taj clearly inferior to several earlier Mogul monuments (which, he complains, the British utterly ignore), and Simpson had such a careful eye and saw so much of the subcontinent that he raises at least a tremor of doubt in one's soul. As he bluntly puts it, "Very few people pay any real attention to the details of architecture." Simpson, who had a rigorously independent turn of mind, could not stomach "Taj-worship."

What to compare it to? Like all buildings it changes as you get closer; with the Taj, the difference is that you care. Unable to keep the naysayers wholly out of my mind, prepared to be disappointed, I found myself instead inexpressibly exhilarated by that snow hill in air, that terrifyingly beautiful white whale surfacing up the sky, that Moby-Dick of architecture....

Agra has two devotions: tourism and the military. It appeared, in relation to other Indian cities, a financially healthy place, if the amount of construction pounding ahead was anything to judge by.

In the Old City, the mottled sandstone ramparts of the enormous Red Fort—both Agra and Delhi have one—still held an air of command, grimacing over the roadway after four centuries. Agra had little importance before Babur, the founding Mogul, fought his way from Peshawar down the rough ancient road, made Agra his capital, and died there in 1530. Akbar, his grandson, had fifty years of rule to consolidate the city, and his vision still defines it.

A mnemonic to keep the principal Mogul emperors in order: *B*ig *H*arems *A*re *J*olly *S*plendid *A*lways. (Babur, Humayun, Akbar, Jahangir, Shah Jahan, Aurangzeb.)

The Mogul architectural achievement is a Muslim inspiration painted by Hindu hands on an Indian canvas. In those monumental buildings you can see the Mogul personality undergoing the same process as the British later on. They come as creatures of ambition and greed; as they get rich, their imaginations are fired by the place and the people; and after a few remarkable achievements all energy is drained away like sap from a tree. Both empires have about two hundred years in power here, both wind up exhausted.

But in the process a marriage of styles occurs, a case of the conqueror being conquered, or at least seduced. Indians today regard the Moguls—who were, after all, invaders—with a kind of proprietary pride they do not have for the British. Perhaps this is because the many Hindu influences on Mogul architecture are obvious, and likewise because the Raj, the former master, is still sharply recalled in living memory. But there is also a wrong-headed sense that India made little mark from within on the British—when in fact it holds their imagination like no other former colony. Even as the paternal sense diminishes, a half century on, the place still fills their fantasies as much as their history books.

The sellers outside the Red Fort are among the fiercest in India. They have devised items that would suit the whims of long-dead emperors, as well as tastes even more extreme. An intricate fan of peacock feathers seems appropriate to the fortress; a long leather whip might be suitable also, but with a fox's ears and snout shoved hideously onto the handle, it was too much. Still, to combine your bestiality and sadism fantasies in one object for only a hundred rupees is a real bargain.

At the mobbed entrance to the Red Fort there was the usual struggle to cram your arm up to the elbow through the ticket portal. Countries where people cannot stand in line are economic failures, and whether this inability is a result of poverty, a cause, or merely another symptom, is an open question. It seems remarkable that the British could leave behind such an obsession with paper bureaucracy, regulations, and good form, without teaching Indians the form of the queue.

Through the Amar Singh Gate at last. Enormous battlements, faded to rust by the sun and no longer "polished like the world-revealing mirror, and...ruddy as the cheek of fortune" as someone noted during the Fort's founding. Some lavish blue and green tilework survives, in flower patterns rather like those on contemporary ceramics in Turkey; one surprise of the Mogul style is delicacy where you least expect it.

Inside, the Red Fort is mostly functional and military, having been stripped many centuries ago to bare walls. In 1857, long after the Mogul collapse, British forces retreated into it and held it without much difficulty during the Mutiny. Apart from a few sculptured niches or ornate columns or bits of floral inlay, it is an empty shell. Tourists roam around as if performing a penance between morning and sunset visits to the Taj Mahal. All efforts at preservation are, rightly, lavished on the Taj, and much of the Fort has been defaced with graffiti—gems like *I love Salma.*

I was tempted, in this Muslim relic, to add an *n.*

The touching aspect of the Red Fort was its view of the Taj. From the most lavish pavilion still remaining, during eight years of imprisonment before his death in 1666, Shah Jahan (b. 1592) could look across the river at the mausoleum of his favorite wife and dream about the black Taj, the other masterpiece which he had intended to build on the other side of the river for himself—linked to the white Taj, possibly, by a bridge.

It could be the finale of a story by Borges: the imprisoned man gazing out at his polished, unattainable dream of black marble. He knows he will die soon, yet he also knows the black shape of his dream will remain to haunt a few other men yet to come. Not a day awaits him when he will not remind himself, staring out at this view, that time's river has made room on its banks not for his own mausoleum but only for his wife's, the white shadow of his dream.

Shah Jahan's story is only partly Borgesian fable and irony. That wife, Mumtaz, had died at thirty-nine after the birth of their fourteenth child. The illness that brought on the fratricidal war of Shah Jahan's sons (which led to his imprisonment in the first place) was the result of his infatuation with a girl of twelve. It was not her youth that was the difficulty, but his age. At sixty-five he couldn't satisfy himself with her. This is how his court reporters express it; her satisfaction wasn't in question. The remedies his physicians suggested took him halfway to the grave, so he shut himself up in the harem with his other wives to recover.

Later, as a prisoner, his favorite daughter was allowed to visit him. One near-contemporary, the Frenchman Bernier, reports that the heartbroken emperor loved her to a point which is hardly to be credited, as the chronicle coyly puts it. He adds that Shah Jahan excused himself by saying that according to his mullahs—doctors of holy Koranic law—a man might be allowed "to eat the fruits of a tree which he himself had planted."

After Shah Jahan's death one son let the daughter in question leave for Delhi via the Sher Shah Road, riding on an elephant. In typical fashion she died almost immediately, probably poisoned. Her father ended up next to Mumtaz in the white Taj.

Within the lavish pavilion of Shah Jahan's house arrest I watched a middle-aged guard hold a fragment of mirror up to a niche to demonstrate for visitors how the interior had once been entirely inset with mirrors. When the local boys each leaned in to look, the guard would gently, accidentally caress their buttocks until they caught on and moved away. He seemed a man who'd found his calling.

As you proceed around the Red Fort you do see extraordinary carved balconies, lattices, marble foyers, brass or copper-capped towers spiked with metal fruit. But the virtue of an abandoned, largely stripped shell is to remind you that the fully furnished palaces of one's own lifetime may someday wear the same desolate look, after a forced and absolute eviction.

"—and he had five thousand girls!" a guide was intoning to his charges in thrilled envious tones as I walked down the ramp and out of the fort.

Early foreign travelers in India, beginning with the Greek ambassador Megasthenes in the third century B.C.—who mentions signposts and distance markers—through Buddhist pilgrims of the seventh and eighth centuries, through European traders of the sixteenth and seventeenth centuries, all praised the road. Most commented on its straightness ("one continued alley, drawn in a straight line") and how it was planted on both sides with mulberry trees, "date-trees, palm trees, coco trees." François Bernier, in a 1663 letter, spoke of caravanserais, wells, and "a double row of trees planted by order of Jahangir... with small pyramids, or turrets, every two miles or so." Seventeenth- and eighteenth-century European maps showed the trees running in an abundant even line down the road.

The most eccentric foreigner was almost certainly a self-mockling, self-hawking, perpetually talking, perpetually walking Elizabethan gentleman, Thomas Coryat (1577–1617). He was befriended and insulted by luminaries of his day like Jonson and Donne; even Shakespeare called him "brave Master Shoetie, the great traveller." Coryat had made a name for himself with his book about a six-month, two thousand mile walk in one pair of shoes through France, Switzerland, Germany, the Netherlands, and Italy. When that didn't make him as famous as he wanted, determined to be the greatest traveler of his day, he set off in 1612 from Constantinople for Aleppo, Damascus, and Jerusalem. Coryat then crossed Persia and, though he'd been robbed on the way, got to India by 1615.

He was now in the territory of "the great Mogul." With typical gusto he ate up what a contemporary called "the Long Walk," from Lahore all the way to Delhi and Agra, forty years too early for the Taj. He then proceeded to nearby Ajmer to meet the Emperor Jahangir—son of Akbar and father of Shah Jahan. This walk of 450 miles on the GT took Coryat only twenty days, at a cost of twopence a day; thus his remarks on the locals' generosity. He had covered over 3,300 miles from Jerusalem, as probably the first European to reach India on foot since Alexander the Great's infantry.

At Ajmer, Coryat settled in with ten fellow Englishmen, local representatives of the East India Company. Any countryman was welcome at a Company table, and they happily put up Coryat for fourteen months while he planned further travels (Samarkand and Ethiopia) and polished his Persian, Turkish, Hindustani, and Arabic. A dedicated wordsmith, he liked linguistic brawls and, usually dressed in native garb, he came to be looked on as "a half-witted English fakir"—a begging holy man—by the locals.

His plan was another book—though all that survived of his Great Walk are a few letters carried home, mostly to his mother, and full of his usual self-praise, energy, humor, and sober observation. Coryat kept walking. He saw Agra again during a plague, and got up to the Punjab; but the climate and his exertions were too much. He had fainting spells and managed to make his way to the East India Company's hospitality in Surat, in the southwest. Their kindnesses did him in. In December 1617 he became the first Western tourist to die in India from a bad stomach, brought on by an English diet of too much local beer on top of meat in hot weather.

Poor old Tom Coryat—butt of contemporaries' jokes, he was so intent on fame he even published a chapter of friends' insults as a preface to his only book. Yet to him belongs the honor of being the first Westerner to visit the subcontinent with no thought of either trade or conquest. He rarely complained of hardship, he was an exceptional linguist, and he traveled not for plunder or science or God but for his own pleasure—the first English travel writer. He was also unafraid of superlatives. As a pedestrian without equal in his time (he claimed), he called the road "the most incomparable shew of that kind that ever my eies survaied."

At Sikandra, a few miles north of Agra, in enormous square gardens the tomb of the greatest Mogul emperor, Akbar (1542–1605), looms right off the Sher Shah Suri Marg. The gardens spread touristless and empty, echoing the raucous cries of peacocks and monkeys amid the standing silence of black buck. The mausoleum has a grand pattern, a successive flow of arches and helmeted kiosks; the effect from the gardens, as you approach through a tall ornate gate, is gradual, regimental, and strong, rising from red to white. Then you get close enough to see it's all in pretty sad condition.

Akbar's son Jahangir supervised the building of the tomb—the second duty of being a Mogul emperor, after fratricide. This "supervision" meant that Jahangir didn't bother to take a look at the site until work had gone on for three years. He didn't like what he saw, and ordered everyone to start over.

Along the periphery of the mausoleum a series of Mogul lotus arches—if you had the place all to yourself as I did—ran like an allegory of time passing, age after age. Through a grand gateway of red sandstone, to the main entry hall, where according to a plaque, a panel had been ornately repaired to its earlier grandeur and the hanging lamp donated by Lord Curzon. There must be hundreds of plaques like this all over India, and they always made me imagine uniformed colonials congratulating themselves on their archaeological bustle and locals standing around picking their teeth and wondering about the purpose of it all. On Akbar's tomb wherever the outer walls were bare they'd been defaced by graffiti.

A tunneling hall slanted at length down to the crypt, which was a bare gigantic room, high ceilinged, with an echo like the Taj Mahal's. The marble cenotaph had gaudy robes laid over it. At the Taj the effect is of a preserved grandeur; here the silence is genuinely entombing. Nothing is left on the stark outer walls to indicate that anyone of wealth or importance was buried in this colossal place, and in any case the remains of the Emperor (who died of dysentery) were looted centuries ago. The eighteenth-century destruction of the Moguls by Sikhs, Jats, and Marathas is writ large here.

On such matters the lone guard was a wall of misinformation. The staircases were locked tight, and he couldn't find the key even after a tip and ten minutes' search, so I couldn't go up to the second story to admire the symmetry of the neglected gardens.

So close to Agra, Akbar's tomb at Sikandra was like an obverse of the Taj, a husk that revealed more of what had really gone on. The outer tilework, of zigzags and stars and abstract flowers; the red that, where not scraped off, had lasted better than on the much-faded Red Fort; the large, white-bearded, dark-faced monkeys patrolling the paths of palms through the gardens; the three out of four gates closed massively, blocking out the world and time; the fact that the Emperor himself was no longer here, but his royal remains scattered to the four winds by enemies; all gave the place an eerie abandonment appropriate to a vanished empire.

Back outside the gardens, I realized there'd been a lot of people here recently. A man was ambling along and said yes, there'd been a fair the day before, spread up and down the road, with debris left by the crowds spilling over into the gardens. It was an annual fair to celebrate the monsoon. So I'd missed a different Sikandra; and I imagined it like a scene in an Italian movie, with the fair all noise and gaiety and the great monument left, little by little receding to its customary silence, with bits of paper blowing about the gardens for days afterward.

A historical footnote to Akbar's popularity. A seventeenth-century Italian doctor in India named Manucci—who claimed (erroneously) to have invented the enema—is describing the kos minars, the road markers that Sher Shah erected along his road. The Moguls had transformed these obelisks for a secondary purpose:

"Every time that a general won a victory the heads of the villagers were sent as booty to the city of Agrah to be displayed.... After twenty-four hours the heads were removed to the imperial highway, where they were hung from the trees or deposited in holes on pillars built for this purpose. Each pillar could accommodate one hundred heads.... In the thirty-four years that I dwelt in this Mogul kingdom I travelled often from Agrah to Dihli, and every time there were a number of fresh heads on the roadside and many bodies of thieves hanging from the trees, who were punished thus for robbing on the highway. Thus passers-by are forced to hold their noses on account of the odor from the dead, and hasten their steps out of apprehension of the living. The villagers were not able to take vengeance on their first enemy, Akbar, in his lifetime, but... they avenged themselves on his bones after his death."

From Sikandra and the Sher Shah Suri Marg a subsidiary trunk road passes for several kilometers through prosperous villages and past fields to Fatehpur Sikri—Akbar's sixteenth-century Brasilia. At one point teams of white buffalo surrounded the car; farther on, boys were training big black bears to dance in the road, the beasts tottering on hind legs.

My guide at Fatehpur Sikri was S. Khan. He was sixty-two years old but his hair was still jet black. He'd been working the tourist trade here for thirty-five years. Skinny, he carried an umbrella which gave him a dapper aspect; his face looked old but the rest of him was wiry and fit, like a London gentleman dressing Indian. When I asked him where he was from originally, he answered, "I am originally from Afghanistan." His ninth grandfather back, he said, a fighting-man, had come from there with the army of Babur—through the Khyber Pass and down the road nearly five centuries ago.

Reluctant to hire a guide, I found myself interrogating him on his life story. He was a Muslim. Had he ever been to Mecca?

"Much too expensive," he said. "I am spending my money on the education of my sons."

His father had worked here for the municipality, he added. Previous generations had often been in the army; he was clearly proud of the military tradition in the family going back to Babur.

"My father had his land taken away in 1947," said S. Khan. That had been the price for staying behind after Partition. "So my family became sellers of wood. Then, in 1965, the government began to allow guides here. So, we have papers to show we are long time family here. So, because I speak Hindi, I become a third-class guide. Then little by little I learn Bengali; I become a second-class guide here. Then little by little I learn English. And so I become first-class guide."

There were twenty-four official guides like himself, working to a government system—in fact I'd had no choice.

He said, "The milkman comes at around six-thirty in the morning. My wife prepares the food and I eat a big breakfast. We are all here, all the guides, at seven-thirty or eight. The problem is that many tourists come from Delhi or Agra with their own guides, so I am often waiting all day. You are the first person I have shown around today."

This was at five P.M. His fee worked out to just over a dollar.

As we walked he kept his black umbrella neatly pinned under one elbow, handle pointing the way, and swung his other arm in time as he talked about his three sons. One was an electronics repairman, one a German-language guide here. The youngest was in school, studying to become a tailor.

S. Khan murmured, "This is very good because it is very expensive to buy a shirt and trousers. At least two days' work. Then you are always buying for nephews and cousins and grandchildren. Very expensive. So we will be happy to have a tailor in the family."

He was full of accurate and detailed information, the only truly knowledgeable guide I encountered in India. His facts, unbelievably, came out not by rote but with purpose, and it seemed a shame that a man of his evident intelligence should be limited to this.

I asked him if there were still local problems between Muslims and Hindus.

He said, "We don't have problems here, we get along and have always got along." He made a gentle gesture with two fingers alongside each other. "Here in Fatehpur Sikri we are fifty-fifty. Ever since Babur's time we are living shoulder to shoulder. Even in Partition we had no problems here."

"But your father lost all his land."

He shook his head. "There were real problems in other places. But not here."

As we walked, he pointed out where Akbar, an illiterate yet most sophisticated man, had ordered a melange of religious motifs in Fatehpur Sikri's architecture. The citadel of local pink and red sandstone was built to be the capital, a celebration of the birth of his son. Akbar planned it like a sprawling and original novel, an allegory for both India and for the world, for here were all the symbols of diverse beliefs. The swastika from Jainism. The Muslim five-pointed star and pointed arch. The eight-pointed star of King Solomon. The Gothic arch from Christianity. The Zoroastrian holy bird. The six-pointed Star of David. The Hindu sunflower and lotus, and the flattened and segmented arch from Rajasthan. The Buddhist mixed motif of elephant, duck, and peacock. Akbar was in search of what he called the Ultimate Faith, and eventually he built a pillar to hold his throne whose four levels were carved with Muslim, Hindu, Christian, and Buddhist designs that envelop each other.

The same impulse led Akbar to take a Muslim wife from Turkey, a Hindu wife from India, and a Christian wife from Portuguese Goa. Akbar's dream was an old one—to build the just city—and his sense of tolerance came at a time of maximum intolerance in Europe. His blueprint was an invented architecture that would combine styles, religions, and peoples in an unaccommodating location, and express India's diversity in one city as well as one life. An Emperor could carry out the personal side of that ideal, but the rest of it was foolhardy and prone to Indian entropy.

The result was a ghost city that took twelve years to build (from 1569 to 1580). It was lived in for only four. Four centuries later, parts of it still look outlandishly modern and experimental. There was an artificial lake and pavilions shaped like a house of cards. Another strange building functioned as both observatory and picnic area. It was five storys viewed from one side, like an Egyptian pyramid viewed from another, like a pagoda viewed from another. A tower tomb housed Akbar's favorite elephant, whose job was to administer justice by trampling or sparing the accused underfoot.

The Emperor, as the story goes, flourished here amid his three wives, sitting in his courtyard by the deep ponds, listening to music and verse. Each of Akbar's wives was given her own house, per the Koran's edict that a man may have up to four wives, but only if he treats them each exactly the same. Much of the architects' task seemed to be to keep the wives happy and free from envy despite the enormous parcheesi game which used dancing girls—my favorite scene in an unfilmed screenplay for the cinema of the mind. Akbar had, after all, five thousand in his harem to choose from.

The usual theory is that the city ran out of water and was abandoned with a parched sigh of relief. S. Khan scoffed at this; he said Akbar had left for Lahore to stop a rebellion and the place had dwindled with everyone away. How, he argued, could there be an inadequate water supply? Surely, he reasoned, the finished citadel, when fully developed, had had much more of a stable water system than during the titanic task of building it. And yet the building force of forty thousand had been kept adequately supplied with water.

The preserved part, known as Sikri, has an immense piazza, with a finely carved marble mausoleum of a Muslim holy man in one corner like a fancy sugar bowl. The piazza was actually the vast courtyard of a mosque still functioning as a mosque. It was a relief to be among the living, and out of the strange weightiness of an abandoned city that seemed to have no center and no order.

From the mosque courtyard S. Khan led me up many steps to a great arch. I looked out with a gulp into sheer empty space—a man-made view to rival the first giddy glimpse of the Grand Canyon as a moment of feeling your stomach drop away and wondering whether it's time to jump. The huge arched gateway, according to S. Khan, was the tallest in the world: 176 feet. The figure is immaterial; standing inside the gate, looking out into pure sky, you feel the arch half a mile above you and absolutely nothing below.

The Koranic quotation around the outside of the arch is in Persian, a quote from Jesus. S. Khan intoned:

> *World is a bridge; pass over it but build no house there.*
> *He who hopes for an hour hopes for an Eternity.*
> *World is but an hour: spend it in devotion.*
> *The rest is unseen.*

Below us was a large stone bathing pool being avidly used by the public. A gangly madman with a pinched face heard S. Khan tell me, "In the old days I remember seeing men dive from the very top, top, top of the wall into the pool for money. Just as in Acapulco."

The madman came over. He had a devastated expression. He began pleading, arguing, proclaiming that he would dive for us from high up there into the pool. He waved his arms to show his technique.

"I can do it!" he insisted. "I can do it! I did it in Acapulco!"

> Sleep was impossible that night in the hotel at Agra; we sat in the lobby drinking quarts of gin-and-tonic and staring limply at the angry red 104 on the thermometer.... By noon the temperature had risen to 115; roaring back to New Delhi.... There were wild peacocks and baboons under the trees edging the road; villages newly burned out by Moslems and Hindus flicked by every few miles; but every ounce of interest and initiative evaporated under the single fact of the inhuman, punishing sun.... The Moving Finger had writ, all right, nor all our calamine lotion could wipe out a word of it.
>
> — S. J. Perelman, *Westward Ha!* (1948)

12.

Krishna's Playpen

At early light, leaving Agra behind. Heading back up the Sher Shah Suri Marg, past the mainstreet fizz of an Indian town already awake. Barbershops and tailor shops and shoe shops and spice shops. Monkeys clattering over the rooftops and being shooed away. Motorcycles and bicycles clogging the artery lanes; for once the voluptuous cooking smells overpowering the usual fumes. A clown's face poster for the Amar Circus, ASIA'S BIGGEST!, coming soon to Agra. Other posters for salacious films, in this little place, that can never actually be salacious enough. This is the India I cannot get too much of.

Campa Cola painted on the walls of immemorial houses. Women in red, yellow, and blue saris, gold studs in their noses, poised by a pond with large jugs on their heads.

Halfway to the Khyber now.

Much of the forty miles to Mathura had been recently repaved, and was the best GT so far. At seven A.M. it was virtually devoid of trucks. The villages were mostly out of sight, far back from the road, down dusty bare brown paths that seemed to lead directly into fields and fields alone.

My driver for the two days' drive of Agra-Mathura-Delhi was a Hindu named Lalit, recommended by my hotel. He was tall and glossy-haired and a bit ill at ease out of the city, with a flair for indecision at moments when the most decisive action was called for.

Mathura starts, like many of the larger towns on the GT, as a dribbling series of truck stops—intermittent dhabas and service stations and shop stalls of spare parts and sundries—followed by a patch of wilderness, a factory or two, a power plant. Just before the town proper we passed an older village and a refueling station with the giant bellies of dead gas trucks lying spent and rusted-through as debris by the road.

Mathura's pragmatic importance is its huge refinery, one of the principal ones in India. Oil goes by pipeline from Bombay to Mathura, where it's refined, then distributed by trucks as very expensive petrol (almost $2.50 a gallon) around the country.

I had Lalit stop for the spectacle of a group of itinerant musicians carrying walking canes, trying to hitchhike. Five young women, five young men, four children, and a dog. They had nine bundles of belongings, in burlap sacks and knotted saris used as suitcases. One man was bowing a stringed instrument—bells were jangling from the bow—and he sang along in unison with the melody. The instrument, called a ravanhatta, had a small sounding-drum at its base and four strings on either side of the reed-wrapped bamboo neck (three for the drone, one for the melody). He wore a blue-checked sarong and light cotton shorts; a gray shawl hung around his neck. His wife was completely covered in a green flowered sari wrapped even over her head, but her full breasts were prominent beneath it. She sang along with the bowed melody, a baby in her arms. They all spoke little English, and I grasped only that they were locals, on their way to a nearby village to work.

The GT may have changed profoundly since Kipling's day with the advent of trucks, but the professional itinerants of the road survive—performing musicians, herders, drivers. No doubt the urgency of earning a living off a personal strip of highway is the same as ever.

On the edge of Mathura the enormous Jagurdep Temple was under construction, all flags flying and workers chaotically filing up and down the combination hospital-cum-prayer ground. Already a sizable tent town of sadhus had arisen in the dust to one side.

It was a massive undertaking—four tall brick towers crowned with tulip domes; loudspeakers on posts; inner and outer staircases; a great bowl at one end; and eventually three long, high stories around an enormous central dome.

"That will be one hundred forty feet high," a man told me gravely. "The tallest dome in all India."

He threw his arms skyward; his gesture seemed to take in all the world.

The claim sounded ridiculous until I checked my guidebook. If his figure was correct, this monstrosity would be even taller than the Taj. They'd worked on it for eleven years already, someone said. It'd be finished in another one or two, maybe. All its domes would be covered in mirrors and the whole temple itself in marble tiles.

Just past it were little houses made of only hay, with wizard's caps for roofs. A man ambled past with buffaloes pulling a small cart that supported a preposterous burlap sack of fodder, a hay house bursting at the laces.

In the congested town, outside my hotel, a boy was wearing a T-shirt that read: MY PAPA SAYS CONDOMS DON'T WORK.

Mathura has been holy to both Jains and Buddhists for twenty-five centuries, but it is of paramount importance to Hindus. For them the town is the birthplace of the god Krishna—the eighth incarnation (the one just before the Buddha) of Vishnu, supreme Lord of the Universe. In this wonderful saga the baby Krishna, pursued by his evil cousin—a king who has already wiped out most of the family—is brought up safely as a cowherd by a nomadic couple. Krishna is a wily prankster even as a child; his foster mother learns his divinity when she finds him eating dirt one day, opens his mouth, and finds herself staring at the entire universe.

All Krishna's boyhood and early manhood occur near Mathura, and there are pilgrimage sites for miles around to prove it. Here Krishna happily grows up enacting miracles. He shelters fellow cowherds from a vast storm by lifting a hill with one finger to use as an umbrella. In local forests (which no longer exist) he kills demons sent after him by the evil cousin, whom he soon disposes of effortlessly. Part of Krishna's appeal as a boy and young man is that he makes it all look easy. The local miracle I liked the most was the erotic story of Krishna hypnotizing and seducing a thousand and one milkmaids in the river—that was one site I was ready to pay to see. And after so many centuries' practice receiving pilgrims, Mathura didn't miss a trick: it had the business of religion totally covered.

The first gauntlet was a huge turn-of-the-century temple, erected (according to the guide who barnacled himself to me) *exactly* where Krishna had been born *exactly* 5,216 years ago. The guide took on an air of practiced reverence whenever he repeated this. By Nagel's calculation Krishna was already forty-four that year, so either my guidebook or my guide was considerably off.

My own travel instincts were useless, as I'd never have guessed that this temple, with its wide palatial stairs and a kind of Mann's Chinese Theater decor, was a supremely holy spot.

In Hindi the word for birthplace *(janamsthan)* means something more precise, closer to the idea of "birthspot." The Hindu pilgrims who were pushing past me to get up the stairs felt they were visiting somewhere very particular and indeed actually sacred.

Inside the temple at one end stood three wax figures of generous donors to the temple, and a seated fat guru, legs folded, also in wax. They all looked like winning politicians after an election. The ceiling was covered in hokey paintings of scenes from *This Is Your Life, Krishna*; little temples like crèches were set in niches and corners of the big temple. It seemed a kind of Hindu products fair, the atmosphere one of commerce, not piety.

Descending the stairs of this first temple in search of the tank where Krishna's baby clothes had been laundered, I ran into a chunky English tourist trying to fend off several would-be guides. He was lugging a backpack, huffing and puffing and sweating. He said to me, "Which is the old temple, which is the new, and which is better?" He'd come on the train and, from the looks of things, was going to give Mathura a wide berth on his next visit to India.

I asked where he was staying.

"Are you joking? I'm not staying the night in this bloody place. I've got another train out of here in a few hours."

Just around the side was a small temple called the Baby Krishna. My sallow guide assumed an expression of greater sanctity as he led me in; he reminded me of one of those sharpshooters trying to sell you Florida time-shares, with a side interest in the religion business. Yes, he insisted, the Baby Krishna Temple was certainly and absolutely built around Krishna's real birthspot, which was a ground-level room that he further claimed was actually 5,000+ years old. It was so crammed with people that the walls were perspiring. It'd been a prison at the moment of Krishna's arrival; I took this element of the story to be the Indian equivalent of a manger.

Here were glassed-in paintings and dioramas of the birth, and one blue-and-silver Hindu version of a nativity scene that visitors threw 50 paise coins at. This featured a little stage with a tinfoiled golden swing like a rock-a-bye cradle, except with a figure inside of Krishna as a young man, not as a mischievous baby. People prostrated themselves before it and occasionally someone gave the little cradle with the gold statue of Krishna a push and it swung back and forth for a moment. Then everyone clapped and oohed.

It looked so ridiculous and yet people seemed so deeply moved; I suppose a tone-deaf man thinks the same way watching people weep over a Chopin nocturne. I found it impossible to give the place the benefit of the doubt. NO PHOTOGRAPHS ALLOWED, the signs said, but it would take more than a reverent warning to make the place look anything but an age-old backyard con.

I asked my guide, whose name was Hari Babu Sharma, if he truly believed this room, these walls, were actually 5,000 years old.

"Oh, yes, sir. 5,216 years old, sir."

There were many variations on a chromolithograph, in happy sepia tones, of the baby Krishna—the same painted photo was essentially reproduced everywhere. Did Hari Babu Sharma also think that was a real photo of the real Krishna?

"Yes, sir, it is an authentic picture."

"So someone was there with a camera to do a picture of the baby Krishna, just about age three or so? Flowing hair and everything?"

"Of course, sir, why not?"

Well, why not? I make fun of the photo business because I found the photos themselves comical, but it was the obverse side of one of Hinduism's great qualities. Their deities are accessible, knowable, approachable, at least as personalities—like the friend from childhood or the distant cousin who's turned out a celebrity, whom everyone can gossip about and feel close to even from a distance, because his behavior, while superhuman, is still so everyday.

I ran into the chunky Englishman again in the Baby Krishna

Temple. He had somehow managed to get in without removing his big blue backpack, though he'd taken off his shoes, and most impressive of all, he was guideless. When he pulled a camera from his pack, people swarmed to admonish him and an argument escalated; he wouldn't give up his camera and went to the floor battling for it. Passive Hindus turned rapidly into aggressive Hindus when a sacred photographic ban was about to be broken: in the end the Englishman decided he'd seen enough of this crowd.

I no longer questioned that the small room was one of the ultimate Hindu sites, roughly on a par with Bodh Gaya. It wasn't difficult to see which holy place had a stronger air of commerce. And there are, apparently, no limits to Hindu kitsch, as students of the Bombay cinema know well.

JUST CLAP YOUR HANDS AND SEE THE MAGIC!

Nor was there much restraint in the items on sale at the Krishna Bazaar around the main temples of the birthspot. The Baby Krishna was available on key chains, in photo displays, on earrings, on posters, in dioramas, on magnetic buttons. It is always startling to see how people who have little to eat will spend some of the little money they have on religious junk. My favorite item was a white temple which lit up when you clapped your hands and stayed lit up until you clapped again.

Shopkeepers everywhere evolve strategies that work on their clients; therein you can read the two opposing psyches. Let us say you are wandering around Mathura's temple bazaar. You show interest in a display of rather costly silverized, colorized magic lithos of Krishna playing the flute, or sporting as a very girlish baby. You are on the verge of buying a few when suddenly the shopkeeper breaks your concentration by waving a miniature Krishna lava lamp in front of your nose. No sooner have you fallen for that when he shows you a set of magnets. For not a minute are you left in peace to contemplate something, so you end up buying nothing, driven mad. I was forced to conclude, however, that Hindu pilgrims must be weak-minded shoppers, easily distracted. Never mind their world-wide reputation for bargaining savvy. Any race of merchants that practiced unsuccessful hard-sell tactics would have died out thousands of years ago.

After a while it became an abiding pleasure to walk deafly, imperviously past the entreaties of shopkeepers, making them clamor louder. Students of kitsch should not overlook Mathura—for my money it has all the other sacred spots beat. Nowhere will feed you more cynical thoughts per hour about commerce and religion, and how rarely the twain divide.

By the Jamuna River, amid a constant barrage from would-be guides, there was no bathing and soaping as along the sacred Ganges. The opposite bank grew sparsely about fifty yards away. Even boats were decorated with Day-Glo pictures of Krishna in heroic attitudes. The ghats descended from a sequence of temples; the Krishna Ghat itself, where he rested after killing the evil king, had a great blue gate hung with bells. The rampant aggression, the out-and-out attack on a newcomer here, left even Benares far behind.

In the town proper many houses were magnificent: elaborately fretted and carved, with starred and flowered lattices, balconies, and columns. That signaled a long career as a sacred destination. But the streets were anxious and tremendously congested, in really punishing heat, for the first time in my journey.

Getting concrete directions in India, even with two helpful Hindi speakers doing the inquiring, is like roulette. A long effort to locate the Mathura Archaeological Museum paid off.

MUSEUM EDUCATES FOR FUTURE THROUGH PAST

Not if it's deserted. The museum, which was exceptional, had numerous carved heads, pillars, and lovely terra-cottas. My favorite stone sculptures included *Beautiful Damsel Mounting On a Dwarf* (100 A.D.)—they meant happily trampling, with her breasts aquiver and vagina exposed. Also *Bust of a Naga Queen of the Serpent Power With Five Energies Emanating From Her* (second century), which wasn't really a bust, but simply all boobs—schoolboys must throw fits over her. Also *A Fish-Tailed Elephant In Sporting Mood* (100 A.D.). But what to make of an inscription like *Life Size Statue of the Snake Deity*? How do they know it's life size?

Some animals that resembled chipmunks ran through the museum and its interior courtyard. There were no other visitors, and at least a half-dozen guards. Who wanted to see the great achievements of their culture's past, when you could look at an itsy Krishna on a swing set?

The museum had been founded in 1874 by a Mr. Growse, "a collector in the district." An Englishman had taken the time and trouble, but chosen a site almost guaranteed to be ignored by the millions of annual pilgrims. I thought he might also have overestimated the interest of the Hindu mind in the concrete past. It is remarkable that the Hindu civilization has gone on as long as it has, but produced a people with historical indigestion. The past is too deep to swallow, so it swallows them.

Or perhaps what I call indigestion is instead a subtle form of wisdom under the burden of few possibilities; a necessary adaptation for living fully in the present moment alone. Which is nearly to say: for happiness.

In the center of Mathura the Hotel Madhuvan (that misleading name again, "honey forest") was a businessman's concrete oven, attractively interiored. You could've baked bread in its corridors; the air-conditioning in the rooms, set permanently on high, gave me bronchitis.

The staff induced paranoia and lunacy.

"Room service?"

I was speaking into a telephone with a deep echo like a well.

"Yes?" The answering voice came from far, far away.

"This is room two-twenty."

"Two what?"

"Two-twenty."

"What?"

"Two two zero."

"Two two?"

"Two two zero."

"Two two?"

"Two two *zero*."

"What?"

"I'd like a tea, and some toast."

"Room?"

"Two-twenty."

"Two tea?"

"One tea."

"Room?"

"Never mind."

"Two two three?

"It doesn't matter."

"Two tea?"

"Good-bye."

"What?"

A few minutes later there was a knock at the door: one of the two fellows who'd carried my bags.

He swept into the room simultaneously as he knocked; in India, no matter how cheap or expensive the hotel, staff have been trained that they can enter any guest's room so long as they knock. It is amusing that so many people, Americans especially, still come to India to meditate, to be alone with their self-ness, since it is almost impossible to get any privacy in this country. If you've taken the precaution of locking your door, they will try the handle over and over, ignoring your pleas for them to go away. It is no use giving an inquiring "Yes?" (which to them means, naturally, "Come in, please") or asking "Who is it?" By this time the fellow is standing in the middle of your room looking urgently around for an excuse to have entered.

"What do you want?"

"Tip for carrying bags."

"I tipped the other fellow."

"He say no."

"You're supposed to split the money."

"He doesn't give me any."

"That's not my problem."

"How much you give him?"

"Forty rupees."

"Give me forty rupees, sir."

"Twenty is enough for each of you. Go talk to him."

"Give me money, sir."

"Get out of my room."

"Money, sir."

"No."

"Please." Imploring as I backed him toward the hall.

"Don't come in again."

"Please."

"Bring me a tea and then I'll tip you."

"Tip now, sir."

"Bring me the tea first."

"Tip, sir. Tip."

"Get out."

He was trying the door handle after I locked it. Krishna's birthspot: a most sinister and uncompromising place.

Vrindavan, a few miles outside Mathura, is sacred to Hindus as the former site of fields where Krishna worked as a cowherd and seduced milkmaids as they bathed and filled water jugs—a frequent image in Indian miniatures. Naively, I held out hope that there might still be some pastoral aspect to the place these days. The GT leading to it was semi-rural, but it was easy to guess from the proliferating billboards when you'd reached Vrindavan.

Typically, an entire village—a mini-town, a going concern for centuries, a way of life—had grown up here. Vrindavan was a favorite with widows; it was said that in two houses of mourning here were two thousand widows who mourned for four hours in the morning and four hours in the evening. My self-appointed guide, a stubby, pushy guy with a mustache and a card-sharp manner, was full of figures.

"Five thousand cows here at Vrindavan. This Lord Krishna's playground. You pay my guide charges, as you like," he kept repeating. "This Lord Krishna's playground."

Up to now in India I'd pretty successfully fended off guides, partly because I cannot look at anything when someone is yapping away at me, and because the most inadequate guidebook usually contains more accurate information than almost any guide. But in both Mathura and Vrindavan I lost the battle, even if I won the war.

The principal temple, down a winding filthy street, contained a kind of crèche showing the entire Krishna family: elder, black-skinned brother in the middle; red-skinned father with a white beard; mother, gold-skinned in a red and gold dress; and Krishna himself, gold, in a silver dress. The trappings of religious idols in Hinduism, and the stories themselves, do not deny materialism to the heroes. The gods may preach spirituality, but the message of the images of Krishna is deeply materialistic, even gaudy, unlike those of Buddha or Jesus. Everything glitters and is abundant.

To be here was to have an image of a forest grove by a river, straight out of a painted eighteenth-century miniature, torn to pieces in one's imagination. The story of the young Krishna and the flock of *gopis* (milkmaids), bathing and coupling at Vrindavan, is one of the most beautiful and compelling Hindu myths; it is hard to find its counterpart in tone or meaning in any Western culture. It resonates as an idea that India itself no longer freely expresses in art, thanks mainly to the combined prudishness of the Moguls and the British.

The images are usually similar: the gorgeous milkmaids bathing themselves on a clear autumn night, disporting naked in the river while Krishna sits on a tree limb above them, playing his flute. There are often a few cows too, peaceful by the water's edge. The thousand-and-one milkmaids (one will prove his favorite) have been summoned by Krishna's melodies to achieve an ecstatic union with the divine. In a kind of trance they have all left their husbands, "abandoning the illusion of the family, breaking through modest reserve, abandoning household duties" as one version puts it, to hurry to the forest grove. He has stolen their clothes, which hang from the tree's branches. Soon Krishna will reproduce himself, a multiplying and ubiquitous lover, making love with the milkmaids in dozens of aquatic ways, to give each gopi the total attention she both desires and deserves in the sacred dance.

This particular flavor, simultaneously pastoral and erotic, the pleasures of the flesh freed from sin and charged with a frank, divine sensuality, will be evoked over the centuries whenever this story is portrayed, in music, in poetry, and in the naturalism of miniatures. "And there where merit-fruit is eaten...Krishna then in love-play lying beneath you..." This idea of the merits of the union with God allied to the merits of sexual pleasure is foreign to the West; they are usually considered contradictory. In even the classical Greek and Roman myths, when sex between gods and humans takes place, humans are often the toys, the sport, the victims of the gods. It is a long way to this notion of ecstasy as a divine rapture which bathes you, and spreads its glow from within.

The closest story is that of Don Juan, with his thousand-and-three women like notches on a pistol. The tragedy of the great Spanish lover, as many critics have pointed out, is that he really does not love these women at all because he cannot know deeply any of them. Thus the story is treated as a condemnation of purely sexual love. The pleasures of the flesh are damaging: the man who loves this way is doomed, as are so many of the women loved by him. Hearts and marriages are broken, lives are destroyed, which is why the supernatural statue punishes Don Juan from beyond the grave, as a gruesome form of divine justice. Yet Don Juan is, in essence, already a dead man.

Consider this instead, from the *Gita Govinda,* the long Sanskrit masterpiece of around 1200 A.D., by the Bengali court poet Jayadeva. It has been called the Hindu *Song of Songs*; it will inspire the miniature painters for centuries:

He has gone into the trysting-place, full of all desired bliss,
O you of lovely hips, delay no more!
Oh go forth now and seek him out, him the master of your heart, him endowed with passion's lovely form.
He dwells, the garland wearer, in the forest by the Jamuna, in the gentle breezes there,
The swelling breasts of gopi girls whom he crushes ever with his restless hands...

Softly on his flute he plays, calling to the meeting place, naming it with notes and saying where;
And the pollen by the breezes borne, the breezes which have been on you, that pollen in his sight has high esteem...

Oh fallen feathers of the birds, on leaves about the forest floor, he lies excited there, making his bed,

And he gazes out upon the path, looks about with trembling eyes,
anxious, looking out for your approach . . .

There on that bed of tender leaves, O lotus-eyed, embrace his hips,
his naked hips whence the girdle drops.
Those hips whence the garment falls, those loins which are a
treasure heap, the fountain and the source of all delight!
He dwells, the garland wearer, in the forest by the Jamuna, in
the gentle breezes there,
The swelling breasts of gopi girls whom he crushes ever with his
restless hands.

The coupling of God and the human, of Krishna and the gopis, is achieved through the ecstasy of lovemaking. The great seducer is neither a cad, nor a tragic figure, but a handsome young man and the incarnation of the Lord of the World. He ravishes each of the milkmaids but every one ravishes and possesses him as well, for there is plenty of Krishna to go around. Each will enjoy the entranced radiance of imagining she is absolutely alone with the flute-playing god, as if she were his favorite, and there not a thousand others to share him with. As Marguerite Yourcenar points out, "This phallic festival is a symbol of the marriage of the soul with God." But marriage is not quite right: it is a mere evening's dalliance that is at the same time knowledge of an eternal bliss.

The mood is of a serene erotic paradise, a luscious and mystical Eden in which the human reaches the god by letting the god do the reaching. The human surrenders but does not become less human. The satisfaction of desire is here a blessed occurrence, a tender mutual orgasm brought on by the divine. There is no deception, damage, or retribution, and no danger. The erotic is not to inspire guilt, but to inspire spiritual hope and sensual bliss, to be enjoyed.

This is what everyone had come to Vrindavan to celebrate.

• • •

The majordomo of the temple ("You can call him a priest," said my guide helpfully) made me sit crosslegged at the front of the amenable half-dozen Hindu visitors in the temple chamber. The walls were mostly uniform marble plaques with people's names and addresses engraved. The pushy priest let me know, without any prompting whatsoever, that only 257 rupees (about $8) would buy me such a marble plaque with my name, prominently displayed. I spied plaques from contributors in the States, Canada, and New Zealand, though the majority were Indian addresses, naturally. There was one from the Patels of S. Mital, Virginia, which didn't sound much like a Virginian town to me.

The majordomo spoke English very well.

"It is not necessary for you to give all two hundred fifty-seven rupees now," he said. "You can give one hundred rupees now and send the rest in foreign currency in several months' time. We will reserve a plaque for you."

"I suppose I can pay all the two hundred fifty-seven rupees in rupees all at once, though. To get my plaque up sooner."

"Of course."

"How old is the temple?" I asked.

"This temple is five thousand five hundred years old."

One year for every cow and then some.

"This very temple?" It looked perhaps fifty, allowing for poor upkeep. "You mean there's been a temple here all that time, surely."

"No! This temple is five thousand years five hundred years old!"

"You must get a lot of visitors."

"Two lakhs people coming here every day. [200,000]. To see five thousand five hundred Vrindavan temples."

It seemed a nice coincidence in the statistics. On my map, Mathura was marked as being merely The Town of a Thousand Temples.

The majordomo priest pulled out a contributions book and lifted his pen. My moment of truth had arrived.

"How much you are giving?"

"Ten rupees."

"Minimum contribution is fifty-four rupees. How much you are giving?"

"Ten."

I stood up to go.

He slammed the pen against the donations book in disgust and snarled, but I was already leaving.

This same expression was echoed by my useless guide five minutes later when, amid exhortations that I could pay him "any guide charges you want, sir," and the additional insight, the only one in his repertoire, that "this was Lord Krishna's playground," I gave him only forty rupees. One baleful glare stopped his protest as soon as it began, and he left me to drink a cold 7-Up in peace.

The usual victim of these guides and priests is not the rare Western tourist but the very plentiful and naive Indian tourists who have often traveled a great distance, at great cost to themselves or their families, for the most important sacred moments in lives filled with religious devotion—only to get taken by these parasites for every last rupee.

So much for an entire profession. Undoubtedly, when dealing with tourists in Hindi rather than in English, these guides have far more to say and a framework of shared religion to which they can refer. But most pilgrims looked set-upon and daunted, and whenever I asked, they complained about having been robbed one way or another. To paraphrase Robert Frost: in India, just as in the West, there's more religion outside the holy places than in.

Back at the hotel there was the agreeable surprise of good music in the restaurant that night, and at a manageable volume. In India the fancy restaurants tend to be mostly those in expensive hotels;

they cater as much to the local wealthy clientele as the foreign tourist. The result often involves overamplified music, and always air-conditioning cold enough to mask the poor ventilation. What a joy it was to hear a superb sitar player in this dire place, while the two traveling salesmen at a neighboring table wobbled their heads in agreement with each other as if their necks were made of steel springs.

> You remember Humayun's Tomb? I had the garden restored, the water channels dug out and refilled and the whole place restored to its pristine beauty. I went to England last summer and, the eye of the master being away, the whole place has been allowed to revert. The garden has been let to a native and is now planted with turnips and the work of four years is thrown away! I shall drive out there, and woe betide the Deputy Commissioner whose apathy has been responsible.
>
> — Lord Curzon, then Viceroy of India,
> in a letter to Lady Curzon (1905)

13.

Delhi

The Haryana border was cornfields and wild brush. Perhaps forty trucks stood idle as their drivers enjoyed tea or a wash or getting their trousers pressed at a dhaba. A good number of tailors were busy in thatched huts, which I took as an ominous sign of bureaucratic delays. A camel pulling a cart plodded past—a tortoise methodically gaining on the parked hares.

A slew of other drivers were lined up outside the squat white bunker of the *octroi* post. Tax forms for passage had to be filled out, stamped, severally approved, signed; even Lalit and I, simple wayfarers, were not exempt.

TOLL TAX	
HEAVY VEHICLES	100 RUPEES
MEDIUM WEIGHT	75 RUPEES
TAXIES	50 RUPEES

After the border the road grew narrow and chaotic. A brightly painted elephant with a long-haired, equally painted man on board was stalled to one side, daunted. By a river, great blue sheets were spread out to dry and women swirled others in the shallows.

We passed a truck with its windscreen and front roof ripped away entirely; only stray bits of metal stuck out. The two drivers, both laughing Sikhs, rolled merrily along through a buffeting wind.

Flocks of vultures congregated on the bare ground. Khaki fields, orphan trees, huts.

Another truck swung by with a balloonlike appendage roped bulging off the back, a canvas sack of fodder; one snap would turn the road into an impassable cereal bowl. It wasn't unusual to see trucks heeling over, not from speed but from precarious overloading. The drivers used their horns like enchanted trumpets that could clear the offending bicycles or rickshaws or mopeds out of the way, and even make those two oncoming headlong trucks vanish.

The land was terribly seared; gone were the generous old shade trees, and Sher Shah's road lay unprotected from the heat like a dried snakeskin. Yet in a bleak village someone of talent had made the effort to draw geometric arabesques in sleek profusion across every inch of one low mud-and-dung bungalow.

In Palwal a bored young man sat coolly, lasciviously smoking opium in the driver's seat of his tempo-taxi.

A capital usually looks after itself first, and approaching Delhi (which has its own state) the road divided into four well-kept lanes, two in each direction, with a gully of green between.

Even twenty-five kilometers away it became evident we were nearing a great city. There was more traffic and relatively fewer trucks, the beer and wine shops multiplied, the villages amalgamated into one continuous clutter. Bicycles, motorcycles, and tempo-taxis proliferated. In vast cantonments of garbage, people and animals grazed equally on the refuse.

The popular Western conception of urban India as unending poverty is misleading. A more accurate image would be of cities surrounded, literally, by garbage on which people subsist and whose stench, from no matter how far away, is always in the air. Most of that garbage has been scrupulously sifted and picked over; it's not waste, since nothing goes to waste in India. You see islands of it in even the wealthier areas, amid office and apartment construction sites, shimmering new hotels, and bypass highways. This taunt alone makes urban poverty more severe than rural.

As the Sher Shah Suri Marg curves through the city it becomes an unbelievable three lanes in each direction, then a genuine modern highway as it passes the Delhi Golf Club.

New Delhi is the early twentieth-century city alongside Delhi, created to supplant Calcutta as capital. I put up at a somewhat weary hotel in Connaught Circus. Connaught is the hub of the city, a white-columned, Edwardian-style complex of several blocks in the shape of a wagon wheel of concentric circles, with stores at ground level, offices and hotels above. It's also the first place that gets scorched here whenever there's a riot, and this has given it a more profound dinginess than a decade ago.

Along Janpath, a main avenue nearby, there is a Damnation Alley of shopkeepers to be braved on foot en route to the Imperial Hotel. There I hoped to enlist a Sikh driver for the road through the Punjab. Once the grandee of New Delhi, the Imperial is set back from Janpath in tall-palmed gardens beside the hall of justice known as the Great Western Court. I bypassed the curio shops and haunted the bookstores, mini-Calcuttas of moldering paperbacks jammed tightly, almost inaccessibly, into the shelves. The dust had been crammed into their skins for so long that these paperbacks imported from the States or the Commonwealth decades ago now wore the same patina of age as every building on the Grand Trunk Road.

No bookshop was too small not to contain unexpected treasures. With the constant devaluation of the rupee, R. K. Narayan's novels could be had for a dollar each, printed on the same low-grade paper as, say, *Seven Keys To Social Success*. Indians are devoted, in their popular self-help literature, to "keys"—keys to fortune, keys to knowing one's future, keys to a good career. Rules of thumb are raised to magician's secrets, as if life might prove a rope trick. Many of those current here dated from a more innocent, pre-computer age, of the winning-friends and perking-up-conversation era. I know no country that devotes more space to self-help books, unless it's the States, where the shelves are full of this or that imported Indian diet of self-realization, the same mulligatawny soup warmed up again.

Since my last visit the rules had changed, for now even the smallest bookstall, even a magazine kiosk on the corner, had a selection of software manuals, and in cities there were ever more computer shops. I saw no books in the business shelves, however, on clawing your way to the top. Success still came from being a decent man—the old Hindu virtues—a person of upstanding character who could talk to anyone.

India still seems to believe, to judge from its advertising, in a kind of homemaking in the style of old television commercials. This, given an Indian twist, is the referent language in the ads and self-help books, and in the notices for suitable marriage partners on, say, page 2 of the *Sunday Times of India,* the Matrimonials section. Here, in the same newspaper as a special report on Supercops ("Introducing some of India's top crime busters") and articles on music ("New ragas: creation or concoction?") and a review of a literary anthology ("Gutsy women's writing in India") were ads like:

> BENGALI Kayastha only daughter of
> Senior Executive, 25 / 165 cm beautiful
> accomplished from noble cultured family

> Resident in Bombay. Convent educated
> National Scholar B.Com LL.B. Advocate
> Sangit Prabhakar Computer trained.
> Alliance sought from brilliant Established
> match from respected family having Indian
> values modern thinking. Write Box G 723.

Most of the ads are from parents seeking a husband for their daughters; these are all "better families" who can afford the newspaper space. Organized under several headings (Cosmopolitan, Bengali, Christian, Brahmin, Gujarati), they have a terminology which pulls no punches. The age of the girl is given, followed by her height in centimeters, sometimes her salary if she's a working girl ("graduate working for foreign bank earning Rs. 6000/-P.M.") and her complexion (usually fair or "wheatish") and her general views ("liberal in outlook"). Some describe the parents ("father Colonel mother Professor") and many request "horoscope particulars" from candidate bachelors, since the stars will in the end determine the suitability of the match. Occasionally they stipulate "no dowry" or demand "vegetarians, non-smokers, teetotallers preferred."

The two most frequent phrases are "homely girl"—they mean home-loving, a nice domestic-minded wife—or "Caste no bar." I took this last to be as much the whole truth as the phrase, "Boy's merit is the only consideration. Medicos preferred." These ads were clearly only aimed at castes who knew how to read.

She was one of those people you fall easily into conversation with without knowing how. She was very tall, with a bell of short blonde hair. I'd ducked into the doorway of a clothing shop to get out of the street air for a moment, as I could not stop coughing.

"Are you all right?" she asked.

"I'll be fine."

"Are you sure?"

She looked Dutch; it turned out she was from South Africa, with a rangy ease about her height. She wore a flouncy pale blue-and-white shimmering pantsuit that was slightly hippyish, the sort a young woman might buy out of enthusiasm on her first days in India. I couldn't tell if she was a jet-lagged thirty or a very healthy forty. Her frank smile confused me, since she was obviously a woman men would often try to pick up. To travel on her own in India, I thought, must be murder.

I got my breathing back and asked if she'd be in Delhi long.

"Oh, no," she murmured, as if no one who knew India would stay in the capital for more than a day. "I'll be up north. Two weeks."

"Is this your first time here?" I asked.

"No, no, I come every year."

Aha.

We were back on the sidewalk now, eating the Indian air. This old expression for taking a stroll has gained another meaning, for according to one study Delhi suffers the most polluted urban air in the world (followed by Hong Kong and Calcutta). Delhi's air has a distinctive yellow presence and sickly aroma, as if the spewed fumes of rickshaw exhaust have grown pallid from being rubbed across piles of dying or decayed animals. Here on any afternoon the air was far worse than on the Grand Trunk Road behind a line of belching trucks. As an asthmatic without the sense to bring a face mask, I felt I was stumbling through a jaundiced fog attacking me from all sides.

"Two weeks sounds like a healthy visit," I gasped.

"'Healthy.'" She smiled. "Maybe you've guessed why I'm here?"

"I can't."

"I'm here to see my master."

Her master! I wondered a lot of cynical things very quickly.

"Who is he?"

She named some guru; legitimate or not, they all sound alike. He was up in a village in the Punjab. She'd be traveling there by train the next morning, early. She wasn't sure how she'd get to him from the train station, some miles away, or for that matter what the station's name was. "It's all in my master's hands. Like meeting you just now. There's a reason for all of it."

"It seemed accidental to me."

"When did you decide to go to that clothing store?"

"Just a minute ago. I couldn't breathe."

"You see? And I wasn't looking for clothes. I just felt I had to go in. So it wasn't accidental at all."

Fearing the answer, I said, "What's the reason, then?"

"I'm just thinking. My master must have wanted me to show you something. I'll be going to him—to his headquarters, I mean—this afternoon." Her English was exact. "I know!" Her eyes lit up. She fished around for her backpack, and pulled out a softcover book. "Have you read this?"

It was a slim paperback published in the U.S., with a title about deep mysteries explained. We stopped walking and I flipped through. It seemed to cover, with great concision, the many conspiratorial connections between Jesus and Socrates, the Eisenhower and Reagan and Bush administrations, Shiva, Buddha, the U.S. Air Force, and a host of U.F.O. sightings. There was also an address where you could send money for more information.

"I guess I haven't read it," I said.

"Would you like this copy? It means a lot to me. Read it, pass it on."

"I'll look for my own copy back in the States. So what'll you do for your master this afternoon?"

She said, "I go to his arrivals center and they enroll me and I spend the night. Then they put me on a train, I guess. Tomorrow morning. I've done this before."

"Many times?"

"Just once."

So when she said she came to India every year, that meant she intended to from now on, if this visit went as well as the last.

"Just a second." She pulled a wallet from her backpack, probably the least safe place she could carry it, and slipped out a photo. "Do you know who this is?"

It was a formal portrait: a straitlaced woman who might've been her older sister, alongside a quiet, serious, much older man, the sort of husband who does not come to India to listen to masters.

"It's you."

She was delighted. "You see! We were just married. I didn't expect Hans to come. But he loves me enough to trust I know why I do come. He sees what my master means to me. Do you know, I sold my own office and my business to come here? Because it was time. It was time to alter everything. To me, I look at this picture and I don't see the same woman as I see in the mirror here."

You're telling me, I thought. "What happens when you go home?"

"I don't know yet. All the dimensions change. And—" She paused. "Hans is very understanding. He doesn't try to stop me."

"What will you do with your master?"

She said, "It's not how people imagine. He's not the sort who tells you what to do. He asks you questions sometimes. But you get to work at the ashram for a couple of weeks and you get to change your life and then you go back and the world is different."

She was paying money to live and work there for two weeks, a sort of pay-per-view kibbutz.

"So your master isn't around today? I'd like to meet him."

"Would you like to come with me to the enrollment anyway? Just to visit his headquarters?"

"I actually have to meet someone myself." I was curious, though, to see the spectacle of her handing over her money. Willing to tell me so much about herself, she wasn't willing to divulge how much her two weeks would cost.

"Oh, really!" She seemed almost beatifically happy. "But that's wonderful. It was so great meeting you. Don't forget to look for that book! I think all these meetings with strangers make a real difference. To everyone's lives."

We shook hands and I watched her stride off through the pale infected air, tall among the Indians, her backpack the only luggage in her life. One more visit, one more year with her very sensible husband, I figured. That would be enough to do the trick.

The week I arrived, Delhi was in the grip of dengue fever: over three hundred dead in a month and five thousand victims on hand. There was a severe shortage of hospital beds as well as of blood for transfusions. This may have been just as well, as there are also fears that as much as 30 percent of India's blood supply is HIV-positive. The epidemic would simply continue until the temperature dropped.

The city's chief minister tried, at least, to kill two birds with one stone. "The fewer street lights there are," he stated, in reply to those who'd complained about the ill-lit streets, "the fewer the mosquitos, and far fewer dengue deaths."

The other catchphrase was "load shedding." This was when the big load of electricity was shed, and the power went off for hours.

I doused myself in mosquito repellent and hoped for the best. A moment's walk away from my hotel one evening, past a boy pissing in darkness under dim street lights, amid the hubbub of sellers and sidewalk amblers eating the ghastly air outside the Regal Cinema, I found the Mechanical Doctor.

Inside a huge stone arcade outside the theater I was pulled up short by a seven-foot-tall machine with a carnival look. Atop a steel trunk sat an illuminated glass case filled with wired-up mechanical contraptions and interlocking gears that whirred and shifted, lights that blinked and a turning red-and-white pinwheel. Above the mechanical device was the motto: HEALTH SPEAKS HERE.

Near the machine, by a dugout corner of pavement where a rat quaintly nosed around, was a small deformed man with impossibly bowed and knotted limbs. As he flopped and flexed his way across the sidewalk, an oblivious old woman tripped over him and there was a brief exchange of pleasantries. Then a boy appeared with the man's own contraption, two wooden planks nailed together with wheels attached. He and another boy shouted and unceremoniously hoisted the folded man onto his little roll-along and he got underway, self-propelled again.

HEALTH SPEAKS HERE. I couldn't figure out what the machine actually did. Every now and then it emanated loud Indian film music. But there was a pedestal to stand on and a warning to wait until the pinwheel stopped its turn. And there was a slot for one rupee. As soon as my coin dropped, music came blaring out and the machine's belly made ratcheting noises. The lights flashed with excitement and the great mechanism spun and lifted and dropped something. *Thunk*. A tiny card slipped through a slot at waist level.

On one side of the card was my accurate weight (73 kilos). The other side pronounced a deeper verdict in Hindi and English: *If you are a woman, you have a rare unapproachable delicacy, poise, and a charming manner.*

Not to mention a weight problem, I thought.

I reasoned that the next card would give me an assessment as a man. So I put in another rupee and enjoyed watching the Mechanical Doctor go through its vaudeville machinations. The glossy music kept playing.

If you are a woman . . .

A fun bout of television one night. First there was the deep pleasure announcers take in dispensing facts, out of context, with great fanfare: for example, that each urban Indian creates seven kilos of waste per day. This would be a meaningless figure even if it were compared to how much waste a New Yorker produces, since the process of waste treatment is so different. And there was a special report on a Delhi go-getter who had opened a workshop of highly skilled painters to turn out copies of da Vinci, Rembrandt, Monet, Goya, van Gogh. On the small screen they looked superb—I liked especially a Mona Lisa the size of a film poster—and accordingly they were proving very popular, at $100 each, with "the posh set."

Then there was the surreal effect of seeing black-and-white comedies from my childhood shown here in Hindi, three decades later. In a prudish Indian context, later programs from the seventies—like the one about the three beauties working as private detectives—seemed almost risqué. No wonder people without electricity ran their TVs off car batteries. And the current soap operas shown every night, or the one about the California lifeguards in tight bathing suits, came across as messages from another planet. Apart from the obvious revelations of health and sex, they arrived from too far off to be decoded, dense with assumptions about a way of life that must seem utterly cryptic to most Indians.

Perhaps I've been here too long, I thought.

I was finding that what suddenly looked incredibly provocative were those squeamish Indian musicals turned out endlessly by the Bombay film industry, in which harem girls waggle and cavort and tease and occasionally show a navel. Though the society regards it as obscene to show nudity or even couples kissing (the centuries of erotic statuary notwithstanding), they get away with a lot via the dances and the constant opportunity to soak a shirt in a rainstorm. To follow the plots an ignorance of Hindi isn't much of a hindrance, because they're like Elvis Presley movies: a guy with important dark hair, surrounded by adoring women, fights off gangsters and finds true love, all the while singing and gyrating.

And yet I was seeing the society at a moment of tectonic shift. Television was bringing the programs of Europe and the States to hundreds of millions of superstitious illiterate villagers. It was being used to convince them that, say, polio was dangerous but the oral vaccine was safe. And it was the latest kind of bribery, as one state politician, a former film star, had bought her constituents 45,000 TV sets with public funds. Most important, other people's myths were being delivered like candy down the throats of people who for hundreds of generations had looked to the *Mahabharata* for entertaining stories. I didn't think the result of this would be the breakdown of Hindu culture; if they could handle eight centuries of Muslim invaders they could outlast thirty channels. But I did look forward to the day when there is a program in Hindi about a poor family from Bihar who discover oil on their ancestral land and move to a lavish part of Bombay, near where the movie stars live, to thrive as hillbilly millionaires.

The best shows are the strictly Indian, of course. My favorite was *The Money Game*. In this one, teams of two businessmen go head-to-head to prove their company has the better sales force. The announcer gives each team a ludicrous problem and a minute to come up with a sales strategy. Question #1: Convince a blind man to buy a high-definition TV. The answer involved persuading him that such a fancy piece of equipment would attract a lot of pretty girls to his house, so that when science actually got around to finding a cure, he'd have his love life already swimmingly in place. This sounds absurd stated so baldly, but the winning team's version took it step-by-step and made it almost as logical as Descartes.

Question #2: Convince Salman Rushdie to go on vacation at an Iranian beach resort.

In Connaught Circus I ran into a ragged man hawking posters on the sidewalk. They were all in bright colors, with line drawings. One showed Red Cross safety tips, another was yoga postures, but the one for me was a guide to road safety. It was aimed at kids, because children were in most of the panels illustrating the mottos. ALWAYS STAND IN QUEUE AT THE BUS-STOP. DO'NT THROW SWEEPINGS & FRUIT-PEELS. DO'NT PLAY, JUMP, & LOITER ABOUT ON THE ROAD.

The one improvement I noticed since my last visit was that the city was less engulfed in litter. More than a fifth of the capital's residents sleep on the streets, so there are more people scavenging than before. Delhi, catching up with Calcutta, will have its own subway soon, though naturally one problem, as the poster seller warned me, is that "when they are digging more than ten feet east, west, north, and south, they are striking only bad things. Filth! Filthy things! You can't imagine the horror, sir."

A New Delhi bookseller in Connaught Circus—fifty paces from the Mechanical Doctor gizmo—pored over a road map with me. It took awhile, but eventually we traced the route of the Sher Shah Suri Marg through the thickets of city roads as it threaded past grand Mogul edifices, briefly switchbacked, then flowed freely out toward the Punjab.

The huge Old Citadel (Purana Qila) is rarely visited by tourists. Its vast interior, surrounded by stone ramparts, is now a half-wild park, interrupted by two buildings built by Sher Shah, a stately mosque and an octagonal tower. This latter was used as a library by Humayun (1508-56), the bookish, opium-addicted Mogul emperor whom Sher Shah temporarily displaced. It overlooks, appropriately, some of Delhi's most modern geometric buildings, with their own triangular ramparts. In 1556, a few months after returning to power, Humayun heard the call to prayer while he was watching the remnants of a sunset, hurried down the steps, slipped, and brained himself.

Like the Old Citadel, Humayun's Tomb stands near the Sher Shah Suri Marg's original route. In white marble and sandstone of several pinks and browns and reds, it looks like a study for the Taj Mahal, though it carries more a sense of loss than of celebration. Here the last Mogul emperor, Bahadur Shah, surrendered to the

British after the Mutiny, whence he was ushered off to Rangoon to wither. Like the Taj, the great mausoleum has a similar imposing platform at the first level, the same sense of a palatial tomb rising from a vast garden. Unfortunately, the pools aren't kept filled with water.

Humayun's Tomb was, in fact, the first double dome in India—meaning an inner dome that harmonized with the interior, then an outer shell with the proper proportions for an outside view. This Persian-Indian blend of styles was also the first version of the garden-tomb concept, with a grid of squares, channels, and fountains. On entering the tulip gateway you see how closely the model was followed later, to culminate in the Taj; Humayun's Tomb looks like a strange fraternal twin in a different stone.

Farther on, the road passes the Red Fort, and Gandhi's memorial. All these together make it a curious highway of power and loss, from Sher Shah through Humayun to that enormous fortress, the centerpiece of Mogul might, which the British used to fend off the Mutiny, and down to Gandhi, who found his own way to defeat them.

THUGS—
THE PUB, NOT THE PEOPLE!

Here, too, was the Jami Masjid, the country's largest mosque, for Old Delhi has traditionally been the Muslim part of the city ever since Mogul days, and it's the area where land ownership is most deeply rooted. The Jami Masjid is ever more graceful the farther one stays away from it. You approach it past sidewalk dentists and palm readers with their signs of disembodied teeth and hands, and a crowded encampment of tented shops selling cheap clothing and bric-a-brac. Up steep steps, past tribal and Muslim beggars, inside the mosque a somewhat forced, painstaking austerity takes over that, for this infidel, three big tulip domes and the complex gazebo towers can't relieve.

Just outside its walls are the first stages of the Chandni Chowk—the Avenue of Moonlight, once a tree-lined canal—Old Delhi's web of narrow tumultuous market streets that dates back to Mogul times. With a festival coming soon, it seemed much taken up by fireworks stalls selling "rockets" with gorgeous deities, animals, and females adorning the packages of Cock Brand portable explosives.

Past it the streets devolved into dealers' alleys of clothes, religious trinkets, jewelry, spices, poultry, and furniture. The problem with a bazaar of a thousand shops is that there's never anything to buy. A few sleeping cows forced the mopeds and cyclists and pedestrians to go gingerly; where once strolled refined courtiers there were now a lot of mangy dogs. I was taken aback at first, in a labyrinthine and musty lane, by the Jain Computer Shop—then it didn't seem surprising after all.

Not so far away, heading toward the Jamuna River, is the Raj Ghat, the memorial to Mahatma Gandhi (1869–1948), built by the spot where he was cremated. A simple marble slab as black as an abyss marks the loss of one of the most effective men of the century. Garlands of flowers lie on the slab. A flame burns perpetually, and a flat grassy courtyard flows to the embankment. Stone walls on all sides carry engraved quotes from the Mahatma: the effect is dull and dutiful. But there is no mistaking the core blackness of that slab. It reiterates that he is no longer here and can never be replaced; a fire may burn but his ashes are gone.

Gandhi's assassination came six months after independence and the partition of India and Pakistan. His life, now, seems of another age, of a nineteenth century whose assumptions lasted stubbornly until the Second World War, when they were killed off and their parent empires became depleted. Gandhi's genius, of using the Indian mass and its passive weight against an enemy whose mind and weaknesses he understood intimately, belongs to an era when governments and people still played by certain agreed-on rules. All three attempts on Gandhi's life were made not by Muslims but by upper-caste Hindus, who feared his elevation of the lower castes. And in the end he was shot by a conservative young Hindu nationalist, who hated Gandhi's defense of Muslims during the communal violence following Partition.

India today deals uneasily with the Mahatma. Shortly after I left, a last wooden chest of some of the ashes off Gandhi's funeral pyre was discovered in a bank vault in Orissa. Originally the ashes had been divided into at least twenty such coffins to be immersed in rivers all over the country; one, though, had been forgotten for forty-nine years. When it was located again it was as if the Mahatma were back, stirring up uncomfortable questions about the country's failure to deal with the core Gandhi issues: the caste system, the religious fissures, the buildup of arms, the pressures of a society ever more materialistic, made wicked by the West and its products.

Gandhi's great-grandson had wanted to take the coffin on a tour of northern India, but the government, fearing trouble, sent it under the guardianship of crack troops straight to Allahabad. There the last of his ashes were scattered at the sacred meeting place of the Ganges and the Jamuna. Thousands—but not many thousands—came to watch, but no political leaders of any import turned up.

What, the Mahatma's descendant was asked, might Gandhi have thought of India today?

"What would he *not* have disapproved of?" said the great-grandson rhetorically. "He would be a very disappointed man."

I got a magic lesson on Janpath, for only two hundred rupees, from Mr. Singh (Yogi).

This was the only name on his business card, safely encased in plastic. It also said: *Has Testimonials From VIPS!* and *So Many International Predictions Came True!* I liked this so much I asked if he had any cards to give me but no, it was his only one.

This struck me as proof he must be in the business of fleecing people. I met him while talking to a sign maker on the street about designing a plaque for my house. Mr. Singh (Yogi), who seemed a friend of the sign maker, joined in the conversation and made some good suggestions about the sign. When he asked if I was interested in a scientific experiment, no money involved, naturally I agreed.

He was a Sikh: intense dark eyes, black beard, rather roly-poly, in khaki robes and turban. A professional air, which must help the scam. A serious black zip pocketbook added to the effect.

"Let us step around this column and into this hallway. Sir. Move in a bit so no one is bothering us. So we can *concentrate*. This is an experiment in time, sir, yes? There is only past, present, and future, sir."

We settled ourselves crosslegged in a cool hallway corner off Janpath, with a staircase a few feet away. Occasionally someone went up and glanced incuriously at us. The hallway was pleasantly dappled with sunlight; just outside, an old man sat on the remnants of a table at the edge of the sidewalk and hummed oddly to himself.

"Past, present, and future, sir. They are meeting in my vast concentration, sir, if we are concentrating together."

"I'm concentrating."

"I too am concentrating, sir. This is an experiment, yes? I do not want your money today, sir. If I am convincing you of my ability I ask you to visit me here tomorrow, because how can you trust me to tell you the future if you do not trust me to tell you the past. Are you understanding me, sir?"

"Absolutely. But I don't need to be told about the past."

"That is not the question, sir. The question is one of trust." When everything was in readiness he said again, "There is only past, present, and future, sir."

Mr. Singh (Yogi) sat only a foot away and drew three swift horizontal lines in pencil on a torn rectangle of white notepaper just like the ones on which my past, present, and future would soon be written.

"I am feeling a certain amount of alarm about the twenty-second of December, sir. You should feel very attentive on that date."

He checked my lifeline and loveline: plenty of thread left on both, it seemed. I should perhaps relieve the suspense by saying now that the twenty-second proved as uneventful as the day before and after, but of course that may have been because I was very attentive.

"Are you concentrating, sir? I do not feel you concentrating."

I'd have felt better about our relationship had I figured out how the trick was done. It involved repeating some magic numbers and my writing down the names of a few loved ones and their birthdates on a piece of paper which I folded, he pressed to his forehead, and then put in my pocket. Some moments later he produced a piece of folded paper from his own pocket that had the same information with some slight misspellings but accurate dates, in his own handwriting. He was never out of my sight, I never saw him write anything down. It was his litany, though, I found magical.

"If you don't believe in what I do, if I am wrong, sir, then I don't ask for money, you don't give me money, God is my witness and God is your witness. If you believe I lie I do not want your money.

As I'd hoped, Delhi's bookstores yielded plenty of old accounts of European travelers on the GT. One of the most vivid and detailed was from a sixteenth-century Frenchman, Jean-Baptiste Tavernier, who was jeweler to Shah Jahan, the emperor who built the Taj Mahal.

Tavernier passed frequently along the road between 1641 and 1668. He wrote that to journey in India was "more commodious than in France or Italy." A traveler then didn't use horses or donkeys, but rode an ox or was carried in a palanquin, a canopied couch like a portable sitting room. Goods similarly were transported either in wagons drawn by oxen or simply on animals' backs. The road was often swollen with traffic: caravans of twelve thousand oxen carrying corn, salt, and rice. Ordinary travelers might have to halt for a few days until the caravan passed. These bovine trucks were driven by one nomadic tribe who lived on the road, bringing their families along with their employer's merchandise. This tribe of drivers owned their oxen just as trucking companies today provide the trucks.

Wealthier travelers, carried in a palanquin by, say, six men, might also routinely be accompanied by an umbrella-bearer and twenty or thirty armed men, carrying bows and arrows and muskets. Hollywood, it seems to me, got a lot of this right.

Tavernier has nothing but praise for the road under the Moguls—though they were his employers, after all. He did have difficulty getting tolerable provisions in the strictly vegetarian Hindu villages. Much journeying was done at night, to escape the heat; hence the bodyguards. Many towns were fortified against bandits, the gates shut tight after nightfall.

Tavernier also describes how mail was carried by runners, a human-footed Pony Express who were faster than horsemen and passed letters on from post to post, about six miles apart (presumably at every three kos pillars). The highway was evident from Sher Shah's trees planted on either side. Where there were no trees, villagers were compelled by the government to heap whitewashed stones every five hundred paces.

An Italian trader on the road in the 1600s, Pietra del Valle, was impressed by the lavish coaches, curtained with crimson silk, and the oxen, who wore bells and (he claims) galloped like horses. This inspired a dream I had one night of being run over by a Tata truck fancily going jingle-jingle-jingle.

A contemporary of del Valle, the British chaplain Edward Terry, described how men of means used mules, horses, camels, or two-wheeled coaches that could carry four passengers plus the driver—

comfortable versions of the traditional tonga. The coaches were lined with quilts and velvet cushions, and their oxen's horns were tipped with silver or brass. He seconds the Italian's estimate of their speeds, and says they could cover twenty miles a day.

I averaged about twice that, by combustion engine.

To even approach the idea of the subcontinent is to fall down a well of mind-numbing figures. In India alone there are over a billion people, though the official numbers are slightly lower. Three out of four live in villages. The population is growing at a rate of over 2 percent a year, 20 million more Indians annually. Efforts at controlling the growth rate through sterilization and birth control have been half-hearted, and defeated by numerous embedded traditions. This is India's real tragedy: all other difficulties spring from it.

China's population growth, by contrast, is nearly flat, a result of severe policies. The two countries invite comparison, for living conditions in them were similar around the time of Partition, fifty years ago. Now China's per capita income is about twice India's, life expectancy ten years higher, and the literacy rate about 25 percent better.

Say what you like about India's forward motion, trade controls, multinationals, joining the next century, etcetera. This one fact—that India simply produces too many Indians—overwhelms all the others, including India's "steady new economic dynamism," as the finance-wallahs put it. (The growth rate in Pakistan, with about 140 million people, is even higher, at around 3 percent.) Nothing that India's thinkers and leaders say or do will make up for this disaster if the population rate is not curtailed. You can argue that India is one of the largest food exporting countries in the world, but so what? Feeding everyone remains far too complicated, even if the country successfully continues to avoid a famine.

Every other Indian is malnourished. Every third Indian may be considered poor by even the most astringent standards. One in four Indians always goes hungry. One in five is an untouchable.

One in eight Indians belongs to an upper caste; seven out of eight do not have clean water or adequate sewage.

Out of those eight Indians, six are Hindus, one is a Muslim, and the last, almost too small to notice, is a child laborer, perhaps working in some form of indentured slavery into adulthood.

There is no guarantee of primary education for most of the population. Not quite two out of three men are basically literate, and just over one out of three women. (In arch-rival Pakistan rates are considerably worse; only about 10 percent of the women can read and write.) Here there are less than two phones per hundred people; in Pakistan there's half a telephone more, plus they work better. (In the U.S., there are nearly fifty-seven phones per hundred people.) One out of two Indians has never made a telephone call.

Phone calls aside, it is still a society throttled by tradition. What started more than three millennia ago as four Hindu orders (Brahmin priests, warriors, merchants, peasant farmers) grew to either over five hundred castes or over two thousand subcastes depending how you count them. Thus a caste structure became ingrained, dedicated to neutralizing the majority of the population through the idea of karma—one's lot in this life is determined by actions in past lives, therefore it must be totally accepted, no matter how awful. It remains difficult to separate the custom of caste from the customs of Hinduism; this is what has given the culture its stability and tensile strength. Even if the average Indian (as one economist insisted to me) may reject the whole idea of caste intellectually, and likewise "doesn't know very much about his religion, really," he is still a prisoner of its many social assumptions.

Take marriage. Because of the expense of dowry marriage, more than one daughter can insure lifelong poverty for a family. Hence many daughters are murdered at birth. Should the daughter live and grow up to be married, she may be at risk from her husband's family if her parents default on part of the dowry—seventeen Indian women are murdered for this every day. (The popular methods are strangulation, poisoning, burning, and electrocution.) The costs of an Indian wedding are staggering for the bride's family—rarely less than $3,000, a decade's wages for many workers. To pay for the dowry through loans, a family will often accept an indentured servitude that goes on for years or even generations after the ceremony.

By contrast, the usual Muslim marriage tradition—the husband's family pays for the wedding, and the bride holds on to her dowry as a kind of insurance—looks a lot more sensible.

No wonder Hindus are so wary of daughters; no wonder there are so many child workers to pay off such debts. Many of these children are simply sold as slave labor for, say, twenty bucks a head. In Bihar, where a family lives on sixty dollars a year, this is a lot. The little boys are often branded, the girls raped. Though the government in recent years has introduced tougher child labor laws, 3,500 (out of 4,000) Indians convicted of violating the laws were fined only five dollars and let off through a convenient loophole: that such laws don't apply in "small workshops" like those making carpets or silver trinkets or leather goods. And with the proper bribe, even a match or a brick factory, a quarry or a construction site may be deemed a workshop and use kids sixteen hours a day—children trying to pay off the debts of their dead grandparents.

Aldous Huxley wrote of this brave new world back in 1926, in his travel book *Jesting Pilate*. "For India is depressing as no other country I have ever known. One breathes in it, not air, but dust and hopelessness . . . generations of peace and settled government have made the country, as a whole, no more prosperous than it was in the days of anarchy." This was Huxley slapping the Raj in the face, laying the blame on British shoulders. He saw millions "without enough to eat, all their lives. Custom and ancient superstition are still as strong as they ever were." But he was also seeing the future when he added, "The educated and politically conscious profess democratic principles; but their instincts are . . . almost ineradicably aristocratic."

Nehru saw that democracy and the caste system were opposed to each other, that "between these two conceptions conflict is inherent and only one of them can survive." He underestimated, perhaps, the ability of the unconscious to embrace two contradictory ideas at the same time, especially in people with minds brilliantly suited to arguing many sides of an issue. Caste in the cities may no longer be as fundamental as it is to rural life, but the society is still deeply stratified. Nature itself and the unchecked population seem to guarantee that—no matter how low people's expectations are—there is usually an exploiter and an exploited. As V. S. Naipaul wrote in another context: "Hate oppression; fear the oppressed."

And here in Delhi, the population has quintupled in the last thirty-five years. At this rate, it may hit twenty million in a decade or so. But it won't catch Calcutta.

At the mercy of my asthma, I found it almost impossible to breathe in this city whose air is the equivalent of a pack of cigarettes a day. I thought I'd seen everything in the way of pollution, but I'd never been to a place where the air actually hung like a stained scrim between me and the other side of the street, where the day's poisonous exhalations seemed tidal, pushed about in thick, choking waves by rickshaws and cars.

Even the GT was safer than this. I'd been coughing my lungs out since I got to Delhi; I realized that one more day of its gangrenous air might kill me. At the restaurant where I ate every evening, two kind waiters hovered tremulously over me as if I might expire between the soup and the curry. They told me that my hacking alarmed them, and they were glad to hear I'd made arrangements to leave the next day.

The air in Delhi gets worse and worse; the bribery, everyone assured me, was also thicker than ever. And yet India had changed, palpably. The mood on the streets was both far more severe and more determined than a few years back. When I remembered the listlessness, the lack of purpose that was so overwhelming when I'd first visited twelve years earlier, I felt I was seeing not only an added desperation but a new sense of people taking their lives into their own hands.

The statistics weren't encouraging. But India did seem less a huge, sleeping, beleaguered series of crowds and more a country of individuals rudely awakened and even stirring to action, at last starting to take responsibility for their individual destinies—no matter what destiny the fortune-tellers might foresee for them.

> See, Holy One—the Great Road which is the backbone of all Hind. For the most part it is shaded, as here, with four lines of trees; the middle road—all hard—takes the quick traffic. In the days before rail-carriages the Sahibs travelled up and down here in hundreds.... A man goes in safety here—for at every few kos is a police-station. The police are thieves and extortioners (I myself would patrol it with cavalry—young recruits under a strong captain) but at least they do not suffer any rivals. All castes and kinds of men move here. Look! Brahmins and chumars, bankers and tinkers, barbers and bunnias, pilgrims and potters—all the world coming and going... such a river of life as nowhere else exists in the world.
>
> —Rudyard Kipling, *Kim* (1901)

14.

Haryana Holidays

I left the capital in the early morning on the Sher Shah Road. Soon it would join up with the British "Military Road"—the branch of the GT I hadn't taken—to become once again the Grand Trunk.

This was an old part of New Delhi, faded, much used, away from the monuments. At a stoplight there was the quick little girl at the window, her hand outstretched, beauty pleading for money.

As we passed a shining white marble temple, my driver, Lucky Singh, said, "The trucks with Sikh drivers always stop in there for a shower and a rest on their way down the GT." Soon both sides of the road became a scraggly desert dotted with yellow work trucks, men laboring on a bypass highway.

I chose a Sikh driver for the last big stretch of the Indian road, about three hundred miles, because much of it crosses the Punjab. At twenty-two Lakhanjit (Lucky) Singh was handsome, with a trim beard, mustache, and glossy dark hair, a frank grin and easy athletic walk. His youth worried me at first, until I met his father, Mohan Singh. Short, hefty, with a lavish white beard and his hair bound up in a turban, Mohan Singh had the calm assurance that makes Sikhs, for me, the most trustworthy group in India, despite years of troubles. My instinct was that this man was not going to raise an unreliable son.

"He is a good boy," Mohan Singh said to me gravely. "And he knows the Punjab very well."

My prior drivers had all seemed terrified as soon as we left their home turf, and I couldn't be put in that position now. I'd been to Punjab state twice before during years of tumult and bloodshed, and it was no fun to be lost there. The Punjab was officially quiet again, but I liked the fact that Lucky was a Sikh who'd cut his hair and didn't wear a turban—a "lightly burdened" Sikh. It made him seem more reasonable.

He told me he'd first cut his hair a decade earlier, not long after Mrs. Gandhi was machine-gunned by her Sikh bodyguards in her garden. The assassination had been sparked by her attack on the Sikhs' holiest site, the Golden Temple in Amritsar; a great deal of anti-Sikh vengeance and rioting had followed.

"I felt in danger," said Lucky. "I decide I rather have my life than my hair."

"What did your father think?"

"He said, 'I have much life behind me, I will keep my turban.' But he did not stop me."

Lucky's older brother, a computer programmer in Delhi, had kept his turban and his hair uncut, following Sikh religious requirements.

Lucky was studying to go into banking; he was going to night school whenever possible after driving during the day. His father owned two taxis, both Ambassadors. The family kiosk in front of the Imperial (the hotel concierge got a cut, naturally) had proven a success. They often took tourists to Agra for the day: the Red

Fort, the Taj, lunch in some fancy restaurant, sometimes Sikandra, but not, oddly, Fatehpur Sikri, unless the tourists specifically asked.

Lucky's father Mohan had come to Delhi from a village in the Punjab; Lucky would be getting his bachelor's degree in commerce and hoped to go to work for the Reserve Bank. A family success story in only one generation, though I wondered if Lucky would be willing, when the time came, to give up the looser hours and the taxi driver's sense of cash in hand.

We passed well over a hundred trucks pulled over for repairs or adjustments, their wheels blocked with rocks. This part of the road ran straight to the Delhi-Haryana border, with old trees even in the green divider. There were a few roadblocks, just to slow the trucks, and at the state border were STOP barriers that no one paid the slightest attention to. The landscape was busy: plywood companies and sawmills, and smokestacks in the trees.

The National Permit legends on the truck· foreheads now included states I hadn't seen listed earlier, Punjab and Chandigarh. Almost without exception, trucks have on the back WAIT FOR SIDE, meaning wait for a hand signal from the driver that it's okay to pass him. Sometimes it works. More often, another inscription applies:

MY GOD, GIVE ME LONG LIFE

In the sweltering heat eucalyptus trees always managed to look cool. Cultivated fields of corn sheaves were fronted by jacaranda trees and white flowers; power lines ran to electric stations standing like steel chessmen in the distance. A tractor was slowly tugging a cartload of saried women.

Murthal was a rank of competing dhabas, which created a jostling pileup of trucks.

Despite accidents the road, for the first time in nine hundred miles, felt relaxed. There hadn't been many moments when the Grand Trunk seemed to breathe easily; I had never expected it up here, with the long history of political strife north of Delhi.

At Samalkha, another unbelievably dismal auto-parts town, there was a Blue Jay Tourist Complex nesting neatly in a service station, out of place with its brick arches and clean curtains. I found myself idly wondering what it'd be like to rent one of its rooms for a few months, to try to write a novel. Could I enjoy struggling through a difficult first draft here?

Only if there were nowhere else on earth.

AVOID USE NO INTOXICANTS WHILE DRIVING

There had been heavy rains recently, by Panipat. The wrecks were more severe—three trucks flipped over, scarred bellies upturned, within fifty kilometers.

Panipat in 1526 was the site of Babur's victory over a bumptious Afghan kinsman who then controlled much of northern India. The battle ushered in the Mogul Empire, and was the fifth time Babur had invaded from his native Samarkand. This time, outnumbered ten-to-one, Babur's cavalry and artillery did in an opposing chorus-line of chained elephants; by lunchtime he'd killed twenty thousand of the enemy and sent the rest running. All the northwest was his as far as Delhi. Babur sent his young son down to secure Agra, and Humayun returned with the Koh-i-noor diamond, the biggest in the world. Babur, a most refined man and ever the fond father, handed back the Mountain of Light. But Babur showed absolutely no patience with his son's poor letter writing:

> *You wrote to me, as I ordered; but why didn't you have your letter read over to you? If you had tried to read it yourself you couldn't have done it, and so you would almost certainly have rewritten it.* It can *be read, if one really takes the trouble, but it is very puzzling. Though your spelling isn't too bad, it's not*

quite correct. Your remissness in writing seems to result from that which makes your letters so obscure—namely over-elaboration. Write in future without so much hyperbole, using plain, straight-forward language; it will be less trouble to you, and less for the reader.

Panipat was large enough for a college and a Psychiatric Centre, but the GT-as-main-street was all truck stops. Even on Sunday it was business as usual, with a flourishing market and lots of new guest houses. I'd rushed through Panipat a few years earlier, right after eleven trucks had been set on fire in a political protest—front-page news in a Delhi paper, which referred to the town as "known for its textiles and pickles." Now things had calmed down appreciably.

Panipat did still live up to a long-standing reputation for flies, which were horrifically insistent in the heat. There was little else to see here, so I went looking for the tomb of a saint named Kallandar. We turned down a side lane and got embroiled in a classic standoff between two bullock carts, one carrying shit, the other carrying dirt. In a back market street I found an old mosque that had been walled-in and was now the home of goats and piles of dung—a local Muslim defeat.

Past a series of bicycle repair shops, barbershops, and a rickshaw graveyard, perhaps a mile back from the town, Lucky and I parked and walked down a muddy path lined with two water canals. Snorting pigs with snouts made brown by drinking were enough to make you forswear Indian bacon forever. I went through a dilapidated arch, across a narrow lane, then into an old pale blue and white compound with a mosque and several tombs.

This was theoretically Kallandar's final address. Across the tiled courtyard, hot under my flip-flops in glaring sun, was the oldest part, guarded by two small snoring men. Inside the domed chamber, ornamented with fine Koranic script ("an example of the calligraphic decorative style" said my faithful old guidebook) was the saint's tomb, covered in requisite red velvet. A padlocked trunk received donations. A worn little yellow sign for Atlas Spare Tires, with a glowing image of a mosque, had been quite earnestly hung on a corner of the tomb's enclosure.

Back in the courtyard's glare a bustling potbellied man in dhoti said, "Yes, can I help you? That is the grave of Kallandar."

"He's the saint of the town?"

"Saint, yes. Like Christ."

"What makes him so popular?"

"Well, he moved the river. That was a miracle."

"How long ago, do you suppose?"

"More than three hundred years, anyway."

"And both Muslims and Hindus admire him?"

"Of course. I am a Hindu. Those men asleep are Muslims. Will you excuse me? I have to get back to my office."

Every once in a while in India the past rears up and gives you a solid whack. In Gharaunda a caravanserai of grand dimensions rose by the road, probably three to four centuries old, and even as an utter wreck it dominated the town. I'd been reading about these serais in all the old travelers' memoirs and expected something smaller, mostly because once there were so many of them. Sher Shah alone had supposedly put up seventeen hundred.

Built in brick, the Mogul serai was now being repaired by local workmen. In fact this was just one "gate" (in the sense of a castle's gate)—the other was perhaps a half kilometer away. Much of the mill town, which looked eroded rather than poor, had been built from the pillaged serai.

The gate was elaborate, with abutments, protrusions, arched stone windows, tulip-shaped gateways, niches, and stone-canopied balconies. Twin rounded towers on either side had peepholes for ventilation and defense—the place had also functioned as a fortress. Thick wooden doors with fierce iron spikes lay waiting to be put back. Upstairs were the domed sleeping chambers.

The government worker who took me around and the man in the town who'd shown me the correct path to its entry both refused money. Most unusual.

Karnal was a medina town of magnificent preserved houses with lattices and elaborate towers and often the Islamic crescent as decor. Of all the old towns I stopped in along the GT, it had the most finesse. In Karnal there was also an active Lions Club, with the familiar insignia. Thousands of Sikhs are members, because all Sikh males bear the surname Singh, meaning lion, so they join. (In the Punjab, the Sikh heartland, there are Lions Clubs virtually everywhere.) I wonder how welcome one of these big fellows with a turban and a scimitar would be in a Cleveland chapter.

Karnal was wall after enclosing wall, less a fortress town than a succession of labyrinths studded with many elegant mansions, often covered with Persian script. I walked through an old gate down Nawaab Chhatta, where a man from a TV repair shop took me into one mansion. Around a small courtyard of cobblestoned brick, beneath fretted balconies with that abstract, art deco aspect of Mogul design, several girls were hanging up the wash. They giggled when they saw me and the repairman led me through an open doorway into darkness.

Eventually I made out a big antique water heater and lofty ceilings with ornate carvings and floral moldings, all begrimed but lovely. We went up a flight of high, narrow stone steps; a small monkey took his time clambering out of the way. The stairs opened onto an upper courtyard and another floor of infinite rooms within rooms. Plenty of home here for the extended family: cousins, uncles, grandmother, heaps of children.

A bare-chested man sitting in a shadowy interior chamber got off his rope cot and came out to shake my hand.

"When was the house built?" I asked.

"Mohammedans," he grunted. "Muslim building. Before 1947. Then they go. And we come."

Those were the three essentials, centered around one date, the Partition and Independence, and leaving out the slaughters.

On the road a truck had overturned completely, sending a black sea of coal flowing all over the highway. The coal had probably come by rail from Bihar to a large city in Haryana like Jullundur, then been loaded onto trucks to be distributed along the GT. The road is often used as a short distance carrier in league with the railroads; for long distances it's cheaper to use the trains only if you're sending an entire boxcar-load.

Shortly after, a sign in both English and Hindi:

ACCIDENT STARTS WHERE SAFETY ENDS

I gave up trying to determine how many people die on the Grand Trunk Road annually. The figure I'd seen twice, of a thousand deaths a year, seemed suspiciously round and suspiciously low. I read that two hundred people die on Indian roads every day; surely more than three of those must be on the GT.

The Karnal Lake Tourist Complex, aimed at Indian tourists, was an amazing vision painted by Magritte: a modern motel by a man-made lake, complete with a few turbanned Sikhs kayaking. From where Lucky and I stood watching, they resembled die-cast toys with twirling Salvador Dali mustaches. A little farther on was a rest stop with a Post Office, an Ice Cream Parlour, a Red Cross Dispensary, a Tandoori Chicken Counter, spotless He & She restrooms, a Liquor Vend, a bank, a Hot Dog Counter, a petrol station, gift shops, fruit and snack counters, and a formal restaurant. Behind it stretched a well-landscaped park.

A sign advertised *Packed Snacks*:

NON-VEG TWITTER TEMPTER RS. 17
VEGETARIAN TWITTER TEMPTER RS. 10

One was suddenly, here at this rest stop, in an India that functioned. There was even a sign on the road with the familiar pictographs for available services—gas pump, taps, fork & knife—though Indians eat with their hands most of the time.

On the road just before Kurukshetra lay the worst wreck I'd seen: a truck flipped over, the front and back ends gnarled and torn, the cabin ripped off like a crumpled soda can beside it. Surely no one had survived that one.

Another five hundred miles of this, I told myself. At least. And these accidents were happening to men who prayed several times a day.

THE ANCIENT AND HOLY CITY OF KURUKSHETRA WELCOMES YOU!
TOURISTS ARE OUR HONORED GUESTS!

I said to Lucky, "I think I know what that means."

Krishna:
I am all-powerful Time which destroys all things, and I have come here to slay these men. Even if thou dost not fight, all the warriors facing thee shall die.

— *The Bhagavad-Gita* (c. 500? B.C.)

15.

Toward the Punjab

The ancient battle of Kurukshetra engulfed one hundred sixty square miles and lasted eighteen days—that is, according to the *Mahabharata*. Everything about the Sanskrit epic poem is on a similarly grand scale. At 100,000 stanzas it's the longest poem ever written, virtually a literature in itself, eight times the combined length of *The Iliad* and *The Odyssey*; it makes the Ring Cycle seem like a hit single. One chapter within it, capacious in its own right, is the single most important work of Hindu philosophy, the *Bhagavad-Gita*, which is Krishna's sermon before the battle of Kurukshetra. This part of the epic was probably the earliest composed; most of the rest dates from around 400 A.D.

Arjuna: What power is it, Krishna, that drives man to act sinfully, even unwillingly, as if powerlessly?

Krishna: It is greedy desire and wrath born of passion, the great evil, the sum of destruction: this is the enemy of the soul.

All is clouded by desire: as fire by smoke, as a mirror by dust, as an unborn babe by its covering.

Wisdom is clouded by desire, the everpresent enemy of the wise, desire in its innumerable forms, which like a fire cannot find satisfaction.

Of the battlefield there was nothing left to see. Instead I was in modern Kurukshetra, which wasn't nearly as opportunistic as I'd feared. My experience in Mathura had made me paranoid.

Lucky suggested I visit, first, the Sannehit Tirath. This was an "artificial lake," meaning a huge tank 1,200 feet long, filled with sickly green water with boys swimming in it. Temples were built alongside the steps down into the tank. The steps and the temples were all very clean; the water was disgusting.

It was lunchtime now, and staggeringly hot. A group of bearded men, mostly bare-chested and scruffy, sat beneath a large tree by the water swapping stories.

A sequence of four plaques proclaimed:

> A mere touch of the Sannehit Tirath on the occasion of the solar eclipse is equivalent to hundreds of yagays. Whosoever visits the holy Sannehit Tirath in Kurukshetra Brahmvedi daily attains the salvation. All the tiraths, holy rivers and tanks collect at the Sannehit Tirath every month....

The fourth plaque was missing.

In an open-walled shelter two men were playing a checkers-like game using gray and red pebbles on a board they'd sketched in chalk. Other men stood around watching. One player kept cagily silent, the other bluffed his strategy aloud. A lot of layabouts were stretched out asleep under the zinc roof.

At Lucky's suggestion—I left him in the car in shade—I walked over by myself to the nearby Sri Krishna Museum.

Closed for an hour's lunch break, it looked from the outside so modern and Western in layout and architecture that it might have belonged to another country.

Rather than waiting for the museum to open, in severe heat I traipsed down a country road toward a bulbous-domed red temple. Eventually I located an open doorway in the outer wall. I wandered into a compound of arched pale yellow buildings in stone, some British, others older. A bearded and long-haired young man in beads and sarong ambled over with another boy. The place turned out to be a hostel for the local Sanskrit university, known officially as Kurukshetra U.

The boy was twenty and spoke a bit of English, but had little to say; he might've been drugged-out. I asked him a dozen questions and got virtually nothing out of him, which is unusual in this country. To avoid the glare we stayed in the shade—I found I'd fitted myself into a niche of a Mogul-style building. "Old house," said the boy with enormous and urbane ennui. That was all he knew, and he clearly didn't care how it had got there.

Funny how buildings in north India, apart from religious sites, seem to rarely fulfill their original function. And how seldom people seem to know what that original function was, or to care.

Unlike the so-called backward Muslim peoples I have traveled among, the Hindu villager seems happily local. He apparently has few interests or opinions outside his home sphere; or try as I might, I could never extract them. A distinct contrast with the most remote desert *bedu* in Arabia, who while I was with them were full of opinions about world politics, getting it all hourly over the radio.

The Sri Krishna Museum, its lunch break over, was full of schoolchildren being led around by teachers. The interior, spacious and airy and comfortable even in the heat, made it seem the newest museum in India, and it would've looked quite at home in

Amsterdam. Most impressive was a tableau of lifesize papier-mâché and bamboo figures showing a moment near the end of the *Mahabharata*. In this scene Bhishma lies on twenty arrows while Krishna, Arjuna, Dhritarashtra, and others stand around listening to the dying warrior's admonition on kingship.

A sign warned: SPITTING INSIDE THE MUSEUM STRICTLY PROHIBITED, and never once in India did I see anyone spit inside a museum.

The one historical site I hoped to find was the tomb of a shaikh at Thanesar, a sister town of Kurukshetra. Why? Because my guidebook mentioned it, and I'm obedient. Eventually, after much maddening back-and-forthing, Lucky and I had to give up. I was always afraid one of these enormous old tombs would be majestic and I'd have missed it. Instead it was sobering how forlorn and weed-choked so many of them were. Anything that's not new in India is broken, and unless it's still worshipped at or can be usefully dismantled, it's considered of no interest whatsoever.

Leaving Kurukshetra the land became very green and prosperous. The monsoon had been generous, but the fields also looked evenly irrigated. A cow stood up to its chest in green water. Hundreds of white birds, as white as the cow, flitted along the surface.

Just after we crossed the sluggish remnants of a river there was a police checkpoint—a man in khaki shielded by a bunker, his rifle pointed at the road. The checkpoint was formed by a log laid on stones which half-blocked the GT, so drivers had to take turns going around. All traffic ceased while an old man rolled along in a one-of-a-kind wheelcart; both arms made the motions of someone jumping rope as he turned its homemade cranks. Indians have an extraordinary ability to get by, to create some original contraption that works really well out of bits and pieces of nothing—an odd accompaniment to their genius for inventing anarchy.

Near Amballa the train tracks made themselves memorable, twenty feet to my left in the green-gold cathedral light of the trees. Amballa was traditionally a flourishing Punjab town due to its location on the GT and its proximity on the rail line up to Simla, the hill station that was the summer capital of the British Raj. As an English country town re-created in the foothills of the Himalayas, for several long months every year Simla was the most powerful place in Asia, the buzzing hive immortalized by Kipling "where all things begin and many come to an evil end." Nowadays Amballa, along with Simla, has lost its old importance, and the map has been redrawn so it lies just inside the Haryana border.

The Amballa Cantonment Train Station stands right on the Grand Trunk Road. The station is an off-white and cream yellow, with brown trim and NORTHERN RAILWAYS in large letters above the entrance. Here, in Kipling's masterpiece, Kim and his charge, the old Tibetan lama, disembark the train from Lahore and begin their walk along the Grand Trunk Road. *Kim* was written in England in 1900 out of intense nostalgia, Kipling inventing himself backward into an idealized boy's childhood in India, the years there that he was denied. It was a fantasy to heal that lost boyhood, for Kim is of the same age as when Ruddy was sent back to cold England for school. Significantly, when the book ends, Kim is the age Kipling was when he returned to India to start life as a journalist.

Throughout the novel Kim must choose between two different ways of life: to follow a spiritual path, or to play a role in the Great Game—the pawn-takes-pawn struggle for control of Central Asia—as a spy in native disguise. Even the ending does not make clear which he will choose. One of Kipling's remarkable achievements is to present the reader—imagine, the turn of the century European reader—with a white protagonist whose own heroes, whom he follows, trusts, and even emulates, are all Indian.

Kim and the old lama don't walk very far on "the broad, smiling river of life... the Great Road which is the backbone of all Hind" before fortune and the Great Game "that never ceases day or night" overtake them, but those pages are some of the most memorable and poetic in a scene-crowded book. In Amballa Kim first makes contact with Colonel Creighton, the spymaster. This train station was one of *Kim*'s few settings on the GT I could be absolutely sure of.

There is still a particular magic to such train stations all across the subcontinent; perhaps it's the air of a happy marriage. They seem the most fruitful and untroubled collaboration of India and England: those far-off echoes (generous arches, seven broad platforms, the whistle of an arrival or departure) but in a tropical clime. Little ever changes in an eternal Indian Railways experience of people sleeping or camped out on the floor, alongside the unusual sensation (for here) of ordered motion and, in the staff, an almost military decorum of uniform and gesture.

As Theroux puts it, Indian railway stations "are like scale models of Indian society, with its divisions of caste, class, and sex." Here was the country in miniature. There was a Waiting Room (Ladies), a Telegraph Office, a Retiring Room (4 Beds Only, 30 rs. per bed for 24 hours); the offices of a Chief Booking Supervisor, a Chief Ticket Inspector, and a Waiting Room (1st Class). There was a Refreshment Room (Veg. & Non-Veg.) There was a machine with tiny colored pinwheel lights which told you your weight if you could figure out how to use it. There was a new digital clock, but the old Roman-numeraled one still worked.

To verify that this would've been the station Kim and the old lama used—for there's another station elsewhere in Amballa—I asked a conductor if this was indeed the one the train from Amritsar passed through and how old the station was. "At least one hundred and thirty years old," he told me, after conferring with another railways employee. "May I ask your profession, sir?"

"I'm a musician."

He had wavy gray hair and a charged expression, as if extra voltage were being sent through his eyeballs. I guessed he might be Anglo-Indian in the twentieth-century sense of the term, of mixed blood. (They already outnumbered the British here from the late eighteenth century on.) Traditionally, Anglo-Indians have had a virtual monopoly on any job of responsibility in the Indian Railways.

"Are you a composer, perhaps, sir?"

"More an instrumentalist."

"Aha! A performer. And what is better in life, sir, than to perform? To free the huddled masses from the daily grind of their rigmarole? To let the soul take flight on the thoughts of great men?"

"Nothing."

"Nothing better indeed! I should have you know, sir, that I too am a great admirer of the performing arts. Particularly the theater. *Hamlet. Macbeth.* An ardent amateur, dare I say it. You are familiar with those plays, I believe, sir?"

"I am indeed." It felt natural to adopt his locutions.

He waved his arms. "*Richard the Third. Julius Caesar.* Do you know, sir, I have committed all those great speeches to memory? 'O noble Caesar, why dost thou lie so low—' And do you imagine, sir, that such art of true performance is appreciated in this country? I tell you it is not! 'Friends, countrymen, Romans, lend me your ears!' Of course not! O India, why dost thou lie so low?"

I had never before seen anyone actually foaming at the mouth. I excused myself and hurried up the platform. A sign had the train hours posted, the names straight out of Kipling: the Flying Mail, the Shalimar Express, the Frontier Mail, the Kalka Mail, the Himalayan Queen. Nor has the overcrowding changed since his day. By my calculations you can seat eighty uncomfortably within a train car with almost no ventilation, and a good fifty on top of the railroad car with maximum ventilation.

I crossed the Grand Trunk from the railway station to have a look around Amballa Cantonment; I had to keep reminding myself what an important hub this used to be. Just down a lane stood the small Hotel Savoy, by what had once been a large British garden.

Nearby was a cluster of low buildings, dignified but weary, from colonial times.

So 'ark an' 'eed, you rookies, which is always grumblin' sore,
There's worser things than marchin' from Umballa to Cawnpore...

The British style of stone arches has worn well, for even run-down buildings have a faded beauty. I have always liked the sense of order these buildings propose throughout the tropics, in hot countries where the natural bent is for chaos or lassitude. I like their proportion to the local fauna, the sense of space from one to the next, their sociable echoes of each other. In India I realized I liked them most in decay.

Ho! get away, you bullock-man, you've 'eard the bugle blowed,
There's a regiment a-comin' down the Grand Trunk Road...

Across the lane, in pale yellow arches, stood the library. The Reading Room was somewhat bare but full of people reading newspapers from all over India; you can't help but think what a benevolent institution the library is, a magic carpet with room for all, when you find one in a dusty place like this.

The British had brought the modern world to India and yanked India into the modern world. Neither the Moguls nor the maharajahs would have. That the British had been well compensated for their trouble did not lessen their achievement: "the life of empire like the life of the mind." Would domination by another imperial power (the Russians? the French? the Portuguese?) have been more fruitful for India, have produced better results and been kinder, or less unkind? Perhaps it was not a professional historian's question, but I wondered. It seemed now—at century's end, and the vicious twilight of the colonial day—rather unlikely.

Wandering in the Cantonment proper, on Alexandra Road I

found St. Paul's Church. One rusted metal door of the tall gate was open, the sign still in place, but the immense Anglican cathedral ("the finest church in India"—*Murray's Guide*, 1898) had been destroyed, struck directly in the Indo-Pakistan War of 1965. For someone like myself who has never gone through a war, it is a shock to see a huge nineteenth-century cathedral in ruins, overgrown with thirty years of weeds.

"It is where a bomb blast hit," said a rickshaw driver, watching me from the road. He spoke with such gravity that it made me think the ruined church's first significance for the locals was as a memento of war. Perhaps it was best to leave it the way it was.

We drove past mostly rice and corn fields; soon wheat would be planted in the same fields for an April harvest. What the trucks carry south from the Punjab—rice, wheat, corn, potatoes—depends on the time of year.

SAFE DRIVING IS A PLEASURE!

Mysteriously, most warning and inspirational signs along the road are in English, which an extremely high proportion of drivers don't read. It can't be to reassure tourists, since there aren't any. Nor are there speed traps or controls; the road itself dictates the rules, from moment to moment. The GT may be a paved law laid down with irregular justice, but it is defied at great peril.

An overturned truck had spilled apples and painted crates from further north all over the road—the chaotic fruit of separatist Kashmir rolling deliciously all across India.

The Kingfisher Motel was the last bastion of Haryana Tourism before the Punjab border. The place was nearly full, with a convention of bull-and-cow fertility experts. But this Haryana Tourism motel was not nearly as inviting as the one I'd passed at Karnal. The health club had been converted into someone's office, perhaps never having been a gymnasium; signs in India are often only for show. The gift shop was doing a brisk business in watches and kitsch porcelain. On the pleasant lawn fronting the GT were swing sets for children. The pool was large, the water a little suspect.

Next morning I ordered tea and toast.

The waiter brought tea only. I asked about the toast.

"Sorry, sir. No more bread."

"No more bread?"

He paused, savoring the phrase.

"Out-of-stock."

Jagatjit Singh, the Maharaja of Kapurthala, weighed 19 stones at the age of 19 . . . the ministers of the Court always employed trained beautiful young women from the professional dancing class to train the Maharajas in the art of love and sex so that they joyfully live sex life with the Maharanis and the concubines . . . . In spite of all the efforts of experienced dancing girls, it was rather impossible for the Maharaja to have sex relationship due to his excessive fatness and heavy weight . . . professional women were brought from Lahore, the centre of fun and frolic, and from Lucknow, the centre of Muslim culture and art, but they also failed to achieve the object. Ultimately it struck an experienced middle-aged woman that . . . due to excessive fatness . . . the pose adopted by elephants could be tried.

—Diwan Jarmani Dass, *Maharaja* (1969)

16.

The Maharajah and the Wedding

Lucky was devoted to his gray-green Ambassador, with its large luggage rack on top. Against all technical reports to the contrary he insisted it was an excellent car, better than the new Novas, with a stronger iron body and a more reliable transmission. He'd taped Day-Glo playing-card images of serene, bearded, and turbanned Sikh gurus to the dashboard, like wise Father Christmases with swords.

With the Ambassadors it is easy to forget that it is their shape and style which is over forty years old, not the car itself. I let drop to Lucky that it was amazing how such an antique could look so spiffy under these driving conditions. I assumed the car was nearly as old as he, but kept up lovingly by his father through decades of hard use.

"Sir," said Lucky with disbelief. "It's three years old, only."

• • •

We came to another Mogul rest house, this one complete and of a staggering size and magnificence. Shambhu Serai lay in green fields, and it was built in ruddy brick around a square courtyard, now a garden, of four acres, and with some ninety rooms, each with a tulip entry. There were domes on the corners and on a two-story mosque in the courtyard. The serai presented the arrogance of a fortress, with battlements twenty feet high crowned with watch-holes. It must've been gossipy when there were plenty of guests and animals and goods everywhere.

The serai was so well preserved I assumed it was from late Mogul times. The idea of rest houses along the GT went back to Ashoka's era, the third century B.C.; his empire had been better run than the Mogul, under a strict civic administration rather than bureaucratic soldiers. The Mogul serais were an inheritance of Sher Shah's extensive hotel chain (seventeen hundred after only five years in power). The Moguls built them even bigger—one serai in Agra could sleep over two thousand travelers and stable five hundred horses. From Sher Shah the Moguls had also inherited a hotel policy: separate areas for Hindus and Muslims, married slaves on permanent staff who functioned as personal servants during a guest's stay, and free provisions according to one's social rank.

Until twenty-five years ago the nearby villagers had been using this huge serai as their actual village and school. Now it was empty, and government workmen were overseeing it. Their small dog trailed me, ceaselessly yipping.

The GT was again lined with flowering eucalyptus trees. The prosperity here was evident. Almost no one walked, there were more private cars than I'd seen outside of cities, more tractors than motor-rickshaws, and more motorcycles and Vespas.

The fields were vast, stretching horizonward with trees marking only a few farmhouses or villages. This was still the most disputatious part of the GT, and always the part most trodden on by invaders over the centuries. Its villagers had lived in terror for more than ten years; only recently, since my last visit, had the state of internal siege been lifted.

At the border crossing for the Punjab, the customs area still in Haryana was a few rude tents and brick bunkers, and dozens of southbound trucks were backed up, blocking the road. By contrast, the Punjab side was the most professional customs post I'd seen, running smoothly with a modern weigh station and rest stop.

Sirhind has a double significance for Sikh truckers. It's the site of one of their holiest temples, and a center for "body builders," the small factories which make truck and bus bodies. A frequent sight around here was a Tata chassis coming down the road, awaiting its new cargo-carrier body like a turtle denuded of its shell.

Lucky already knew the way to the Fatehgarh Sahib Temple, one of the holiest Sikh sites after the Golden Temple in Amritsar. Dedicated to the tenth and final Sikh guru, it was built around a white marble flagstoned piazza-platform. The temple had four white corner domes and a central golden one. Sikh temples are always extremely white, a strong color in a country where nearly everything is either dirty or colorful.

Within was a white marble kiosk and a smaller golden kiosk within that. Silver vessels with flowers, a white–bearded priest; faithful men and women kneeling, praying, strolling around the chamber to the music of two keyboardists and a drummer. Only one sang, broadcast loudly all over the very large temple complex.

Narrow steps took us underground. People brought offerings to a smaller chamber with another golden kiosk, an inner sanctum where the two children of the tenth guru had been walled-in to their deaths for refusing to convert to Islam. A convincing stretch of old wall remained. The priest, an old man in a blue turban, held the Sikh holy book, the Granth, and a whisk to keep flies off. He read aloud and swatted at non-existent insects in the cool underground chamber.

According to Lucky it took three days to read the entire book. "If you start now," he said with a smile of pride, "you finish the day after tomorrow."

Sikhism began here in the Punjab around the turn of the sixteenth century as a one-man reform movement led by the first Sikh guru, Nanak. Rather like Martin Luther a few years later, he was trying to declare a path to God as ultimately available to any man and free from religious cant. Nanak's quest was originally a democratic attempt to bridge Hinduism and Islam and eliminate the caste system and idol worship.

It was a doctrine founded on service to the community and the idea that any man could, through daily meditation and prayer and real action, have a personal relation with God. Though the Sikh God is single, abstract, and unknowable, every Sikh feels he can talk on a daily basis with him. And though apparently a highly masculine religion in its tone and trappings, Sikhism holds women as equally important in the temple structure. One reason Sikhs are bigger than everyone else, it's said, is that by breaking down a lot of the taboos against diet, Sikhs ate meat and just got brawnier.

The religion also made them extremely confident. As Khushwant Singh, the journalist, historian, and novelist, puts it, to a Sikh, "There are no saints, no priests, no prophets to intercede for us.... Any ragtag, betel-chewing, fornicating bumpkin off the farm can meditate and talk to God.... If we are good enough to talk to God, if we have the notion or conceit that he actually cares about our views, our wishes, then why on earth should we cringe before any mortal?" They also all carry tangible reminders of their faith. Every man is required to follow the five disciplines of uncut hair, to carry a comb and a sword (a dagger will do), sport a steel bracelet on the right wrist, and wear what a brave man might call undershorts but what a Sikh thinks of as warrior-style breeches.

Sikhism may have begun as a bridge, but historically it quite rapidly became the sea wall against the ever-rising Muslim tide—and when I got to Pakistan I would see how deep the anti-Sikh feeling still ran in Muslims. Most Sikhs were in fact Hindus who had converted, beginning in the Mogul era, and because of this, certain aspects of the Sikh personality (no smoking allowed, but lots of drinking encouraged) arose as efforts to separate themselves from the Hindus.

As the Moguls collapsed, a brief Sikh empire was established in northwestern India under the one-eyed Ranjit Singh for the first four decades of the nineteenth century. After Ranjit's death the Sikhs could not hold out against the British and soon decided they liked being part of the Raj army. In any case, it gave them an enjoyable opportunity to fight old enemies like Afghans and Kashmiris.

Their strongly unified identity far outweighs the fact that they make up only 2 percent of the Indian population, perhaps around 20 million. Most Sikhs live in the Punjab and are further united by the Punjabi language. Strong military traditions go back to pre-British times and have made them ornery, proud, gregarious, literate, and independent-minded. About half of India's army officers and Olympic athletes are Sikh, and Sikhs like to tell jokes about what big dumb animals Sikhs are then go on to boast that any one of them is equal to 125,000 of anyone else. It makes perfect sense that a lot of the Grand Trunk Road's truckers—and plenty of New York taxi drivers—are Sikh.

While Sikh men share that lion surname (though not all men named Singh are Sikhs), most Sikh women are surnamed Kaur, meaning princess. Men are required never to cut their hair—thus the beard and turban—but anti-Sikh attacks following the assassination of Indira led many of them to go turbanless and beardless, to make themselves less of a target. Once in the habit, some stayed with it.

• • •

The trappings of the religion are much more sober than those of Hinduism—though without the keep-out-of-this-holiest-temple mentality—and virtually uncommercialized, though these people certainly mean business. To enter this temple I'd had to cover my head with a shiny cloth, and remove my shoes. On the way out Lucky reverently touched a tall marble pillar wrapped in orange cloth.

A small wizened man in blue wearing a large, curved silver sword was just coming in.

Due to this centuries–old murder of the tenth guru's children, the Sikhs have a long-standing grudge against Sirhind. Traditionally every Sikh was supposed to carry away a brick or two of the town when passing through, to eventually erase the place from the earth; these people think in long temporal terms. There were certainly many Sikhs in town, and their temple was kept at a glorious blinding whiteness, like a mountain of snow rising from a sandlot.

Sirhind these days could, I thought, be counted a full Sikh victory, for the new town, utterly without charm, had totally obliterated the old.

Khanna was a dust-bowl of steel mills, makeshift foundries, and stopped trucks. Outside the hammer-and-tongs town the road ran pleasantly past unremitting wheatfields being harvested, a few old villages, and an occasional gleaming white Sikh temple. These often had a clock with Roman numerals on high, giving the curious effect of a church steeple. The Sikhs always have their eye on the clock, for they believe that the entire world will convert soon, in ten years or so, to Sikhism.

Ludhiana, famous for "hosieries manufacturing," was a crowded industrial city, of smoking mills, overpasses, factories, and auto showrooms. It stank worse than anywhere else in India—a big statement—from burning tires and all those mills. According to posters, that evening there would be an international hockey match at the stadium: Kenya versus Punjab. I spotted a kos minar stalwart among the tool-parts shops: a relic of the age of emperors on horseback, stranded in the age of punctured tires and broken axles.

Outside Ludhiana thick forests edged the GT, and a sign showing claws and a snarl promised a

TIGER SAFARI UNDER CONSTRUCTION

Meaning they'd bring two poor striped beasts up from South India.

The Ambassador was finally, after about a thousand miles, almost alone on the road. The middle lane of green was so tall it obscured the parallel road flowing in the other direction.

We crossed a long bridge over the sand-banked Sutlej River, the opposite side manned by police in khaki uniforms, with rifles. This was the first of the five waterways that gave the region (and since independence, the state) its name, for Punjab means "Five Rivers" (just as *punch* refers to its original five ingredents: water, lime juice, spices, sugar, and arrack, a local liquor). Three of the Punjab's rivers are now in Pakistan; all drain into the Indus.

Sikhs are by nature responsible, civic-minded people—until they go to battle. In Gorada their Lions Club, full of Singhs, had put up a bus stop and the Rotary Club had contributed a policeman's traffic pedestal. The town was all ball bearings, electric, and iron works. The dhabas were few and far between, though I guessed there were more than on my last visit here, five years earlier. In those days, during the Sikh wars of the 1980s and early '90s, with thousands murdered annually, absolutely no one had wanted to sleep by the roadside in the Punjab at night, even on the GT. Now the scarcity of dhabas was only because we were nearing a conclusion to the Indian road. We weren't far from Amritsar, and soon after that city the country ended. No Indian trucks were allowed up the Grand Trunk Road into Pakistan.

The British cantonments ("cantoonments") were always well-organized, self-sufficent, and private. They were the military half of each settlement of British India, that went with the so-called Civil Lines. Together they made up a complete dreamsville: a grid of broad avenues, uniform buildings, open greens, private clubs, bungalows, and shade trees, miles upwind and well separated by a road from the local town they controlled—that assault of native exoticism, disease, temptations, and confusion. In Jullundur the old cantonment, its main street as usual called the Mall, was now off-limits to civilian traffic, unlike cantonments most everywhere else. Here the GT curved around the sprawling city, which was gargantuan and out of control.

Oddly enough, the writer Lawrence Durrell (1912-90) was born and lived his first year in Jullundur. His father was an engineer on the Indian railways for about fifteen years and later founded his own company, which built the huge Tata Iron and Steel complex in Jamshedpur. Durrell's parents had married in India and Jullundur was the first place they lived as a couple. The family eventually ended up in Darjeeling, the hill station on the lower slopes of the Himalayas where Durrell had his early schooling. I'd heard that one of those cantonment houses near the railway station here might have been his family's, but had he lived in Jullundur long enough to recognize it, I still doubt he would've recognized it now.

A mile before Kartapur we turned off the GT for two hundred meters to visit cousins of Lucky's. My hiring him had been fortuitous for both of us, because his relatives were preparing for a wedding the next morning, and this way there'd be someone there from the Delhi arm of the family. He'd told me he'd been at school in Kartapur, years earlier, and often visited his maternal uncle and family here.

The village of Kalma was perhaps a thousand people and a hundred fifty houses. Most were brick; a few were new and concrete, a few weathered with old doors. Most houses had TVs—antennae sprouted everywhere—and some also had refrigerators and "air coolers." The village lay on the edge of big fields of wheat, rice, and corn. The village was entirely Sikh; to protect themselves elsewhere, many men had cut their hair short but still wore their turbans at home. This district had avoided the bloodshed of the Amritsar District, but even around Kartapur, until a couple of years ago no one moved around at night who didn't have to.

The cousins' house was two adjoining buildings, both small. Lucky ushered me into a room with high rope daybeds on wooden posts and a tall studded chest, a wedding gift handed down through the family for a century. A fan had been plugged in for the guests' comfort, its raw wires pushed alarmingly right into the wall socket.

About twenty fanciful pictures of the ten Sikh gurus hung on the walls. Copper and tin vessels were arrayed on a high shelf. The walls were painted a cooling blue; unframed family pictures, some faded and decades old, were taped to them.

Tea was brought in by Auntie, the young wife of Lucky's maternal uncle. Auntie was accompanied by two little girls, both cousins. They were taking care of a baby, with familiar roughness.

Auntie and Uncle spent time apart, as he had his own family house up north. He would be here the next day for the wedding.

The old lady who followed the girls in was not in fact Lucky's grandmother, though he called her that. He treated her with great affection and greeted her with a low respectful bow, hanging his right arm lengthwise against her. The old lady told us about the wooden chest, a marriage gift to her from her parents. Her body was slack but full, undisguised in billowing lavender robes.

I had a conversation, translated via Lucky, with a stocky, resigned, smiling man in his thirties, his hair black and cut short like Lucky's. In Kartapur he'd been a successful sweets-shop chef for three years. Married to Auntie's sister, he was trying to get to Canada to cook in an Indian restaurant. He told a labyrinthine saga of trying to find his way through Canadian immigration procedures. My impression was that they were scamming him without his realizing it (he remained only enthusiastic about his chances) for the hard currency it cost every time they made him reapply. He was using up his annual savings with each application, and the Canadians were too self-serving to explain that no, he would never be allowed in and should give up.

He had no illusions about the costs of living abroad; he knew that financially he wouldn't come out particularly ahead. Why did he want to leave? I wondered.

"Because of the troubles," he said. "The troubles began in 'eighty-four. For nearly ten years the government wasn't able to put a lid on the troubles, they only got bigger. And who knows? Maybe they'll come back one day."

Not too far away there was a maharajah's château—apparently the literal reproduction of a French château—that I didn't want to miss. So from Kartapur we turned down the empty road nine miles for Kapurthala, past railway tracks with abandoned antique train carriages and venerable trees.

The maharajahs are a pre-Independence institution that still limps on. When the British arrived they found 560-odd princely families that had managed to maintain independent states by cutting deals with or fighting off the Moguls; all told, they controlled about 40 percent of the subcontinent. As Mogul power dwindled and the maharajahs' power in their private states solidified, and India became British, the princely states were still allowed to be independent, and many bargains were struck. Some states were as large as Kansas or England or half the size of France; others were downright tiny. Most of the maharajahs, whether Muslim, Hindu, or Sikh, were absurdly rich, in cash, jewels, elephants, wives, tiger rugs, eccentricities, personal staffs that often numbered in the thousands, private regiments if not armies, harems, polo ponies, Daimlers and Rolls-Royces.

They managed to weather the 1947 storm of Independence well. Part of the arrangement was that they were allowed to keep their titles, their houses, and at least some portion of their land—meager by their standards, lavish by anyone else's. They lost their political role but in return were guaranteed annual government stipends ranging from a few dollars a year to hundreds and hundreds of thousands, depending on their property. They also remained exempt from petty annoyances like taxes and customs duties and gun licenses. They no longer, however, were allowed to whimsically put their (former) subjects to death.

In 1971 Mrs. Gandhi did away with most of these privileges and there are now only a few of the big spenders left. If everyone looks the other way while they still call themselves the maharajah of this or that, if many of their palaces have now become expensive hotels or 1,500-room government buildings, if their "privy purses" have all been eliminated, they occupy a quaint role as a reminder of the pre-democratic past. It is still easy to find villagers who speak of them loyally and fondly, repeating stories of some favor done for their grandparents. They will kiss their maharajah's feet if he lets them and cry out that things were better, less corrupt, in the old days, and at least you knew where you were....

Kapurthala was formerly one of the most famous princely states, about half the size of Rhode Island; these days there was a large army cantonment near the château. Tents were everywhere, and military buildings commanded both sides of the road. The large gate to the château grounds lay at the end, as if the road all the way from Kartapur were nothing but a nine-mile driveway. But there was also a real town edging it, and cross streets, and a tall church that now bore the sign: JAGATJIT CLUB—MEMBERS ONLY.

Jagatjit Singh was the enthusiastic maharajah who'd built the château around the turn of the century. Descended from brave

Rajput princes and even from the moon herself, he had (it was said) been grand in all things. At age nineteen he weighed nearly three hundred pounds; the days were far off when he would wander the great hotels of Biarritz and the gardens of his Paris villa in the Bois de Boulogne, a svelte and dashing figure with an intense seducer's gaze. His early copulatory problems solved by the construction of a tilting steel bed with silken ropes (which earned his chief engineer a stipend for life), Jagatjit was shipped off to Europe for the rest of his honeymoon. He owned the biggest topaz in the world, the best emeralds in India, and a turban built out of three thousand diamonds and pearls; he occasionally cheated at tennis. He enjoyed Spanish dancers, and married one who later left him for one of his sons by another wife. According to the memoir of his chief minister, the brightest light of his harem was "the beautiful blond Miss Stella Mudge, an Englishwoman he'd met while she was playing the piano in a cabaret show." Like the Buddhists, the Jains, and the Sikhs, the maharajahs found their own idiom for liberating themselves from the caste system.

The sturdy gate to the maharajah's château indicated it had for some time been turned into a school. The château was set way back on the grounds, hidden by trees; I got only the hint of a grand roof. A sign said: VISITING HOURS WEDNESDAY AND SATURDAY, 10–12.

The guard dog at the gate refused my request for a brief look and my pleas for him to telephone the school officer. I had no choice but to come back the next morning.

A day in the life of a Sikh wedding, which is always held in the bride's village.

At eight-forty A.M. the groom and his family, due to arrive from their village, weren't in Kalma yet. Heavy storm clouds were threatening rain, the brooding forehead of the monsoon. A white mutt on a rooftop was barking at all the human commotion. It was an arranged marriage, set up six months earlier; the bride and groom had never met.

A tall Sikh in blue said to me in one breath, "How do you do? Quite well, thank you," and repeated both remarks as he walked on.

Men were sitting idly beneath a big tree, not for the wedding, but due to the weather. "There's water everywhere when it rains, so they won't be able to work in the fields today," said Lucky. "They might as well be near home."

A dapper gray-haired man in fine tie, rings, and wristwatch, the uncle of the bride, was here from the U.K. He'd brought his Indian wife and British-raised son and daughter for two weeks' holiday in this, his home village.

His full name was Karnail Sarbjit Kahlon Singh, of a London suburb near Heathrow. He'd worked many years for ICI, the industrial chemicals company. He was acting as father of the bride since the real father, his brother, had died a few years ago. The bride's mother was still alive, sequestered with her somewhere.

Karnail had been back to the village only once in sixteen years, until a few months earlier when he'd come to arrange the marriage. He had the urbane aura that simply living in another country provides, a gentle sheen of ease, wealth, and knowing.

High winds in the village, at nine o'clock.

The plan was that once the groom and his entourage arrived, the two families would meet for about thirty minutes, then the ceremony would take place in a small new Sikh temple. Her family would provide presents and furniture for the house. His family would provide bracelets and gold jewelry for her.

The two newlyweds would live in his village, five kilometers away. His family were farmers, like most families around here.

Lucky's mother's brother—whom he referred to simply as Uncle—was of the same generation as Karnail, but staying here had made him more of a swashbuckler. He was a hefty man with jet black hair, a good-time guy whose house was a natural gathering place and who, by being away regularly, was one whose company would always seem a bit of a party.

I asked him what he thought of the groom's family, due at eight. By nine-twenty there was still no sign of them.

He said, in a cheerful man-to-man way, "I think it's a good idea to make a woman wait a little. But not *too* long—"

The wedding would clearly be awhile getting underway, so we decided to slip off and try our chances with the maharajah's château again. As we turned off the dirt road from Kalma onto the GT, we spied the groom's car parked by the wayside, waiting for other relatives to show up. The groom, whose hair might've been cut that morning, looked appropriately traumatized.

At the maharajah's gate the same Cerberus of a guard was on duty. It wasn't enough that we were there on the right day and at the right time; he still couldn't let us in without permission from the headmaster's office. Could we telephone the office? Why, no. He didn't have a telephone in his guardhouse, nor would he leave his post to go ask permission on our behalf. Could he give us the phone number? Well, he supposed he could do that.

No, he didn't know where the nearest phone was.

The number he gave us, after much driving around searching for a public phone, turned out to be incorrect. Eventually we got through and were given permission for a brief visit.

Of course the entire routine had been a charade. We went back to Cerberus, who simply took us on our word that we had permission from the headmaster's office to visit. He made us take a slip of paper (after noting our names and passport particulars in a ledger along with the license plate of the Ambassador) to be initialed by the office and returned to him on our departure.

This school had been built as a "French Renaissance" château, a small, sub-Himalayan fantasy version of Versailles, by Jagatjit from 1900 to 1908. Thirteen years after the maharajah's death the

Sainik School, as it was known, had opened here in 1961. There was some connection to the military, and it was perhaps no coincidence that Jagatjit's grandson had become an army colonel.

The château was in pale sandstone with white sculptured nymphs everywhere, a preposterous and lovely building that made me think of those millionaires who have an Indian palace transported stone by stone to a Caribbean island. It was parents' day, mothers and fathers formally visiting their children on the château grounds, and all those nymphs lent an absurd air to the proceedings.

This was a government-aided school, mainly Punjabi boys and girls, all boarding students, from the 6th to the 11th forms. Life was marked out in little divisions for the young: on one side a post office, computer cell, audio-visual department, electric store, text bookstore. It was impossible to look at the fountains, the erotic statuary, the subsidiary buildings used famously by the maharajah for uproarious escapades, and not wonder what the little boys and girls in navy blue and white uniforms wondered.

The entry from outside was a marble staircase with two lifesize wooden horses on either side, wearing leather saddles. A painting of a female nude hung near a tall, gold-framed mirror. It had the air of a place that'd been efficiently if selectively stripped, yet it was easy to imagine it (as one Viceroy's wife noted) as "one mass of gold with nymphs disporting themselves on vaulted ceilings and innumerable Sèvres ornaments and vases."

I got my permissions slip vetted upstairs by the assistant headmaster, who also—Land of Coincidences—happened to be the headmaster's son. I was allowed to look around for *only* a few minutes, he said, but *not* allowed to go into any classrooms. It reassured me to see that the vanity and constant self-flattery of many second-rate British boarding schools have been so successfully exported to India.

Some rooms were grandiose, with screens and paintings and vases left over from the maharajah. Other rooms were utterly bare and the paint close to peeling. Downstairs the grand ballroom was now the school library, with a great chandelier, a gigantic stained-glass ceiling, and a carved balcony intact. Mirrors sent the lavish room back at itself, ornament on ornament; every inch was covered in floral moldings and hung with paintings of maharajahs. The floor was inlaid with the motto *Pro Rege et Patria,* and there was a big model of a battleship named, rather surprisingly, H.M.S. *Queen Elizabeth*. The card catalogue and the long table for students to read at seemed out of place, but I was most surprised at how ornately Indian the room was inside the French mise-en-scène.

A framed sign on the veranda:

GENIUS IS NOTHING BUT A GREAT APTITUDE FOR PATIANCE.

The wedding finally got going around eleven forty-five.

In the small Sikh temple, the women in green and saffron long dresses and veils sat on the left, the men in yellow and orange turbans on the right. The place was packed. The priest kept flicking flies away from the sacred book. He sat behind a stepped altar on which a little blue ceremonial canopied bed was raised; around the altar were fringed and embroidered cloths. Its steps were draped in a white sheet, on which lay some money, several copper goblets, and five rusted straight swords. The wedding was being captured on video by professional cameramen.

The bride, nineteen, wore crimson and gold trousers and gold high heels. She was small, wobbly, even more unsteady and nervous than the groom. Her face was hidden by a veil of gold and silver tinsel; many-colored bangles and decorations dangled from her legs. Beneath the veil a gold chain was strung from one earring to a gold bead in her nose. Her hands were hennaed in stripes, and she wore gold rings on all her fingers.

The groom, twenty-two and very shaky, wore a peach pink turban. The two looked straight ahead, not at each other; and it was right that everyone referred to them as "the girl and boy."

The bride's family picked their way through the throng seated on the floor and presented the groom with a winking gold ring on his finger and a gold necklace around his neck. Still he stared resolutely and ritually ahead. He looked more nervous than ever. It was noon and very, very hot in that temple.

"He is thinking about what he will say to her," said Lucky beside me, sotto voce. "When they go back to his house. Maybe he's so nervous because he isn't sure what to say to her."

It amused him, for there was no special young lady in his life. He'd told me he doubted his father would press an arranged marriage on him—that odd idea of meeting the person who'll probably become your best friend for life by the act of marrying them.

One by one men got up and filed behind the couple to offer a gift. I dropped a hundred rupees in the groom's lap. Photos were taken of each well-wisher with the happy newlyweds, so somewhere there is a photo of Lucky and me peering over the groom's shoulder.

The men filed out of the temple first, then the women. Right away a band of five men standing outside—trombone, trumpets, and drums—started playing a sort of loose Indian mariachi. Then the music became surprisingly bluesy (full of flatted 3rds, 5ths, 7ths) and resembled early jazz—the Punjab meets New Orleans.

In a relaxed gesture of accomplishment, the groom removed his turban. His hair was cut short, and he ran both hands through it.

It started to rain; everyone looked up. Just a few drops. Then, very considerately, it held back.

After the ceremony several of us sat in the uncle's house drinking Guru Beer (made in Lucknow, and accurately marked FOR SALE IN PUNJAB ONLY—SUPER STRONG) and Binnie's Fine Whisky, also available here only. When music started up again outside, we went back to the girl's family's house for sweets and food. We agreed that the stars had been indeed propitious for the marriage and, as a result, for the party. In an inner room, intense lights kept flashing; the women were being photographed.

Outside the house where all the photos were being taken and more food was being laid out, I asked the British-emigrated aunt of the bride, "Is she nervous?"

"She will be." The aunt giggled.

"Is she happy?"

"She will be! The boy and girl saw each other for the first time only today. The girl will be happy because she is brought up to accept, you know. This afternoon they go to his family's house. Tomorrow she comes back to her family's house for a few hours. Then she goes back to his house. Then perhaps she comes back next week for a week or so, by herself. In this way she becomes accustomed. But she will be happy."

I told myself that for them there must be enormous eroticism in this situation, beyond the evident strangeness and trauma.

The sky was starting to drip again.

Finally, on a rooftop, the newlyweds were photographed together. They looked like what they were: two strangers forced next to each other. When they were shot with her now seated, him on the arm of the chair—a somewhat loutish, scowling guy—it was the photographer who had to arrange his arm around her shoulders. She looked down demurely, patiently, eyes darting anxiously, not sure where to look. Aside from her family, this was probably the first man's arm she'd ever felt around her.

It began to really rain, but everyone still crowded around on the rooftop. Only when he sat, and she could stand behind him, her knuckles on his shoulders, did they both seem more relaxed. In the community of rain, of getting wet, they both genuinely smiled. At last they had shared and survived something together besides the wedding, something that was not memorized ritual, but their own private invented behavior as a couple—the photographic ordeal.

I asked the wife from the U. K. how her kids were faring, staying in this Punjab village. The boy had a high fever; the girl, about fifteen, seemed to enjoy being the most chic and worldly girl here. "But my children missed fish and chips so much I took them to one of the big hotels in Jullundur. Just to have a proper meal!"

We left as the storm began driving down in gusts, the monsoon sweeping across the Punjab. It was a spectacle to see how life carried on in a torrential rain through which people still walked, or trudged pushing their bicycles, or repaired their trucks in, or drove conservatively through. The air was made of water, and no one moved who didn't have to. The shop-stalls were mostly shut, and the roofs of buses bare. We passed a colony of tent dwellers, in humped mushrooms of plastic and canvas sheets lashed down; they had a terrible season ahead of them.

A transformer suddenly blew in a shop, exploding smoke up into the rain.

We passed, in the downpour, a public bus with no windscreen or windows and a half-munched front end.

When the rain finally stopped, the road looked newly ironed, steaming, with little traffic. After Kartapur the Grand Trunk was the gentlest I'd ever seen it. As in *Kim*: "By this time the sun was driving broad golden spokes through the lower branches of the mango trees; the parakeets and doves were coming home in their hundreds."

A blue-turbanned man chiding his bullocks on was passed by a tractor piled with Sikhs. Steady colonnades of trees, the late afternoon light making them fresh again after a wearying day.

This was why I'd spent the last days roaming the Punjab, wondering why I was there and taking a note now and then in those dusty truck-stop towns. To end up invited to that quiet village and a wedding of strangers who knew each other about as well as they knew me. To remain forever as a white phantom in their photos, the American in the sweat-soaked shirt whom cousin Lucky had invited and they'd made welcome.

It seemed an awfully long time I had been on this road. Even though I couldn't say what I'd learned, couldn't feel in my bones what all the different kinds of belief and desperation I'd seen added up to, still, to stand outside in afternoon heat waiting for the monsoon to come and hearing those men in the village band blaring out their music, improvising their way together through a kind of Indian ragtime while a dog howled back at them—for me that was enough to be happy.

We're marchin' on relief over Injia's coral strand,
Eight 'undred fightin' Englishmen, the Colonel, and the Band;
Ho! get away, you bullock-man, you've 'eard the bugle blowed,
There's a regiment a-comin' down the Grand Trunk Road;
With its best foot first
And the road a-sliding past,
An' every bloomin' campin'-ground exactly like the last...

— Rudyard Kipling, *Route-Marchin'* (1892)

17.

The Golden Temple

After eleven hundred miles of the road it struck me that the most essential part of Lucky's Ambassador was the staccato horn. If that broke on the GT and couldn't be immediately replaced, then better to give up the car and shoot it like a crippled horse.

SPEED THRILLS BUT KILLS

The land continued to green with corn, potato, and wheat fields. The Grand Trunk was here an anonymous country road. Except for the many turbans, it could've been Iowa.

There was little drama to a brief bridge over the narrow Beas River, but this marked the beginning of Alexander the Great country. The river was as far east as he'd managed to penetrate. From here on the Grand Trunk Road was mostly the route he'd followed on his last momentous expedition. After winning his way across Turkey and Persia with a series of arduous victories in 325 B.C., his soldiers were disheartened after battling across the other four rivers of the Punjab. They yearned for home; he wanted characteristically to press on.

To avert a mutiny, Alexander turned back at the Beas without ever crossing the river, and led his men down the Indus to his eventual death on the way home two years later in Babylon. It must've been right around here that he made that decision. Apart from a few Buddhas in togas two hundred miles to the west, the Greek invasion had made little impact on Indian culture. Still, for the next dozen centuries, nearly every blue-eyed Indian was a descendant of Alexander the Great's men.

The books are filled with names of kings.
Was it kings who hauled the craggy blocks of stone?...
Young Alexander conquered India.
He alone?

At 4:15 the light was already weaker under a cloudy sky. There were now virtually no dhabas, only a few khakied and turbanned Punjab Police standing about, fully armed. A few miles from Amritsar a boy stood by the roadside, playing a little forlornly with a kite.

I had come this way once before, in 1991, during one of the worst periods of the troubles. The Punjab had already been a stronghold of violence for nearly eight years, and no one would've predicted that would slack off a mere two years later. Now, in 1996, it was difficult for me to reconcile these two Punjabs, to not see the possibility of the earlier violence everywhere.

This part of India is soaked in blood. During Partition in 1947 hundreds of thousands, maybe a million, had died in the Punjab as Muslims tried to cross westward to safety in the Pakistan-to-be and Hindus and Sikhs tried to come eastward into the India-to-be. That had little to do with the recent Sikh troubles, but after many centuries certain regions seem to attract bloodshed, and you wonder if the violence comes out of the earth even as the blood flows into it. This is literally true here, for every group since the earliest settlers of the subcontinent has struggled to own the Punjab.

Physically it resembles the American midwest; socially it is a land of blood feuds; agriculturally it holds great riches that everyone wants to control. Back in 1991, every day the newspapers reported twelve villagers gunned down here, three policemen's relatives kidnapped there, seven militants arrested, two more to stand trial. The murder rate was higher than ever. And after nearly a decade of this, and though no one wanted to use the term, the Punjab was suffering a civil war.

It had begun in earnest back in 1984, when Amritsar underwent an army attack on the Sikhs' holiest site, the Golden Temple, and the violent death of the Sikh militant leader Bhindranwale. His death led to the assassination of then-prime minister Indira Gandhi. Ever since, the people of the Punjab had been caught in a dangerous and unending crossfire between militant groups and the government. Behind much of it, or so the press frequently asserted, was the fantasy of Khalistan, the Land of the Pure—for most Sikhs share the dream of an Indian Punjab remade as an independent Sikh nation.

Amritsar begins unpromisingly with a welter of trucks, and a series of hovels and ruins and unfinished mistakes in brick. Barely four centuries old, it is a large, harried, hard-pressed city. It was still a relief to at last see it as a city to be enjoyed, at peace with itself. "No more dinner by seven or going to bed hungry because you have to be off the streets!" a Sikh shopkeeper exulted to me. I remembered it as a place where shops were already shut for the night at half past four, with soldiers every fifty feet, in bush hats, with rifles slung over their shoulders. In the Punjab khaki is the color of government action.

On that earlier visit I'd been unable to get a room at the Ritz Hotel—on the Mall, just down from St. Paul's Church. Instead I'd stayed around the corner at the Moghun Palace. Grand names, but in those days the city's two modern hotels were worn and tired and the staffs visibly nervous.

I'd left the hotel to walk in what little daylight was left me before darkness fell and it would not be wise to be on the streets. Amritsar had been busy but visibly on edge, and half-stunned. Its streets were narrow and its tone hysterical; everyone was living in a siege state that had become a status quo, with the pressure from both within and without, and unlikely to be relieved anytime soon.

Apart from the Sikhs' Golden Temple, Amritsar would prove a very ugly city, ugly even for India. A Gandhi Gate—twin red castle towers from British times—led to a main shopping street with a semblance of calm because it was one way. A block of concrete bunkers was made up entirely of three- and four-story hotels with names like Hilton and Standard, featuring "Decent Rooms with Air Coolers." There seemed an unusual number of large-scale ads for body-building formulas and visa advice—the Punjab obsessions of power and escape.

Because business was so bad the rickshaw drivers had asked astronomical prices, but I managed to convince one to take me to the Golden Temple and wait to bring me back for a reasonable price. I didn't want to get caught walking here in the dark. He dropped me at an elbow in a congested avenue, among soda pop stalls and shops that sold cassettes of Sikh music alongside cards and posters and anything else on which the Golden Temple could be reproduced.

Outside the wall of what seemed an enormous white palace, I followed a roped-in sidewalk to get to the entry, past a few souvenir sellers and several khakied policemen keeping an eye on people coming in and out, no firearms please.

At a sheltered area you turned in your shoes and received a little tag. If you had no head covering an elderly man beckoned you to turn round and he tied a scarf over your head; there was no charge for any of this. Before the marble entry was a marble basin for washing your hands and feet, and at the entry, a brief pool of running water that you could step across if you were in socks or dip your feet in if you were barefoot. In a country of unending everyday filth, all the Sikh temples, no matter how urban, were impeccable.

Going through a many-domed wide marble entrance, you are suddenly confronted with a shining vision out of dreams: a golden temple glowing in a spacious pool of serenely brimming water, surrounded by an expansive white colonnade of tall arches above luscious tulip gateways. People gently wash their faces and hands in the water, maintaining their dignity—no Hindu gargling and lathering—but still partaking of the holiness; some reverently touch a few old trees, the living things which have grown longest at this spot. Birds sweep across the pool from perches of white to a perch of gold. Turbanned, bearded men, some aged ones wearing swords and daggers, some accompanied by wives and children, walk along a white pier to the small and ornate golden jewel box.

As the heat of the day wanes it becomes more golden in its pool, surrounded by its adoring palace of white columns, arches, and domes. Music echoes loudly and without cease across the reflecting water where fish play—the Golden Temple echoed too, shimmering in the pool which is itself sacred, the nectar of the Sikhs.

It is difficult to exaggerate the Golden Temple's beauty against the supreme ugliness of Amritsar. The first sight of it is glorious and astonishing, to be measured against the first view of the Taj Mahal. It is initially even more impressive because it has not been corrupted as a visual image. To an outsider this seems a religion untarnished by acquisitiveness, and everyone coming to take part looks ennobled by the holy place.

I crossed the white walkway to the small floating temple in the pool. The outside of the Durbar Mindan, which dates from the late eighteenth century, is marble to about ten feet high, with a decor of flowering vines growing from the mouths of dogs and lions, or borne on elephants. Above that it is gilded copper, blazing in the sun, with an arched window on all four sides. The temple's size makes it accessible, an intimate shrine for an extrovert religion. I followed a steady stream of happy visitors inside and climbed narrow stairs up a single story.

Upstairs, the floors were white marble with red and orange star patterns. From this narrow gallery you looked down to the inner chamber through three geometrical arches on each side, as from within a harem. A complex chandelier hung down over the enclosure where about twenty men and women sat near a priest who remained motionless except for the flicking of his large *chaur* to keep flies off the sacred book. Two keyboard players and a drummer played and sang without let-up, broadcasting out over the water their haunting solemn music, eerily and absolutely together.

It is not through thought that He is to be comprehended
Though we strive to grasp Him a hundred thousand times;
Not by outer silence and long deep meditation
Can the inner silence be reached;
Nor is man's hunger for God appeasable
By piling up world-loads of wealth.
All the innumerable devices of worldly wisdom
Leave a man disappointed; not one avails.

How then shall we know the Truth?
How shall we rend the veils of untruth away?
Abide thou by His Will, and make thine own,
His will, O Nanak, that is written in thy heart.

On this upper gallery, beneath arched ceilings of blue and gold, the lower walls are marble, with black, red, and pearl geometries and flowers; the upper walls are engraved with an almost Victorian flower and lion pattern of great intricacy. People sat reading sacred texts or contemplating the music. Fans whirled above, and bird calls tinkled in from across the pool.

At twilight the nine pairs of gold lanterns on the walkway to the temple came on, glimmering in the water. On that first visit five years earlier I had stayed a long time, long after darkness fell, to the anxiety of my waiting rickshaw driver.

I had arranged, on that trip, to meet a very experienced journalist, who I hoped would brief me on the situation. This was Avinash Singh, the Reuters stringer in Amritsar and local correspondent for the *Hindustan Times*. He joined me for a late dinner at the hotel, braving what amounted to a curfew throughout Amritsar—given the choice, few people went out after dark. He bustled into the lobby looking piratical: short, sturdy, turbanned, bearded, with an energy and savvy that I trusted immediately. He was obviously used to explaining the Punjab to outsiders and relished doing so.

He ordered a beer for himself, gave the waiter some commands, and got right to the point. The situation in the Punjab was worse than ever. The murders had climbed steadily to over three hundred a month; it had reached that level only once before. Now, said Avinash, they were back up to more than ten a day—"mostly locals and militants, a few cops."

Even those estimates would prove conservative, for by the end of 1991 the killings for the year would climb to over 4,500. In seven years of violence well over 14,000 had died in the Punjab.

The popular impression was that the Punjab was predominantly Sikh, and that the violence was directed against Hindus; the bloodshed was taken at face value as a separatist war. But the total population figures in the Punjab are 41 percent Hindu, and 42 percent Sikh, the rest varied; there is also still a significant Muslim population. (In the Punjab's cities the population is 60 percent Hindu, in rural areas only about 15 percent.)

According to Avinash, what was generally left unsaid, and the most telling figure of all, was that 85 percent of the deaths were Sikhs. It was outside the public comprehension of the situation that the so-called civil war had become a complex war of Sikh against Sikh.

In the Punjab, a land of individual militias and great wealth, the idea of a Sikh nation had arisen in the 1800s, leading to a series of Anglo-Sikh Wars. Because the Punjab is the granary of India, everyone has always wanted to reap its riches. In the seven years since the death of the militant Bhindranwale, in Mrs. Gandhi's much-criticized army storming of the Golden Temple, much of the Punjab had gone back to private militias and blood feuds. The stakes are always high here: not only feeding the country but holding it together. If the Punjab ever successfully broke off, other parts of the country with deep separatist tendencies, Kashmir first, would undoubtedly follow, and India might conceivably fall to pieces.

I asked Avinash how many of the "militants" were truly politically motivated.

"About 3 percent, maybe 5 percent," he scoffed. "Most of them are simply opportunists. Hoodlums and goons. You have to understand: everyone profits from the situation. The militants steal and kill and extort whatever or whomever they want, and their criminal acts are called political terrorism. The police can pick someone up and hold him silently and illegally for two months, put any criminal acts they want on his head, then when the reward money for his capture has run up high, they shoot him and collect. This happens all the time. The government bureaucrats who should investigate make money on the procedure, also. On the GT, the small-time police stop any truck they want and collect 50, 100, 200 rupees—no driver will object, he might be shot objecting. And the militants, the gangs, do whatever they please."

"So who is the man on the street here worried about most?" I asked.

"It's what, not who. The man on the street in Amritsar is worried about extortion—from militants or from the police. Nowadays, if you want something done, or someone owes you money, you send him a threatening letter and the implication is clear. The villagers are the most victimized. The terrorist gangs come round and ask for money and shelter for the night. If they don't get it, those villagers are killed. It's that simple.

"The profits here of the last twenty years have produced a farmhouse culture that never existed before in the Punjab. Instead of living only in villages, as before, a farming family who are successful may live in an isolated and large house or compound, which is particularly vulnerable to this kind of attack. Lately the police have started going round to villagers disguised as terrorists, asking for help. Anyone who gives in, afraid they might be killed, is arrested and taken in on the spot as accomplices. Then those family members get held for a kind of ransom.

"The police kidnap innocent people just like the militants do. They'll hold young men or even old ladies on suspicion of something or other for a ransom of one or two *lakh* rupees. [A *lakh* is 100,000.] Say, four to eight thousand dollars in a country where some people earn that in ten years. Or they'll bring in one of the militant's many relations to hold for ransom, who doesn't have anything to do with the situation. The result is that many Sikhs have moved away, given the chance. I know of a Sikh man who moved himself and his family to Rajasthan to escape the local troubles. He was an innocent man, but the troubles found him there, and he was murdered.

"You see, the death of Bhindranwale has been used by everyone as an excuse for everything. Frankly, he's proven much more dangerous dead than alive. And Sikhs are very aware of the way the perception of them has changed. Before, if a few women in a train carriage elsewhere in the country saw a couple of Sikhs sitting at one end, they thought: 'Aren't we lucky? They'll guard us if anything happens.' Now they think: 'Oh, no, we've got two militants with us.'"

"This must have a disastrous effect on the Punjab economy."

"The Punjab is not so terribly affected economically. It's affected to the degree that ten years ago a Punjab businessman could buy on credit elsewhere in the country and sell on cash terms. Now no one, say, in Delhi, will sell him any goods on credit. They'll say, 'Why should I sell you goods on credit? You might be dead when it comes time to pay—cash only, please.' For the same reason they're trying to *buy* crops from that man on a credit basis. They might get lucky and not have to pay, if the fellow gets shot. And the Punjabi has to give in, he has no choice.

"I will tell you something. Here in the Punjab we can have three degrees centigrade in the winter and forty-seven degrees centigrade in the summer." He chuckled. "This is a land of temperature extremes—is it any wonder it produces extremists?"

"And what happens if the Punjab explodes?"

Avinash shrugged. "India cannot live without the Punjab. The government must realize this and relax a little. Settle down to dealing with the Punjab only on a law and order basis. Because on a political basis, accusing everyone of political crimes, it gives the militants an excuse to do what they please. You can't imagine how the atmosphere here has changed in the last few years. Amritsar is the only city in the Punjab with any life left, where anyone is out of their house after eight o'clock. This isn't to say that people aren't extremely careful. Anything can happen here."

He'd ordered dinner for both of us, playing the kind host, generous enough to offer a fellow writer insights it would've taken me many months and much luck to come to on my own. Now he smiled wickedly and pushed a plate of curried brains toward me.

"You've hardly touched these brains. You must try some more. You know, like my brains?" He pointed to his head and laughed heartily.

We'd been speaking for two hours. I wondered where Avinash stood in all this—if anyone was caught in the middle by seeing all sides clearly, it was he, and I knew he'd been lucky to live this long. He sat there across from me in his turban and mustache and beard speaking of pointless local butcheries and snapped his fingers when I asked him how easily India might fall apart.

He struck me as a difficult man to offend, so I put to him the accusation that—looking back at the history of the Punjab for the last three centuries—there must be something in the Sikh religion which, though ostensibly peace-loving, in a crisis splinters easily into violence and armed gangs and people taking the law into their own hands.

He looked straight at me and said quietly, "I cannot deny this."

But that had been five years ago, and much had altered. After 1992 had seen more than two thousand dead in the Punjab, the local government had changed and the police, the army, and paramilitary forces had stepped up the pressure. Many of the so-called separatist leaders were slain or captured, and by the end of 1993 things were quieting down. They were now, I was assured, back to normal. The price paid had been a reinforcement of the power and the tough (and sometimes extortionist) tactics of the Punjab police and the army. But this calm was preferable to that tension.

And how different Amritsar looked when not under siege! With a million people and awful or non-existent architecture, it still had little particular charm save the Golden Temple. But it did have enormous hubbub and energy; stores were open until ten and the whole city had a lit-up excitement with an approaching festival. Now I noticed how many shop or company names were echoes of the part of the Punjab lost to Pakistan—Lahore Tailoring,

Peshwaria Market. The Indian TV channels, when not showing decade-old American soap operas or those bikini girls saving lives on a beach, were full of reports on new political upheavals over in Islamabad. India's primary fear (China notwithstanding) is that Pakistan will suddenly go berserk and start lobbing atomic missiles at them.

A mutual fear, naturally.

This time I stayed at the Ritz—MOST UPTODATE HOTEL IN THE CITY OF GOLDEN TEMPLE! as they put it, but that wasn't quite true. It looked about as old as I, and as tired, with airy gardens that were being loudly and aggressively excavated for some doubtless higher purpose. The Tibetan man who carried my bags to the room brought me tea almost constantly for my cough, which had worsened.

Lucky agreed to stick around for another day on me, then head back to Delhi. He'd found a decent place to stay around the corner and was happy to have time to himself in the holy city. My idea was to get him to drive me to the Pakistan border; the less unknowns in that situation, the better.

I had some research to do the next morning, and decided to try the library in the compound of old municipal buildings. These British relics of dirty pale sandstone were as run down as any I'd seen in India. The library was three floors of disorganization. In a dusty, enormous single room, unlit, with a few shadowy reading tables for newspapers, old framed portraits of Nehru and Gandhi hung prominently, listing a little, looking down on jumbled, tattered books. A card catalogue, partly in Hindi, partly in English, seemed to have been completed many decades earlier; most of the entries were in one spidery British hand.

Above was a large gallery whose volumes were all in Indian languages—Hindi, Punjabi, Bengali. On the gallery landing I stepped around a great rumpled pyramid of unfiled books. The third floor held non-fiction and fiction, almost all pre-Independence and in disrepair. Research was chancy in such a place unless one had months, because few books were near their proper places. They were old, mildewed, and chaotic, but they were readable. In India great minds, especially in science and mathematics, constantly arise from the slums; a man of talent and hunger could still educate himself here, even after fifty years of disorder.

I paid a visit to the Jallianwala Bagh—the garden on the site of the famous massacre of April 13, 1919. This was when fifty British riflemen (most of them Indians) fired on an unarmed Indian crowd of many thousands who'd gathered to protest the Rowlatt Act, by which people suspected of "sedition" could be imprisoned without trial. About three hundred eighty men and boys were killed—Hindus, Sikhs, Muslims—with perhaps as many as fifteen hundred wounded. The lieutenant governor of the Punjab, O'Dwyer, who'd ordered a crackdown of "fist force" on these peaceful rallies, had as a young civil servant nearly come to blows with an insulting young journalist named Kipling decades earlier in Lahore, which just shows how good the writer's instincts were.

Back then the Jallianwala Bagh was a huge, low, dumping ground enclosed by the walls of houses, many of which still stand. The massacre evoked the protests of many Indian leaders, including Gandhi and the writer Rabindranath Tagore, and fanned the flames of the Indian nationalist movement as only a senseless massacre of unarmed people can. Twenty-one years later O'Dwyer was assassinated in London by a survivor of the Jallianwala Bagh, who was hanged.

Today a pale blue Edwardian gazebo protects the deep well down which a hundred twenty people fell to their deaths trying to escape or evade the shooting. Along a shaded memorial walkway, men of the town were bickering and laughing the afternoon away. At one end a small Martyrs' Gallery museum held a reproduction of a letter of protest Tagore had written to the British Viceroy on May 30, 1919. "I stand by the side of my countrymen," he wrote.

The museum also had a painting of the massacre in the style of those "Custer at the Little Big Horn" tableaux, though it didn't convey the size of the crowd. Nor the pandemonium, for the Jallianwala Bagh is reached via a narrow lane of tall houses, and there was a stampede to get away from the British soldiers who'd placed themselves right at the way out. This led to many more dead from trampling than from being fired upon, perhaps even another five to six hundred; Indian and British estimates differed wildly.

The place seemed nowadays to flourish as a quiet park in an overheated, nervous city in need of respite. A faceless brown pillar to remember the dead had been erected at one end of the gardens. But the old houses' walls, and the Edwardian gazebo over the wide echoing well, had more sense of blood about them. One marker near the entry said PEOPLE WERE FIRED AT FROM HERE and another proclaimed:

NOTICE:
THIS PLACE IS SATURATED WITH THE BLOOD
OF ABOUT 2000 HINDU SIKH AND MUSLIM PATRIOTS . . .

Outside, a hardware store had recruitment posters propped in the windows: INDIAN NAVY WANTS SAILORS and INDIAN AIR FORCE WANTS HELICOPTER PILOTS.

My guest at dinner was Harpreet Singh, the new Reuters stringer here who'd replaced Avinash, who was now down in Delhi. Harpreet was younger and more buoyant, having come in at the tail end of the Sikh troubles. He had a rather handsome woman journalist with him; her husband was a doctor based elsewhere, and they were both leading busy young professional lives with no children. She'd been writing articles on the sexual abuse of working women for a Punjab newspaper. "You can't imagine how frequent a problem it is," she said, shaking her head. "It's in the blood."

There seemed something mildly risqué about her being in a hotel room with two males, neither one her husband, even though Harpreet was happily married and I was similarly spoken for and, anyway, all that we were discussing was how pistols were smuggled under the seats of the twice-weekly train from Lahore and where to go for dinner.

Harpreet had invited me to give a lecture in the morning to his students at Khalsa College, before I crossed the Wagha border into Pakistan. I had agreed, assuming my bronchitis let me; I generally felt best in the morning. Harpreet, turban and all, had visited Lahore, barely forty miles away, several times as a journalist. Very few Indians have done this.

"It's the same as here, really," he said. "The Punjab looks just the same, the food is the same, the people are the same. Their military bosses are something to worry about, though."

I pressed him on the Sikh troubles: no one visiting Amritsar now would guess at the state of internal war it endured not long ago. He admitted that there was no reason the bloodshed couldn't come back someday, in one year or twenty, as part of a recurring Sikh cycle. These days he had to work hard to come up with stories that might interest the international press; Avinash had had a lot more business as the Reuters stringer. Once the bloodshed ceased, as Harpreet put it, the Punjab was no longer newsworthy. His days were filled with running a Punjab weekly and being the local correspondent for the nationwide *Indian Express*.

The three of us ate at a sleek restaurant that looked like it'd been transported here from Miami Beach, only full of amiable gents in turbans: I was tempted to yell, "Phone call for Mr. Singh!"

The food was about the same. The clientele look stranger in Miami, but it's easier to find a taxi—a rickshaw, anyway—in Amritsar.

My final night in India I went to the Golden Temple for one last visit. Past the Sikh policeman looking for firearms; past the old attendant who accepted my shoes and loaned me a head scarf since I wore no turban; down the marble steps of the many-domed, almost Victorian entrance: the Golden Temple, burning in its pool. At twilight people sat around enjoying the hypnotic music and contemplating the glittering reflection as swallows darted.

Abruptly, clocks on the steeples of the white palace gonged. Everyone knelt and put their foreheads to the marble as the amplified priest prayed for about two minutes.

It is in the words that we write and speak about Thee,
In words on man's forehead
Is written man's destiny,
But God who writes that destiny
Is free from the bondage of words.

Then the music started up again, and lanterns came on. Five years ago when that happened people had hurried home before the virtual curfew made it risky to be out, or else elected to stay at the Golden Temple for dinner and sleep, to wake to the morning's inevitable headlines of violence and loss.

Now people took their time.

As night came down I happened into conversation with a husky young Sikh while we were both handing in the tags to get our shoes back.

He said quietly to me, "Which country." His intonation made a statement of every question.

"United States."

"Tell me what you think of Khalistan."

The magical name for the dreamed-of, independent Sikh nation. He had grown up with the separatist fantasy, then; he too was taking his time.

"Tell me what you think," I said.

"You must recognize us. If any of the superpowers recognizes Khalistan, we have a chance to succeed. If not, we have no chance. What do they think of Khalistan in America."

"I'm not sure people know enough to think anything."

"What do you think." He added flatly, "Do you think we will succeed."

"I don't know. The world changes. It changed in 1947. Perhaps it will change again."

He accepted this a little reluctantly. With a policeman eyeing us, it didn't seem the right place or time for a foreigner to say, "Viva Khalistan!" just to make him happy.

I asked, "Are you married?"

"In six months, thanks to God, I will be married."

I wished him many sons, warriors-to-be of Khalistan no doubt, and scurried back to my three-wheeler rickshaw. As I did, the power went out all over the city. In darkness only the Golden Temple, with its private generator, stayed illuminated—an independent source of power, even when power seemed periodically to fail in the rest of India.

Khalsa College, fronted by a spacious green, is a triumphant polygamy of Victorian, Sikh, and Persian architectures in russet sandstone, each fantastical style suiting the others. It was built in 1892 not by the British (as I'd assumed) but by Sikhs, with Sikh money. Harpreet ran a graduate class of journalism students theoretically destined for newspaper work. "Of course," said Harpreet, "there aren't remotely enough jobs to go around. Only the more ambitious ones really understand this." The girls were much bolder and more outspoken than the boys. Each sex had its own rows—on the students' natural inclination, Harpreet assured me. (Were there ever relationships between students? I asked him after the class. "Only in secret," he said. "And usually quite innocent. When you mentioned 'going out on dates,' they didn't really grasp what you meant.")

After I talked for a while the students asked plenty of questions, some about writing, many about my perceptions of India.

I said that what I disliked in so many travel books on India was that they were written out of a kind of obsession with all things Indian, which I found grating and not very clear-eyed. Didn't I love the country? one girl asked. I said I did, but that I thought there was a profound difference between sober love and silly love. She accepted this and asked if Americans thought her country was as described in E. M. Forster's *A Passage To India*. This struck me as roughly the same as a Parisian asking how Americans' ideas of France were shaped by having read Proust. I assured her that Mr. Forster's book was usually read as a novel, not as a precise report on the India of that period.

A bearer came in with a vast tray of little steaming glasses of sweet coffee and passed them around. At Harpreet's request one girl came up to the podium and gave a brief speech thanking me.

I thought I did well, considering that a few hours earlier I was curled up on the floor of my hotel room toilet drenched in sweat, shaken by a spiking fever, wondering if I could or should complete the journey.

Afterward Harpreet took me to a young Sikh doctor who gave me several days' worth of antibiotics and told me I possibly had a viral fever and should really stay put for a week or two. Or, he added, it might be dengue fever; it would be wise to get a blood test for that once I reached Pakistan, since I'd told him I was determined to cross the border that afternoon.

What happens with dengue fever? I asked.

Your temperature hits 105 and pus shoots out of your eyes. Then, if not treated, you die.

Packing, I stole a look back at my thick pile of Indian notes, many of them in a handwriting difficult to decipher—shaken by my trying to scribble in a jolting Ambassador.

What seems most difficult to convey is the extraordinary complexity of the Indian scene, especially in cities—the visual overload, as if a fervid photographer has crammed a frame with two million items in several thousand colors so that the eye cannot possibly take it all in.

And no matter what new energy I might see in India—everyone who's anyone carries a pager now—the problem is bigger than any social theories, than any change in government, than the economic liberalization which took place a few years ago. It still comes down to human numbers, and these do not go away. ("The government's been totally ineffective at curbing the population problem," Harpreet said. "We're slated to overtake the Chinese by the year 2000. At least we'll be Number One in something.") There seems no way out of the trap that there will be ever too many Indians, with conditions ever harder for most.

The Bombay skyscrapers may resemble those of the West, but they are constantly offset by the cultural fury and fear that can tear down a mosque, protest an international beauty pageant by self-immolation, and turn out rioters by the thousands who hope to keep out multinational corporations trying to invest in India. The bureaucratic logjam and mental constipation left by the British are still firmly in place, and won't disappear, not for many generations. They go all too naturally with Indians' own tendencies, and block colossally any forward movement and the possibility of helpful outside influence. In the end the strength of India is that no matter what, it remains resolutely Indian; but this is also its weakness as well.

They are a resilient people who have withstood a lot and, unbelievably, held on to a continuous civilization for a good thirty-five centuries. The result filled me with despair. It may be that I come from a soft country, and have no experience with such explosive pressures, but I didn't believe that anyone could stay so resilient forever. I thought that things here would only get worse, and much as I admired and enjoyed the people, I was glad to have seen it when I had. From what I'd witnessed, the future for most Indians looked like hell.

Less than twenty miles to Pakistan.

On the way to the Wagha border crossing there was almost no traffic, since practically no one crosses by road. We passed several military trucks and a few men on bicycles with brass milk-pots hanging. Harpreet had told me that very few trucks crossed the border daily from Pakistan into India. "Two or three. Not many. Carrying dry goods or canned fruit. But never from our direction."

There was so little traffic, actually, that a dog chased the car. The first time that had happened in twelve hundred miles.

Past the police station at Gharinda the countryside was mostly scattered villages and corn and rice fields with bullocks snoozing, crisscrossed overhead by power and telephone lines, ready to communicate war or the rumor of war.

ATTARI 3
WAGHA BORDER 5

Incredibly, even a few rickshaw drivers were here for the little local traffic from village to village. It was as if the country, usually crowded, was sighing at having so much space, relieved at not having to do any more. For weeks I had been hoping for, dreaming of, an empty road. Here, where India ended, I got my wish.

Another army outpost. A lone water buffalo basked, up to its snout in water on the edge of fields.

Attari was the bare minimum of a border town: a few tents and stalls, and a sign proclaiming 21ST CENTURY MALT WHISKEY. I told Lucky Singh that I wanted to do the last bit of the Indian road on foot to the border, just to enjoy it in the slowest way possible. I suggested he drive on ahead with my bags and wait for me there. He nodded, a little reluctantly, and I watched him head out of sight in the Ambassador—how much sentiment, I suddenly realized, I had attached to that faithful machine.

Just ahead, off the road in trees was a considerable cluster of army tents. The Attari checkpoint was a folding card table, two khakied policemen, and a raised barrier. The two policemen went through my papers and handed them back with the job-well-done look on their faces.

It was already very hot, even though it was barely noon. I hadn't walked for very long when the Ambassador reappeared in a flurry of dust. The border would be closed for a good hour, said Lucky. Someone was having lunch. What should we do? I said that I still wanted to walk there.

The opportunity to stroll the last Indian kilometer of the Grand Trunk Road was too good to let slip by. Lucky called out to the policemen, parked the Ambassador in the shade of a tree near the card table checkpoint, and caught up to me. After so long in a car it was liberation to be sweating this final empty stretch on foot together, walking past more army tents toward Wagha and the end of India. There were no more villages visible through the trees.

We passed a small police compound of earthen walls. The Punjab Police inside—turbanned Sikhs in khaki—called out to us to come inside for tea or cold drinks. We chatted for a minute and promised to do so on our way back to retrieve the Ambassador and my bags, once the border opened.

At Wagha Border the only war of nerves was between Limca (BIGGER BOTTLE!) and Campa Cola (TASTE IS BETTER THAN SIZE!).

Still, even asleep in noon heat, it was a border. MONEY

EXCHANGER / PAK CURRENCY / CHANGE HERE was painted on a little bunker. And here, incredibly, was the Neem Chamal Tourism Complex, a motel-restaurant that must be the emptiest in India, since there is rarely a reason for anyone to hang around for longer than a soda.

There were three identically khakied officials on duty—from the Punjab Police, the Army, and Customs. A few hundred meters up the Grand Trunk, past identical barriers on this side and on that, stood their Pakistani counterparts.

I asked, "Lots of traffic from Pakistan?"

The customs man said, "Two, three, seven, eight buses and trucks come over the border. They don't go far, anyway. None go from here to there. Only European cars going that way."

There must have been very, very few of those. Holders of Indian passports simply aren't allowed to enter Pakistan by road, but only by train or plane, and very rarely.

"Is this the end of the GT?" I asked.

"Not at all," said the customs officer. "It goes all the way to Peshawar."

Nearby, sitting on the grass or getting themselves lunches from a food stall, were blue-smocked porters, known locally as "coolies." The porters were drinking as friends now, but once the border opened the competition would be extremely intense for very little business.

Now that I was at last here I was overcome with the sensation that I had seen nothing; and yet I knew I had seen all I could. It was exactly what India had made me feel every time. At least it was a small achievement to be ambling along in this remote place near the border, in the easy heat of early afternoon and the unexpected quiet of the road here.

We headed back toward the Attari checkpoint to get the car. I would not have long to wait now.

Lucky and I were approaching the earthen-walled police compound where we'd been invited for refreshments when sharply, suddenly from within came pleading shrieks of pain that shattered the pastoral stillness of the day. The howls were unearthly, and stopped us cold. In no time porters were gathering beneath nearby trees to listen and watch from a safe distance.

From the road I sneaked a glance inside. The Punjabi Police were beating a bare-chested man with a wooden "enforcer" like a cricket bat. There were loud whacks as he was struck again and again. He was still able to cry out. Through the opening of the compound I saw him rise and try to hobble away, imploring, gulping, clutching at his spine. Several policemen stood around, laughing, hemming him in, edging him this way and that like players kicking around a soccer ball; one swung the enforcer at the man's naked back and he tumbled.

Lucky insisted we start moving again, inconspicuous off to the side of the road. I asked him, perhaps a little loudly, whether we might not go into the police compound for tea or that promised cold drink. Lucky shook his head and kept me walking swiftly, past the porters and out of earshot of the compound. A short ways up the road we heard from an old fellow driving a horse cart that the man being beaten was "accused of being a thief." And that was my last memory of the Grand Trunk in India: a man's shrieks in gathering heat, to the clip-clop of a horse's hooves on the old road.

Warning!
Improbable, you say?
No, fellers.
All improbables are probable in India.

—G. V. Desani, *All About H. Hatterr* (1948)

18.

Order at the Border

The border itself had me a little worried. For a few days, I—who rarely remember my dreams—had been hit with vivid nightmares in which I was denied either the right to leave India or to enter Pakistan. I am not a nervous traveler, but these dreams took on the sting of prophecy. And the more I read about this disputatious border—from Indian accusations that Pakistan steadily armed Sikh militants to, back in 1965, the three-week war that culminated in Indian tanks roaring eighteen miles up the GT as far as Lahore's outskirts—well, the more I read, the less I slept.

Such struggles were the heritage of Partition, when the wealthy Punjab was divided as Pakistan and India were born, at midnight on August 14–15, 1947. Overnight Britain made two independent countries by drawing a new line on the map. What began as "the most complex divorce in history" and the "lovely dawn of freedom" was soon communal slaughter. Much of that bloodshed was in the divided Punjab.

The carnage was mainly Muslim-Sikh and Muslim-Hindu. About half a million were killed in the Punjab alone—acid was thrown on people's faces, entire villages were machine-gunned, whole fields of farmers were castrated, children's throats cut while they slept, city blocks torched and people hammered, beheaded, roasted on spits. The butchery was almost unimaginable in its horror, and still lay close to the memories, even if secondhand, of everyone on both sides of the Punjab.

It was never mentioned and always there. Forty-nine years ago, right where I was traveling, perhaps six million people had migrated in each direction, with the resulting massacres. That year the Punjab vultures stayed fat. The GT was the path of the crisscross migration, and all its truck wrecks today were nothing compared to the summer and autumn of 1947. The war-hardened correspondent of *The Times* of London would write as he passed along it, "I had the impression that it had been visited by vast swarms of locusts . . . . I had never before seen anything so horrible."

In Peshawar ten thousand Muslims and Sikhs died in a week after one soldier's gun went off by accident.

And those massacres lay in spirit behind wars fought between the two countries—in 1965 over Kashmir, still disputed between them; and in 1971 over Bangla Desh, originally the eastern half of Pakistan, which declared independence and broke away. Both times Pakistan lost. That hadn't prevented the two countries from entering the nuclear arms race, though India's eye was on a greedy China as well. They were also still busy with a forgotten, ongoing war for glacial crags far north in Baltistan; Indian and Pakistani soldiers were fighting and freezing to death in no man's land at over 21,000 feet.

So I wondered how friendly their sole border crossing point would be.

• • •

Lucky left for Delhi, anxious to make a dent in his journey in the several hours before dark, and I gathered my energies where he dropped me, at the Wagha border.

There were other reasons for things to be a bit tense. This was turning out a bad week for the subcontinent's prime ministers. Tuesday morning a presidential decree had toppled Benazir Bhutto's government—she and her cabinet were sacked and the Pakistan national assembly dissolved. This had happened to her once before, though anyone who survives a father's assassination and remains in politics has staying power; doubtless it would happen to her again. For the last half century no Pakistan government has managed to finish out its term, and for half those years the country has been ruled by military dictatorships.

Troops had surrounded Benazir's house, turned her supporters away at the gates, and cut off her phone; cellular phone service throughout the entire country was also shut down and the airport sealed. It looked like a peaceful coup despite televised images of shots being fired in Islamabad, the capital, by the so-called man in the street.

"It was politics and business as usual," rumbled the Indian TV news commentator, meaning the fourth dismissal of a Pakistani government in eight years. Bhutto, emerging at last from house arrest, claimed that her husband—who still hadn't been seen—was not only kidnapped but tortured. She also invoked her late brother, shot dead some months back by the police (and, some implied, on her orders). "The bullet that was meant to eliminate my brother physically was meant to eliminate me politically."

She was accused by her successor of "corruption and nepotism and mismanagement." Her husband, a minister in her cabinet, was being called the most dishonest man in the country. This is a huge claim, since Pakistan is considered the most corrupt country in the world after Nigeria, and no Pakistani denies it deserves such status.

Meanwhile, former prime minister Rao of India was kept busy

battling a court order that he be arrested on charges of forgery and vote-tampering. It had been an eventful week.

I hadn't reckoned that the virtually total corruption of the Indian Police would extend to foreigners.

From now on I'd be on foot. The first border post was a little table where three khakied Indian Police officers—all Sikhs—were seated. Before I could get to them I was approached by a money-changer offering to buy up all my Indian rupees, which weren't negotiable in Pakistan. His rate was only fractionally low, as it turned out. A blue-jacketed porter would carry my bags to Pakistan. He wore a copper arm badge that said L.C.S. (Land Crossing Station) and his number and the designation PORTER, ATTARI ROAD, which is what they call this Checkpoint Chapati.

By now the area was swarming with porters. A steady stream of those blue jackets was filing across from the Pakistani side, enormous bales and crates of almonds on the men's heads. They scurried along with a kind of seaman's gait, a low center of gravity to compensate for the massive load above.

My porter was a grinning young man whose strategy, I soon saw, was to maintain a lighthearted enthusiasm in the face of constant setbacks. It was two o'clock now; the border would close at four. This seemed like plenty of time, but when it was obvious my porter was a little worried about having only two hours to go less than a kilometer, I started to worry also.

One Sikh policeman took my passport and began writing down the usual information. His colleague glanced at my bags. He was the first of several Indian officials who demanded a bribe.

"What is these?"

"Posters."

"Posters? For wall?"

"That's right."

"I am liking posters. Oh, very much, posters very good! I am liking one, two posters. I will take a look."

He didn't like my posters.

A little farther on the process was repeated at another table, this time with Mutt and Jeff Singh. Mutt asked me to write down an accounting of all the money I had with me. My porter pointed out that Mutt Singh was a very, very kind officer and kept pointing this out until Mutt barked at him and told him to stop being so sycophantic. Thus far this approach had worked.

Jeff Singh looked gravely at the amount of money I said I was carrying and said that didn't look correct to him and he thought I must have some extra money on me.

No, I told him politely, I don't have any extra.

Are you sure? said Jeff Singh.

The porter hied me away from this conversation.

Our next gauntlet along this, the sole pedestrian strip of the GT, was a bland modern glass-and-concrete building on the right. This was the Customs Station.

IMPORT OF FIRE ARMS AMMUNITION AND EXPLOSIVES AS BAGGAGE IS PROHIBITED

CARRYING OF NARCOTIC DRUGS IS STRICTLY PROHIBITED

OBSCENE AND ANTI NATIONAL LITERATURE IS ALSO PROHIBITED

Another sign had a much longer list, which included exotic birds, beef, tallow fat—that old bugaboo of the Mutiny—and human skeletons.

The porter led me into a lobby area of the Customs Station that was all but deserted—not surprising, since only about twenty people cross the border here every day, foreigners all. A few privileged Indians and Pakistanis with visas could cross by plane (Delhi and Bombay to Karachi and Lahore), or near here by railroad, twice a week. This was the famous cross-border train which ran from Amritsar over to Lahore and back. After the partition of British India, during 1947 and 1948 it often set out carrying hundreds of Muslims to the newly created Pakistan or Hindus and Sikhs back to the new India and would arrive carrying nothing but butchered corpses. Thousands had died on that train.

The porter put down my bags carefully and directed me to an official window with no one behind it. I waited a moment, then took a seat. Eventually a Sikh policeman came to the window and I went over to give him my passport. He put it down without looking at it and walked away.

He came back about ten minutes later, glanced at me, and with nothing else to do, examined my passport as if it were a lump of asteroid. Satisfied that it was not a forgery, he then barked at my porter, who ushered me up to take it back. I was careful to thank the officer for his attention: he had not asked for a bribe.

My porter then showed me to a window ten yards away. Soon another Sikh officer hove into view. He had a slightly smarmy manner, which denoted simply another approach to the problem of extracting money from the wayfarer. He shook my hand and grinned enthusiastically. "America first class! USA number one okay!"

He went round behind his window and took my documents.

He leafed through the passport with some leisure. Several foreign visas merited extensive scrutiny and he wrote down some numbers. He also noticed my gray waterproof zipper coat, in one of those soft artificial fabrics. I had made the mistake of putting it on the counter between us.

In an instant he had pulled it over to his side of the window and was guilelessly examining it.

"Where is this from?"

"From America."

"Really? How much is costing this coat?"

"I don't know. It was a gift."

He smiled. "Is gift to me."

"I'm sorry, but I need it."

His smile broadened. "Is nice gift for me. I keep."

One corner of the coat was still draped on the counter. I tugged it firmly back across.

He accepted this with equanimity. He returned to my passport. He came at last to the page wholly devoted to my Indian tourist visa—a multiple entry, good for three months, similar to the previous one. In copying the number of my passport onto the visa itself, the consular official in New York had made a slight error on one digit which had been neatly corrected. This was pounced on.

"This is your writing, sir?"

"What do you mean?"

"This here."

"No, that is Indian writing. Your consulate."

"This *your* writing!"

"No."

He reflected. "This no good, sir. I cannot let you pass."

I didn't say anything, because I couldn't think of anything.

He shook his head. "You see here, sir? You are writing here where it is *official* visa. You are forgering. *Forgering.*"

"I am not forgering. I didn't write that. Your official in New York wrote that. He got it wrong, then fixed it. Look, it matches my passport number."

Another fellow had come up, a Sikh in bedraggled robes who had the air of being merely a step up from a porter. He seemed to want only to observe what was going on.

The official said suddenly, "You have Indian rupees, sir?"

"A little bit."

"How much? You cannot take to Pakistan."

Like someone who shakes a tree every which way to see if any fruit will fall.

"Ten rupees," I said.

"You should give to this nice man. It will make him happy."

"Will it make him happy?"

The newcomer actually looked uncomfortable at being included in this minor extortion, about thirty cents.

"It will make him *very* happy," said the official.

"Well, all right then."

A satisfactory truce had been reached. A worn ten rupees was handed over and my passport duly stamped. I was now about a third of the way into successfully, legally leaving India.

Now for the baggage. An up-to-date, enormous X-ray machine with its own glassed-in shrine, larger even than the one at Delhi Airport, would electronically examine my bags to make sure I was carrying no explosives, no exotic birds, and no human skeletons. First, though, the proper official would have to be found; and in front of me were the Nigerians.

They were clearly a time factor that had my porter worried. These four young Nigerian men were at pains to appear well-dressed students but were, my porter assured me, workers who'd found no jobs here. They were hoping for better luck in Pakistan. He'd seen their ilk before. Two Nigerians had sent their bags through and were arguing pathetically with officers on the other side of a glass barrier in the actual customs inspections hall. The other two stood around morosely on this side. They knew they were done for. No Nigerian would avoid paying bribes as easily as an American with a strong embassy.

A portly Sikh policeman came back to the X-ray machine. He said to me, "Where is your passport?"

"You've got it."

My porter was busy putting my bags on the conveyor belt before the X-ray machine. The portly officer growled at him. He removed them hastily.

One of the Nigerians came up and murmured a timid protest. The officer said, "I've only got two passports here. There are four of you."

"Sir, the others are already inside. You gave them their passports, you see."

"I see four of you here and I only see two passports. I can't let you through under these conditions. Don't bother me."

He walked away for a rest. A moment later, re-energized, he

came back and took up the problem of my passport again.

My porter said to me very quietly, "Those Nigerians will have to pay one hundred dollars each. Maybe more. Or they will not get through."

I wondered how long the four Nigerians had been in India, what it was like to be an African here looking for work. After all, Africa was full of Indian merchants and tailors who'd done well for themselves for generations and been hated there for it.

My porter had at last succeeded in getting my bags allowed on the conveyor by the portly officer.

"What do you have in these bags?"

"Souvenirs. Books. Clothes."

"You have camera? Machine is filmsafe."

I am a camera, I thought. "I've got a computer." I removed my diskettes before the bags got trundled through and the machine zapped them. Instantly another official, in plainclothes, materialized. He said, "You have what kind of computer? IBM?"

He looked as young and innocuous as a graduate student.

"Something like that," I said.

In fact he was the most dangerous of all.

"You must let me look at floppies."

Reluctantly I handed them over.

"What is your occupation?"

"I'm a musician."

"Why are you traveling with a computer?"

It didn't seem propitious to admit I was writing about his country.

I said, "Americans never go anywhere without their computers."

He accepted this and darted inside another glass shrine. I realized he was going to be really looking at my diskettes—he was seated at a computer with a big screen. He shoved the diskettes into the portal one by one and tried to read them; his screen showed only staggered truncated lines that must've been gobbledygook. This didn't deter him, and patiently he tried all of them.

Meanwhile the portly officer with the X-ray machine was making me watch while he examined the blown-up, negative image of each of my bags on a big screen.

"What is this line? This thing here?"

"I think it's a book. Why don't we open the bag and see?"

"And this? The electronics?"

"That's my laptop."

"I would like to be able to buy a laptop."

He was about to suggest I make a contribution to the Punjab Police Laptop Fund (Wagha Border Chapter). Fortunately the grad student plainclothesman trying to read my diskettes called out, "What are these files you are making? 'Delhi' and 'Amritsar' and this sort of thing?"

"I keep a journal about places I go. Interesting people I meet."

He handed back my diskettes and grimaced, bored with the American problem.

Meanwhile, behind me, one of the Nigerians was pleading. He had his hands clasped before his face and looked ready to cry. The Sikh policeman who'd wanted my coat turned away in disgust.

My porter said to me softly, as if imparting a secret, "*Sir.* You can go through now. I will meet you on the other side. We must try hurry, sir. *Hurry.*"

I passed through the glass airlock of a metal detector into the customs inspection lobby just as the last of my bags emerged upended on the other side of the X-ray machine. The X-ray screen showed a frozen image of my laptop and a thin line that was a box holding the notes for this book. At that moment it felt like a bomb in my bowels, waiting to make itself known.

It did not help my state of mind that all this time I was racked with coughs and asthmatic wheezing.

My porter, hurrying around the building outside, bustled into the customs area and retrieved my bags from the X-ray. He moved me and them over to a customs inspection table, a long metal slab, deliberately choosing the one farthest from the other officers and nearest the door to freedom.

It was now three.

Another Sikh policeman, an extremely tall man, wandered over after remonstrances from my porter about the time.

"Open it."

I unzipped one of the two large bags. To my astonishment the policeman started pulling out its entire contents as if searching for something he'd lost. Out came everything I'd bought in India: scores of books and souvenirs. These were mainly little wooden toy statuettes of gods and goddesses, Christmas presents. Hand-painted, visible behind clear cellophane windows, they were obviously fragile. They each had their own little red box tied up with string and it couldn't have been more evident that they were inexpensive and nearly identical, all having come from the same government-run crafts store.

"Where these from, sir?"

"New Delhi."

He shook his head and opened them, one by one. The table was now a mess and getting filled. My porter looked disconsolate.

"Look, they're all the same. Here's the store receipt."

"These not Indian. Where you smuggle from?"

"Of course they're Indian. Those toy soldiers are Sikhs, aren't they?"

He was either very obtuse or very cunning.

"Hari!" He called over a colleague and handed him two red boxes. Over they went to the X-ray machine.

At this point I started losing my temper. Beanpole Singh unzipped my other bag and pounced on the batch of Indian newspapers I had on top.

"You cannot take these to Pakistan. They do not let you bring them in."

Good work, Sgt. Singh, I thought. A week-old *Times of India* is an incalculable security risk.

He shoved them aside, his suspicions about me confirmed. He

started pulling out my clothes, a decision he soon regretted, as I hadn't done any laundry for a week.

"Why this many books? All these books on India."

Some were political, and I began to wonder if he could read. As it turns out, virtually every book published in India, no matter how controversial, is available in Pakistan.

He moved on to the case with my laptop. The computer itself didn't interest him. He pulled out the box with my notes and fortunately opened it from the back. He riffled through the apparently blank pages but eventually noticed the chaotic handwriting on the other sides. As the pages were upside down as well, the Indian place-names sped by unrecognized; and perhaps he could not read.

"Why you write all this?"

I said indignantly, "I didn't write that."

A dimwit thing to say, but I hadn't anticipated such scrutiny. The portly officer came back from the x-ray with the two red boxes of toys. The set of Sikh infantry and the gods Ganesha and Lakshmi had passed with flying colors. The gods protected me: Beanpole Singh laid them atop the other boxes of toys he'd unearthed and forgot my manuscript.

He pulled more envelopes of my research materials from the laptop case but couldn't be bothered to look inside, fortunately. Then he hit paydirt: an American humor magazine that had on the cover, quite misleadingly, a semi-nude portrait of a famous actress. I'd been discarding magazines brought from home as I traveled, and this was the only one left. Still, would a real spy carry a magazine by that name?

Beanpole called out to his colleagues, who hurried over. In a moment I was in an officers' convention.

It was three-thirty now. I could feel my porter's courage flagging.

On the other side of the glass airlock, the two Nigerians looked ready to immolate themselves. Their compatriots on my side had gone on ahead, perhaps at some prearranged understanding.

"You have more magazine like this?"

We were joined by a middle-aged plainclothesman and the computer grad student one. They were all taking turns leafing through in search of more risqué photos. Theirs was a pointless quest, and the text would be totally without humor—or meaning—to someone who hadn't lived in the States. But why spoil their fun? I only wished I had several inkless pens to offer them, too.

"You want the magazine?" I said. "Keep it."

The Sikh policemen huddled together in their dirty magazine quorum. One gave a little dismissing wave, and my porter started hastily, quietly, efficiently packing my bags alongside me. I was now free to go. It struck me that I had better get to Pakistan before disappointment over my modest bribe set in.

The porter and I scurried out. In a moment we'd left the Customs Building behind and were headed down the Grand Trunk Walk again, flowers and trees on both sides, the border just up ahead. Porters passed us in a steady stream, crates on their heads. They called out jokingly to my porter, who would undoubtedly make more from me than they earned all day.

I said, "You're very good with those policemen."

He managed to shrug even with my two big bags balanced on his head. "They are very crooked men, sir. Very crooked. They love nothing but money. Only money, money, money."

He made it into a song. I passed him several dollars as we came to two conflicting signs, one facing away from us—

WELCOME TO INDIA, THE WORLD'S LARGEST DEMOCRACY!

and a little ways on, before a cluster of heavily ornamented and rainbow trucks, from which porters streamed in a neat line—

LONG LIVE PAKISTAN!

My porter smiled happily. “Pakistan,” he said. He indicated a swatch of grass across the border. “Good lawn. Green color.”

There was one last card table of Indian officials. They checked my passport, stamped it again, confirmed that I wasn’t carrying any loose currency. My porter shook hands with me and passed my bags over the invisible line in the road to a taller and skinnier Pakistani porter. They exchanged a few words in Punjabi and we parted.

It was ten to four. It had taken us nearly two hours to go less than half a kilometer, making this arguably the slowest stretch of the GT, especially considering the lack of traffic. I wasn’t part of a pile-up of a hundred trucks coming from both directions—this afternoon had been only me and those four Nigerians. 60 percent of us had gotten through.

And the end of the fight is a tombstone white
with the name of the late deceased,
And the epitaph drear: “A Fool lies here
who tried to hustle the East.”

A Pakistani officer glanced quickly at my passport and waved me on. Up ahead was a lovely old British residence on the left. A fellow in the trousers and long smock-shirt which nearly every Pakistani man wears hurried out. “Medical card?” he inquired. I produced it, he approved of my many inoculations, we walked on.

We then came to a compound that had clearly seen better days during the Raj. There were tall mango trees and a new bank, shut tight, and a long veranda of empty offices. My porter shooed me into one. It had a motionless fan, peeling paint, and a weary map of Pakistan on the wall. There was nobody behind the desk, on which rested an ashtray and a list of international terrorists and check bouncers to watch out for.

“Just a moment,” said the porter, and vanished.

Here we go again, I thought. Now for the low-tech version.

I sat down. A moment later my porter shuffled in. He was sweating, but then it was still hot.

He was followed by the chief border officer, who was not sweating.

I handed him my passport. He scowled at it but took it. He scowled at my photograph, he scowled at my visa, he scowled at me. He pulled out an enormous inkpad and an official seal and scowled at what he was about to do. *Bang, bang.*

He grinned. "Welcome to Pakistan. This is a customs post. Anything to declare? No?" He handed back my passport. "May I at least offer you some tea?"

> In many respects the Mohammedans surpassed our rule; they settled in the countries which they conquered; they intermixed and intermarried with the natives; they admitted them to all privileges; the interests and sympathies of the conquerors and conquered became identified. Our policy has been the reverse of this; cold, selfish and unfeeling; the iron hand of power on the one side, monopoly and exclusion on the other.
>
> —Lord William Bentinck (1837)

19.

Where the Kites Come Down

New country, same landscape: the empty, indifferent green of the Punjab. Brick kilns rose just off the road, with tapering gray chimneys. At first I mistook them for very tall kos minars, until I noticed the pirouetting smoke.

The first task, crossing into Pakistan from India, is to set your watch back a half hour while keeping a straight face.

My taxi, hired at the border, took me through a crowded town a few miles later. It was all in hideous brick that matched the dirt, with a tent market spilling onto the GT. The air was thick with dust, turned up by tractors and decrepit old *ekkas* (two-wheeled pony- or donkey-carts) which you see more of here than in India. There were more *tongas* (horse carriages), too, though this didn't improve the air; ponies and horses have their own fumes. But no Ambassadors—how much I unexpectedly missed them.

The great revelation was the elaborate, almost formally dense, maniacally colorful, and astonishingly total ornamentation of trucks—flamboyant, mobile art galleries that made those painted Indian designs I'd admired for so long seem lazy, casual, and incomplete. These have Muslim competitive edge.

DON'T RUSH DEATH

On the outskirts of Lahore, by the walls of the Mogul-era Shalimar Gardens, there was no order whatsoever on the GT, just a confused assault of every vehicle for itself. After the gardens the steady stream of tongas, ekkas, scooters, cars, sputtering motor-rickshaws, and ornate buses and trucks spewing murderous fumes was split by a raised divider. Both sides became quite spacious, with auto works, leather-hide and vegetable markets, cages of doomed chickens.

As we reached Old Lahore, the rabbit warren bazaar part of the city, the GT narrowed, devolving into side streets with British names like Cooper Road or Bull Road. On Fleming Road I had my first glimpse of what amounts to a national posture. A man lifted his long smocklike shirt, squatted, pulled down his baggy drawstring trousers just enough, and peed as the traffic squirmed past. This is the only effective stance for anyone in a *shalwar-kameez*, which nearly every man and woman wears.

Then the Grand Trunk collapsed into mud and potholes, and even after weeks of fine weather it was difficult to get through the muck. "All the government ministers should have to live on this road," a man told me the next day. "The worst drainage in Lahore. I call it the digestive part of the GT, because you get a bad stomach from jiggling down it. Or cholera, if you get stuck there long enough."

No sooner had I reached Faletti's Hotel, in the gathering gloom of a hard day, with bags and money mostly intact, than the electricity promptly went off. The management—two clerks straight out of Dickens Central Casting, one tall and funereal, with spectacles and hennaed hair parted in the middle, the other small, with a whispered oily geniality—assured me that the power cut, across most of Lahore, would only last five to ten minutes. Instead it went on till midnight. So my introduction to Kipling's city was the groan of generators.

As in British times, Lahore is still capital of the Punjab—Pakistan's Punjab, anyway. Because Pakistan remains an idea in search of a nation, its four provinces make even less sense as an entity, either tribally or culturally or linguistically, than India does. After the Punjab, the GT would take me through the North-West Frontier Province as well, but I wouldn't see Sind and Baluchistan, to the south.

India, with several serious separatist movements going on at once, sometimes seems strapped down with duct tape. What holds Pakistan tenuously together are the glue of Islam, the popular and successful national athletic teams, the army and the police, and a shaky centrifugal force given a shove every now and then by two long-standing political rivals, who seem to go round and round like two bullies in a schoolyard. These are the venerable Muslim League (founding-era equivalent of India's Congress Party, run by the Nehru dynasty), and the People's Party (which produced the Bhutto dynasty, and is cast in the same spoiler's role as India's Bharatiya Janata Party). The Pakistani method of changing governments by deposing or executing the leader is only the Mogul habit of fratricidal warfare brought up to date.

The viral chest fever I picked up in India had gotten worse but it seemed absurd to go to bed, having spent so much energy to get here. Faletti's at least was well suited to candlelight, with traditional stone arches and a little private garden out front. Around the side a couple of bleak souvenir shops were crammed to the rafters most optimistically, since the hotel was deserted. It had been started (or so the story goes) in 1860 by a Neapolitan who fell hard for a Lahore courtesan. In back was a flagstoned courtyard with an older building and occasional flocks of hangers-on standing around. A semi-destroyed grand piano sat tucked away beneath a terrace that ran the length of the second story. My upstairs room was spacious if pretty basic, with a Koran in the closet. What won my heart was the promise of a hot shower and the framed, worn pastoral print of winter ice-skaters in Canada.

So, with almost no street lights operating, I went for a walk, stopping every few paces to cough my lungs out. A block away from Faletti's is the square traditionally known as Charing Cross—though locals say it and sometimes write it as Cheering. Emanating from it in both directions is the Mall, the principal boulevard built by the British in the 1850s, when the Punjab became theirs, and now given a second, Pakistani name. Darkness only made evident how drivers use their cars and motorcycles as weapons. Headlights get turned on only as a polite gesture an instant before impact; the roads have no lanes.

This part of the Mall seemed predominantly footwear stores with catchy names like Mr. Big Shoes or English Shoes. Gaily lit-up, generators grinding away, they were doing a booming business in the blackout. There were more couples strolling about than in, say, Delhi or Amritsar (a misleading first impression) but no dresses or short sleeves, much less anyone stripped to mere loincloths: you just don't see a lot of human flesh in this country. Or beggars, either.

I saw, in fact, only one beggar in Lahore, for in Pakistan a small percentage of everyone's bank account, a *zakaat*, is taken out for the poor. A second inner road for both pedestrians and cars runs along both sides of the Mall, a truly dangerous innovation in lieu of a sidewalk, and here the beggar heroically stationed himself. His legs were torturously deformed, yet he fearlessly perched right in the middle of this roadway and shouted and shook his fists. It was a bravura show of chutzpah and technique—he simply faced the oncoming traffic and screamed at it as he pulled himself along. He was so low he was practically invisible until it was too late; all that signaled his presence in the darkness was cars swerving abruptly at the same spot. He was living proof of what Kipling's

Kim had said about Lahore's beggars: Those who beg in silence, starve in silence.

When I handed him 10 Pakistani rupees—25 cents, but a meal here—he stopped screaming only for the amount of time needed to grab my bill. Then, mostly drowned out by the car horns and engines roaring, he started screaming again.

A few shopkeepers stood in their doorways, amused at the spectacle. It struck me that this beggar was expressing what nearly every Pakistani probably felt like doing, were there no consequences. Given an excuse, I bet half the country would sit in the road, wave their fists, and scream.

Another day at Faletti's under the threat of hot water in the pipes—a promise that I suspected might not materialize. I suggested they really should rectify this before December sets in. This must be the hotel where Claude Lévi-Strauss stayed on a prewar visit to Lahore ("interminable avenues, tree-lined, villa-bordered") described in *Tristes Tropiques*. It reminded him of a stud farm, "doors opening directly on to the road . . . like so many diminutive stables." Paul Theroux was kinder to Faletti's twenty years ago, but counted forty-seven tables one evening in the torpid restaurant, all of them empty. That was still true today at breakfast.

Today was a public holiday—the fifty-eighth death anniversary of the poet and philosopher Iqbal, who first put forth the idea of a Muslim homeland on the subcontinent back in 1930. Naturally I'd expected a certain amount of quiet and inactivity in the streets this morning. But nothing seems to please a Pakistani, no matter how early, like the spit and mutter of a gasoline engine. Could it be the implied power, a pleasant sound to people always feeling like the underdog next to India?

Or maybe Pakistanis just enjoy noise.

• • •

The only expectations I had of Lahore came from Kipling, and if you throw in thousands of homicidal cars and motor-rickshaws and some postwar concrete, the illustration fits. Then one descends to facts; there was that same surprise I constantly got in India, when I'd arrive in a smallish city, open my guidebook, and learn it held more people than Manhattan. Lahore, though I'd never have guessed, is a city of 5 million, the second biggest in Pakistan. It is half the size of Karachi down south, which is where most Muslims who came over from India settled after the Partition. The Lahore that Kipling described as "a tide of unclean humanity" ready to "burst through its dam of rotten brickwork and filth-smeared wood" is forty times larger a mere century later.

English is still the official government lingo here, which made it easy to enjoy the nightly TV news broadcasts that showed ministers speechifying while getting arrested. It was difficult, though, walking around, to find young people with serviceable English. Here, unlike in India, the language seemed to be rapidly disappearing from the street. This was doubtless due to the short British rule in this part of the subcontinent, which was just under a century; it takes more than three generations to plant a language firmly in a region with so many already. Urdu, the national tongue (a vacuum-cleaner soldiers' language with Turkish grammatical roots, Hindi structures, and words from Persian, Punjabi, and Arabic; *urdu* means "military camp") is spoken "by most educated people throughout Pakistan." This was according to an old schoolteacher, who added patronizingly that around here "our common folk get along with Punjabi."

The Mall was fluent with English architecture, anyway, and suited the vague watercolors I had mentally painted in Kipling. The High Court was that typically extravagant imperial melange of Gothic, Mogul, and Victorian styles: the unmistakable message was that Gormenghast plus Hajii Baba plus Quasimodo adds up to justice. (One example is the fellow three years ago whom a Punjabi court sentenced to death for claiming he was Jesus; he was given an additional three years in the clink for saying that *The Satanic Verses* was all true.) Around the corner, a huge cathedral with extensive lawns sprawled behind an English wrought-iron fence. The post office, the town hall, the university, and the museum were likewise high Raj grandees, a reminder of how the British adventure here was as much romance and make-believe as it was greed. This polygamy of styles, united in a rhubarb brick, manages to be at the same time ostentatious, liberating, fanciful, powerful, and silly in a cartoonish way, and I could not fathom what the British meant to imply with it. Perhaps that they were learning here, as well as teaching.

Outside the museum was the huge bronze cannon Zamzamah, popularly known as Kim's Gun, since the novel, set in the late 1880s, begins with the boy defying municipal law by playing on it—as Pakistani boys still do. The museum (started in another building a block away, by Kipling's artist father Lockwood) was chock-full of spacious room after room of Nepalese brass statues, exquisite Mogul miniatures of emperors' wives, huge stone Hindu gods, tribal daggers and armor and swords and silks. Its predecessor in *Kim* was called "The Wonder House" by the street urchins of Lahore, and the name was even more deserved now. There were hookahs galore, and Tibetan temple banners, and ornate jewelry and coins; and after an hour I decided I would gladly back this museum against any in Asia.

The most impressive collection was sculpture from Gandhara, the large Buddhist kingdom which spread out of where Pakistan and Afghanistan meet from the fourth century B.C. to the fifth century A.D. The art was largely the result of Alexander the Great's invasion, when many of his men stayed behind; the result is the earliest representations of the Enlightened One, Buddhas with flowing Greek robes and the profile of Apollo. The most powerful is a gruesome, fasting Buddha, a severe masterpiece in blue-black stone whose cavernous eyes and tranquil suffering I found more horrifying than ever because of the statue's artistry. I watched a little boy go through the museum reverently touching various statues, happily constructing his own subtle theory of criticism. While his father followed and made sure he didn't break a piece off anything, he went directly from the emaciated Buddha in swirling robes to a statue of Queen Victoria that had stood for years on the Mall—from the begging bowl to the punch bowl.

The museum hammered into me this question: why does much of the subcontinent's refined art simply halt during the British takeover? Few books address this head-on; it is mentioned in passing, as if it were natural that people should stop painting extraordinary miniatures after several centuries. I suppose it's because the artists subsisted on a patronage system, and the latter-day patrons, the princes, became increasingly Europeanized (modernized) in their tastes. Why pay for a miniature when you can have a photo? The art historian Coomaraswamy put it sharply back in 1913. Craftsmanship, he said, is no less than a mode of thought, and he warned that "nearly every force at work and every tendency apparent in modern India is consciously or unconsciously directed towards the destruction of all skillful handicraft."

It made me wonder if the day would ever come when the bric-a-brac of the West would so penetrate India that even its Hindu and tribal folk art, which are mostly religious and thus so stubborn as to be all but invulnerable, would dwindle away. Pakistan, like many modern Muslim societies, produces little art that is not functional first, like carpets; the flowing Persian aesthetic that invaders brought for century after century survives nowadays mainly on the painted sides of trucks.

Lahore used to be a fortified city of twelve massive gates, whose names have outlived the largely pillaged walls. It has been a great city for at least a thousand years; one ancient proverb claimed that if Persia's Shiraz and Isfahan were united, they wouldn't make one Lahore. It was conquered, manhandled, occupied and ransacked by the Sikhs when they took advantage of the Mogul decline in the eighteenth century to seize the Punjab. They held it as their capital until their wars with the British in the mid-nineteenth century, after which they happily settled down to being the most reliable and tough soldiers in the Raj alongside the Gurkhas. At Partition most Sikhs went to India, or died trying.

It was illuminating to come to Lahore straight from the Indian Punjab, where the Sikhs run the show, for they are spoken of with disdain and deep annoyance here. A Pakistani mother who wants to frighten a misbehaving child will still let him know that So-and-so Singh will come get him unless he straightens out. When you've been into your fifth great mosque or palace or tomb that morning and found that once again the Sikhs had stripped it bare of the semiprecious decor two centuries ago, then used it as 1) a whorehouse 2) a storehouse 3) a public dump 4) a public stable—well, you do begin to get the point, no matter how much you might have enjoyed yourself in Amritsar.

Of course the past was still alive in these people. How could I have thought otherwise? Sometimes they were nothing but past. They all still distrusted—if not hated—each other, from end to end of the subcontinent.

Old Lahore is the dense, tottering, bazaar-city of Kipling's stories, and some of his titles, like *The Gate of a Hundred Sorrows*, could serve as name plaques every few steps. It was architecturally not as old as I'd imagined—this was because a lot of it got burned to the ground during Partition. Still, it was every bit as anarchic, boisterous, crammed, decrepit, exuberant, and aromatic. Clearly collapse had for centuries taken the place of city planning: lattices collapsed, towers collapsed, age-old balconies collapsed, roofs collapsed, entire buildings collapsed, and some makeshift replacement or other put up. The effect was of an eighteenth-century bazaar, with few houses actually that old. The wiring looked, on the other hand, totally original.

The most popular items in the little shop-stalls seemed to be fanwheels of paper rupees pinned together for wedding gifts.

Every other shop sold silks and cottons even more elaborately embroidered, spangled, encrusted, and ornate than their Indian counterparts; but in color, subtlety, and sheer beauty they were nothing compared to the glorious Bonnard universe of the Indian sari. One homeopath kept a live and extremely sedentary lion caged in the window, alongside other taxidermied animals; when I did the requisite double take he merely shrugged. He also sold powdered lion penis, only 5,000 rupees a gram ($125). The sleepy one in the window was a lousy advertisement.

The Wazir Khan was a mosque entirely on a small scale: a beautiful squarish courtyard, four towers, and brick walls with a painted fresco work as ornate as the decor on trucks, showing trees, flowers, urns, and verses from the Koran in Persian.

Remove thy heart from the gardens of the world, and know that this building is the true abode of man.

Around it was an intricate jumble of old brick and stone work, the upper stories of Old Lahore—fallen-in roofs, lots of satellite dishes, and kites fluttering and swooping and attacking each other above the old city. Colorful paper kites were one of Lahore's liberations. Popular throughout the country, they were an obsession here; Lahore hosts a huge kite festival every spring. The idea really was to attack: each kite string was made with ground glass, paste, and flax, and with great skill you could use your deadly twine to saw through another man's kitestring and send his treasure plummeting to the ground. Many power failures came about when children's kites flew into the rats' nests of convoluted electric lines. In the rainy season people often got electrocuted, trying to untangle their kite-strings from the naked old wires.

A motor-rickshaw to the Shalimar Gardens, just outside Lahore on the GT. Among donkey carts and shaded tongas packed with families for the afternoon. On the road's edge in a square of busy shop-stalls a barber was squatting and shaving a courageous man with a straight razor. In India this would be a good way to get mortally infected.

In a city of so many gardens the only ones built by the Moguls are the Shalimar, with the same fabled name as those over in Indian Kashmir. These Shalimar were built by Shah Jahan around 1642, midway through the construction of the Taj; few rulers have commissioned so much beautiful architecture. The walled gardens were peaceful and full of people strolling, mostly men. They wore that look of stupefied repression and frustration which comes from having your sexual fantasies fed on a public diet of film posters and the occasional slip of a veil; it made me think these must be the most unsensual people in the world.

I stood trying to picture the gardens all in bloom, before the marble that was once everywhere had been pillaged. The Mogul gardens tend to be planned rather like an elaborate board game, on several levels and with an almost classical symmetry. Eventually I realized that what my eye was missing in the formal garden layout was statues, which are forbidden in Islam. When the British came they used the Shalimar as a honeymoon site and turned some quarters into dak bungalows; they also tore up lots of centuries-old mango trees to make way for a rose garden. At least they somehow resisted building a bandstand. (In Lahore's Government House, built around the tomb of a Mogul khan—a cousin of Akbar—they had not been able to resist using the carved marble sarcophagus as the kitchen chopping board.)

My hope was to see the Shalimar fountains playing and avoid the buffalo, which are used to drag the lawnmowers here but wander around a little too freely the rest of the time. The fountains were dry, the buffalo were resting, but I did meet Aamer.

He was a young man, mid-twenties, in blue jeans—one of four pairs I saw in the entire country. (This is not the case in India, where the young especially try to be up-to-date.) We were both standing above the Hall of Light, an enclosed chamber in the middle of the trilevel gardens. Water sluiced from the upper level through the chamber, whose walls had hundreds of candles set in niches on three sides. The effect by night must've been dazzling: the musicians playing in stereo by a little pond with a stage like a lotus leaf, on which dancing girls cavorted before tossing clouds of gold dust on the guests. One satisfying thing about Mogul emperors is that they used their power to ensure pleasures that most of us, were we in their slippers, would choose as well—from dancing girls to gardens of paradise to enemies' heads impaled on kos minars.

Aamer said, "Are you English or American? I hope so."

"Why do you hope so?"

"I don't speak French or German. Don't worry, I'm not a guide."

"What are you, then?"

He shrugged, and laughed ruefully. "I'm an airline pilot, actually. Out-of-work, is that how you say it? Some problems with... well, with bribing the right people for a job. We'll see. Meanwhile, I'm meeting a friend here and wasting my life."

I explained that I was doing much the same thing.

He said, "It's too bad for you the fountains aren't working. I've seen those guidebooks that tell you which hours to come for the water. But I haven't seen these fountains working for weeks. I don't understand why the Moguls could do it and we can't, four centuries later. Back then every tree had its own gardener, can you imagine?"

"Cheap labor."

"So what? It's that way here now. We'll see how things change with the different government."

The ease with which he brought up the touchy subject of last week's coup surprised me; all the talk of corruption had made me imagine that talk too had been corrupted. I couldn't have been more wrong. Total strangers were comfortable telling you exactly what they thought, just as in India.

I asked how he'd vote in the coming elections, assuming they were held.

"Oh, they'll have to be held. Maybe a bit later than they say. I'll vote for Imran Khan."

This was a Pakistani cricket hero, a handsome playboy in his forties who had retired to London and recently married the young and very lovely daughter of one of the richest men in England. Now, returning, he was being talked about as a fresh breeze in Pakistani politics, rather as if Bjorn Borg were to marry well in Monte Carlo then go back to Sweden to run for prime minister.

"He's a good man, a straight man. And he doesn't need more money now, right? So we can trust him. Not like Benazir."

A country of sports fans, but they wouldn't vote that way.

"What about you, Aamer? Are you married, like Imran?"

"I've got a girlfriend."

"Will you marry her?"

"Maybe. Probably." He was evasive, but perhaps he wasn't sure himself, and I guessed she was the friend he was here in the gardens to meet.

"I thought most Pakistanis had arranged marriages."

"That's true. Most of the time. But, you know, my father's an eye doctor, and her father's a businessman. Our families are modern. I've got a sister in Texas. Married to a Pakistani doctor with a green card. So the families understand. We're lucky."

He seemed a little nervous and it occurred to me I must be making him late. We shook hands and he said, "You ought to do something for that cough. Just a moment." He wrote out a word on a slip of paper. "Ask for that at any little store. An old herbal remedy. As old as the Shalimar." He grinned. "You see? And these fountains have a cough today, too."

A dizzying morning of coughing and sleeping fitfully, waiting for the Indian antibiotics to take effect. All those gas fumes yesterday.

In the end Aamer's remedy—a teaspoonful of a powder called *joshanda* that looks like the bottom of a hamster's cage—did the trick, mixed in hot water.

LATEST ELECTRONICS!
MOBILE PHONES & GUNS!

The street heading down to Anarkali Bazaar, one of Kim's old haunts, led from a tires bazaar into a bicycle and small arms bazaar, where one store sold ingenious wheelchairs, handcranked on both sides. I nearly fell into an open sewer when an old man on a bike let out a blast on his horn, which was attached to a bicycle pump that made it louder than all the cars. Throughout Pakistan I was constantly amazed at the complex melodies of the vehicle horns: they ran with great velocity up and down the pentatonic and whole-tone scales, or through intricate Oriental flurries. I was told of one that played *Never On Sunday*.

On the Mall a corner display had newspapers hung so people could stand and read for free, and along a sidewalk was a mini-bazaar of outdated foreign magazines. There was also a Jewelers' Row, for much of Islam has a deep faith in gold bracelets and a deep distrust of banks. The paradox was that even though Pakistan economically looks pathetic on paper, worse off than India, to someone just strolling around, people looked much better off here. Perhaps there's a more equitable distribution of what little money there is, for I was rarely confronted with the bone-breaking poverty I saw at all times in India.

A few of the old private clubs from British days, like the Punjab Club where Kipling was a member, do still exist, but they have been forced over the years to shift their premises from those embarrassingly grand edifices on the Mall to obsequious lesser quarters on side streets. The enormous white mansion that was the Punjab Club, where Kipling went to drink after writing the newspaper all day—"the old, wearying, Godless futile life at a club—same men, same talk, same billiards"—is now a government staff headquarters a blinding block long. Men who might not have been permitted into any London gentlemen's club could relax in one larger than any of them; it was here that the young sub-editor nearly got into a fist fight with O'Dwyer, the bully partly responsible years later for the Amritsar massacre.

Kipling's years in Lahore (1882 to 1887), in his teens and early twenties before his big promotion to Allahabad, were spent on the staff of the *Civil and Military Gazette*. It was where he joined the Freemasons and also had his first encounters with Indian "courtesans." As half the newspaper's editorial staff, he had to painstakingly correct the Muslims, Hindus, and Sikhs who set the type by hand and had little idea what it all meant. The building where he worked, like the large bungalow where he lived with his family, has been demolished. "Outside during the day everything is dusty and redhot," he said once. "You drink there for the liquid, and not for the liquor, and the minute you drink it you feel it coming out through your shirt." There were the fans, too, blowing every piece of paper but kept "ceaselessly going to prevent suffocation." And there was also the cholera, that killed foreigners off regularly. No wonder (although most of the Indians around him and in his stories were Muslims) that a core idea of Hinduism and Buddhism, the illusory nature of this world, seeped into his bones; *Kim,* with the lama's spiritual quest on the GT, is saturated in it.

The best way to see how the British relaxed here was to visit the main public library on the Mall, whose staid white arches and columns look rather formal and parliamentary on the outside. Once the Gymkhana Club, it could easily be the national assembly of some medium-size country. Inside, though, the arches go up, up, up past five glittering chandeliers, the balustraded mezzanines of books look over grand lawns and tennis courts, the ceilings are a dreamy swirl of flowers and skylights and inset flower mirrors. It makes a serene and pretty library, warm with sunlight pouring in, full of English books and foreign magazines immaculately kept, and quiet reading nooks with standing lamps. You sit there trying to imagine it as the private club for a membership of several dozen, served by turbanned waiters and the rest. Or in later years, just before Partition, when Lahore was full of bars, cafés, cabarets, theaters, and a fashionable red-light district; and when here in the Gymkhana Club under British auspices, according to one historian, "the distance between the communities was often reduced to the thickness of a sari as Sikhs, Moslems and Hindus rumbaed and did the fox trot together."

Then the muezzin goes blaring off outside and you are really not sure where you are, or where this ever was.

The key to a mosque's beauty lies in the proportions, and they make the Badshahi Mosque sublime, with a soap-bubble perfection to rival the Taj Mahal and a sense of religious exaltation to equal the Golden Temple. It was all in red Jaipur sandstone with scalloped tops and tulip windows and three fat floating tulip globes. I heard it claimed that the vast courtyard could hold 100,000; but it was the absolute balance of all the lines that was so exquisite, and I stood there gaping to the clack-clack of men making slate slabs for the courtyard.

The mosque was built by the emperor Aurangzeb (1618–1707), who'd once sent his brother's head, gift-wrapped, to his imprisoned father Shah Jahan. As the last Mogul with any real power—he wore a disembowelling claw on one arm—he was the equal of any when it came to pithy remarks. "There are only two men in India," he observed, "who are not drunkards: myself and the Chief Justice." In fact that Italian doctor Manucci, the self-styled enema inventor, was sending the Chief Justice every day "a supply of the spirits, which he relished in secret." So much for the illusions of emperors.

In the middle of the mosque's stately courtyard was a fountain where men were busy with pre-prayer ablutions. A Muslim must pray five times a day, but he must also three times daily wash his mouth, his nose ("Sniff out everything that's inside!" the gent who was explaining all this to me pointed up his nostrils), his face, his right arm up to the elbow, his left arm up to the elbow, his hair and neck and ears, then his right foot and his left foot. One of the most remarkable things about the subcontinent, which is filthy, is how often everyone washes. But this is probably the moment to point out that, street for street, Pakistan is much, much cleaner than India.

The lavish exterior of the Badshahi Mosque is covered with delicate white floral designs and curlicues raised off the ochre stone. Entering one of the prayer chambers I realized that the interior is in reverse: colors on white. These interior frescoes rising from fluted columns, chamber after chamber of them, are a chain of flowers that hover on the edge of abstraction and grow more complex as one moves outward from the innermost prayer hall. The marble-floored chambers were later used, naturally, as a Sikh bordello.

The enormous Royal Fort, built mainly by Akbar in the 1560s and considerably embroidered by his successors, is so large and new looking it might be a film set. The main gate, with big chess-piece towers and crenelated walls, faces the Badshahi Mosque and dominates a large square which, with its broad burgha trees, dogs, and children playing, forms a kind of historical summary of power. There is the poet Iqbal's modest tomb, and the mausoleum of the Sikh leader Ranjit Singh, their one-eyed Thomas Jefferson, who filled the Shalimar Gardens with good-looking girls and boys and every night drank a signature mix of opium, corn liquor, musk, and raw meat juice. His grand ornate tomb here was inaccessible unless you were a Sikh, and then only twice a year. There was also an elaborate Sikh pavilion in the square, now filled with Muslim men snoring away the morning.

Inside the fort you are confronted by lawns with cannons, which pretty much sums up the Mogul philosophy. This fort was the typical combination of gardens, fortress, royal apartments, and ship of state. The scale is expansive but intimate. Every building was open due to the climate, and gives onto the gardens, which flow everywhere. Here were Shah Jahan's stately sleeping quarters, with a little fountain for the cooling effect and also for the secrecy of conversation ensured by the babble of water; there a parking area for elephants, and the large Hall of Public Audiences, later used as a hospital by the British. A harem had its own small and once-enclosed garden of cypresses and fruit trees exclusively for the women. The Hall of Mirrors was room after room of thousands of small petalled mirrors in arabesques. On a starlit night the torches must've made it like inhabiting a prism.

To look at such architectural comforts raises a shiver at the thought of the congested, cold life of European royalty in drafty old castles. A lot of the Royal Fort's interior is patchy; a large quadrangle lost many of its foundation stones when one of Ranjit Singh's sons, in an intramural war with another Sikh, bombarded it from the nearby mosque's minarets and destroyed a lot of buildings which even the British couldn't repair. What comes across, still, is the elaborate Mogul use of public space, seemingly improvised but careful in its air of constant surprise, that makes the British approach to public spaces in New Delhi or Calcutta seem lifeless and unyielding.

Outside you could see one wall of the fort as it once was, prior to the Sikh renovation. In a mosaic of semiprecious stones and bright blue, red, yellow, green tiles, elephants and horses battled or marched in procession. Below them on the street, men were grinding sugarcane for juice, to mix with fresh lime.

In Kipling's day Lahore was considered, like so much of the British Indian Empire, a hardship post. As the center of government for the Punjab, it still required only a few hundred British civil servants and army staff; the mind-boggling fact about the Raj is how few British there actually were. And as much as Lahore has grown since Kipling's day, there are only about two hundred fifty expat families here, many of them teachers, doctors, missionaries. The rest run national branches of international corporations like airlines, ad agencies, soft-drink manufacturers, and candy-bar makers, one goal being to provide as much long-term work as possible for local dentists.

And Lahore is still considered, for foreigners, a hardship post, even though there are gardens and parks everywhere—as omnipresent as in Paris—and the city's mood is leafy, open, nonhysterical. This hardship status is partly because Pakistan is an extremely lawless country; the wealthy are prone to kidnappings, murders, and robberies. It's also difficult to get alcohol, much less good alcohol. The only place I found, full (as it turned out) of these multinational foot soldiers, was the American Club, where I managed to wangle an invitation at the thirsty end of the day.

The name was misleading in a Lahore context. There was no sense of social pretense, and no one a century from now will ever turn this anonymous house into a great library. There were ties to the U.S. Consulate down the road—this was in a developed new area of the city where there were few power failures—and security was tight: a barrier at the entry, an I.D. check, the mirror-search for bombs beneath every car that entered the grounds. But half the men rappelling their way along the fully equipped bar were Australians.

"Make yourself at home, Yank. Grateful to you. If it weren't for this little shack there'd be no sanity in Pakistan. It's even worse here than the bloody Middle East. At least there if you can prove to them you're an alcoholic they'll let you buy the stuff for medicinal purposes. Here . . . "

"Put that away, mate, your money's no good in here. It's all chits. Alf's good with numbers, he'll do the buying. We'll all share the drinking. Welcome to Pakistan."

"Numbers? You want some numbers? Try one hundred forty million people in this bloody country, how many bloody taxpayers would you expect? Go on, guess. Go on. Not even close. Try eight hundred thousand, mate. Half a percentile. Missing a few zeros, wouldn't you say?"

"I'd say so." I pointed out that in India there were a whopping 12 million taxpayers out of a billion population—a rate twice as good, if good is the word.

"Last year old B.B.—that's right, except I call her Brigitte Bardot—paid taxes on thirty-eight thousand rupees. Do you believe it? That was her reported official income—about ten thousand dollars U.S. Meanwhile she goes and buys a three-million-sterling property over in U.K. Presumably with all she saved on taxes, right? And she wonders why they took away her cell phone and threw her out. Not to mention dancing on her brother's grave."

"You know what they call her husband, don't you?"

"Who might end up her late husband, by the way."

"Or her formerly-a-free-man husband."

"Mr. Ten Percent. 'Cause that's his cut on every deal in Islamabad. There's a couple's made loads of friends."

"Meanwhile the government just bought a few submarines to defend the country against nuclear attack. Which could seem a bit excessive if you have a gander at the coastline. I mean, let's just say they've got slightly less beachfront than Sydney on a windy day. Third of the bloody budget goes to defense, if you believe the papers, which seems mighty absurd."

"On the other hand, if I've got to be stuck here for two years, I don't mind being defended. Problem is, there's nothing to bloody do once you are."

"I'll defend you, Alf, don't worry."

"Have you seen the newspapers? The ones in English. They're not bad, all things being equal—I mean, they almost say what they like, at least some of the time."

"They had that business about being the second most corrupt country in the world right there in a headline the other day. They were actually *proud* of it. And the India rivalry's there every bloody minute, on every page."

"But that's what keeps them going, after all. Remember Kashmir, eh?"

"Who could forget her!"

"Still, must drive 'em bonkers to watch Indian TV every night and see how much fun the Hindus are having. Not to mention all their fellow Mossies who stayed behind. Not that polo and Shiva and that cobra music is my idea of fun. But at least you can buy a drink down in Delhi without having to file a bloody certificate."

It was the paperwork that seemed most absurd to expats. If you were a non-Muslim foreigner you could buy locally made beer and spirits at certain licensed places, and you could bring a certain amount of the good stuff in every time you entered the country. Fortunately a lot of these men were flying over to Hong Kong or Singapore every other week. The Pakistani booze left much to be desired: the infamous Murree Beer, started by the British in 1860, was an eloquent example. The back of the label, legible after you'd finished the bottle, said GUARANTEED GLYCERINE FREE.

As a foreign tourist I was at one of the few hotels in the city licensed to serve me alcohol, but it meant filling in forms and having it in my room so as not to torment the Muslim guests. I couldn't drink at the modern hotel a street away, despite my passport, because I wasn't a guest there. The Pakistani government was like a pesky old great-aunt who, while you're visiting her for a few days, will do nearly anything to keep you sober. For all these resident Australian and European and American businessmen and their spouses, survival was absolutely predicated on the existence of this club. They could depend on the bar most evenings, so the few bottles of quality whiskey they brought in were preciously hoarded at home. Any terrorist who wanted to get, say, Pepsi-Cola and British Airways and the rest out of the country would do more damage at the American Club than by bombing any twenty offices.

There was also a sizable old Christian Pakistani community who could buy all the non-glycerine beer they wanted, as could the tiny percentage of Hindus. According to the Aussies, these two efficient groups together had the black market well covered. Aamer had told me the day before that occasionally he'd splurge and buy liquor from a Christian peddler at vast prices.

Much to complain about here, but from a business point of view the foreigners were left alone, compared to other places. One soft-drink executive pointed out to me that it'd taken only a couple of months to get business underway in Pakistan; in India, with its terror of multinationals, even though they were now officially "welcome" there'd been two years of red tape.

As the evening was winding down I remarked that the streets seemed surprisingly well-kept after India, and there were moments when Lahore felt almost sedate—not many, mind you, but still . . .

"See that couple over there? Typical story. Couple of kids, comfortable house not too far from here. You can easily afford a full staff in Pakistan. So they've got a gardener, a cook, a cleaner. And, of course, two guards to make sure there's no trouble. Some expats prefer 'em armed, these people liked 'em unarmed. Doesn't matter. In fact the guards were robbing the house themselves. Took a few months to figure it out. Now the couple's really skeered. They've hired the guards through an agency, they let the agency know what's going on, but the really delicate part is getting rid of the guards without repercussions. Get 'em arrested and you've got serious problems. Transfer 'em to another household and *those* people have problems. So the agency very nicely transferred the two guards to the other side of the country in a corporate post, a factory or somewhere, essentially a promotion, then let 'em go one by one so they'd never suspect a thing and not come back to exact retribution. But it's touch and go here, all the time. Let me tell you, mate, *my* bloody guards are armed."

> Its people have no good looks; of social intercourse, paying and receiving visits, there is none; of genius and capacity none; in handicrafts and work there is no form or symmetry, method or quality; there are no good horses, no good dogs, no grapes, muskmelons or first-rate fruits, no ice or cold water, no good bread or cooked foods in the bazaars, no hot baths, no colleges, no candles or candlesticks.
>
> —Babur the Tiger (1526)

20.

Any Friend of Flashman's Is a Friend of Mine

The Faletti's people rewarded me with hot water my last morning. I thanked them by stealing a lovely green ashtray.

After a couple of hours spent in search of more antibiotics and joshanda and a detailed road map (the latter impossible to come by; someone must fear an invasion), I left at noon. Great weather this season: seventy by day, sweater-cool at night.

It took a lot of bickering over price, but at last transport for the hundred eighty miles to Rawalpindi was arranged via Faletti's. A green Toyota Corolla, ten years old, driven by the gentle, imperturbable Khalid Pervaz. Gray hair, the usual smock and trousers, an aquiline look and rudimentary English. I couldn't wait to find out if the GT here was more dangerous than the Indian road; Pakistanis have the edge in reputation as being the worst drivers on the subcontinent.

Along the Mall past Kim's cannon, past the huge British cathedral ("There is no cathedral here," a man had told me in puzzlement, a block away), and finally onto the GT. Soon we were skirting Old Lahore, threading the hot anarchy of densely painted "flying" buses, three-wheeled motor-rickshaws, bicycles, tongas, and motorcycles. I started keeping a list of images seen on these rickshaws, which are the modern equivalent of ekka pony-carts. The images are mostly unwelcome in official Islam: airplanes, eagles, cutlasses, butterflies, hearts, fish, flowers, minarets, camels, eyes, teapots, tigers, a mongoose and cobra in mortal combat. Someone should start filling a museum with these contraptions. They should also outlaw leaded gas and put up a monument, a giant set of lungs, to the Unknown Rickshaw Driver.

As we crossed a new bridge I spotted a vast herd of water buffalo below on one shore. The Ravi, which is spoken of as a real river, becomes virtually an estuary at this time of year, and one lone buffalo, standing halfway across, was wet only to its knees. This was the same view that Kipling described in *On the City Wall*, his story of a Lahore prostitute: "...you saw all the cattle of the City being driven down to water, the students of the Government College playing cricket, the high grass and trees that fringed the river-bank, the great sand-bars that ribbed the river, the red tombs of dead Emperors beyond the river, and very far away through the blue heat-haze, a glint of the snows of the Himalayas."

I couldn't spy any snow through the pale pollution haze, but before leaving Lahore there was a last Mogul edifice I wanted to see: the tomb of the emperor Jahangir (1569–1627), remembered for his love of the natural sciences, his calm, his drinking problem, and his habit of having enemies impaled on stakes, torn apart by elephants, chewed by dogs, and bitten by serpents. All were perhaps a result of his father Akbar keeping him under house arrest as a young man while having his lover, a dancing girl, buried alive.

The emperor's tomb lies in Shahdara, a few miles from Lahore after a turnoff from the GT. A busy wood and steel market and a homeopathic skin clinic gave way to an area of palms, great filth, and jumbled do-it-yourself architecture, the men walking in dull colors, the women in bright. This squalid town provided much of the milk for the people of Lahore; I saw cows standing up to their knees in sewage and was glad of my many vaccinations. One of Kipling's earliest Lahore articles had been about dairy hygiene and the typhoid problem.

The Moguls always built vast gardens around their tombs, an earthly paradise to match the heavenly one. In Shahdara the outer gardens had been enclosed by walls to form a serai with frescoed gates, a hundred eighty rooms, and a mosque, all shaded by old burgha trees. It had a bit of the feel of Spanish missions in California—and in much the same way subsequent armies, in this case Sikhs and British, had used it as a military encampment.

The equally vast inner garden held Jahangir's Tomb at one end, built by Shah Jahan a decade after his father's death, in 1637. (Jahangir was the first Mogul emperor that Europeans met.) I have seen the long, low tomb called dull, dismal, or else the great masterpiece of Mogul building after the Taj. It resembled none of the others—a stark, sleek, one-story platform, with eleven shadowy arched portals on each side and four very tall corner towers, all in red sandstone with inlaid white and yellow marble in ornate zigzags and geometries. The effect is very red and sober, with nothing grandiose but with enormous power. To my eye it was a deeply haunting design, masterful and very moving.

Though the interior, a series of vaulted compartments, had once again been picked at by Ranjit Singh to ornament the Golden Temple in Amritsar, it didn't look ravaged. There were colorful floral frescoes and *pietra dura* inlay everywhere, and the actual tomb was a slab of marble inlaid with realistic and delicate flowers of semiprecious stones and the Ninety-Nine Names of God. My 1883 guidebook was poetic enough to provide some of these:

Who Causes Death.
Who Knows the Hidden.

The Long Suffering.
The Rich.
The Guide.
The Greatest.

Among the mango and palm trees schoolboys were playing catch with an empty Pepsi can.

The stalwart Elizabethan walker Thomas Coryat had earned the sympathy, admiration, and charity of Jahangir one morning at the emperor's regular appearance before his people. This was down in Ajmer, near Agra, when Coryat's need was great: he had all but run out of money. Coryat's Persian, though, was abundant, and he spoke of the ruler's "glorious court" and said he'd come all this way to see "Your Majesties elephants" and the Ganges, "captaine of all the rivers of the world." He had on his journey "sustained much labour and toile, the like whereof no mortall man in this world did ever perform, to see the blessed face of Your Majesty."

The speech worked. Jahangir replied in Persian and threw him a hundred silver rupees, about ten pounds sterling, which was a fortune in terms of local prices and Coryat's needs. Later the English ambassador complained to Coryat that it was most, most unbecoming for a countryman to beg. Coryat was used to fending off the insults of wits like Ben Jonson and John Donne; he could eviscerate a mere bureaucrat. "I answered . . . in that stout and resolute manner that he was contented to cease nibling at me."

At Gharibwal a line of trucks bearing steel coils was pulled to the side waiting for inspection. Abruptly we were free of the city—the GT's four narrow lanes separated in two directions by seared trees down the middle. This, after the Indian road, seemed remarkably insightful. The land was brown and uneventful, with clusters of shops around an occasional gas pump. As in India, you drive on the left and pass on the right. That is the theory.

The Pakistani dhabas are much the same as Indian ones—free rope cots, food, fire, open ground. The Urdu phrase is "truck driver hotel" or "highway hotel," though *daaba* does occur too. In Punjabi it's called a truck *ada* ("island"). The trucks are mostly six- or ten-wheelers. Many are Bedfords, with plenty of Mercedes and Isuzus as well—engines, chassis, and wheels imported, the bodies made here. They often sport chains off the back and the high-protruding front, like short skirts of hanging chain mail, and little good-luck talismans—bells and amulets. Their painted inscriptions often invoke Allah, but there might be romance, too—LOVE IS MY PROFESSION, or an imprecation against lawyers, faith healers, and lovely women, or a plea to a beloved: DO NOT CONFUSE ME ON MY LONG, LONELY JOURNEY. IS THIS YOUR FACE I SEE BEFORE ME, OR THE SHIMMERING, RADIANT MOON?

The working landscape was like Bihar: beyond trudging water buffalo, the barbed wire and rude brick houses of a chemical factory or a brick kiln pouring smoke. There are several thousand such kilns in the country, with perhaps half a million workers—and as in India, most are essentially indentured slaves who, despite court rulings, are imprisoned in the system for life, like at least another million Pakistani slave laborers.

Every town was tough and looked as if it were just being built, its engineering works like exposed intestines and nothing painted. The GT as main street was usually a mess of open sewage trenches, piled branches for burning, giant vats and unattached plumbing, a textile mill, a bank, and a few shops selling sodas, blood oranges, cigarettes. Smokestacks would be pouring filth, with the relieving glamour and gore of a lurid film poster. Mosques in these road towns had a fanciful, elaborate, almost Hindu quality to their architecture—exaggerated by the eerie soundtrack of truck horns ripping up and down their arabesque riffs at astonishing speed.

And amidst it all, the balanced pose of a man or boy in a smock, standing on the rocking wooden platform of a horse cart, the rope reins held easily, gently chucking the willing animal along, as if being pulled through the air on some moving walkway.

So far the road in Pakistan was safer and faster than in India. The trucks held more, and weren't overloaded.

Starting in Gujranwala, the GT turned into a modern highway, studded with power lines—as if the World Bank had arrived last year with fistfuls of cash. The divider of venerable trees became a concrete barrier one meter high, studded with reflectors and storm drains. There might as well be a sign announcing Western engineering. This safety barrier must drive the locals crazy, to have to clamber over it to get from one side of town to another.

At Wazirabad the landscape changed radically, with cultivated fields on both sides—a Punjab I knew. A toll booth got us before we crossed the Chenab river. ("The force of the current of the Chenab will be observed; the alligators are large and numerous," said my 1883 *Murray's Guide*, after recommending I stay where there were "fewer fleas," in the special quarters fitted up for the Prince of Wales, who'd opened the bridge in 1876 with a gold hammer and silver rivet.) The British Raj was, fortunately, an empire of engineers; in the stretch from Lahore to Peshawar alone, the Grand Trunk had required 550 bridges and tunnels through six different mountain masses. It was not a fully bridged road from Calcutta to Peshawar, possible for cars without detours, until the 1930s.

In Kharian Cantonment, I saw a yelling military policeman forcibly yank a man out of his car and onto the road as a crowd shrank back. Khalid shook his head at my request to pull over, and I realized he was trying to do us both a favor.

The terrain grew hilly and the GT became a single disputed roadway with men repairing it on one side. Suddenly there were escarpments all around, where the road had been cut through the hills. A train of old cars labeled PESHAWAR-LAHORE-KARACHI went rattling past, above the road—the passengers staring down with the easy superiority and relaxed air that train travel bestows.

In Sarai Alamgir an accident had blocked the heart of town—a truck lay crumpled and wretched on its side. Nevertheless, this was only the second accident in about a hundred miles.

Having dealt with the Sutlej and Beas in India, I was now knocking off the other three rivers of the Punjab quickly. The Jhelum felt like a real waterway, with a modern bridge and an even more modern one being built alongside. Alexander, probably the first foreign invader to use the road, had fought a great battle to cross it; his tireless horse Bucephalus, favorite of schoolboys everywhere, was buried nearby. He had died either of wounds or of strain on an old heart, having been with Alexander since age fifteen; he had carried his master in full body armor across the Jhelum in full flood on a hot June day, and sustained him through the battle. A couple of towns near here were disputed as being the one named in the horse's honor.

Every conqueror coming in the opposite direction, even the poet Babur, had raced through these rocky hillsides. This was the end of the generous Punjab, the fields that stretch down across India. From here on the landscape was bleak and hard.

A woman with a curvaceous golden pot balanced on her head, striding along an embankment behind her child.

Dina was the biggest place so far, a dusty town with large concrete pipes lying everywhere and half its buildings collapsed into rubble. Its disassembled urgency matched the chaos of the lunar landscape, whose only life was the odd wheat field and scorched acacia bushes.

Soon we came into a jumbled plain of gouged ravines, with scraggly kikal trees and sweeping undulations of woodsy terrain.

In Gujar Khan I saw my first kos minar; later I decided it might be the only one on the entire Pakistani GT. Someone had surmounted it with a crucifix, of all things, and painted the whole pillar in stripes and built an enclosure for it as for some statue. But it was still a kos minar.

It was nearly five: at last the light was mellowing, the day cooling, the "truck islands" starting to fill with drivers who didn't want to pass Rawalpindi tonight. Even vultures were on their way home; another busy day of roadkill done. The sun was setting rapidly on our left, a brilliant yellow disc, with a hazed yellow wash falling like a shroud across the countryside.

A marble foundry by the road: billowing clouds of white dust blew about the bodies of men drowning, choking, wavering in it.

At Riwat (the name indicated a serai was here once) a branch road hooked right, toward Islamabad, the new modern capital built in the 1960s. I stayed on the GT for the much older sister city, Rawalpindi. Dust was everywhere, blowing from the fields, from the embankments where men were working on the road, from more marble foundries, from the sky and the hills. It was a light gray dust the color of the sky and soon it covered the world.

At twilight I was glad to be getting off the GT. The wooded outskirts of Pindi, as it's popularly called, were like a diplomatic congress of Pakistani public life. There was a UN Military Observer Group for India & Pakistan; the Rawalpindi Golf Club; a Royal Canadian School, a polo club, an Odeon Cinema; and, still, the ex-British army messes. The new Cardiology Hospital had a gory sculpture of a heart out front. The Haj Complex was where pilgrims on their way to Mecca camped for a couple of days, got organized, then flew to Jeddah. And there was a good mile of army cantonments with a long colonnade leading in and armed sentries before a very grand colonial-era military headquarters. Superficially at least, even more than the railways, the Pakistani army had taken on the Raj skin, from buildings and layout to rank and file. Pindi remains, as in British days, one of the most important military towns in Pakistan; here in 1849 an entire turbanned army surrendered, ending the Second Sikh War.

At a traffic light we followed an old black and yellow taxi, a Morris Minor three decades old, into the cantonment. The Grand

Trunk Road took on airs and became the Mall. There was a church, a cricket club, tall cypress trees. Then Khalid slowed, and we turned into Flashman's Hotel.

LOOK INTO THE FUTURE WITH PROFESSOR GHARI
ASTROLOGER PALMIST HOROSCOPE SPECIALIST
PLEASE ASK THE FRONT DESK FOR DIRECTIONS

But to find Professor Ghari you already had to be able to look into the future, because he was taking the night off.

One remark by Khalid—who left for Lahore immediately after dropping me off—stuck with me the next day. I'd asked him how far the Grand Trunk went. He thought for a moment, realizing it was a serious question, and said, "The GT Road goes Delhi to Kabul." To these people Kabul, over in Afghanistan, is a reality; when someone over there falls sick, a couple of hundred miles away, someone here gets a headache.

Apart from the spangled name, Flashman's Hotel has nothing romantic about it. It was started in the 1850s or 1860s, was later one of the Cecil chain throughout British India, and is now one of four old hotels run by the government. Unfortunately it lost whatever architectural charm it once had by being covered in ribbed white concrete not long ago; today Flashman's resembles an ice-skating rink or a bowling alley. As at a motel, you drive right up to the room, which lacked a Koran but which did have hot water. It was the first hotel I'd stayed in since Bihar that was actually on the Grand Trunk Road.

When I asked about the name, assuming it was called by some wag after the character in *Tom Brown's Schooldays*, the desk clerk said, "Not at all. It was owned by a Mr. Flashman about a hundred years ago." A century from now, will someone come along and wonder if the hotel was named after the fictional character of our era? After all, Pindi is part of that cavalryman's stomping ground; and the real Mr. Flashman will by then be totally erased. Old soldiers don't fade away, they manage the front desk.

A gray stucco marker in the shape of a shield, or an open book, stood in the GT's divider outside Flashman's. It was the only such oracle in fourteen hundred miles. It said GRAND TRUNK ROAD. White panels showed thirty-five places, in random order, on both sides:

KABUL	393	KM
LAHORE	275	
AMRITSAR	337	
MURREE	63	
DELHI	785	
ATTOCK	82	
PESHAWAR	167	

The air in Rawalpindi was clearer than in Lahore—crisper, with a faint hint of winter behind the heat. It got me up for a dewy early morning walk. Mists were lifting as young cricketers did laps around the expansive green playing pitch across the road from Flashman's. Down the lane past an English church, a school was receiving its walking flock: the boys in white shirts, dark blue pants, and V-necks, the girls with sky blue smocks and white trousers. Outside the school the older students parked their bicycles and scooters organized by model and by color.

Rawalpindi, at least along the GT, still felt like a British garrison town, a place resolutely following a colonial example. There was the manicured look of the army cantonments, replete with flowers and freshly ironed lawns and solidly barricaded gates. There was the tired sweeper with a rag, polishing the huge howitzer set as decoration right on the road: army surplus as modern sculpture. At seven-thirty he pocketed the rag and was off—with a new spring in his step, as if done for the day. And on one corner loomed a big sign for some imported English item I didn't understand: STILLMAN'S SHAVING-FRECKLE-BLEACH CREAM.

Number 13, the Mall, was an imposing black wrought-iron gate with brass medallions, so gleaming I thought there must be a grand mansion behind. When I peered over there was only a decrepit abandoned bungalow, its fountain full of leaves. It looked ghostly and forlorn, like most British sites here that hadn't been taken over by a government agency or the military. The neglect seemed never quite as total as in India—not as if a half century had gone by but only ten years; not as if several generations had passed, but as if the heir had run out of money a while back and been forced to move on.

Beside it I wandered round the garden of St. Paul's Church (dated 1908)—the edifice in red brick with a tall steeple, Church of Scotland; services Friday and Saturday, which are the Muslim weekend. Then someone threw a piece of tarmac at me—unless bits of the GT were dropping out of the trees. I glanced about; maybe a schoolboy prank. Yellow roses were thriving, and parts of the garden were being used for makeshift greenhouses and a furniture maker's lean-to. But the church was shut tight today.

Across the road from Flashman's was an artillery officers' mess and an athletic training field for the army from which two helicopters were lifting. There was also a cricket pitch where a team of young men, age sixteen to twenty or so, was now training. Pakistanis everywhere are obsessed with the sport, except in the North-West Frontier where they're only fanatical about it.

The coach, whom I'll call Mr. Argileh, was a dark-skinned man in his forties who, according to his players, had been one of the country's finest. He'd lived a decade in the U.K., playing on a county team, and spoke a rapid-fire English no doubt garnered from arguments with old league mates who were Oxford grads. He was a voluble critic of the old government, the present interim government, and any new government that might have the misfortune to come along and be raked with the crossfire of his scrutiny. When I asked about the nickname I'd heard for Benazir's husband ("Mr. Ten Percent"), he shouted, "Mr. Ninety Percent! That's how much he takes! Out of every deal that passes across the surface of his fucking bureau! Mr. Ninety Percent!"

We talked about his team's prospects in upcoming matches in Karachi and Lahore. If the corporate-sponsored team did well, the better players would have a shot at the national team, one of the finest in the world. Cricket was these boys' main chance in life, their ticket out of poverty and perhaps abroad, as it had been for Mr. Argileh. I assumed he'd run out of money over in the U.K.

In no time he was back on the subject every Pakistani was ready to speak about openly. "Do you think we are ever going to have a decent government in this country? Don't you believe it, man! Not a goddamned chance! Things can go down the drain and they stand by the sink and wash more bloody water after!"

I asked if he, like my Lahore friend Aamer, thought highly of the political future of his colleague in sport, Imran Khan.

He spat. "That guy. Always looking in the mirror. We don't have to worry about him, eh? Now he's got that beautiful English girl with all her father's bloody millions, do you think he's going to make a real politician? Not a prospect! The damn-you damn-me cheek. Every one of our politicos is dishonest, one after the next. You can go to sleep for years in this country, you wake up and it's still the same story. Listen, I'll tell you the damn truth. Our politicos are always bloody rich people or they're poor people who end up bloody rich. I promise you! One day I want to see an honest politician who ends up poor. Otherwise, fuck me, I tell you, one day, fuck all this, time to get out."

He was full of invective; but if his speech had no direction his anger did. This is a Muslim strength: they are ready to do something. So much of the simmering Hindu rage seemed ready to express itself in futility—burning down a mosque, or setting oneself ablaze in protest, or marching by the thousands. As a more artistic people, believers in immobile eternal law and the inevitability of rebirth, the mere expression could be purpose enough. But my cricket friend here was just getting started. He would take action at some point, even if that action was to leave again and send money home, like millions of Pakistanis. In a situation of genuine futility, with little prospect for true democracy, they would do something eventually, even if it blew the country apart—which was why Pakistan often got held together at gunpoint. This was not a country of people standing around waiting and hoping, no matter how much they might trust in Allah.

The first moments inside a Pakistani motor-rickshaw are amazing. What looks so crudely made, if fancifully painted, on the outside, is in fact quite sophisticated on the inside. They are, to start with, much more enclosed and comfortable and better put together than the Indian variety. Though essentially a shell fitted over a scooter, you feel as if you're traveling in a tiny roomette, with enough space for two short people on its couch. There is a tilted oval mirror so you can admire yourself. Dozens of aluminum tubes, pipes, braces and bars are painted and wrapped and studded and have green, yellow, blue, and red wrapping and plastic gewgaws. The driver alone has eight personal mirrors to examine his own reflection in while steering his scooter handlebars, which are set in an actual dashboard. There are big springs boinging gaily all over the place.

Heading to the Old City part of Rawalpindi, my rickshaw bridged the winding Leh River and I had a glimpse of green riverbank that could've been Scotland, except that those highlands don't have local women swathed head to foot in black. The so-called Kashmiri Bazaar was a helter-skelter of stores: refrigerators, stereo equipment with handmade speakers, gun belts. Toilets were sold on the sidewalk, alongside squatting dentists with painted metal signs showing a set of grinning teeth. Cigarettes were for sale individually.

Behind one rank of shops was the quiet enclosure of a church in a secret courtyard. I found it only because I noticed a table selling Billy Graham books in Urdu, and—having a literary bent—I ducked into the shadows. The First U.P. Church Pindi was a Presbyterian church built in 1835, white up to its knees, then red brick. It was open, at least, with a quiet interior of vaulted carved beams. A few holes in the roof needed repair.

"A question of money, of course," the minister said. "Over the years all the other Christian churches stole members from us—the Catholic, the Anglican. So what can you do?"

He invited me to a Sunday service, but did point out that it would be in Urdu. I said I'd be in Peshawar by then.

In Old Pindi I found Nanakpura, a lovely cool interior street of Kashmiri Bazaar that belonged to another century. Its shoulder-to-shoulder houses were in pastel colors, with overhanging balconies, heavily filigreed lattices, elaborately outlined windows and carved doors with seven interwoven circles etched in—a symbol of something, since it was everywhere. Several boys were playing badminton, dodging the pooled water and trench sewers, and a single kite was flying above the snarled electric wires.

For a few moments there was an American playing badminton in the street with the Rawalpindi boys.

When I sat down on a doorstoop to rest, one of two heavyset Pakistani women in robes and half-veil approached me and, in a thick Scottish accent, asked where I was from. Her accent seemed unbelievable at first, issuing from that draped figure, but she turned out to be from Glasgow, born of a Pakistani family there just under fifty years ago.

She said, "Do ye like this street? It's an old Indian street, ye know. Can ye tell? From the Indian time, back before the Partition."

"Beautiful houses."

"I suppose." She sniffed and gave a wan smile.

"And do you like living here?"

"Well." She gave a slight nod over her shoulder, which seemed to communicate to the other woman that she'd not be long. "To tell ye the truth, I don't like it. I've been here thirteen years. But my husband's here."

"He's from Pindi?"

"I'd not be here otherwise! And how I miss speaking English. Oh, ye can't imagine."

"Do you ever go back to Scotland?"

She shook her head. "Not once. That's part of the trouble, I guess." She peered at me. "Are ye traveling alone? No young lady with ye?"

"I'm afraid not."

"That's a dear shame, that is." She said it in a way that made me think she just might have an unmarried niece.

Behind her the friend spoke in what I took to be a chiding tone. She said wearily, "Well, I'll not tarry ye no more."

"It was nice to meet you."

"Likewise." When I reached to shake her hand she shook her head. "I can't do that here, ye know. This is Paki."

She laughed with a great natural exuberance, and her eyes sparkled. Then she stopped laughing, and rejoined her friend.

> In the hills it was always holiday and life was lived in a round of balls, races, picnics, excursions, sketching parties, drinks at the Club, tea on the Mall, amateur dramatics, art exhibitions and gossip. For once in British India there were almost as many women as men; the average age was very young; the gaiety was infectious; it was no wonder that flirtation flourished, and young men who spent the rest of the year cooped up in dismal cantonments, or alone with a few more bachelors in awful backwaters of the Raj, let themselves go in the hills, and ornamented many an otherwise plainer tale.
>
> — James Morris, *Hill Stations* (1972)

21.

To the hills

I felt no need to linger in Rawalpindi. The antibiotics and joshanda were at last kicking in, and now that I felt better, I was itching to get to Peshawar, the frontier town near the Khyber Pass and the end of the GT. But part of me wanted to let the itch grow more insistent, so I decided to reward myself with a detour and a couple of days' rest. By now I felt a desperate, almost physical need to get off the road, to breathe air devoid of truck fumes; some days I had coughed so much that I felt I could no longer think. It would be an hour's winding climb of only thirty miles up to the quiet hill station of Murree, in the lowest reaches of the Himalayas, and a good spot to restore my energy.

Flashman's rang up someone's cousin with a taxi to drive me. The route off the GT would also pass Islamabad, the new capital ten miles from Pindi. Its reason for being built here was ironclad: the other two candidates for Pakistan's capital, after Partition, had serious drawbacks. Karachi, way to the south, felt remote from most of the country; it would've been like making New Orleans the capital of the United States. And Lahore was much too vulnerable, less than twenty miles from India.

WELCOME TO THE
CITY OF THE 21ST CENTURY
— Islamabad —
Environment Friendly City
The City Getting Even Better

Islamabad was all roundabouts and domes and ring roads and pipes and the future being built, excavations and sacks of cement and those huge irrelevant open spaces that are a feature of prefab cities. A massive convention center was going up; a contender for the title of largest mosque in the world, looking like a giant spaceship exhibit from a 1960s World's Fair, was already done. Islamabad didn't look or feel like part of Pakistan. Every local I asked agreed, and added that it was boring and a den of thieves, and joked about having to go through immigration to get in. No horse carts or rickshaws were allowed here, theoretically. One architectural victory was the planting of gum and flame and jacaranda trees, which gave a pastoral order to the city, though after thirty-five years the whole operation was looking faded.

Policemen in royal blue sweaters stood by a central roundabout with a huge sign of a man holding a machine gun and firing away. Unfortunately Pakistani political art displays none of the exaggeration, breathless melodrama, or heated colors of their film posters; at best they have a selective imagination, as in the army propaganda that use the famous Churchill quote, omitting the tears while keeping the blood, toil, and sweat.

Political kitsch was squashed by the truck we were following through the edge of Islamabad. Painted on it were flowers, eyes, birds, a mosque, roses, lakes and trees and mountains, peacocks, human faces, horses, butterflies, bird feathers, a cat, eagles, tigers, one of Columbus's ships under full sail, and prayers to Allah. To paint one truck could easily cost a thousand dollars, but part of the point was to proclaim the owner's financial stability. On the truck's forehead were eight shiny medallions, and apart from the windscreen, every inch of metal body was packed as densely as a sentence by Joyce, covered with studded and painted panels riveted into place. Even the inside of the high-fronted cargo bay was painted. Fifty years from now, the galleries of Soho that make folk art chic will be displaying the panels of these trucks, and there will be monographs, and more picture books, and trends analyzed. Some of the trucks I saw will still be trundling along, and the air will be even worse.

In no time we were in countryside, for Islamabad isn't old enough to have munched the natural beauty around it. Thickly green hills hemmed in the narrow winding road; ahead rose plum-colored mountains. Bullocks ambled past a lone dusty monkey chattering from a safe distance by the wayside. Every now and then the road was interrupted by the splatter of a village, a few collapsing houses and shops that reminded me of rural Appalachia.

Much more than in India, one feels assaulted in Pakistan by international brand names, indiscriminately painted on walls everywhere like an unending shout: FANTA PEPSI KNORR AGFA COKE KODAK MOUNTAIN DEW KONICA MAGGI SUZUKI! It is exhausting to the eye and seems pointless, since it's not as if there's a lot of local competition. In a poor countryside these brand names appear to be invoking merely a better-off society and little more; they represent not products but a glossary of mostly Western success that is welcomed here—more so than in India. But to paint COKE on a four-hundred-year-old stone battlement adds neither to the prestige of the soft drink nor to the majesty of the battlement.

Still, they were welcome here, while in India people rioted about multinationals coming in. To investors, India seemed attractive for so many reasons. It had legal, accounting, and political systems that were comprehensible to Westerners. It was a democracy. In '93 there'd been steps taken to attract multinationals, but the process never went smoothly. Either Indians rioted because they didn't want Western soft drinks corrupting the society, or else powerful people held things up and you were stuck waiting for the paperwork for two years to get the business out of quarantine.

Pakistan had never looked as attractive for Western companies. They were a small market compared to India or China; their rare versions of democracy always looked like a military dictatorship. On the other hand, they didn't have the Indian prejudice against Western investment: they were open. And the nature of the government kept it easier to handle the legislation and paperwork of setting up shop. India's democracy made it into a multi-headed beast—a company trying to invest there was eaten at either the federal or state level. In Pakistan, as the Aussie businessmen at the American Club had explained, things didn't get mucked up. The Pakistanis were just happy to be at last included.

WELCOME TO MURREE HILLS

After a toll stop the road began winding more extravagantly, and to climb steeply. Signs with names like Mount Pleasant, the Olive Tree, Shangrila, Blue Pines Inn, Kashmir View, Snow View, Fairyland Hotel, Pine Hills, Blue Moon began to appear; there was that pine-forest sense of dripping water. We crossed a little bridge and spacious green valleys started to proliferate, row on row, and the route became a series of paper-clip turns going up. The evident danger of the road, with the drops getting ever more inviting and fatal, kept drivers more sensible and sometimes there were even warning honks from up ahead. Valleys became more stupendous and alarming; suddenly we were deep in forest, monumental trees rising past the road, misted mountains below.

A few kilometers from Murree there'd been a landslide of big boulders. We waited while workmen dynamited and bulldozed the road clear. The happy surprise was to turn a corner, past signs for Hotel Viewforth, and Lady Roberts' Home, and have just enough time to wonder at the incongruity of it all. From the principal road there was a momentary flash—a glimpse only—of the snowy Himalayas.

Architecturally the British hill stations were of a type: a clutter of wood and stone structures hanging preposterously by their eyelids off the main roads and apparently out over chasms, with lesser, poorer structures dribbling down switchback lanes on the hillsides immediately below. All the stage scenery was still in place in Murree, at 7,400 feet. The main road was called the Mall, dominated at its upper end by one of the largest churches I saw in Pakistan. There were gazebos, and a lookout point, and a steep-roofed stone telegraph office, and a rickety library with a hypnotic view of kneeling mountains and locked glass cabinets of antiquated English books being crowded out by the Urdu. Around the roads were hiking trails and a convent. You could hire Lady Roberts' old home—once an officers' club—if arranged in advance down below in the capital.

There was a Ritz, and a Mall View, and a Majestic, and a Brightlands and a Lockwood, and other hotels with homesick titles. There were ironwork British lampposts that had once held gas flames, and cottages that would've been at home in Somerset or Keswick, and trees brought halfway round the world to give the illusion of an English summer in reach of the Himalayas and the Hindu Kush. In its era every visitor had arrived by horse; and in faint homage to that, there were almost no motor-rickshaws. Murree was still a place where people walked.

I put up at the most illustrious of the dowagers, this being the off-season. The Cecil Hotel was a classic hill station establishment, formerly a sister of a hotel I knew from Simla. It was built to last, in gray stone with columns and gaslights and 1851 over a monumental door and fretwork wooden balconies; the style was that hill station mix of the country cottage and the grand panjandrum. Past what had once been a lower tennis court, it looked across lawns to commanding views, having chosen the best location. Down one side were folded and undulant brown-green hills, like skin stretched loosely across an animal's back; facing out the other side, past pines and the groan of traffic from the road winding below, were snowy mountain crags with frost and sharply etched summits.

My room echoed those heights. It would've been two stories in an ordinary hotel, right up to the wooden crossbeams. Double doors led into a palatial bathroom. Huge old leather armchairs framed the fireplace, but a plug-in heater was provided as soon as I arrived, and that night I would leave it on.

"I am your Room-Bearer, sir." In his uniform he looked like a living antique, waddling around, offering me tea and knocking hourly. He was old enough to have learned his profession under the Raj, and he spoke at top speed. "And if there is anything you are requiring, sir, you will not hesitate to ask. I will not disturb you! I refuse to disturb you! You are our honored guest, Hotel Cecil sir. Thank you, sir."

The term he'd used was one I knew, having been studying my 1883 *Murray's Handbook of the Panjab*. This English equivalent to Baedeker was one of four early guides to British India, written by a tireless Captain E. B. Eastwick beginning after the Mutiny. Eastwick seems to have gone over every inch of the subcontinent with a magnifying glass. In later editions, the four regions got compressed into one book and also included Burma and Ceylon; but those first volumes were amazingly thorough, the result of a critical mind inclined, after thirty years' travel here, to question everything and everyone, be they Oxford don or Bangalore merchant. My Punjab volume was far more detailed than any modern guidebook. ("This is the great northern Sanatorium of the Panjab," it said of Murree. "The journey from Rawal Pindi is made in 5 hours. . . . The climate is well adapted for Englishmen.")

It was also a time machine, and revealed the expectations of the Raj. ("A travelling servant who can speak English is almost indispensable. . . ") One assumption was that anybody who came out here did so for a length of time, and might learn something of the local languages. After a hundred pages of fine print and historical analysis, the 1883 guide offered a twenty-page primer in English, Punjabi, and Hindi. There was an extensive vocabulary chock-full of legal and governmental terms, in which the roots of India's bureaucratic logjam were evident. It was followed by a series of imagined dialogues in the three languages. You could follow the career of a newcomer, from landing at Bombay and going to a hotel to hiring servants, washing, dining, exploring the country, and finally, inevitably, falling terribly ill.

Will you take me ashore? These boxes are all mine.
Go quickly, but don't shake the palanquin.
Torch-bearer, run a little before me.
Don't let the torch flare in my face.
If you overcharge I will complain to the Magistrate.
Hold your tongue.
Of what caste are you? I am in want of a servant.
Have you any friends who will be surety for you?
You must keep exact accounts.

Have water ready for a bath.
Pour it over me from the leather bag.
Where are my bathing drawers? The razors and strop?
Before you close the mosquito curtains, beat out all the mosquitos with a towel.
Let the feet of the bed stand in water, to keep the ants off. The bearer must pull the pankhah all night.
If he does not take more pains, I will discharge him.
The bread is bad and gritty. I am going to dine out.
Mind you stand behind my chair and attend to my wants.

Tell the bearers their reward depends on their conduct.
If they go quick they shall be well paid.

What is the name of that village, fort, or mountain?
Is there a European bangla or a native inn for travellers?
Are there any bugs, fleas, or other insects?
Is there any epidemic in the village?
Is there small-pox, cholera or fever?
Has any sick person slept on this bed lately?
Call the sweeper and let him clean the place.
Are there any snakes, scorpions, or other reptiles here?

I have got a fever.
I have great pain and giddiness in the head.
My skin is very hot, and I have great thirst.
I have great clamminess and a very bitter taste in the morning.
Is there any medical man in this place?
Is he a native or European?
Send for him whoever he may be.

The last phrase, presumably, was groaned in desperation, just before death; but they knew what to say until then, and how to demand a proper cup of chai.

In Murree, in the fading shadow of the Raj, I gratefully let my Room-Bearer bring me a pot of hot water, and I made myself another joshanda—which, were I an ambitious man, I would import to the West. It was already chilly in the room; I took my antibiotics, put on my sweater, and went for a twilight walk.

Even more than in Calcutta, there'd been an attempt to re-create a teatime, cookie-box England in the hill stations. They looked like country villages that had gone a-wandering—albeit ones designed by military engineers for their wives. Beneath the perfume of cheroots and wine and officers' clubs and dances and flirtations and tattling servants, there was always a profound melancholy at being so far from home. The hill stations exuded total self-confidence; they were also vulnerable as only a tiny place can be to the power of gossip, superstition, and disease. Kipling had written, "Murree has a merry ghost, and, now that she has been swept by cholera, will have room for a sorrowful one . . . "

Murree was like a small-scale sketch of Simla, and it wasn't surprising that the larger hill station had supplanted it in 1876 after only twenty-three years as the summer capital of the Punjab government. Simla had more space to expand, built on a series of long, steep connecting ridges; it was also more accessible to Lahore, Delhi, and ruling Calcutta, which accounted for its later grandeur as summer capital of the entire Raj. Murree was compact and intimate, and not well located except for Lahore, Rawalpindi, and Peshawar. It hadn't been important for long enough to still hold any air of power, as Simla does. It was simply a modest summer resort whose purpose was to provide relief from the heat of the plains. ("Like meat, we keep better up here," was how a Victorian put it.) By the time I arrived the season was over. The wind whistled and there wasn't much to do besides try to keep warm, stroll the Mall, and see if you could find anything worth buying. No one who was anyone was still here.

I asked at Raja Bros. Toffee-Biscuits-Store about that item still mysterious to me, advertised everywhere: the Bleach Cream.

"Stillman's? It is skin whitener, sir. For purifying the skin."

"And their freckle cream?"

"For the pimples, sir."

"Do people buy a lot of them? I see ads all over."

"They are most extremely popular, sir."

I expressed surprise at their popularity.

"But everyone wants to have lighter skin, sir. This is why it is so very popular."

I said, "Everyone in my country wants to look like they have a tan. Well, almost everyone."

He smiled, as at a child.

"Our set-up is different, sir. Everyone wants to look like you."

Murree wasn't a busy enough hill station to have Simla's huge rabbit warren of lower bazaars, but there was an extensive bazaar for nuts and dried fruit—a local specialty. You could buy Turkmen earrings, or Kashmiri shawls—a strong undercurrent of disputed Kashmir here, for Srinagar was only 160 miles away. You could buy bedspreads from Sind and carpets from Afghanistan, or locally carved walking sticks for those traditional hikes to an impressive lookout point. You could get your nose pierced, or buy popcorn, or even a cup of espresso, which is not an option you encounter every day in Pakistan. One evening I watched two boys outdoors duel with espresso machines five paces apart. They stood letting off blasts of steam with gusto and shouting in a macho attempt to outdo the other and attract customers. They put on a great show, and people stopped walking to marvel. When I walked past them again an hour later they were still at it.

There were also pirate videocassette shops galore, for there was little activity here once the season ended in late September. Until spring the place would be mostly empty and roads to the Gali hill resorts would be made inaccessible by snow. The huge church was shut tight today; but a public toilet, which had been built in its courtyard, was open. Murree had been a center of Christian evangelism, with six hundred missionaries still here a decade after Partition. Most were long gone, though there was still the legend hanging around that a hilltop grave was that of the Virgin Mary—a highly extreme etymology of Murree's name.

Farther down the Mall were two bookstores competing with each other, where I came across the only soft porn I saw in Pakistan: a few mild magazines and paperbacks, including a purported nineteenth-century soldier's "very erotic and truthful" memoir, *Venus In India*. There was an Aladdin's Fun House with rides for kids, and a pop music store full of bootleg cassettes. Four men sat outside playing a table game, pool-cum-shuffleboard, with sliding disks and corner pockets. Numerous jewelry dealers with open stalls were trying to keep warm with propane gas heaters, but it was already downright cold here, just a short drive up from the heat of Pindi.

I asked an elderly man in one shop if he could recommend a good restaurant for dinner. He named several and I asked about the dining room at the Cecil. It had looked so empty and unused I couldn't imagine they were serving anything off-season.

He said, in an of-course way, "But that is top of the mark, sir! The best hotel in Murree Hills."

"Really?"

"Naturally, sir. It is top of the mark."

When I got back to the Cecil the dining room was deserted, and two waiters couldn't get the heat going. I ate a chicken tikka in my room with the electric fire on full blast. Later the wind howled, really howled; it was insistent enough to rattle my room's massive doors. This was a discomforting sound to try to fall asleep to, but what kept me awake all night was the ceaseless clatter of the rats, the rats in the walls.

It was a relief to leave such unexpected cold. In an hour I was back at Flashman's for breakfast and organizing a driver for the afternoon's hundred miles to Peshawar. This would be the last big stretch—afterward there was only the short push through the Khyber Pass to the Afghan border, and how difficult could that be? For days now my dreams had been filled with horrible accidents. It was beginning to sink in that I might successfully avoid disaster.

The countryside came rapidly after Rawalpindi. A wide belt of trees, withering in the heat, separated the two halves of the road. To the north, the Margalla Hills rose in sharp thistly ridges. A quarry for crushed stone filled the air with dust.

Fifteen years ago the United States had supplied the Afghan mujahidin with advanced weaponry, sent up the GT, from Pakistani Intelligence headquarters and warehouses right on the road somewhere nearby.

Almost immediately we were in the Margalla Pass, a cut reinforced by Sher Shah after Babur had come along here. A tall obelisk stood on its own outcropping, the memorial to General John Nicholson, a nineteenth-century British hero who'd fought at Kabul in the First Afghan War. In his twenties he'd led Pathan tribesmen against the Sikhs in two wars; he died in Delhi during the Mutiny, age thirty-four—"mourned by two races with equal grief." This wasn't military cant; he was liked enough to inspire a local religious sect who called themselves Nikalsenis.

There was still a heavy military presence. At the entrance to the Taxila cantonment an army truck had gotten stuck in a ditch. Taxila's heritage, however, was far older than cantonments or Muslims: one of its three unearthed ancient cities went back at least three millennia. It was where the Grand Trunk Road converged with the ancient silk roads which ran from the north out of China and all the way to the Mediterranean. This region had been called Gandhara, with Taxila at its heart.

Here in 326 B.C. a Hindu king had played host to Alexander the Great, welcoming him en route east from conquering Persia and crossing the Hindu Kush. Many Greeks stayed here, but by the third century B.C. the Macedonians had been dethroned by the Mauryans, who held most of the subcontinent. Ashoka, who made the Mauryan Empire into a Buddhist empire, planted the religion firmly in Gandhara. In the next couple of centuries the area went through many hands—Bactrian, Scythian, Parthian—but the ones who mattered were the Kushans, who reestablished a Buddhist heartland here in the first century A.D. This was the golden age, when Gandharan art built on Greek prototypes found its way east. Taxila survived changing political fortunes as a pilgrimage center until the Huns arrived in the fifth century. At that point Buddhism had retreated up to the isolated Swat Valley.

Gandharan art had flowered under mingled Greek, Indian, and Roman influences, and Taxila's museum was full of gray stone sculptures from the first to the third centuries, its high point.

These statues, among the earliest images of the Buddha, showed a synthesis of the Buddhist sense of peace with the strong Greek illumination of the individual in bodies and faces. Stylistically it was a powerful combination, and many of the large stucco Buddha heads held a profound, almost abstract tranquility.

Behind the museum a classic British garden of tall cypresses gazed out to blue forgotten hills beyond.

Of the vast Taxila ruins I chose to see Jaulian, a later part, where atop a hillside were several piles of gray rubble that corresponded to a monastery, and a sequence of plaster reliefs of Buddhas large and small around a massive central stupa. A seated Healing Buddha had a hole in its navel where you stuck your fingers, like the pre-joshanda pilgrims of antiquity, to get cured. From the stupa complex I got a full view of the Taxila valley, its lush green fields limned by hazed mountains.

On the way down the steep hillside path I was accosted by a couple of local young men selling crude fake "antiquities." The last thing I wanted was a lion paperweight, and the price for a delicate, very small Buddha head was even more outrageous, but by walking away it went down to a few bucks. At that point it seemed like a charitable contribution to the men who had, they admitted, waited several days for a tourist to come along. In my several weeks in Pakistan I doubt I saw twenty foreign travelers.

Soon the GT became one disputed roadway, dangerous again, with a new version being built alongside for most of the way to Peshawar. Every few towns there was a sign in red and black like a giant shopping list, detailing vast amounts of rupees (all those zeros) that the government had spent in nearby villages.

Just before Kamra were fields of people living in tents; and some dwellings were of thatch, with camels alongside, trying to eat the houses. These were the poorest people I saw in Pakistan, and the white laundry hung on ropes, flapping in a breeze, only made their situation look more forlorn.

The Indus River and the giant fortress at Attock had the stately grandeur of a historic spot. The Indus marked the end of the Punjab, and into it, further south, the region's "five rivers" drained. I'd been crossing them with ease thanks to British bridge-building, but for millennia these had been the parts of the road traversed with difficulty and defended with the most ardor. You could be immune to history and, standing here, still feel like an explorer in a child's adventure book, from the titanic view of mountains to the left, past where the river met the ankles of an enormous Mogul fort here on this side of the river gorge. Until Sher Shah's time the GT hadn't run along here at all; the crossing point of the Indus which both Alexander and Babur had used was twenty kilometers upriver.

Up to the right the Indus was a rich blue, curving through the land with whitecaps dancing—a beautiful turn in one of the signal rivers of antiquity. To my left the river was straighter, and just above me on the hillside was what seemed the gateway to a smaller fort. In fact it was a serai, attributed to Sher Shah.

The serai perched over the road. Its huge courtyard had many rooms intact—perhaps about eighty in its heyday. The remains of a mosque were crumbling in the center; a cricket pitch had recently been cleared in the grass. From the upper level it had a broad view over the parapets, turrets, and crenelated walls of Akbar's Fort, now used as a prison, and down to the water. Until the British the crossing was by ferry, and the Indus was famous for treacherous floods, rising a hundred feet toward the fort.

The area was also known, according to the old guidebook, for snakes and scorpions, which had a habit of molesting British soldiers when the Mogul fort was their headquarters. Attock had held one of the most important concentrations of British might. Here, if Russian forces ever made it past five hundred miles of Afghans and penetrated the Khyber, they could still be held at bay. On a long-gone English double-decker iron bridge, with the road below and train tracks above, as James Morris wrote in *Pax*

Britannica, "the infantry [had] swung by, the commissariat carts, the cavalry with their lances and fluttering pennants; on the upper deck the troop trains clanked their way towards Peshawar, bare-headed soldiers lolling at their windows, or singing bawdy songs inside. There were block towers, gun emplacements, watchtowers along the ridge, and often the roads over the escarpment were cloudy with the dust of marching platoons."

From the other side of the modern (1925) replacement bridge it was clear how gigantic the fort was, stretched along the lazy Indus, with fat corner towers and a matching watchtower on this side of the river. The fort nearly resembled, as my old guidebook claimed, a baronial castle, with mountains rising dramatically behind it and smoke twining. You could just make out where the brown Kabul River and the blue Indus joined, a swirl of historic waters.

Now I was in the North-West Frontier Province. This was the territory of the Pathans (rhymes with 'batons'), though they also call themselves Pushtuns or Pukhtuns. These are about two dozen sub-tribes, spread across the North-West Frontier and eastern Afghanistan. They make up one of the largest tribal societies in the world, close to twenty million, and they are famously and historically ungovernable. They have defeated Moguls, Sikhs, British, Russians, other Afghans, and anyone else who had the misfortune to start an argument. They love to hate and they love to fight. One on one, they are good-humored, extremely friendly, helpful, and totally confident. They have their own languages and consider themselves descended from a few legendary warriors (hence the sub-tribes) and sometimes even speak of themselves as Israelites. This is not something to dicker about.

The modern result is that about a quarter of the NWFP is designated Tribal Areas, in which the rule of the particular sub-tribe—like the powerful Afridis—is all that matters. Pakistan national law is conveyed, if at all, via subsidies and spokesmen in Peshawar; in the end it counts for little. This had been the situation under the

British too, because there was never anything to be done about the Pathans, even after many of them were fighting with great heroism for the British all over the world. Nowadays the Frontier Police, tribesmen themselves, might be visible in extreme situations within a Tribal Area, but they were essentially powerless and without any authority more than a few feet off the road. Most Tribal Areas as a result were closed to foreigners, including non-Pathan Pakistanis. The Khyber Pass, I knew, was an exception, an open Tribal Area.

The romance of the Pathans had all come via the British, who admired their *pushtunwali,* their code of behavior that was more rigorously followed than any set of Jain strictures. It was built around a tribe's council of elders, who could throw together a posse if they had to, and was based on enforcing several lasting principles. These had to do with hospitality, revenge, self-abasement in defeat and mercy in victory, and the protection of honor, usually meaning women's honor; often Pathans ended up killing off their own family members to preserve it. As they like to say, "Revenge is the food which tastes best . . . cold."

There were all too many stories about someone getting their throat slit, sometimes a continent away, as the last stage of restoring honor for a naughty glance or an insult or an abducted sister several generations ago. The Pathans were brutal, cunning scoundrels. Unwaveringly independent, they made their own rules, and everyone who'd ever fought against them spoke admiringly of their relentless bravery and their fierce refusal to submit to anyone. Their enthusiasm and loyalty, their brilliant thievery and the warmth of their friendship, were legendary. This part of Pakistan was Pakistani only on sufferance, and the writ of law existed no more tellingly now than it had in British times. The Pathans in every sense had always been their own masters: of no one else I had met on the road could this be said. They only made you welcome if they felt like it. I couldn't wait to meet them.

• • •

Pakistan definitely does not look as poor as its neighbor; only now were towns occasionally echoing the rural decrepitude I'd seen so often on the Indian road. It was also time to conclude that Pakistanis were not quite as foolhardy drivers as Indians, at least on the Grand Trunk. And the road here was in much better shape—newer, better maintained, and because of single-direction lanes much of the way, immeasurably safer.

The Kabul River kept peeking through the shade trees on the right. It was like a scene out of Conrad: the sluggish river unreeling, the slouched hills, the low-slung lean-to home of a family. Then a School of Armour and Mechanized Warfare would intrude, and a densely armed strip, with tanks in front of a sprawling ex-British military cantonment.

This was at Nowshera, a large town. It also was one of the oldest, with an enormous and elaborately Italianate building covered in floral frescoes, and many antique British residences. I realized I had clung to such emblems of age on passing through these uninviting truck-stop towns, because they alone could give me a tactile sense of the history along the GT. It usually did me little good to know that a famous saint or warrior had been born here nine centuries ago, because the last decades would have ruthlessly obliterated most signs that anyone had been here then. It was amusing to speculate on some Englishman recognizing a place from a few decades back, but whenever I glanced at my old Punjab guidebook from over a century ago I shuddered to think what its author's reaction would've been, traveling alongside me. To disapprove of the barbarian conquerors of history razing this or that spot to the grassblades is to underestimate what people in this century cheerfully do to their own hometowns.

SPEED THRILLS BUT KILLS

The same sign as in India: one road after all, lined with the odd palm surrounded by spindly lachee trees. The happy clanging of a man on a bicycle, pedalling home in the warm gloom; the sun descending nobly in orange fire.

SEEK HELP FROM ALMIGHTY ALLAH
DRIVE WITH CARE

Horse carts trotted easily along, despite a flurry of horns. The fortress was an immense walled bastion that dominated the entrance to Peshawar and looked capable of withstanding any siege. The tribesmen wandering beside it in the gathering dark looked like they might try an assault just to have something amusing to do that night.

GOD'S LOVE IS LIMITLESS promised one last sign. We turned off the GT, past a cream-colored old railway station. Ten minutes later I had my feet up on the veranda of my room at Dean's Hotel, staring dully past the lawns at the stone wall and the road beyond, and sipping my joshanda like a man who'd just missed being hit by a thousand painted, merciful trucks.

> Let us be frank, however, and say that of the thousand and one sins of Peshawar most are unmentionable and some are unbelievable. They are the sins of opium and hemp and dancing-boys and jealousy and intrigue and that deviltry which gets into men's blood in certain latitudes. They are the sins of battle, murder, and sudden death, of gambling and strange intoxications, of savagery, sentiment, and the lust of revenge that becomes the strongest of all passions.
>
> — Lowell Thomas, *Beyond Khyber Pass* (1925)

22.

The Piccadilly of Central Asia

Peshawar has an almost stately grace and calm in the morning, which is a wonderful surprise since its reputation is for howling tribesmen just over the frontier waiting either to disembowel you or sell you a hundred kilos of opium. There are really three Peshawars: the Old City of bazaars, the British cantonment of spacious green avenues, and the modern University Town of spies, diplomats, and relief agencies. There is also the Peshawar of Afghan refugees, who live by the hundred of thousands in so-called camps that resemble moderately prosperous Indian mud villages but are far more dense, organized, and closed-off.

All coexist in a businesslike hubbub wherein you can, given savvy and a good deal of patience with complications, readily buy carpets, guns of all sizes, hard drugs, Herat bracelets, local information, unsafe passage beyond the Khyber Pass, and the odd Gandharan Buddha that will rival nearly anything in the museum.

Even though Peshawar is a city, it feels like a town; you have the delight of being in a complex place it's possible to get to know, and after a few days here people start to recognize you. There weren't many places along the Grand Trunk Road that made me immediately want to return—the traveler's overnight nostalgia before he has even departed—but Peshawar, despite Kipling's calling it "the city of evil countenances," was one of them.

Dean's is one of those venerated hotels whose best qualities are age and calm in the face of a local melee. It wasn't alluring or particularly comfortable, but for over a century nearly every foreigner had stayed here, since it was practically the only white man's hotel in Peshawar. You could learn more here in the lobby than by reading the morning's *Frontier Mail*. The hotel was a cluster of low, tile-roofed, many-gabled white stucco buildings with cypress trees and a lawn with chairs for tea. The boxlike rooms, every one a suite with a little veranda, were in a couple of ranks like attached bungalows. A clock at the front desk was permanently set at check-out time (one minute before noon). Over it hung a painting of tribesmen on horseback charging across a khaki landscape. There were slipcovered chairs, ceiling fans, harem-style hanging lamps, and a bedraggled carpet; a portrait of Jinnah, the country's founder, with warm eyes and a cocked cap, surveyed guests from over the carved-wood fireplace. In the dining room stood a decayed Bechstein upright that must be the worst example in the world of that august piano: the keyboard looked as if a tractor had dragged it through a field.

Nevertheless, Dean's was recognizable as the place where Robert Byron in 1934 had sat "drinking gin fizzes in the marble lounge" at the end of his road to Oxiana, on the way out of Persia and Afghanistan. Likewise Paul Theroux in 1973, who wrote affectionately about kicking back on a veranda, sipping a beer, and getting the blood circulating in one of those chairs with a swing-out extension while watching the sunset. Clearly, if you were coming from Meshed and Kabul, it was like reaching Paris.

I had three personal missions to accomplish in Peshawar. First, to enjoy myself in a place I'd heard and read wild tales about since I was a kid. Next, to see Darra Adam Khel, a nearby village where the Afridi tribesmen, practically while you wait, will make you working copies of any armaments from nineteenth-century British rifles to Stinger missile parts. And finally, to get through the Khyber Pass, where the Grand Trunk Road at some mystical (or arbitrary) point ceases to be the road across the subcontinent, the road to India, and becomes instead a different road, the way out, to Afghanistan, to Kabul.

That would be the end of the Grand Trunk Road—of my road, anyway. After all these miles, despite the dangerous name, I did not see any difficulties with the Khyber Pass.

At least until, after a lazy breakfast, I ambled past an immobile watchman who sat sipping tea to the small tourist office near the hotel grounds' entry, and read a handwritten sign:

NOTICE

All Tribal Areas are closed
to foreigners including Khyber
Pass and Darra Adam Khel.

I read it over several times, even though there was only one sentence. Maybe it was an old sign.

The bearded, swathed man on duty within, Mr. Salhuddin, was eloquent on the impossibility of my going to either place. Darra, he implied, the village of arms makers, was much too dangerous for foreigners—I did not remotely believe this—and the famous Khyber Pass, he asserted, was quite dull. "Anyway, nothing to see there," Mr. Salhuddin insisted. "Wastage of time. Don't worry. You are not missing a thing." He looked genuinely gloomy on my behalf, then brightened. "Have you been to the museum?"

He was not unfriendly or unhelpful. He was simply stating the iron policy of the Khyber arm of the North-West Frontier Province government, which applied to everyone. How could I not have found this out before? The restrictions had been in force for a long time; all my guidebooks, which spoke of daily tours to the Khyber, were from years ago. Those tours had been scrapped. Wasn't there anyone I could talk to about special permission? No, the situation was too dicey, the tribesmen too busy. That meant guns and drugs. Who could even remember when the last foreigner had been given permission to go through the Khyber? *Impossible. Nothing to see. Wastage of time.* It was almost a mantra.

So I took Mr. Salhuddin's maps and brochures and went for a walk. This was not like being shut out of one more Hindu temple: at that moment it seemed to render the entire journey futile. I could not think what door to hammer on.

At least I was in Peshawar. It did not seem a very wild and woolly place. Outside Dean's there was a gaggle of shoe shiners, both boys and men sitting on their little unrolled patches of cloth in the shade. After fifteen minutes of the ministrations of the eldest, my feet shone as they hadn't since Delhi. Behind them, the wall of Dean's compound hid the hotel's bungalows and led along one of the town's principal streets. Here were enormous carpet emporiums for the European tour groups who descend on the town for a day or two during the autumn and spring. By now the tourists, such as they were, wouldn't be back for months and the only customers were Pakistani women in couples, Mama and daughter up from Pindi for a better deal on a big Afghan carpet. Or else the rare foreigner, usually a man trying to look like a mercenary or a foreign correspondent.

Two of them were the only foreign guests at Dean's: they came and went during my week, and at first I thought my memory was playing tricks on me, so similar were their outfits. This was the standard garb of the macho traveler, usually American, usually a man, who desperately wants to be mistaken for a war correspondent. Part of the outfit involves wearing clothes too hot for the climate, to imply that heat doesn't bother you as it does normal people. Long-sleeved shirts with lots of pockets for all those *laissez-passers* and *baksheesh* money; clodhopper boots for scrambling up mountain passes; the ubiquitous camera even at breakfast; aviator sunglasses but no hat; a two-day growth of beard and a kerchief knotted around the neck to soak up sweat (this was on mild, ideally balmy days); the trousers always a dull brown or gray-green, baggy, rumpled, and very dusty.

The most conspicuous and necessary part of the outfit—and Peshawar merchants may be excused for thinking that all Americans wear this as a national uniform—was the reporter's jacket. It was always thick, bulky, sleeveless, with a hint it might stop a few bullets if necessary. It boasted a vaguely military aspect and made anyone look burly and battle-hardened; it had subsidiary pockets and main pockets and extra pockets all over and loops for rolls of film or to attach binoculars to and one special pocket for your passport in case you had to slip over the border. It was a jacket you could drink in and dodge bullets in and sleep in and it looked ridiculous on anyone who was not a war correspondent. There were virtually none here anymore, now that the Afghan-Russian war was long over and Peshawar no longer a reporters' base, to relax in and file stories from.

I wondered if I was being overly critical of my fellow man until a party of French tourists came through for a day, on their way up to Swat, and they were all dressed normally, comfortably, enjoying fine Peshawar weather. Meanwhile the Yanks playing at journalist left urgently—decamped, rather, in full kit—on different days, carrying several carpets each.

In this I could concur, because it was an ideal town for Christmas shopping. Even my old guidebook spoke of the "great transit trade from Kabul and Bokhara and Central Asia" and recommended the bazaars, "both for the objects they contain—many of them not seen in Central India—and for the fierce-looking and picturesquely-dressed tribesmen." Peshawar was still the capital of old Asia, not the Asia of Hong Kong and Singapore and international stock markets, but the Asia of goods traveling overland, silk and spices and camels and semiprecious stones and opium and gold bracelets and automatic rifles and people on the move carrying their family carpets. Alexander and Marco Polo and Babur and everyone else had passed through here; the ruin of the largest Buddhist stupa on the subcontinent was on the outskirts. It was still the ultimate crossroads, whose role had not changed for millennia, dictated by mountains and tribal geography. The town was like a doorman with radar instincts and many hidden pockets. Peshawar was on the way to everywhere, and no missile systems or airplanes would ever render it obsolete.

It had more secondhand wristwatches than even Istanbul. This was farther down Saddar Road, past a succession of antique shops selling the spoils of people fleeing Afghanistan: a lot of old Bokhara porcelain, damaged Russian military equipment, and rugs which sometimes showed helicopters attacking horsemen wielding automatic rifles. After a few tea-stalls, clothing shops, and a sunglasses vendor, suddenly there'd be three men competing against one another with cubicles selling about a dozen new clocks and, on a large sunken table as if they were shellfish being rinsed, a thousand old watches. They came from all over the world and were apparently priced by whim or the shopkeeper's aesthetic judgment, which sometimes placed a souvenir watch from an Arab economic conference above a fine Bulova. Many were Russian army surplus, and I imagined some Afghan mujahidin delicately removing the watch along with the wrist. It is amazing how much useful bric-a-brac gets left behind when an invading army next door gives up and goes home.

GHULAN MOHAMMAD DOSSUL & CO.
DEALERS IN ARMS, AMMUNITION, STABILIZER & ELECTRONIC ITEMS
EST. 1843

The Pathan features are distinctive: skin that looks seared by the sun; a grave fastidiousness in the facial gestures, as of an actor who has been studiously preparing for a part; a slightly sour, recalcitrant, or at least highly doubtful regard for what's going on around him; likewise a masculine flair in the beard, a swagger in the headgear and turban, and an extremely relaxed and loose-limbed gait that has no hurry about it. The old men walk as if pacing off the extent of their terrain, the young ones as if hoping the fellow at the other end of the street will draw first. And though you can't always tell, Pathan men almost all carry guns. They wear arms the way a nineteenth-century Londoner wore a pocketwatch, or a necktie, as part of the normal apparel. Some men, of course, openly sport weapons slung over their shoulders.

This is not to be confused with the Sikhs and their swords, or the Yemenis and their curved daggers. Pathans use their guns.

The men invariably wear the long pajama smocks with trousers that usually match, in some dull color—off-white, or gray, or light brown. Sometimes they wear a vest over this outfit, or even a Western-style jacket, and some men are swaddled in robes on top of the whole get-up. Their headgear identifies them by tribe—little skull caps, or turbans, or double-layered flat hats that resemble two *naan* breads squashed together. Most men have mustaches, and many bear the severe, naturally intense features one expects from the violent Pathan history. They seemed surprisingly ready to smile.

This part of downtown leading to the old British cantonment area was full of eateries, and travel agencies, and the odd hotel—Green's, for example, ripped apart by a bomb a couple of years ago and back in business now. A gaudy cinema from another era was showing an American thriller about husband-and-wife spies. With certain scenes cut for moral reasons the action yarn must've made little sense, but there'd be enough explosions and mayhem to keep this audience happy. A couple of bookshops were remarkably vast and well stocked, with a broader selection of titles on the history of the subcontinent than I'd seen in any shop in Delhi. Many volumes were Indian publications, imported somehow, which showed an open mind and confirmed my impression of the discursive and free press in the daily papers. What the bookstores weren't free to carry was anything to do with sex or female flesh—Pathans are notoriously touchy on this subject—though the shelves held the complete works of Harold Robbins and quite a few foreign fashion magazines. Here they looked downright lascivious.

The Peshawar Club, along the broad, tree-lined Mall within the British cantonment, was at the end of a long driveway and had a gatekeeper who was happy to let me in for a look. The club itself was a low-slung faded brick affair from the turn of the century, the color of sand, and formerly the Raj Club. It nestled gently around an open area where carved tables and wicker-and-wood chairs were laid out. The lawns had been carefully clipped and there were grass tennis courts in fairly worn condition, a few palms, and surrounding magisterial trees.

I tried to do what every gentleman was supposed to on arriving in Peshawar: register at the club.

There was no one at the club office. There was a dining room of some elegance, a Ladies' Parlour, and a Hairdresser. Most important, hidden somewhere on the grounds was one of the town's two swimming pools—though I'd inadvertently come during the morning hours for ladies, who swim in purdah behind a curtain.

The club library was one of those leather-armchaired salons with books numbered and arranged non-alphabetically in glass cabinets. No one in there either. There were yards and yards of travelers' tomes from the last century and a few old amateur paintings of local scenes. A yellowed beer-ad calendar for the Murree Brewery in Rawalpindi was turned to the mildewed but correct date and was clearly pre-Partition. There were several portraits of Beefeaters and tribesmen in full military rig, and two Pakistani tourist posters from the fifties. Most impressively, row upon row of huge animal horns—Thompson's gazelles and such—were ranged atop the bookcases.

I went back to the office, which was still deserted. I was curious what it cost to join and what the restrictions were. Its reputation was of being very expensive and having a traditional membership of ex-military officers. Outside on the lawns, one table now had six Pakistani men, mostly Pathans, seated around it, reading newspapers and saying almost nothing to one another. Several were smoking pipes. They looked like a club committee.

One of the men called out, "May I help you?"

I went over and introduced myself and before I got very far another man had brought me a chair. Four of the men were lawyers, one a retired professor of history, the other a retired army colonel. I said I thought it was a lovely old club.

"The lunches aren't bad," said one.

"It's not as old as it looks," said a lawyer. "That main building is—what? 1902, I believe. The three bungalows in the rear went up in 1862. Near the swimming pool."

"You know the only problem with it," said the colonel. He sucked on his pipe. "See if you can guess."

"No liquor allowed, I suppose."

"That's right!"

"You know what we say? We say, 'The bar is barred.'"

"You have a good library," I said. "And the pool."

"Squash," said another.

"Billiards."

"A card room."

"Tennis. But we need a new net."

I said, "What do you all think of the Taliban? They seem to be tightening their grip on Kabul."

The Taliban were the new force in Afghanistan, an army of arch-conservatives who had taken much of the country in recent months and were yanking women out of schools and executing men for petty offenses against Islam. This was only a hundred miles away.

"Well, you see, we all know them."

"You know the Taliban?"

"Not all of them. Their leaders. You see, their families are here in Peshawar."

"And you don't worry that they might start trouble here?"

"No, no," said the army officer. "Why would they do that? This is where their families live."

"Are any of them members of this club?"

"The Taliban," said one of the lawyers firmly, "would not enjoy this club."

I said, "That country seems devoted to fighting. Even with the Russians gone."

The professor shrugged. "Afghans don't need an enemy. When they don't have an enemy they fight among themselves."

I asked if they could recommend a good restaurant in town.

"That's the problem, you see. Most of the good ones are real Afghan food. You might not like it."

"I've liked it in the States. It's probably different here."

"That depends," said the colonel gently, "on whether you like fried dog meat."

I said, "So if I were to move to Peshawar, do you think I'd be able to join the Club?"

"A member would have to propose you. You would have to be voted in. That's not a problem. And there's the membership fee."

"Is it high?"

"About a hundred rupees," said a lawyer—less than three dollars. "I believe that's right. Is that right, Mr. Ali?"

"You know," said Mr. Ali, "I'm not sure I remember."

I took a motor-rickshaw to the Old City. This rickshaw had a mongoose and snake painted on the back; the one in front, whose fumes I inhaled, showed an open Koran, the face of some muscular violent film star, and beneath them, doves and a tiger. At the time, the images all made sense together.

On the edge of the Old City were a lot of dentistry offices all run by doctors named Camphor, with gruesome painted signs of grimacing teeth. Near them slices of sugarcane were being sold off carts. Past a sequence of yellow, red, and blue film posters (machine-guns, kick-boxing princesses, skyscrapers, a bomb, and leathery men wearing headbands), I was rapidly in a shadowy back-alley universe of pool halls, printers' shops, and video games squeezed into the bellies of tottering buildings. Eventually I emerged and found my way down Khyber Road to the bazaars.

Peshawar gets a lot of mileage out of its status as an aged frontier town. In truth its older atmospheric streets, like the Qissa Khawani, the Old Storytellers' Street—once called the "Piccadilly of Central Asia"—simply don't look old, only rundown. This is partly because Ranjit Singh in 1818 torched most of the Old City (he wasn't even twenty). Under Sikh control, before the British took over in 1849, the population was cut in half. The area also tends to experience regular small earthquakes and the buildings aren't put up very solidly. The past survives architecturally as a few moldering carved second stories among new concrete constructs of one or five decades old, covered in Pepsi ads or Urdu signs for shoes, metalware, suitcases.

The Pathan town has been somewhat overwhelmed by the Afghan refugees, who are also mostly Pathan. None of the tribesmen recognize the Durand Line separating the two countries as anything but a musty, irrelevant British fiction which Pakistan (another semi-fiction) inherited. Still, the refugees from over there, who are fairly permanently installed over here, probably outnumber the Peshawaris, and the town revolves around this fact.

Once you begin to walk through the interior streets there is an Arabian Nights aspect, though the Copper and Brass Bazaar is simply another stretch of another street. And while the Old City is hardly labyrinthine, it is enclosed, complex, and largely self-referential. The bric-a-brac of Western pop culture—movies, TV shows, and pop music—have not arrived. Instead the eternals of the world are here in their own articulate bazaars: dates, nuts, sweets, woven baskets and ropes, and endless tiny shoe stores.

In the jewelers' quarter, run by Afghans, each narrow shop could easily have equipped several harems with tribal silver in elaborate, clanky designs from Turkmenistan and Uzbekistan, from Bokhara and Herat, and all the other fabled names. The cerulean blue of lapis lazuli was inset everywhere, the workmanship of high quality, the prices low because the materials were lesser grade as was the gold that Pathans used to make their wives into mobile, jangling bank accounts. There was a lot of beauty here, and a few shops held treasures that'd somehow survived the decades. Delicately painted Persian ceramics, say, that had made it through a half century's upheaval to arrive here on camelback.

There was a fruit and vegetable bazaar crammed with garlic, apples, bananas, grapes, potatoes, green oranges, peppers, eggplants, cauliflowers, tomatoes, onions. Through it all I trailed an old bewhiskered gentleman stumbling along in a pre-Partition British army sergeant's jacket, and when he crossed my path going the other way he gave me a flash of a mock salute.

And of course Peshawar is famous for making everything else most readily available.

"What you want, sir?"

This was at the Chowk Yadgar, the Place of Remembrance, and within sight of a British-era clock tower. The man was short, in late middle-age, with a florid face, and he had gripped my arm as I was hurrying down some steps. He did not look like the sort of man who carries a gun; perhaps he was not even Pathan.

"What you want, sir? Hashish, sex, no problem."

"Hashish?"

"Good hashish. Anything you want."

"Anything?"

"Anything."

"Girls?"

"Of course. Pretty girls."

"Pretty girls and hashish no problem?"

"How many you want, no problem. Where you from, sir?"

"What about boys?" I said.

"Boys, of course, no problem. You are English, sir? Anything you want."

"Can you show me which way to Andarshar Bazaar?"

"Tell me what you want, sir."

"I want earrings. Special earrings."

"Ear-ring?"

"Turkmen earrings. Special ones. Long ones."

That was straining even his imagination.

"For my girlfriend," I said, and he realized he was being made fun of and clucked at me and moved on.

We have boys & girls of special kinds,
White, brown & black, fragile or fair or strong:
Their bosoms shame the roses; their behinds
Impel the astonished nightingales to song

Still, it's in the Old City that you have the most chance of seeing that unusual thing, a woman—seated behind her husband on his scooter, or walking hand in hand with him, or with her children trailing her; hardly ever alone. Sometimes the woman is totally covered by a kind of bedsheet with an embroidered thimble of fabric that fits over the top of her head and is called a *shatelkoq*, which it resembles. Or sometimes half the face may be daringly exposed, but this is mostly old ladies. Only very rarely do women meet your glance; in this society you see even fewer roaming around than in the Gulf States. It makes sense that here where blood feuds can last for generations because someone looked a tad askance at your sister, Islamic multiple marriages are uncommon: it would seem a mathematically efficient way of limiting the circle of potential enemies.

Very occasionally you do see a couple of young women, perhaps from Lahore or Karachi, who only wear scarves over the tops of their heads. Naturally every man does his best to stare at this unexpected sight of the Unseen Mystery while trying not to get caught at it and gunned down. Presumably the only place where a repressed bachelor may get a reliable idea of what a woman outside his family might look like is in a few foreign films or magazines. The visual imagery of his fantasy life must, then, be very strangely upholstered indeed.

I watched a couple of women struggling with two metal tanks in the middle of the street. One tank was oblong, the other looked like part of a water heater. The women made a strange spectacle. They stopped beside me and wrestled the two tanks with strips of cloth, trying unsuccessfully to bind them together to make them portable. It was a battle they kept losing. Perhaps they couldn't afford a rickshaw. There was no shortage of men nearby observing their struggles with dismay and pity, including a policeman, but no one dared step in and assist them. To speak to them, to accidentally touch them, could easily mean death both for the man and for the women.

Nothing folkloric or pure or quaint at work here, just unwritten, steel-clad tribal law. On the other hand, anyone who tried to persuade the Pathans to change their behavior got annihilated, from Akbar's Moguls to the Sikhs, to the British army for a century, to the odd Pakistani tax collector every now and then. So the point would appear to be moot.

Be straightforward and honest with women;
They will be deceitful and wayward with you.

Give them a thousand gifts and caresses;
They will sulk at one untoward word.

Seek balm from their sweetness;
They will poison your life.

Although they resemble man,

They lack humanity...

Soft and beautiful on the outside,
They are venomous serpents within.

From the amount of loud hawking and clearing of noses and throats, I wasn't the only phlegmatic one in the bazaars. Men here spit all the time, perhaps not as much as the Chinese but enough to keep you on your toes.

The Chowk Yadgar was also the black-market money bazaar, which was right on the sidewalk and swifter and more efficient than the banks. It had been here since Partition; now there were 350 money dealers, many with offices overlooking the square, and almost half were Afghans. The impetus was to protect against constant fluctuations of the *afghani*, essentially a non-currency unless you lived there. Here at the Chowk Yadgar huge amounts of money, in the many hundreds of thousands of dollars, were changed every day. The exchange rates were good and the money-laundering rates reasonable via Pathan family members all over Europe and the U.S.—5 percent, no paperwork—thus the many porters, lugging big sacks of cash like the weight of the world.

The oddest achievement of the Pathans of Peshawar, that hardly any journalist mentions, is that they have dominated a world sport for nearly fifty years: squash. I couldn't think of another area of achievement that people competed in worldwide and which belonged so handily, in its top ranks, to people of one tribe and from one town. The first of the dynasty, Hashim Khan, had learned to play as a boy at the Peshawar Club, where his father was chief steward. Since 1950, numerous Khans (some related, some not) have brought trophies back to Peshawar, and usually to a nearby village, Nawa Killi. Most of the last twenty world championships have been won by Peshawaris; in the rest they were the losing finalists. Their wives and mothers never, ever got to watch them play except on TV.

One morning I decided to learn what might be done for the Khyber Pass situation, which I'd been fretting about constantly. The U.S. Consulate was in the leafy, airy cantonment area not far from the Khyber Road—the local name the GT takes on as it heads toward the pass. It was a pleasant walk through the huge cantonment, all calm, broad boulevards and trees and open sewers running healthily along the spacious roadside. It was in every way the antithesis of the Old City, principally used by the military, by the government, for schools and the wealthy and a few old Christian churches and cemeteries.

And consulates. At mine a raven-haired Pakistani woman, her head uncovered here on U.S. soil, was manning the window for American citizens. Clearly she saw very few of them. She said to me in astonishment, "You look just like Imran Khan."

I was so startled to find myself speaking to a woman in this country that at first I didn't take in what she'd said.

"Who's that?"

"Don't you know Imran Khan?"

"Ah, right. The champion cricketer."

"Everyone in Pakistan knows him. He just married a wealthy English girl."

"So he did. Lucky man." But I was thinking: He's five or six years older than I am, I must really look exhausted.

"Really," she said. "You should see his photograph."

She went to fetch a young American woman, a vice-consul, who turned out to be full of information. The most helpful thing she could do, she said, was offer me a few days' membership in the local American Club. Like the one in Lahore, at least it would guarantee me good food at dinner and a bar if I needed one.

As for the Khyber Pass, it was pointless to try to sneak in. I'd be caught right away, and locked up until the Consulate persuaded them to let me go—assuming I wasn't shot by some zealous tribesmen for sniping practice. No, my only prayer was to throw myself on the mercy of the North-West Frontier Province department in charge of the Khyber, at the Civil Secretariat, and explain why I needed to go through. You never could tell; six months ago they'd let someone else have a look at the pass.

"If you're lucky, and they say yes," she said, "they'll send a gunman with you for protection. Just be certain not to step off the road, because then even he can't protect you. Only the road is legally under the jurisdiction of the government. Twenty feet off it you're at the mercy of anyone who doesn't like the way you look. So be really careful. If you stop somewhere and you sense people staring at you and gathering, don't wait around till they start shooting. Things can happen really quickly there, and one gunman on your side might not be enough. But—" She paused. "I'm sure nothing will happen. And maybe they'll say yes this once."

"Surely no foreigners have been shot there recently."

"That's because foreigners aren't allowed in, unless they're on their way to Jalalabad or Kabul, over the border. And things have been tense up in the Khyber since the tax inspector problem a few months ago."

"I thought they weren't taxed, up there."

"It was a problem with taxes owed on property in Peshawar. That some tribesmen up there owned. Anyway, after a few weeks they sent the tax inspector's body back."

"They'd killed him?"

"Technically, I think they only kidnapped him. Let's say he died in their hands. It was probably just an accident. And in retribution some villages got bulldozed." She smiled. "So which hotel did you say you were staying at? We always like to know."

The taxi driver who took me to the American Club that evening had learned his English caddying as a boy. His name was Shafi, and when I suggested in an offhand way that I might be interested in going up to the Khyber Pass and no, I didn't have a permit, did I really need one? he only laughed.

He said, "There are plenty of Afghans who've never heard of the Khyber Pass. They only know Torkham, at the border. To them it is all their main street!"

I said, "But it's the Grand Trunk Road, right?"

"That is right, GT Road."

"How far does it go?"

He hesitated, considering. Then he said, "Calcutta. How far you want I take you?"

University Town by night, with the large modern bungalows of international aid agencies for refugees and consulates and the residences of foreigners, was quiet and well guarded. Many houses had watchmen smoking calmly in chairs out in the fragrant night air, with guns laid meaningfully across their laps. The American Club was a bit better protected than most, but much more relaxed than the one in Lahore; the ping-pong table stood out on the front veranda. Downstairs there was a library and somewhat worn dining rooms, full of Westerners speaking German, French, English, Australian, and American, and looking mightily relieved to be there. Upstairs was a TV room and a darkened and gloomy bar aswirl with cigarette smoke.

I watched TV on a massive screen for a few minutes with an American boy and a Pakistani man who must've been his family guard, or an employee of the father's company—locals weren't allowed in here because of the alcohol. Most of the TV channels you could get were Indian, so every Pakistani with a television is bombarded with glimpses of a high life they are denied: polo matches, sexy girls dancing at cocktail parties, the Indian high spirits and a kind of fun that is just not permitted here. It must be sheer torture—and perhaps their happiest dreams end up filled with Hindu women.

The bulletin board's handwritten messages were full of expat problems and amusements:

Are you looking for a mali and / or chowkidar who is willing to be on call day and night? We are vacating our home and no longer require Rahib G—who has worked for us for two and a half years. . . .

The Peshawar Kipling Society presents a Raj Garden Party
Friday Nov 29
1.00 PM Raising of the Union Jack
1.30 PM Afternoon refreshments

Chowkidar means watchman; most who could afford one, got one. So a Canadian ecologist told me dourly up in the bar. He'd been here for several years and had about had enough, though he spoke quite glowingly of the government's attention to wilderness preservation. He looked spent; he couldn't wait to get home for Christmas. He normally took out a good dozen carpets every time he went back to Canada, to give to friends or sell at a firm profit. He hadn't been whacked by Canadian customs yet; somehow living here turned everyone into a smuggler.

What worried him most was getting caught on the Grand Trunk Road in darkness. He said, "I bet twenty, thirty people a week die on the GT at night. Of course you don't read about it."

I didn't have the heart to tell him how much worse the road was in India. "What about the other kind of violence?" I asked.

He said, "It's hard to keep track. Someone threw a bomb in the American Center down in Lahore a while back. Maybe, oh, twenty-five hundred dying in a two-year period? Something like that. There's lots of violence here, man. It gets blamed on the various political factions, or the army. You don't always know. And then sometimes it's just obvious. You're sure who did it. And you turn out to be wrong."

He had adopted a local air of fatalism and finality—none of it ever made sense, period. Not ever. At the end that was all you were left with. It was nearly time for him to go home.

Until the sovereign has cut off many heads,
The plains and mountains of the land will not be still.
Either others will mourn at your door for your death,
Or they must weep for those slaughtered at your hand...
It is better that bleeding heads should lie
On the battlefield
Than that live hearts should carry evil blood.
Either like a man enfold the turban on your head,
Or wear in its place a woman's veil.
Oh God! What use my writing? Who will heed me?
Yet have I said what must be said.

—Khushul Khan (1613–1691)

23.

The Wild West of the East

The Khyber Pass begins eleven miles west of Peshawar and winds for another twenty-four miles to the Afghan border: so close, it seemed to me, and yet so far. It had become clear, after visiting my consulate and making inquiries in the bazaar, that there was no chance I was going to sneak or bribe my way successfully through the Khyber Pass.

Still, it seemed absurd to miss the end of the road after coming all this way. I was reminded all too ruefully of the old rhyming slang, at the core of the best Kipling parody I know:

It's tradition in the ranks to protect each other's flanks
Like the Roman legions done it by the Tiber;
But you've never known the charms of the fellowship of arms,
Until you've 'ad it up the bloomin' Khyber!
Up the Khyber, up the Khyber,

It's a man's world up the Khyber,
They'll find out if you can take it
Up the Khyber!

So one morning I went looking for the Civil Secretariat's Home and Tribal Affairs Department. These were administrative offices for the entire province, and I spent a muddy hour roaming the back lanes of the quarter by the museum and the High Court getting conflicting directions from Pathan police and civil servants. The Civil Secretariat had moved in recent months, and no one knew where it was now. I felt the frustration that I'd kept mostly bolted down through many weeks of wearing travel come up in my throat; I wanted only to lash out at someone, anyone, though this is not a healthy frame of mind around Pathans. All these miles and I would not be able to finish the damned road because I couldn't find some stupid building and in any event the right official would not be there. It seemed unbelievable and yet an explanation for everything, that no one in Peshawar knew where the most important building (to me) stood.

And then there it was, right across the road from the Anglo-Oriental-style museum. I'd walked past its anonymous modernity several times. The blue-gray sign was propped sideways by the door, so if you weren't going in anyway you'd never spot it:

GOVT: OF N. W. F. P.
HOME & TRIBAL AFFAIRS DEPTT.

Mr. Kamar Ali, the Deputy Sec'y of Home and Tribal Affairs—as the sign outside his tiny office referred to him—was typing very fast on a large electric machine when I walked in. I was so relieved to be here I was ready to drop the story of my life on him. He was dark-haired, about my age, with a kind of scholarly gentility that seemed unusual. I had never seen this man before, yet he stopped typing and stared at me as if he'd been waiting urgently for me to materialize.

He blurted, "Can you spell deficit?"

I said, "D-e-f-i-c-i-t."

"Not f-e? Are you sure?"

This seemed somehow significant.

"I'm sure," I said.

"One f?"

"One f."

"As you say, then. *Deficit.* Please sit down."

He typed at extraordinary speed without the slightest excess motion, as if he were merely pouring tea. As I sat down he zipped the paper out of the machine and wound in another.

He murmured, "I'm very sorry. I must finish these forms for the new Home Secretary, who will be starting tomorrow morning." He paused as if carefully considering what he was about to say. "Perhaps you have heard. We had a change of several government posts quite recently."

"I did read something about that."

"Then you understand. Just one moment."

Another burst of typing at full speed. He tore the paper out, grabbed the first, and was gone. I looked around the little office. Over his desk was a bulletin board with photos of poppies and, fixed to the wall near my chair, a tribal map of the North-West Frontier Province with a few telephone numbers jotted along the bottom. His clutter had a certain economy and energy. It made me think that Mr. Kamar Ali was undoubtedly a most effective man.

While he was gone I decided that it would be pointless to try to fabricate some story about innocently wanting to see the Khyber Pass. If I were missing the proper press credentials then so be it; it would do me no good to pose as a curious tourist. Still, what chance did I have? Why should the new Home Secretary bother with me on his first day? He hadn't even started yet. People were probably lining up to try to bribe him.

Kamar Ali came back in, apologizing and rubbing his hands. "I have sent for some tea. Perhaps you would prefer coffee? No? How may I help you?"

I introduced myself, explained the GT Road, the many miles, the idea of my book. I said that for me the Khyber Pass was the final chapter. He listened very attentively as if memorizing what I was saying, nodding every so often.

The tea arrived, brought by a tea-bearer. Kamar Ali thanked him and waited until the boy had gone. Then he explained that the prior policy had been that no foreigners were allowed, etc., etc.

"But," he added, picking his way through a minefield, "I do not know yet what the attitude of the new secretary may be toward a request such as yours. It is . . . too early to tell."

"What do you suggest I do?"

He took a sip of tea and thought for a moment.

"I need you to write a letter. You must explain it all as you have explained it to me. You must be convincing. You have come a long way to write the end of your book as you wish it to be. And then I will take this letter to the Home Secretary this evening, at his first meeting. And we shall discover his mood, though I can promise nothing, you understand, because no foreigners are permitted in the Khyber Pass. And you will call on me at this time Thursday morning and—"

"And?"

"And perhaps we shall know more then," said Mr. Kamar Ali.

There was one four-star hotel in Peshawar, a kind of homegrown Hilton with a large modern lobby and a sign:

HOTEL POLICY.

Arms cannot be
brought inside
the hotel premises.
Personal Guards

or Gunmen are
required to deposit
their weapons with
the Hotel Security.
We seek your cooperation.
Management.

I had dinner there that evening with a luxuriantly white-haired French journalist in his sixties, back in Peshawar for the first time in seven years. He had the thoughtful gait and glow of a deeply intelligent man who has seen the world and is relaxed enough to take his time in any situation. A veteran war correspondent for *Der Spiegel* and *Paris-Match*, he'd had his decades in Indochina, his decades in Central America, his decade in Afghanistan; during the '80s he'd virtually lived in Peshawar, like so many reporters covering the Afghan-Russian conflict; he was the sort of man who can never retire. For him, Peshawar was a somewhat forlorn and depressed place now, without the buzz of a nerve center—his elite corps of friends, both Western and Pathan, were all gone. It was still a place of great sentiment and memories for him: colleagues who'd died covering the war from here, colleagues who'd survived and died elsewhere. He'd met his wife here, a younger American doctor, when she was running an aid camp for war refugees.

I had told him about my difficulties in getting permission to go into the Khyber Pass and mentioned that I was sure it was not like that in the good old days, and anyway, what had those good old days been like?

He smiled and said, "That was, for people like us who do this work, an adventurous war and even a romantic war. There was none of this business about getting special permission to go through the Khyber Pass. I went into Afghanistan with the mujahidin I don't know how many times—there are several ways in and we would go with one group or another. It was a war that was very good for the young reporters because the older reporters, my contemporaries who weren't as fit or as determined as I am, just couldn't do it. They'd see that they had to climb up five-thousand and six-thousand-meter passes in terrible conditions with those Afghan horses sliding on icy trails and falling to their deaths, and sleeping on the ground, and no hygiene at all, you can't imagine how filthy the Afghans are, no hygiene for days until you had every possible microbe you can have, and the big journalists would say *Forget it. For a story on page five? Forget it.* So for the young guys with energy and backpacks, it was a great era and they produced great reporting.

"Peshawar was a different place, you see. Things were so well organized for journalists because there were so many of us here for so long. University Town was like an international section where we could do whatever we wanted. There were nearly a hundred international aid agencies here, with all their people, and dozens and dozens of journalists, a real international elite. We all met every evening at the American Club. You'd make it back after your long weeks in Afghanistan getting bombarded by Russians, you'd be filthy, you'd get back to your house or to Dean's or Green's Hotel and wash as best you could and get to the American Club and immediately start comparing notes."

"No rivalries?"

"Not here. Not then. What was wonderful was that we all shared information: the aid workers, the political people from the consulates, and especially the journalists. Because we really weren't in competition with each other—someone writing for a French weekly is not in competition with someone from an American daily or a Swiss monthly. You could find out absolutely everything, absolutely everything. And Peshawar was full of spies, too. It was one of those strange places that crops up in a war that goes on for a long time, where you can learn and get hold of anything if you know how."

"Was it as inexpensive here back then?"

"To give you an example, when the Afghan war with the

Russians really got going, you could rent a house here—which I did—for two hundred dollars a month. Say, 1982, '83. By about '89 the same house was up to twenty-five hundred dollars. You see? But there were special stores, too, where we foreigners could buy alcohol or where we could send our servants to buy alcohol for us. They were all selling some off on the side. Now all that has closed down. Even so, Pakistan in general is welcoming to journalists, because they know they need us. To report on wars from here and then to tell the world how poor they are. Pakistan has been strict and rigid ever since I can remember. In places in the north it's as strict as Iran. But everyone knows that in Iran things are loosening up. Here, not so much; it's not as if there's some secret loose living here, behind closed doors. There isn't."

He was here on the trail of an Islamic story that stretched around the world and finally to Afghanistan, where he hoped to go during the next few days. I was sure he would find his way in, whether through official channels or by a usual route through old friends. "What I want to see is not the Taliban leaders at the front in Kabul or Jalalabad who are just going to give you their latest press release, repeating what they heard in the mosque. I want to talk to the people and see how they're taking this new strictness there. That's the way to find out what the future of the Taliban is."

"Do you think the Taliban can hold on to power?"

"It's hard to imagine they're going to succeed, though they might for a time—and with Afghanistan you never know. People joke about how war is the Afghans' national sport, but it's simply what they know, it's what they do, and they've been doing it since Alexander the Great and they'll keep on doing it. It's a bit difficult to say why. What I saw, all those years, was a huge amount of fanaticism and stupidity. You'd go off with a group of fighters over a certain set of mountains with a plan to attack some Russian position the next morning. The weather would be awful and they'd have chosen the wrong way because they knew Allah would protect them. And halfway up the crags they'd lose a few of those horses that they always treated so abominably—you can always tell what a people are like by how they treat their animals—and most of their ammunition would go crashing down into a valley and maybe a few fighters would fall too. These men, most of them, weren't real soldiers. They were just fighters. And you'd emerge on the other side and find you were smack between two Russian positions, in the wrong place."

"So then what?"

"So you'd turn around, and they'd throw away the rest of their equipment. And days later you'd finally turn up back at the mujahidin camp and they'd tell everyone that they'd fought to the last bullet, that so-and-so and so-and-so died martyrs' deaths back there, and that everyone else fought like heroes and won a great victory. Thus everyone was either a hero or a martyr, which is what they want. That's why as a journalist you'd find yourself in these unbelievable situations. Exposed out on a plain under Russian bombardment, with the night all lit up with these slow-moving Russian Christmas trees (we called them) that descend and illuminate everything. It's very beautiful and you do notice how lovely it is while the roof of the mud house you're huddling in, trying to dry your clothes, is being blown away. So then you're getting bombarded and the mujahidin are blazing away and dying around you and it's all through some stupid mistake. And even now, still, Islamic guerrilla groups from all over the world send their people there to train. The Russians were like the Americans in Vietnam, you know. They didn't lose the war there on the ground, they lost it at home. So they had to give up.

"What happens as a journalist in Afghanistan, and I'm sure I'll get stuck somewhere because of this now, is there's a king in every valley. To travel you've got to get permission to go from valley to valley, and they're all fighting each other, and you sit there for days and days and smile and smile and then for some mysterious reason one day they say, okay, you can go."

I recognized his summoning up of the past—my father, an

American war correspondent for many decades, had always shown a similar nostalgia and horror at all he'd seen.

We had been talking for hours; it had been kind of him to share a dinner with me. He had two final gifts for me. One was an image.

"What I always remember first when I think of Afghanistan isn't the dead or the explosions or the filth or the waiting. There was one time we were going over some mountains and it was incredibly cold. And we came upon one of their horses, frozen solid, standing up, like a ghost in a glacier. Just standing there, covered in its ice. I have a photograph of it somewhere, and if I didn't I almost wouldn't believe I'd seen such an amazing and ghastly thing. I will never forget it: it haunts me still."

The other gift was when I pulled out the small fake Buddha head I'd bought for a few dollars back at Taxila. This journalist had a collection of Gandharan art he'd brought back over the years and had authenticated back at the Louvre; he knew it well.

"How much did you pay?" he asked, turning it over.

"Two hundred rupees. Five dollars."

"That's a lot of money to them, you see," he said quietly. "It's genuine, all right. Beautiful."

"Genuine? Are you sure?"

He smiled and pushed back his mane of white hair. "These people make imitation Kalashnikovs. Not imitation Buddhas."

Darra Adam Khel was where they made those guns. It lay in another forbidden pass, the Kohat, about twenty-five miles away. I'd heard that you could at least drive through the one-road town and if you didn't stop, no one would bother you. If so, at least I'd get a quick look at the great armaments bazaar. In Pakistan more people know how to use a gun than know how to speak Urdu.

First I had to secure a driver. By chance I found Zarar Shah—the name means "King of Emergencies"—on one of the streets by the

Civil Secretariat, wiping down his white Suzuki van. He was an unshaven young man, bronze-skinned, with black hair and mustache; he wore a leather jacket over his tan shalwar-kameez. When we both nearly got hit by a crazy rickshaw he made a joke about how dangerous it was to even stand still in Pakistan, and in a minute I realized he was an ideal driver. I told him what I'd heard about simply driving through Darra, not stopping; nothing illegal about that. No, no, said Zarar. He knew Darra well. Once he got me to some friends of his there would be no problems about seeing much of the town.

Soon we were heading due south of Peshawar, through farmland with slate-gray crags behind, and cemeteries with markers shaped like those crags. The rare houses were mud-and-stone fortresses with watchtowers, surrounded by battlements with gun holes and heavy doors. In a field of golden haystacks some boys had piled rocks to make cricket wickets.

Like many Pathans, Zarar Shah had several incomes. I did not find out about all of them. I did learn he also worked as an informant for a German narcotics squad; he had taken a bullet in the knee a year before and was hoping to make his way to Germany, which seemed a sound idea considering the nature of blood feuds around here. He was also going to get married in about a year, to a girl in his village. "But the problem is," he shook his head, "I have some girlfriends in Peshawar also . . . "

Darra is a one-industry town, rather like Hollywood. At first it looks like any other bustling Pathan middle-of-nowhere road strip, a mile of harsh, messy main street with fields, hills and bleak mountains surrounding. The street was lined with squarish wood, mud, and concrete shops of two stories with a few narrow lanes leading behind them. Had I not been paying attention I might not have even noticed what the shops were selling. Then a guy in robes and a turban suddenly stepped onto the street, raised a pistol and fired off a few rounds in the air. No one even broke step. He shook his head, rubbed his beard, ambled into the shop, and reemerged with a Beretta shotgun. Then he had a go with that, aiming nearly straight up.

None of this was reassuring, as we'd just stopped and clambered out of the Suzuki. People can also get killed by bullets falling.

GUNS AND UMBRELLAS
MUJAHID ARMS STORE

The loud ripping of test shots was intermittent as Zarar led me hurriedly down an extremely narrow path between mud walls. I'd had only a glimpse of weapons in racks, lined up like skinny dark soldiers. Behind the main-street row of gun dealers we were in an earlier century, a courtyard of open, reed-roofed mud houses. Here the guns were totally made by hand, in little work-stalls.

Zarar ushered me into the first, to the usual greetings and embraces with the men inside. I felt him relax; now we were safe. There were worn wooden chests on the stone floor, a couple of hanging bulbs, a ceiling fan, an open wooden door and shutters. The place was remarkably bare for a workshop. It was perhaps the size of a large bathroom. There was one old, dog-eared copy of *Soldier of Fortune* magazine.

Our host was a gun maker named Haq Nawaz. His father and grandfather had also made guns here in Darra, and his four sons were already helping him in the profession. He had a wide-eyed grin and wore a white knitted skull cap, as did his eldest son, who looked about thirteen. They squatted on the stone floor and we all sipped tea. Behind them a swath of aluminum foil had been tacked to the wall to increase the light. Above it was a long color foldout poster of a fancy hotel with chairs and a garden. It might've been Japanese, and in this context it seemed highly unreal, like a vision of the paradisiacal afterlife.

From the main street came the *crack-crack* of test shooting.

Had this man been a potter, or a weaver, there'd have been

nothing strange about the scene. Instead there was a bowl of bullets in front of him, and dangling from nails or laid out on the floor were assorted files, saws, what looked like primitive tools and some obviously good vises inscribed MADE IN ENGLAND.

"Darra people very fast for mind," said Zarar with a shrug. "But no facilities."

The handmade result of this lack of facilities was lying on the stone floor between us. The son handed it over proudly: a copy of a Kalashnikov that looked very convincing. I got Zarar to translate for me. It had taken five days for Haq to make the gun. He'd sell it for 5,000 rupees, about $125. The Kalashnikov was easily the most popular weapon in these parts, the gun of choice, mostly because it was so simple to deal with. The more difficult M-16 was more expensive, about 7,000 rupees ($175). Haq could buy a template in the bazaar for any gun in Darra and then copy it in a few days, right down to the serial number and original maker's insignia. The estimates ran to as many as forty thousand gunmakers in the immediate area; Darra's gun cottages turned out over five hundred guns a day, of remarkable workmanship when you considered how they did it.

"My father also worked with these guns," said Haq. "With only a drill and a saw and a few files. Now at least we have milling machinery."

"In Tribal Area everyone has guns," said Zarar.

Not you, I thought, but at that moment he reached under his robes, pulled out a pistol in a holster, and removed the clip so that Haq Nawaz could clean it.

"Any shape, any gun," said Haq. "We can shoot down a plane for you." Darra was producing not only pistols and machine guns but rocket launchers, hand grenades, anti-aircraft guns, and even (he claimed) the shells for Stinger missiles—luckily the guidance system computer technology was out of the question. If it was an actual gun they couldn't get hold of to copy, the Darra smithies could make it from blueprints laid out in copies of *Soldier of*

Fortune; I assumed the Darra elders maintained an air mail subscription. The mujahidin and the Taliban and everyone else came here to buy, as well as people from Karachi who needed protection, or even farmers from down in Sind who found it amusing to blast away at ducks with an AK-47.

It seemed absurd: mid-twentieth-century weapons being produced under early nineteenth-century conditions. These homemade guns had the reputation of being less reliable compared to the originals, but clearly they were reliable enough. I found myself continuously flip-flopping between an admiration for the do-it-yourself craftsmanship and a sense that these people were crazy and this was no place for a mother's boy.

"Tribal Area is free area," said Zarar. "Darra people make their own rules. Always. There is no Pakistan law here."

There was only Pakistani pressure, for until recently there'd been more of the drug trade passing through this town. The same held true for much of the Peshawar area, as the drug route had altered from east-west to more north-south, and also grown proportionally in Southeast Asia. There were lots of drug labs hidden away in the NWFP for processing opium—I'd driven past several en route—but there was less wholesaling of merchandise here than in recent decades. Drugs still account for more foreign exchange cash in Pakistan than all the country's legal exports put together. With the population doubling every twenty years, there is no reason to think that such professions will drop away. To the Pathans they aren't illicit; what we call "smuggling" they call trade, and so on. Poppies always grow very well here, like guns—the town was known for its hashish, too.

Darra has been a gun bazaar for at least a century. Around 1897 an Afridi named Sher Din Shahabuddin decided to start making cheap rifles that the tribesmen could afford, copies of the British Lee-Enfields. (Frontier tribesmen had been making long-barreled muskets for a century already.) There is a vague and perhaps apocryphal story that the British decided to leave Sher Din

Shahabuddin and his five sons alone up here in their gun-making gorge in return for safe passage on the main roads and a sense that perhaps this way, far fewer British rifles would be stolen by Afridis. The result was a British fort in the Kohat Pass, but beyond it was tribal territory where the Afridis made their own rules. Those five sons apparently quarreled, each setting up his own "factory," and thus Darra Adam Khel grew.

Lowell Thomas came through in 1924, and his description sounds up-to-date. The methods have changed little, the prices have gone down a lot, and as he put it, "To see these men boring out barrels on a wobbly hand-lathe, shaping a breech-block with a chisel and a broken file and holding a stock between their toes while they whittle away at it with a knife, is to see a miracle in the making." He added, "The Kohat Pass will never become a hive of industry. The Pathan does not believe in industry... men need only for their happiness... a rifle, a wife, and some land to till."

It looked a lot like industry to me. Haq made a selection of Chinese pistols in the five hundred to three thousand rupee range ($12 to $75). He copied and personally thought highly of a German bolt gun, the Mauser; the American M-16 automatic; and the black, almost elegant Beretta 12-bore (MADE IN ITALY, it said; $125). He was also fond of what Afridis call repeater rifles, like American shotguns, for about 6,000 rupees ($150). For old times' sake, there were always the Lee-Enfields, which were still superb for picking off an enemy from a Khyber crag at a great distance.

When Haq started coughing I said, "Be careful! Tobacco is much more dangerous than guns." Zarar translated and everyone laughed and we all agreed that cigarettes were bad for you.

Haq's colleagues were clanking and grinding away in the workshops next door. One held a milling machine for making the breech of the gun—a lapis necklace draped over part of the machine for luck, operated by an intent fellow in a little hat. These mud-brick hovels were full of shaky equipment that looked assembled from pumps and buckets and old bicycles and sewing machines. Nothing stood up straight; wheels and lathes and belts were worn down and crooked yet somehow got the job done.

Outside a forge, men were stirring the metal in a long trough of coolant that looked like muddy water. At one point the men of Darra had gotten their steel by buying old disused British locomotives. They had also traditionally forged gun barrels from stolen railway lines.

I was introduced as Zarar's good American friend.

"Washington is beautiful!" said a young man whose brother lived there, and with a green card, no less. "I am moving to that city one day. But New York, I hear every person says, has lots of thieves. So I don't go there—very dangerous!"

Crack-crack.

A bullet maker was patiently organizing his product—at a dime each—into piles. He sat on the ground, bullets in different baskets around him, while a customer sifted through them, slowly examining each one as if it had its victim's name engraved on it.

The inevitable offer came up, to which the best excuse I could give was that since automatic weapons are made for right-handed people, if a lefty tries one it spews spent shells with enormous velocity directly at his face. This either convinced or confused them, because they stopped trying to get me to fire off a volley.

Zarar suggested we give the main street shops a try. Haq's brother Habib-Ullah's stall was particularly well stocked, with a small .222-caliber M-16; a small, elaborately engraved hand-sized shotgun that looked very nineteenth century; and a 75-bullet tommy gun like in the movies, which he called a "pash-pasha."

After a while it can become almost normal to hear automatic weapons going off all around you, so long as they're aimed elsewhere. To be in a place like Darra, where people think nothing of stepping outside and firing off fifty rounds at the nearby hillside (with luck no one happens to be hanging out the wash) does make you consider. It is, by extension, just as natural for these people to have nuclear weapons—bigger hillsides—and any Indian who spent ten minutes in Darra would go home with even more to worry about. Having seen Darra, having seen the Indian police in action, why any third power thinks it can persuade either of these countries to give up their atomic warheads is beyond me.

Another shop carried antique British Army cutlasses, English and French bayonets, old Afghan swords (*tulwars*), Russian truncheons, canteens, and wrist compasses. I bought a little Russian foldaway magnifying glass and passed up some binoculars, which looked about as solid as my Calcutta sunglasses. As Zarar astutely pointed out, though, they had survived their owner.

The most remarkable items though, were the walking stick that became a rifle—a traditional Darra favorite—and the small pen gun. This counterfeit of a fountain pen had more heft and was inscribed MADE IN JAPAN—an artistic touch, I thought. You unscrewed the writing end, pulled back the dingus at the other end, put in a tiny bullet. Then you simply pressed on the shirt-clip to fire. You could kill a man with it. I imagined the ads: *No pen too small! No plane too large! Shop Darra and send a clear message! We leave the shooting to you!*

I had to admire a cottage-industry town of tribesmen who, despite their reputation for limited ambitions, had done their best to expand. With every unexpected blood feud, every fresh generation, every decade's immortal struggle, old customers were dying and new customers were learning to shoot. And there were always unexpected worlds to conquer from this isolated pass. According to Zarar, for a while the Darra craftsmen were even trying to manufacture planes and military helicopters, until the Pakistani government said: Boys, that's enough.

Of all the places I saw on the road, this was the strangest, made more so by being one of the most dynamic.

Zarar and I were just leaving when two of the local police showed up, stern in their berets and well armed. From the precipice of impending arrest, he talked them into believing I had official permission to be there, with the inevitable result that they insisted on showing me around for another two hours. Meanwhile the test firing from all quarters made it sound as if a guerrilla war for control of the town had erupted. In the end I gave the two policemen a good deal of money and as we were driving off they came hurrying back, waving their arms, barring our way. That's it, I thought. Let's not shoot it out, please.

"Big trouble," said Zarar.

But they'd bought us lunch, some steaming spicy lamb wrapped in newspaper. They passed it through the windows and then we were roaring out of Darra. And I'd forgotten to ask about hashish prices.

That afternoon at Dean's I fell into conversation with an antique dealer, a refined man who said he hoped and dreamed that one day India, Pakistan, and Afghanistan would be finally one country—which just goes to show that some people never learn. Yet it was a haunting idea; it had almost been true under Ashoka twenty-two centuries ago, and after a fashion under the British.

Almost. Later that afternoon in Peshawar I found myself walking down the road from the hotel, through the usual busy stream of people, when suddenly the call of the muezzin went off from a minaret somewhere, the sidewalks emptied and in a moment there were five hundred men praying on their knees, in neat rows, in the middle of the street. At that point in my trip it was less the devotion than the sense of order that impressed me.

I had a peculiar dream that night on my cot. It was a dream of offspring, of two children born from one great earth mother whom I took to represent the British Raj—the earth mother as massive shield emblazoned with a coat-of-arms. Behind her stood a panorama of husbands, of fathers, stretching off into infinity (in the dream this was mathematically possible). My dream was a kind of subcontinent creation myth, done up in full technicolor animation, and the result was two offspring.

One was a many-armed god, a shape-changer. The other was

dull-looking, and dutiful. They stared at each other and didn't see how they could've sprung from the same earth mother, the one ever-changing, the other ever-plodding. One son was flow, the other was power. They looked on each other with enormous distrust and little understanding, and the family resemblance that outsiders noticed only exacerbated the sense of being two unrelated creatures.

I knew which offspring would always have more appeal to my turn of mind, but I also knew that an outsider could not see under the skin. Each unhappy family is different: I had at least been able to measure the family resemblance.

This journey had become a sequence of encounters with the past, often only the shadow of the past, or an odd relic poking up out of the earth with the present blaring around it and ignoring it. It kept me wondering what some traveler following this road five hundred years from now might find, what might survive from this century. Would he say: Ah, there was a bazaar here, or a hotel with rooms off a courtyard, or a kos minar, or a mosque or temple or stupa or cinema?

It was astounding how the past here got transmogrified, so that Pathans could wind turbans around their heads without any sense that they were a link with the Buddha's hairdos on statues in the museum. And these were still extremely fluid societies in which very little had been decided. I felt I could predict with certainty that there would be Houses of Parliament in London for some time to come, but apart from the farmers, nothing looked particularly stable here, and certainly not the lines on a map.

I thought the Grand Trunk Road would outlast anything. It was occasionally beautiful, at times it appeared almost timeless, but mostly the only thing at all poetic about it was that it was still here. There had rarely been much peace along it. It was still a road of great danger for the people who lived near it and those who traveled on it. Death in the form of outside invaders and now disease was carried along it, and it was still one of the most accident-prone highways in the world. That God had chosen to spring up on the Grand Trunk in so many utterly different guises over the millennia, that so much wisdom had grown up along it, was its great mystery and still its great contribution.

I had always seen it as a whip laid across the subcontinent, alternately stimulating and punishing. Perhaps it was also an antenna, picking up and sending out signals.

So much wisdom, so much human thought: that such a pressure of ideas, after thirty-five centuries, could lead to this result was its great sadness.

Or perhaps it was just a road, nothing more; and anyone who stared too long at its dust was bound to find, in the end, only his own shadow. That dust would not be in my eyes for much longer. It was time to finish, if I could.

> As passes go, the Khyber is invitingly mild. It is this which makes it the theatre of such stupendous works....Not one, but two graded roads wind up and down the length of the defile: the one of asphalt, as smooth as Piccadilly and flanked by low battlements; the other, its predecessor, abandoned to camels, but still such a highway as we had not seen since Damascus. ...It was the spectacle of common sense that thrilled us amid the evil heat, the eyries of the tribesmen, and the immemorial associations of pilgrims and conquerors.
>
> —Robert Byron, *The Road To Oxiana* (1937)

24.

Up the Khyber

It was too sunstruck a morning for anything bureaucratic to go right; and so I vowed that at the very least I'd accomplish something before I got the bad news from Kamar Ali at the Civil Secretariat. I had put off going into the Peshawar Museum, saving it as my ace in the hole, my last place to visit before the Khyber Pass was denied me. It was architecturally as lavish a melange as the one in Lahore, though much smaller and ill-lit. I also got the sense, from a few emptied cabinets, that pieces of Gandharan art might be making their way overseas. Then again the town itself—the dirt underfoot—was full of the stuff, for Peshawar had at one time been the Gandharan capital.

More haunting were several enormous, ghostly, wooden standing figures from Chitral, up north in the Hindu Kush. I checked my watch: the Civil Secretariat would have a reply for me by now. On the way out I found myself in front of a glass case containing a gray block of stone with traces of weird, chalky lettering.

Inscription No. 45

> The inscription, in Sacada Script, was presented to the Museum by Sir Aurel Stein. Its find place is unknown. It appears to be a Memorial Stone. It does not give connected sense and is not dated but it impresses upon us the instability of everything. It records that fame alone can make you immortal.

At the Civil Secretariat's Home & Tribal Affairs Deptt. I found Mr. Kamar Ali already well underway on a bright morning. He stood in the hall outside his office, talking to a couple of European men. I kept my distance and couldn't make out what they were saying. They weren't in the customary flak jackets of would-be journalists, which made me think they might be professionals.

He saw me and raised a finger and said with evident concern, "Can you wait one moment?" Then he resumed his conversation with the men. It struck me that he was too polite to dismiss me in front of others. The two Europeans spoke urgently at him for a moment. He listened carefully, then gave a half shrug of genuine regret. "I am very sorry. There is nothing more that I can do."

It also occurred to me that just perhaps he didn't want to give me good news in the face of a refusal to them.

They turned on their heels and left rather abruptly, passing me on the way out. Kamar Ali ushered me into his office and said gently, "Do please sit down."

Here it comes, I thought, the decorous apology.

He said, "Well, the new Home Secretary has read your letter very carefully. Not last night. Just this morning. And he said to me, 'This gentleman has come a very long way up the Grand Trunk Road to write his book. Now he wishes to finish his road and his book. It is our first day. We must not disappoint him.'"

"So this means—"

"This means you can go to the Khyber Pass, as far as Michni Point, on one condition."

"Of course."

"A gunman will be provided for you by the government. A tribesman. For your own protection. There will be no charge."

"This is all very kind of you. Please thank—"

"First we will issue you the permit. Two copies. You will go to the office of the Political Agent for the Khyber Pass. You know where it is? No? Near Peshawar Stadium. His office has been there right from the British times. The Political Agent will take one copy of the permit and you will keep the other one with you. He will then provide you with a gunman. You will have to arrange a driver and transport for yourself and the armed escort. Someone from the area would be best."

"Thank you very much."

"I will convey your thanks to the secretary. And now," said Kamar Ali. "Do you know when you would like to go?"

"Is today all right? I mean, now?"

"Today," he said solemnly, "would be a good idea, I think."

He led me down the hall to another office to get the permit typed. An elder in a white cap presided behind a large old desk covered with eternal files. A typist sat in the corner, a dark, quick man who made a huge clacketing manual machine sound like automatic weapons fire. He took my passport, spread it open and read my name aloud and repeated, "U.S.A." He sounded the syllables out carefully once again and we smiled at each other. On shelves and cabinets overstuffed files of papers were stacked right up to the ceiling. It pleased me to think a carbon copy of my permit might find its way there too.

Kamar Ali shook my hand. "I will leave you here now. All will go well, I am sure of it."

"I am sure of it too. Thank you again."

"It was my pleasure. We were very lucky this time."

No. 3/5-SOPT (HD)/96

Government of N.-W. F. P.
Home and TAs Department.

Dated.... 14/11/1996....

PERMIT

The following foreigner (s) is/are hereby allowed to

visit Khyber Pass upto Michni point on 14/11/1996. from to PROGRAMME

Serial No.	Name	Passport No.	Nationality	
1.	Anthony Weller	Z 6675104	Americain	

Coordinating Agency

1. The foreigner (s) shall enter the Agency through the specified route *i. e.* in case of Khyber *via* Jamrud, Bajau *via* Timergara route, North Waziristan Agency *via* Bannu-Miran Shah road, South Waziristan Agency *via* Jandola, and Mohmand Agency *via* Yaka Ghund;

2. Foreigner (s) shall contact the Political Authorities at the entry points and take levy/Khassadar personnel for security escort;

3. The foreigners shall not travel before sunrise and after sun-set;

4. The foreigner (s) while on tour in the Agency shall contract the Political Authorities both at the time of arrival and departure.

5. That the foreigner (s) are not allowed to take photographs of prohibited areas/sensitive installations.

(SECTION OFFICER, SPL-II)
Ph: 601404 · 27/5/96

Endst. of even No.
Copy forwarded to:–

1. The Commissioner PESHAWAR Division.

2. The Political Agent/~~Deputy Commissioner~~ KHYBER
It is requested that necessary security arrangements may be made during the visit.

(SECTION OFFICER SPL-II)

GS&PD., NWFP. 202; Secy. Home, 5,000 F. 10-6-95—(14)

The Political Agency for the Khyber was on Stadium Road, a boulevard that abutted a newer area with international relief agencies and private homes of foreign diplomats and university teachers. The boulevard itself was old Peshawar with road fever: shade trees, blue rickshaws, rainbow trucks, tongas, tumbledown markets, shop stalls, political offices, a few service stations. At one of them I saw a white Suzuki van I was sure I recognized.

It was as if he'd been waiting for me to appear, alerted by bush telegraph.

"Of course I can take you," said Zarar Shah. "I have family relations near the Khyber. Cousins."

In Pushtun the word for *cousin* is also the word for *enemy*.

The Khyber Agency was a forbiddingly iron-gated compound. Tribesmen in robes chatted out front with a couple of policemen in dark gray. Inside, even more tribesmen milled about the old British verandas off a small court of open ground. Everyone was armed, but by now this didn't matter to me unless they were actually shooting. A corner office in the back was the nerve center, with the weary ex-colonial aura of wooden furniture, old clocks and telephones, and dingy walls apparently unchanged since Independence. A lot of men stood around waiting.

The Political Agent signed my permit with a diagonal slash in two places; an assistant walked me twenty feet to a shadowy room full of men in charcoal gray trousers, smocks, and berets. It was like wandering into a film about the Foreign Legion. The assistant barked a name and the men stopped talking. One came over. He took his time and did not seem perturbed or remotely interested that he was going to have to leave here immediately to protect a foreigner for the next two or three hours.

"Athar Khan," said the assistant. "Your gunman. He will look after you. But you must ask him before you get out of the car or go into a place. If there is a problem, he will not let you go."

Athar Khan was from a small village far up the Khyber. He was absolutely relaxed and looked bulletproof. He might have been forty-five or fifty; his dark mustache was tinged with gray. He had a seamed brown bloodhound's face and long eyelashes—Pathan men often have beautiful, almost feminine eyes. In sandals he had a lean, sinewy way of carrying himself, and when he stood still he clasped both hands behind him as if he were about to give a speech. He wore a copy of a Kalashnikov over one shoulder, high enough so that his hand could rest on it. Leather pouches around his neck contained a pistol, ammunition, and binoculars. His charcoal beret and the epaulets of his charcoal jacket bore the initials K.K.F. and the red insignia of a fort and crossed swords, signifying the Khyber Police Force. He was like a compact version of Sherlock Holmes fitted out as a tribesman, carrying an automatic rifle instead of a magnifying glass. He said nothing, merely gave an economical nod in greeting and swept me at a glance as if appraising what an intelligent sniper might aim at first. He did not smile.

I noticed that when he and Zarar Shah met outside the Khyber Agency compound, they did not shake hands. They nodded, spoke for a moment—each identifying the other's village and ascertaining that there was nothing amiss between them.

Once the GT leaves the old heart of Peshawar and heads to the British cantonment and the Khyber Pass, it's known as Khyber Road, though soon it becomes Jamrud Road, named after the fort.

Peshawar had the largest cantonment I'd seen, as befitting the biggest military outpost in British India. Its principal Christian Cemetery was wildly overgrown. Enormous trees spilled over the walls and a tulip gate; a colonnade of palms stretched through gravestones where vegetation ran riot.

"British people," said Zarar Shah. "Old times."

Heading toward the modern University Town, the GT was a broad and busy thoroughfare that gave no indication it was about to enter Afghanistan. It was lined with photographers' studios and shops specializing in tinselly wedding paraphernalia. Islamia College was another in that Oxford-meets-Akbar style, rather like the college back in Amritsar. Boys in white were playing cricket and hockey in a big field alongside. Just after came a gigantic Afghan refugee camp of mud houses and tented streets, fenced in by tall sheaves of wood like giant breadsticks.

"Fifteen years this camp is here. Kachagari camp. Since 1979," said Zarar Shah. "Since Afghan people are beginning the war with Russia." He counted off years on his fingers and shook his head. "Eighteen years."

"How many people in it?"

He shrugged. "One hundred thousand? Two hundred thousand? No one can tell you."

Athar Khan kept his eye trained out the window and waved at someone he knew every now and then. I wondered if his job bored him: clearly nothing was going to happen on his watch.

Just after the vast refugee camp there was a tree nursery by the road, an oasis of green against the khaki and gray of the rocks and dirt and mud. Along the GT, Afghan kids were playing cricket using long sticks as bats. Another camp of refugees' tents was just starting across the road. In no time there'd be mud houses and in a year it would look, as the other did, like a permanent, secretive, and highly organized town—and it would have a town's rules, bazaars, and clout.

Then we were in a teeming new shopping hub, and the Jamrud Road got clotted. Karkhanai Bazaar was also popularly called the Smugglers' Bazaar; it was modern, with concrete buildings of two and three stories lining the GT. Its goods made little sense together: hanging meat carcasses alongside new electronics goods in original cartons, shining bicycles beside satellite dishes, fabrics piled next to videocassette machines and yellow plastic toys. There were gun dealers galore in a conglomeration of decrepit shops, and even a large emporium that some Pathan in a waggish mood had christened Marks & Spencer. If a lawsuit ever results, I want to be on hand to watch the London owners of the trademark come to collect damages.

The so-called Smugglers' Bazaar was in fact a transplanted market, brought down from the Khyber town of Landi Kotal. These were the mostly untaxed goods brought legitimately into the port of Karachi a thousand miles to the south, bound for Afghanistan. Brought up by truck, they crossed the Khyber and, once across the border into Afghanistan (and frequently before, to save time) they would be swiftly unloaded and brought right back through the Khyber, either on trucks or piecemeal a few yards off the road, where the Pakistani Police officially had no jurisdiction whatsoever. The result was that it could be cheaper to buy a Sony television set here than in New York.

The Pakistanis left this untaxed trade alone—it was too firmly aboveground to be called "smuggling." It was simply part of the price of using the Khyber Pass. Pathans are often described as a kind of Asian version of the Cosa Nostra—the feuding families, the codes of honor, loyalty, and revenge—and in the Khyber they were running a protection racket, as they had for centuries. Some goods, and people, did get through to Afghanistan. Some didn't.

ATTENTION
ENTRY OF FOREIGNERS
IS PROHIBITED
BEYOND THIS POINT

Michni Point, the limit of my permit, was about forty-one kilometers away, overlooking the Afghan border down at Torkham.

The road narrowed in no time to two slow streams of trucks. Now the landscape was sparse bushes, and mud walls with gunslits. A few feet to the right the tracks of the Khyber Railway, opened by the British in 1925 and closed since 1986 due to bombing in the Afghan-Russian War, followed the road. The little train had run one day a week from Peshawar to Landi Kotal up in the pass, about thirty miles via several W-shaped zigzags and thirty-four tunnels. All the tribesmen had been able to ride for free as part of the peace. A few free train tickets were worth it to supply the main British line of defense easily all throughout the Khyber.

Abruptly the road became dusty with a wilderness of thistle bushes and tumbled land on both sides and the Suleiman Hills up ahead. Every few hundred meters in the middle of nowhere there was a lean-to mud picket, with a braided cot and a relaxed man with a gun and a beret, watching the road. In British days these were often marked HEAT-STROKE HUT.

The Baab-i-Khyber at Jamrud—the Khyber Gate—is an image reproduced on matchboxes and the Khyber Rifles' insignia. The actual gate was pretty unconvincing. In blanched brick that wanted to look like medieval stone, it resembled a child's illustration of the gate to the Khyber: Two towers like chess rooks spanned by an arch, with a flag and parapets along the top. It was dated 1963. A century from now it may look suitably ancient, though still with the profile of a toy. Just before it stood a mosque and a sequence of stores, many specializing in medical supplies. There was also a fruit market where proprietors prominently sold a substance in dark, gooey pellets called *naswar*. I took it to be hashish.

"Not hashish," said Zarar Shah.

We had stopped and gotten out so he could buy cigarettes. I noticed that Athar Khan did not leave us for an instant and he kept his hand on his Kalashnikov. In an Indian guide I would have taken this as theater to increase the size of his tip.

"It's not hashish?"

"No, no," said Zarar Shah. "It is like—what do you call it... snuff."

"You put that up your nose?" This seemed unbelievable.

No, up your Khyber, you bloody foreigner....

"No, you put it here." Zarar tugged back his lower lip to expose discolored gums. "You leave it there as long as you like. Then what is still there, you spit it out. You want to try?"

He wasn't suggesting I buy some; he pulled a little ball of the stuff out of his leather jacket pocket.

"I don't think so."

Later I found out through a friend who'd lived with the mujahidin that naswar as used by the Pathans was a high-powered chewing tobacco, liberally improved with opium and plenty of other stimulants. It could also be addictive. A tiny amount—and once was enough—had left my friend dizzy, nauseated, and coughing uncontrollably for hours.

At the Jamrud Gate was a checkpoint where I got out and met everyone, from an official in aviator sunglasses and a gray pin-stripe vest over his smock to a couple of other gents dressed and armed like Athar Khan. The checkpoint looked pre-British: white-washed walls murky with smoke, wood rafters, rope beds.

Above us on the right was the rust brown Jamrud Fort, built originally by the Sikhs in the early nineteenth century with walls ten feet thick. Perched above biscuit bastions, the entire fort looked edible, like a big gingerbread battleship. Just through the Khyber Gate were six marble tablets with the history of the pass thoughtfully written in English and Urdu.

> *All these tribes, for whom, as it were, the land was made, not men for the land, are well-armed warriors, with Spartan virtues and vices, who live more or less a camp life in thick, yellowish-grey houses behind mud walls with a watch tower for each compound. These hillmen are men who can outpace any man in a deadly, manly struggle for existence, hence their survival through the ages.*

All around the plains were dotted with baked-mud, thick-walled, windowless houses like sandcastles with rifle slits, for a man's home was his fortress. A worn Russian truck, one more spoil of war, came rattling at us. A bus lurched past on the way to the border at Torkham. From there to Jalalabad took two hours, according to Zarar Shah—a long time to reach somewhere no farther across the border than Peshawar was on this side.

Another checkpoint, manned by an officer in the khaki uniform of the Khyber Rifles, which are part of the army. His assistant insisted amiably on being photographed outside his picket of blistered stone and mud: an old man in blue robes, white-bearded, ramrod straight.

Up till now the Khyber had seemed simply a road with hills nearby. Now it began to snake and double and rise around the contours of those jumbled and barren hills, which rose suddenly on both sides in vast smudges of gunpowder gray. When I briefly got out to take a photo, looking back to the green Vale of Peshawar, the gunman got out too. Alongside the GT lay the remains of the oldest road, a dirt track for camels.

The texture of the pass walls was lunar and severe as the road climbed and switchbacked repeatedly, following the folds of the Khyber. It was unlike any other portion of the Grand Trunk. Men from Alexander's Macedonians to Tamerlane's warriors to the British had made their way through, again and again; fear of being caught in the pass had filled their undefended nightmares; it was like an unpredictable animal that sometimes let men go and sometimes ate them. Zarar Shah was humming something under his breath, and I wondered if it might be the Pushtun song that runs

> *Your eyes are two loaded revolvers*
> *And your narrow smile has destroyed me.*

The narrow smile: that was the pass, a crooked and elongated smile across deadly mountains that were the edge of the Hindu Kush, the "Hindu-Killer." The pass was, after a few miles, almost dull, but this dullness was an insinuation and a dare. Extreme temperatures, the dire heat and hurtling cold for which it was famous, would give it an intensity missing on this balmy

November day. The British had had to spend thousands of men to barely control this place, this "imperial migraine," even as late as the Third Afghan War (1919). Yet how could they ever hope to control it when one to two hundred thousand tribesmen strung their *kafilas,* their caravans that were sometimes five miles long, through the pass every year?

And for once along the GT the principal traffic coming at me was not lethal trucks but wobbly bicycles, many of them skirting the road. There was a bicycle transport business from the Afghan border all the way back to Jamrud. Each bicyclist, according to Zarar Shah, got paid 60 rupees ($1.50) to bring in—"smuggle" seems an absurd word for someone pedalling uphill in the sunshine—a new bike and whatever stuff he could balance on it at the same time. They could nip over from the good road and negotiate the ancient dirt track easily at any time, where they were officially off the books. One happy lesson of this part of the world is that every law is illusion. Like a mirage it shimmers and looms, yet you can walk around it or make it vanish entirely if you concentrate.

The large, high-walled Shagai Fort had a railway platform; the hills above were decorated with the large plaque insignias, plastered in place, of regiments that had served here. This decor began to crop up frequently, as if the Khyber ridges were wearing clusters of glorious medals on their chests. Many plaques, with their coats of arms and Latin mottos, had been put up in the 1920s when the fort was built, and some as recently as the last decade. The fort looked over an extremely complicated valley that the road wove through, with tribal forts and mud outposts and watchtowers on every outcropping.

KHYBER RIFLES WELCOMES YOU
TO KHYBER PASS

Meaning keep your head down and pray the naswar spoils their aim.

Then, still rising, we were shaken through the most dramatic and narrowest funnel of the pass—thirty meters from one cliff wall to the other. Across the riverbed on our right, ledges for a return road and the railroad tracks hung like shelves, halfway up the cliffs. The road itself was barely wide enough for one truck, but this was a British improvement, for its ledge had originally been only wide enough for one laden camel. It reminded me of an old photo that showed a Waziri "camel throne"—a double basket of wood, padded with blankets, that fit sideways on a camel, carried several veiled wives in purdah, and stuck way out on both sides. Many harems must've been pitched into the stream here.

I was also reminded of how little the reality of the Khyber Pass conformed to how I'd always pictured it, for it was mostly quite broad and only 3,300 feet at its summit. Still, it was the easy corridor through impenetrable terrain.

Easy for some: a friend of mine's cousin, a traveling Christian minister from Bermuda, had died in the Khyber Pass in 1956, trying to bike through with his blonde Swedish fiancée, who had likewise disappeared. It was not difficult to imagine why.

Another British fort, the Ali Masjid, surveyed the gorge from on high. From it soldiers could see up and down the length of the Khyber Pass. Still a military installation, the fort was off-limits, as was its cemetery, full of British soldiers who died here in the Second Afghan War (1879). Just off the road was a fanciful little mosque in shade trees, for which the fort was named. More regiments' insignias were stuck like commemorative badges on the shoulders of rock—Gordon Highlanders and South Wales Borderers, Punjab and Dorsetshire and 22nd Cheshire Regiments, their dates of service here covering the last seventy years. Just by the road, on an abandoned stretch, concrete dragon's teeth from World War II poked up—sharp pyramids of cement to prevent any German tanks coming through in an invasion.

At this fort around the turn of the century, long after the British had started paying off Afridi workers with large wages to reduce the danger, there was apparently one sole sniper left. He favored the crags over the fort, purportedly an old man armed with a *jeza-il*—a long-barreled single-shot musket—who racked up a tally of British corpses and was impossible to catch. A reward went up: a thousand rupees. Still, even the Pathans had no success, until a teenager in the Khyber Militia took a walk one morning. A single shot was fired; soon the young man accepted his reward from the British political agent for the Khyber.

"I don't deserve any credit," he said. "I had no trouble finding him, because I knew all his little ways. He was my father."

We entered a long, impressive valley where even the lowliest mud and stone dwelling was fortified for generations of tribal war.

"This village, people very rich," said Zarar Shah. "Drugs."

We passed a line of four camels following the power lines, plodding toward Afghanistan. The tall hills all around were gray and khaki—the word itself means dust—with scrub trees. The village, its road suspiciously well tarred, rapidly lost all resemblance to any that had come before. Fortress-houses were set on the undulations like heavyset soldiers going for position. Not a single person was visible, which made it eerie moving through the landscape. And the scale of the houses was sometimes enormous; an outer mud wall could go on for a quarter mile.

"*Very* rich people," said Zarar Shah.

Athar Khan merely blinked.

The road now had taken on that blankness I'd sensed in the Punjab, coming to the end of India, on the verge of another country. I could see it as personal only because it had taken me so long to get here. The valley had fallen entirely silent but for the groan of our van, and I felt the collective baggage of all the miles and weeks behind me like a great weight I was about to shed.

"This is the station of Sher Shah," said Zarar Shah. But it wasn't. He was pointing up a hillside at the huge remains of a

Buddhist stupa, like a shattered stone bell, that was well over a thousand years older than that.

We were passing through a principal Khyber village of fortress compounds, a place called Zarai. They each looked ready to withstand a month-long siege and certainly no one was moving in the pebbly desert they seemed to grow out of. I'd read accounts of Khyber women going proudly unveiled, but I never saw a female in these baked villages, and few signs of life; it was rare even to see children playing. The only motion was on the road, our white van and a truck or two crawling along.

"Don't draw any photos," said Zarar Shah. I had raised my camera. He pointed out the window. "This is my cousin's house."

What kind of cousin? I wondered.

"What does he do?"

"He... uh, he transports of goods."

"I see."

"Before he was transporting of drugs. Now it is simply transporting of electronics."

"Aha."

But I had no chance to get into complex family relations, because I was transfixed by a wall far longer than that of any serai I'd seen on the entire Grand Trunk Road. It went on for at least a half mile. I made some remark about the size of the village inside. Could five hundred people live protected in its walls?

"The biggest house in Asia," said Zarar Shah. "For one man. Drugs. He has a private plane. Sometimes you see it land there."

Athar Khan shook his head slowly as we passed.

The tall, iron-studded wood fortress gate had been open just enough for me to have a passing glimpse within—the intimations of a classical oasis, with trees, fountains, a private mosque.

Soon there were the crumbled remains of a Mogul gate—as if here, at the end of the road, emblems of some of its many movements, Buddhist and Mogul and British, had their little souvenir-like wrecks to show that no one had controlled it for very long. This road could reduce the past, the great empires and religions, to a few wobbly names and piles of rubble. On a sunlit autumnal morning in the Khyber Pass, it seemed touching and a bit depressing that there was not much left here besides the present.

A wheezy truck lumbered past us heading to Peshawar. I glanced back—its painted license plate read *Kabal*.

Landi Kotal was the last gas before Afghanistan, four miles away, and a real frontier town. Strictly speaking, it has little to do with Pakistan. It was also the last station of the Khyber Railway. A century ago, its huge fort had been at the epicenter of the 1897 "uprising" of Afridis, when it took 35,000 British troops to quell the tribesmen, and right through the 1920s they were still cheerfully picking off the Queen's soldiers with a bullet through the brain, fired from overlooking crags whenever the whim took them. Lowell Thomas, passing through in 1924, recounts how in a Khyber village a feud between two families separated by the Grand Trunk Road went on year after year, as the families had only a lone ancient cannon each and thirty-two cannonballs to work with. The cannonballs would lodge one by one in the opposing family's fortress without doing much damage, get retrieved, and then the siege would start up again from across the road.

We got out here and walked around. For the first time Athar Khan fell into conversation with a few people and his sense of caution lifted, which made me suspect his home was nearby; he actually turned his back for a moment to make some purchase. The town was built as much below the level of the road as above. The GT had the usual incomplete ugly concrete disasters, but down paths to the left were busy lower levels, canopied bazaars and cobbled streets. Occasionally I even saw a young woman shopping for the morning's fruit and turning her half-shawled face away. I sensed no tension from men at a foreigner's presence; everyone was as urbanely friendly as in Peshawar, and there was for me the childhood scent of mulberry trees.

Landi Kotal had worn the nickname of "The Town of Ten Thousand Thieves" for a long time, but most of the smugglers' business had moved close to Peshawar to be more accessible. The market had the cleared-out feel of a place that had had its day, though you could still easily get imported film, wristwatches, perfumes, liquor (if you knew whom to ask) and plenty of auto parts, shoes, medicines, cheap china, guns, used cars, and name-brand electronics.

You could also easily get hashish, because a lot of people were smoking it. Naswar was on sale, naturally, big bricks of the stuff. One rupee (two and a half cents) would get you a 25 gram brown square, which would keep you high for days and vomiting till you got used to it. It was also legal; the hashish was not. Landi Kotal, at 1,100 meters, was the highest point of the Khyber Pass in every sense. (In the old days, of course, the Indian drug trade was controlled by the British—first John Company, then the Crown. It was their number one export for decades; the headquarters was Patna, near Benares. Bales of opium were brought down the Ganges to the large Calcutta purifying factory, from which it was shipped in chests and sold to Number One Customer, China.)

There is a photo from a few years after World War I showing a British soldier in knee socks, shorts, and pith helmet on a dusty crossing of what had been the Landi Kotal cantonment. A sign reads *Trafalgar Square* and the soldier has both hands up, as if directing traffic. By the mid-1980s, despite the presence of the government Khyber Rifles at the fort, the town had become arguably the largest heroin emporium in Asia. It was the ideal haven, for poppies had been grown and opium produced by the ton around here for centuries. The town was on the GT, but a hundred feet off that road was under tribal jurisdiction: thus it could serve production on both sides of the frontier and even worldwide distribution via Karachi. A kilo of quality heroin could then be bought in Landi Kotal for $100 and sold for ten thousand times that in New York. Now much of that emporium status was gone from the town—and some of the drug trade had moved west, or to Southeast Asia's Golden Triangle—but many walled fortresses through the Khyber Valley were still active opium factories.

Most of the morning commercial activity I saw was destined for Jalalabad, the first city of consequence across the border. Big plastic drums of diesel fuel were being strapped onto complaining camels to make the two-day journey. Other camels lashed with bundles were arriving from there in a long and steady stream. On the hillsides behind the town were the dark holes of train tunnels, as if someone had methodically poked a finger right through the mountains. There was still a lower road for traffic heading to Afghanistan and a higher road for those returning, wiggling around the rocky slopes that towered above.

We drove on toward Michni Point, along my final stretch of the Grand Trunk Road. I was trying to remember how I had felt when I started. I had hoped for luck; I'd been lucky all the way. I hadn't been in a wreck, I'd seen most of what I wanted, I hadn't gotten sick enough to have to stop and give up. My stomach had behaved. I hadn't spent all my money. I was exhausted, but I might have been nearly as tired had I stayed home. Yet mentally I was depleted; and from living off my nerves all this time, the journey felt like an entire career.

ATTENTION
ENTRY OF FOREIGNERS
IS PROHIBITED
BEYOND THIS POINT

I reckoned that the unending reiteration of that identical message, every few kilometers, must be so that whoever caught you would have something to point at with his tulwar ("Can you not read?") while you whimpered and pleaded for mercy.

At the Michni Point checkpost there was a bamboo pole to block the road. Now it was pointing up. A boy lay on an old braided cot and a man on the roof of the mud and stone hut was repairing the electric wires. Bits of furniture were strewn higgledy-piggledy.

Below us and about a mile away were the fortresses and a few trees of the Torkham border. Complex hills stretched off into crags and haze and dust, the occasional glitter of a windshield moving in all that hard vastness. A couple of crags had numbers painted on them, a *2* and a *3*, and these marked the end of Pakistan; one ridge bore the remains of what looked like a cairn. Beyond lay Afghanistan, a flat rocky expanse that in the pale haze looked unremittingly bleak where the road curlicued on.

When you're wounded and left on Afghanistan's plains,
And the women come out to cut up what remains,
Jest roll to your rifle and blow out your brains
An' go to your Gawd like a soldier.

At Athar Khan's suggestion we skirted an edge of the hillside by the checkpost and climbed a little to get a better view. Just beside the stone hut, avoiding the main road, a line of grumbling camels were being led down a path—a track following the most ancient of all these roads, below the present GT.

I stood there looking out over the last stretch, the way out of the Khyber and the subcontinent, where so many men had walked or ridden to their doom, and asked myself what all these miles of the GT added up to. I'd expected to feel more connection between India and Pakistan. All along I had tried to see how these people were living with their profound pasts, pasts they were largely unaware of except for an inherited residue of blind emotion and mutual distrust and habitual gestures—so little wisdom passed on, after all those centuries of civilization. To remind myself that this last century was hardly one for, say, Europe to brag about only reinforced such a judgment. There was no natural drift toward better things: that was the age-old lesson of the subcontinent. The times of wisdom, the fruitful centuries, were only bumps in the road.

To travel here was a sober reminder, to someone from a secular country, of how powerful religion could be. It could shape the mind and drive the personality in automatic ways that might come to seem secular but which were fueled by differences going back thousands of years. And in people with little control of their own lives, with fewer choices or alternatives than in the West, that part of each person which was uncontrollably shaped by history became more important, and assumed a weight that it had not rightfully earned. Here the face of man depended to a frightening degree on the unexamined face of God.

The road was still a whip across this land mass. Ideas that had come down it centuries ago—holy men and warriors long vanished into dust—still had force here, were still its masters. Later masters of the road looked more and more like short-lived wayfarers, whose surviving relics rapidly became strange items whose purpose was too easily forgotten.

The dream of a road uniting both ends of this subcontinent is over thirty centuries old. Today's road was only a shadow of that dream, for only an outsider now could do the journey I'd made. Then again, for most of its life, the road had always been dangerous in one part or another. Those who had strived to make it wholly passable had been unable to make the unity last. The Grand Trunk Road was an illusion, for it was really only a very long local road; everyone had their little piece of it, but few people had answered me correctly when I asked how far it went. And in trying to prove to myself that it was a single long road I had, in the end, persuaded myself only of its fragmentation.

Both India and Pakistan had inherited the laws of one recent world empire and the architectural masterpieces of another. But a half-century on those laws of architecture were not being put into practice and the architecture of laws was failing the two countries in their own singular ways. That nearly a quarter of the population of the planet was living united by a distrust largely of their own creation, armed to the teeth, seemed a terrible legacy. It was mitigated only by what I had felt, week after week: a profound sweetness in the people of both countries, an easy intimacy that was no less real for being offered so quickly and naturally—these people's doors really were open. That had counted for a lot.

Bells jangled on donkeys being shushed down the track. This was a sensible place to call the end of the Grand Trunk Road, with the crumbled remains below of what Zarar spoke of as "Sher Shah's prison" and a flag flying, these few empty cots, an ambivalent wind. Black plastic bags blew across the landscape and got caught in the thistle bushes. It seemed arbitrary to stop here, but there was no way I'd be allowed any further, and anyway, the subcontinent effectively ended at this point of the pass. It looked truly like nowhere, surrounded by crags like a set of serrated teeth in some of the most forbidding terrain on earth. I thought it the perfect conclusion for a road that began fifteen hundred miles away in tropical heat and lush botanical gardens.

I realized, absurdly, that the Khyber Pass was the only part of the entire Grand Trunk I had ever felt safe on. There was no speed, no haste, little traffic, the road was good, and I had a Pathan gunman with me ready to kill on my behalf. It was a sensation to be savored, as I did not imagine coming back. It had been worth coming this far to experience.

Twelve camels roped together came plodding down the ancient path, with hooves like floormops, lovely mascaraed eyes, and red, yellow, and blue braided headdresses. It had probably taken them a couple of days to come up the Khyber. I squinted at the packs on their backs, trying to guess what they were carrying.

Athar Khan was looking at me impassively. He said something under his breath to Zarar Shah, who smiled and quietly replied. They both laughed. Perhaps they were chuckling over some particularly well-executed and savory vendetta, perhaps over the sight of a man standing in the Khyber Pass and writing down whatever struck his fancy, here with the wind blowing from Afghanistan.

One of the camels spat.

"Well?" I murmured.

Athar Khan said nothing. He was regarding the enormous view. His eyes were alive: I wondered what he saw in it that I did not.

"If we leave now," said Zarar Shah delicately, "perhaps we can be back to Peshawar for lunch."

"Good idea," I said.

Acknowledgments

Many people smoothed the road for this book.

In India, Lakhanjit Singh, R. P. Gupta, Avinash Singh, a doctor in Amritsar whose name I didn't catch, the Reuters staff, and Harpreet Singh were particularly helpful; in Pakistan, Denis Reichle, Zarar Shah, Warren Carey, Faridoon and Saeed Hussain, Lynne Tracy, and Kamar Ali. I am most deeply in their debt.

I also wish to thank the North-West Frontier Province administration in Peshawar for understanding my predicament and breaking their own rules to allow me through the Khyber Pass.

I am grateful to the following people and institutions for assisting either with my journey or my research: San Abele, Thomas Bailey, Halil Baştuğ, Chris Baumer, David Benjamin, Kevin Buckley, Henry Dunow, Martial and Lucette Dussart, Steve Gottlieb, Chris Hunt, Ralph and Molly Izzard, Mara Lurie, Ian MacNiven, Pauline Neuwirth, Dan O'Connor, Raghubir Singh, Philip Swanson, John Weber, John Zuill, *Smithsonian* magazine, and the Widener Library at Harvard; Chris Buckley of *Forbes-FYI* magazine and Duncan Christy of *Delta SKY* magazine, in whose pages, greatly altered, excerpts from the book appeared; and Allan, Mohammad, & fellow sons of the East, still quartered safe out there at the Dragon House Society (Kyrenia branch).

A number of friends with acute radar were kind enough to read the book in process; these faithful allies always saw what I did not. Peyton Houston, Diane Fassino, Jonathan Miller, Valérie Moniez, George Weller, and Donna Wolfe scrutinized early versions and asked difficult questions. Geo Beach, Barnaby Conrad III, Reuel Gerecht, Edward Lazarus, Emmett Thomas, Ron Wright, and Diane Zeleny brought their vast experience to later drafts and taught me a great deal. Kylée Smith not only read critically but kept me moving healthily and happily forward against all odds.

Finally, to those many people along the Grand Trunk Road, named and unnamed in this book, who stopped whatever they were doing to make me welcome and to share their lives, my thanks.

Further Reading

The field is so vast that rather than listing many sources in a lengthy and dutiful bibliography, I have selected a few works (alongside those cited in the text) that gave me particular pleasure and which are also in print, likely to be found in a good library, or available in India and Pakistan.

THE GRAND TRUNK ROAD

The Grand Trunk Road: A Passage Through India, Raghubir Singh (photographs) & Jean Deloche (historical essay), New York, 1995.

The Grand Trunk Road, John Wiles, London, 1972.

GENERAL

The Wonder That Was India, A. L. Basham, London & New York, 1954.

The Autobiography of an Unknown Indian, Nirad C. Chaudhuri, London, 1951.

Freedom At Midnight, Larry Collins and Dominique LaPierre, New York, 1975.

A Goddess In the Stones, Norman Lewis, New York & London, 1991.

Portrait of India, Ved Mehta, New York & London, 1970.

To the Frontier, Geoffrey Moorhouse, New York & London, 1984.

Passage To Peshawar, Richard Reeves, New York, 1984.

India: An Introduction, Khushwant Singh, New Delhi, 1974.

A History of India (Volume Two), Percival Spear, London, 1965.

A History of India (Volume One), Romila Thapar, London, 1966.

No Full Stops In India, Mark Tully, London & New York, 1991.

MOGULS & MAHARAJAHS

Delhi & Agra: A Travellers' Companion, ed. Michael Alexander, London, 1987.

The Maharajahs, John Lord, New York, 1971.

A Second Paradise: Indian Courtly Life 1590-1947, Naveen Patnaik, New York, 1985.

THE BRITISH RAJ

India Britannica, Geoffrey Moorhouse, London & New York, 1983.

Stones of Empire, Jan Morris, Oxford, 1983.

Hobson-Jobson, the Anglo-Indian Dictionary, Henry Yule and A. C. Burnell, 1886, reprinted London & New Delhi, 1996.

THE NORTH-WEST FRONTIER

The Pathans, Sir Olaf Caroe, New York, 1958.

Khyber: The Story of an Imperial Migraine, Charles Miller, New York, 1977.

The Way of the Pathans, James W. Spain, Oxford, 1962.

GREAT TRAVELERS

Visions of India: The Sketchbooks of William Simpson 1859-62, ed. by Mildred Archer, Topsfield, 1986.

Edward Lear's Indian Journal, ed. Ray Murphy, London, 1953.

The Life and Adventures of Thomas Coryate, Michael Strachan, London, New York, & Toronto, 1962.

ARTS & LITERATURE

An Anthology of Indian Literature, ed. John B. Alphonso-Karkala, London & Baltimore, 1971.

The Jain Cosmology, Collette Caillat and Ravi Kumar, New York & New Delhi, 1981.

Exploring India's Sacred Art, Stella Kramrisch, Philadelphia, 1983.

The Ramayana: A Shortened Modern Prose Version, R. K. Narayan, New York, 1972.

The Mahabharata (Retold), R. K. Narayan, New York, 1978.

Indian Art, Philip Rawson, London & New York, 1972.

Room For Wonder, Stuart Cary Welch, New York, 1978.

That Mighty Sculptor, Time, Marguerite Yourcenar, New York, 1992. (contains an essay, "On Some Erotic and Mystic Themes of the Gita-Govinda").

KIPLING

Quest For Kim: In Search of Kipling's Great Game, Peter Hopkirk, London, 1996.

Kipling's India, ed. Thomas Pinney, London, 1986.

CONTEMPORARY POLITICS

On the Grand Trunk Road, Steve Coll, New York, 1994. (Also contains a travel essay, "The Grand Trunk Road.")

India: A Million Mutinies Now, V. S. Naipaul, London & New York, 1990.

From Raj to Rajiv, Mark Tully and Zareer Masani, London, 1988.

Quotes

Certain poems are briefly cited without attribution in the text. Here are the sources, to whom I am most grateful.

The opening epigraph is quoted by Alexander Frater in his *Chasing the Monsoon* (Alfred A. Knopf, New York, 1991).

The verses in Ch. 9, pp. 106 & 113, originally in Sanskrit, are by the poet Basavaṇṇa (1106-1167). They may be found in *Speaking of Śiva*, translations by A.K. Ramanujan (Penguin, London, New York, & New Delhi, 1973).

The verse in Ch. 12, pp. 156-7, are from Canto V of the Sanskrit masterpiece *Gita Govinda* (Song of Govinda), by the poet Jayadeva, from circa 1200. The translation, slightly modified here, is by George Kyt and may be found in *An Anthology of Indian Literature*, edited by John B. Alphonso-Karkala (Penguin, 1971).

The passage on pp. 194-5 in Ch. 15 is from the *Bhagavad-Gita*, Stanzas 36-39 of the "Discipline of Action" section. This translation is by Juan Mascaró (Penguin, 1962).

The couplets quoted later in Ch. 15, p. 201, are from Rudyard Kipling's *Route-Marchin'*.

The quote about the life of the mind, on p. 201 in Ch. 15, is from the sixth poem in the cycle, *An Apology For the Revival of*

Christian Architecture in England, by the poet Geoffrey Hill, from the volume *Tenebrae* (André Deutsch, London, 1978).

The verse in Ch. 17, p. 225, is by Bertolt Brecht, adapted from his *Questions From A Worker Who Reads*, from the volume *Svendborg Poems* (1935). Translator unknown.

The passages in Ch. 17 on p. 229 and p. 239 are by Guru Nanak (1469-1538), and are taken from the First Book of the Granth, the Sacred Book of the Sikhs. The translation is by Trilochan Singh et al., *Selections from the Sacred Writings of the Sikhs* (Allen & Unwin, London, 1960).

The verse on p. 260, Ch. 18, is by Kipling, from *The Naulakha*.

The verse on p. 329 in Ch. 22 is the infamous deleted stanza, 'The Chief Humanist,' from *The Golden Journey to Samarkand,* by James Ellroy Flecker (1884–1915).

The verses pp. 330-1 in Ch. 22 are by the Pathan poet Khushul Khan (1613–1691) and may be found in James W. Spain's *The Way of the Pathans* (Oxford University Press, 1962), translator unknown.

The Kipling parody in Ch. 23, on p. 336-7, is by Sean Kelly, taken from "The Man Who Would Be Queen" in *The Book of Sequels* (Random House, 1990).

The verse on p. 373, Ch. 24, is the final stanza of *The Young British Soldier*, by Rudyard Kipling.

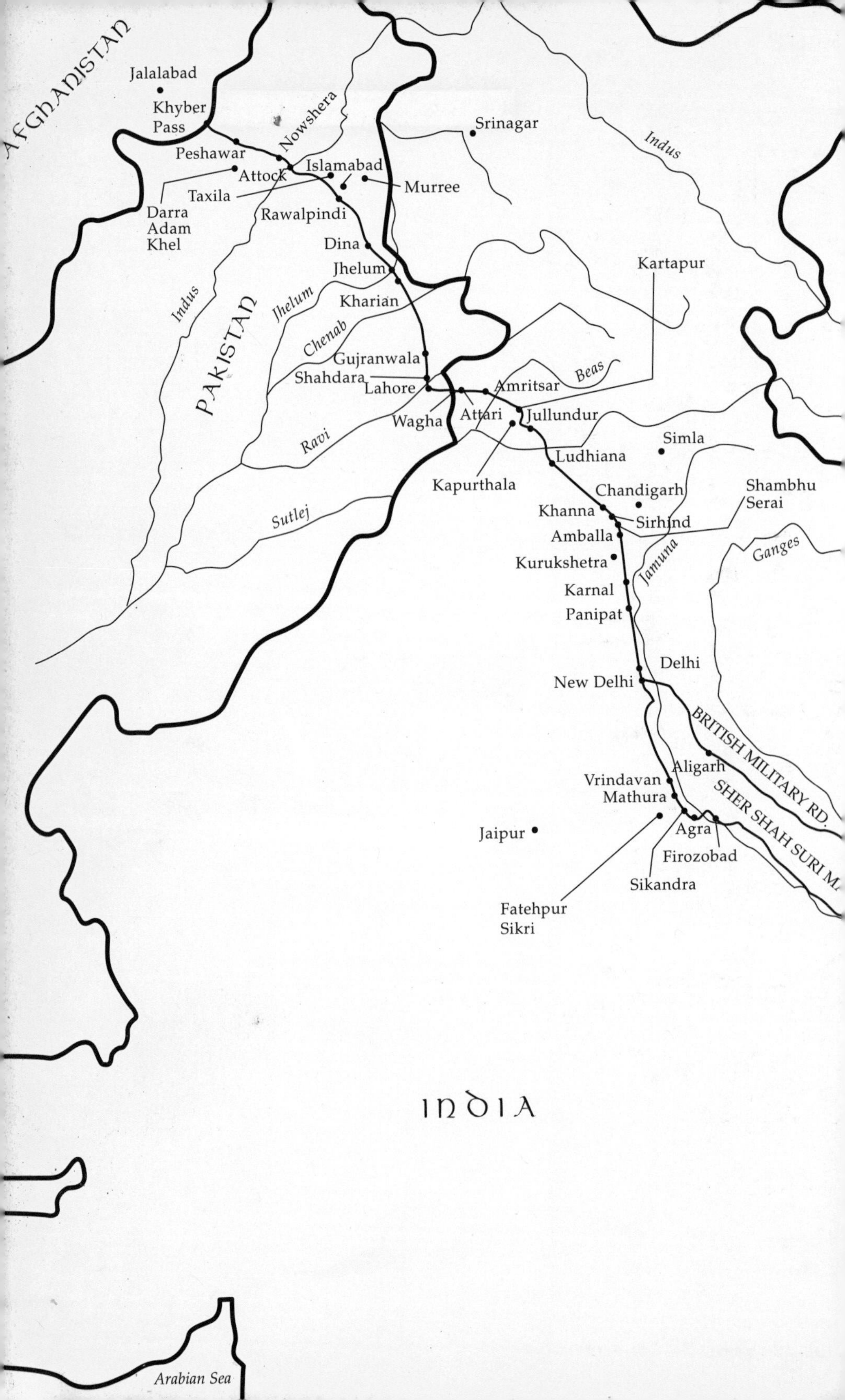

AFGHANISTAN
Jalalabad
Khyber Pass
Peshawar
Nowshera
Attock
Islamabad
Murree
Taxila
Darra Adam Khel
Rawalpindi
Srinagar
Indus
Dina
Jhelum
Kharian
Kartapur
Indus
PAKISTAN
Jhelum
Chenab
Gujranwala
Shahdara
Lahore
Amritsar
Beas
Wagha
Attari
Jullundur
Ravi
Simla
Ludhiana
Kapurthala
Chandigarh
Shambhu Serai
Khanna
Sirhind
Sutlej
Amballa
Kurukshetra
Jamuna
Ganges
Karnal
Panipat
Delhi
New Delhi
BRITISH MILITARY RD.
Aligarh
Vrindavan
Mathura
SHER SHAH SURI M
Jaipur
Agra
Firozobad
Sikandra
Fatehpur Sikri
INDIA
Arabian Sea